BOTTLERS AND BOTTLES, CANADIAN

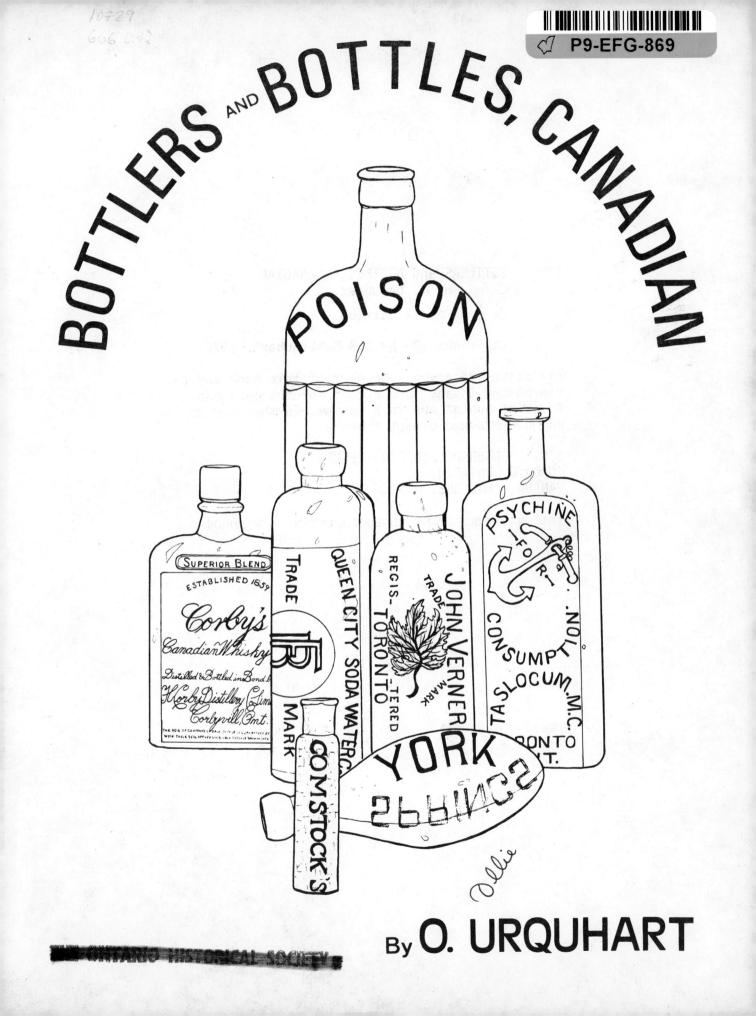

By O. URQUHART

BOTTLERS and BOTTLES, CANADIAN
    by O. URQUHART

    First Edition.

Copyright © by S.& O. Urquhart, 1976.

S.& O. URQUHART, 10 FIR AVENUE,
TORONTO, ONTARIO,
CANADA, M4E 1B5.

INTERNATIONAL STANDARD BOOK NUMBER 0 9690604 0 8

CALEDONIA SPRINGS, CANADA.

THESE celebrated Spas are situated near the Ottawa River, about eighty miles above Montreal, from whence Visitors arrive in one day of easy and interesting travel. They are also approached from Kingston through the Rideau Canal to Bytown, thence down the Ottawa in six hours to the Springs.

Although the travelling on this route above Bytown is not rapid, the magnificence of this great work of art, designed as a Military communication between Lake Ontario and the Ottawa River, in case of a War, well repays the traveller. The romantic situation of Bytown, its lofty banks overlooking the Basin, the Chaudiere Falls, the Suspension Bridge, and termination of the great Rideau Canal, in a succession of the finest Locks in the World, are singularly bold and beautiful.

Nothing can exceed the scenery on the Ottawa, the Lake of the Two Mountains, Mount Calvary, the St. Ann's Rapids—("*Row, brothers, row,*")—are all matters of history, and the whole route to the Springs is full of interest.

The Caledonia Springs are surrounded by a dense forest, and present novelties and attractions rarely to be met with in the woods. The Baths, the variety and beauty of the Springs, and the unrivalled efficacy of their waters in the cure of disease, point them out as the future great watering place of the North, and where already, every season, may be found the best of society and a fund of amusement.

August 11.   WILLIAM PARKER & Co.
                                                                                                    138

ACKNOWLEDGMENTS

I am grateful to Crush Beverages Ltd., and Mr. W.N. Gilchist, Vice President Marketing of that firm: Mr. R.A. Pitt, Manager, Corporate and Consumer Affairs of Canadian Breweries Ltd.: Mr. Cooper, Sales Manager of Charles Wilson's Ltd. Toronto: Mr. J. Kennedy, Toronto, formerly of Rexall's: Mr. McGillvray Sr., Streetsville, of Northrop-McGillvray, Toronto - once Northrop, Tuttle & Moses and for many years Northrop & Lyman: Alan Wilson, Milikan, for information on early Lindsay bottlers.

My deepest gratitude to Janet Holmes, Toronto, of the Royal Ontario Museum, who not only found time in her busy life to read and gently suggest - but also to give material for use in this book.

John Sheeler, Toronto, for help, encouragement and advice along the way. Dorothy Gamble for material on the local bottlers of Peterborough. Olive Jones for the use of her "Glass Bottle Push-ups & Pontil Marks" and a very interesting day at the National Historic Sites Service, Ottawa.

Madeleine Thomson, Ottawa - for the picture of Caledonia Springs, and to Newt Coburn, Montreal for my first 'Caledonia Springs' bottle.

I am further grateful to the Toronto Public Library (Main Branch) and in particular, staff in the Canadian Room: The Toronto Archives and staff.

My grateful thanks to the following people for, or use of, bottles in their collection - Lillian Nicholson, Harold Wase, Elizabeth Payne, Ken Judges and Claude Lunau, Toronto: Don McKitchum, Caledon East: Madeleine Thomson, Dave Perch and Bob Rosewarne (late), Ottawa: Eunice Millard, Peterborough: Joan & Al. Wilson and Don Cummings, Milikan: Sandy Kline, Fort Erie: Dave Parker, Caledonia: Betty Cain, Zepher: Audrey Clark, Sutton: and Fred Spoelstra, Beamsville.

I am also grateful to the following Dealers. "Mollies's Antiques & Little Treasures", "Gemarie House Antiques", "Mona Carrol", "Sandy's Cracker Barrel", "Old York Bottles & Antiques", "Journey's End", "Red Lion Antique Shop", "Doris Robertson Antiques", "Steptoe and Wife", "Markham Antiques", "Joyce Gator" and "The Generation Gap", Toronto: "Kinghorn Antiques Ltd.", Richmond Hill: "Brices Antique Bottles" and "Jack's Pine", Whitby: "McCloud's Antiques", Markham: "Village Forge", Buttonville: "Jug & Basin", Unionville: "King's Lynn", Uxbridge and Barbara Gonyou of "Ray's Shoppe", Sarnia.

In particular, I am grateful to Janet Morse for typing and editing this book.

Last but not least, I am grateful to my husband for patience unending and other help.

I

BIBLIOGRAPHY

Article

Jones, Olive. Glass Bottle Push-ups and Pontil Marks. National Historic Sites Service, Ottawa. Published by The Society for Historical Archaeology, Lansing Michigan.

Sheeler, John. Mallorytown Glass Factory - 1839-1840, -1967.

Books

Baudoin, Philibert. Incorporated Bodies. Montreal Notary of Department of Agriculture, Montreal.

Beck, Doreen. The Book of Bottle Collecting. Hamlyn Publishing Group Ltd., London, New York, Sydney, Toronto, 1973.

Chambers, W.& R. Chambers' Encyclopaedia; Lippincott & Co., Philadelphia - W.& R. Chambers, Edinburgh, 1873-4-5.

Chambers, William & Robert. Chambers Information for the People. William & Robert Chambers, Edinburgh, 1842.

Fountain, John C., & Colcleaser, Donald E. Dictionary of Spirit & Whisky Bottles. Ole Empty Bottle House Publishing Co., Amador City, California, 1969.

Index to Companies (hand written - no pub.), Toronto.

Moorman, J.J., M.D. Mineral Springs of North America, 1873.

Munsey, Cecil. The Illustrated Guide to Collecting Bottles. Hawthorn Books, New York & Prentice Hall of Canada, Scarborough, 1970.

Savage, George. Glass - Pleasures and Treasures, Weidenfield & Nicholson, London, England, 1965.

Grantees Longueuil Township, Prescott, Ont. 1845-55.

Toulouse, Dr. Julian Harrison. A Primer on Mold Seams, reprinted from the Western Collector, 1969.

Wills, Geoffrey, English and Irish Glass, Doubleday Publishers, New York, 1968.

Wills, Geoffrey. Antique Glass for Pleasure & Investment, John Gifford Ltd. London WC2, 1971.

Papers

Belleville Phoenix - 1831 through 1833.

Brockville Recorder - 1834, 35, 39, 43, 44, 46.

Bytown Gazette - 1836 through 1845.

Bytown Rideau Advertiser - 1836.

Caledonia Springs, Life at the Springs - June 15, 1843, Sept. 8, 1846.

Chatham Journal - 1841, 42, 44.

Chatham Tribune - 1866, 79, 97.

Chatham Weekly Planet - 1847, 56, 84.

Cobourg Star - 1843 through 1849.

Duart, Ont. The Musical Visitor - 1887.

East Kent Plaindealer - 1880 through 1904.

Grand River Sachem - 1850 to 1867   (random papers)

Halifax, The Times - 1835 through 1843.

Hamilton Gazette - 1851 through 1853.

Hollowell Free Press - 1830 through 1832

II

<u>Bibliography - cont'd.</u>

Kingston Chronicle & Gazette - 1843 through 1845.

Kingston Commercial Advertiser - 1845.

Kingston Gazette - 1810 through 1832.

Lindsay Post - 1973-4, articles.

London Chronicle (Eng.) - 1766 through 1770.

London Daily Register (Eng.) - 1784, 85.

London Times (Eng.) - 1842 through 1844.

Montreal Advertiser - 1838.

Montreal Herald - 1811 through 1819.

Montreal Pilot - 1844 through 1849.

Montreal Pilot and Evening Journal of Commerce - 1844.

Montreal Transcript - 1836 through 1847 (issues missing from April, 1845 to April 1846).

Newark, Upper Canada Gazette - 1793 through 1798.

New Brunswick, Westmoreland Times - 1862.

Nova Scotia, Yarmouth Herald - 1833 through 1867.

Ottawa Citizen - 1851.

Picton, Colonial Patriot - 1829.

Quebec, La Gazette de Quebec - 1764 through 1817.

Sandwhich, Western Herald and Farmers Magazine - 1839 through 1843.

St. Thomas Liberal - 1832.

Three Rivers Gazette - 1814 through 1817.

Toronto, The Evangelical Churchman - 1889, 1890.

Toronto Examiner - 1840 through 1853.

Toronto Globe (and name changes) 1843 through to 1921.

Toronto Herald - 1841 through 1847.

Toronto Morning Star & Toronto Transcript - 1841 through 1845.

Toronto Star - 1844 through 1846.

Uxbridge Journal - 1870 through 1879.

York, United Empire Loyalist - 1827.

York, Upper Canada Gazette - 1799 through 1835.

York Weekly Register - 1822.

Scobie's Canadian Almanac, Toronto 1848 - 55.

Various City Directories listed at end of check list re Bottle Users.

CONTENTS

I   <u>EARLY GLASS</u>

The earliest glass bottles known were found in an Etruscan tomb dating from about 150 B.C., and the finest early development of glass making is credited to Syria, in particular Sidon about 50 B.C. Tools similar to those early craftsmen are still in use today.

Glass producing centres flourished in Germany and France during the Roman occupation and continued after the Empire fell but few of the Roman decorating techniques survived. Around the tenth century, sources of alkali began to be used by the glassmakers of Germany and these have become known as 'forest glass' or Walkglas and being greenish or dark brown in colour.

In England, a craftsman from Normandy, Lawrence Vitrearieus began manufacturing Verre de Fougére, similar to the Waldglas of Germany in 1226 by the Surrey-Sussex border. Window-glass seems to have been his primary out-put as it is recorded that around 1240 he was making glass for Westminster Abbey. The glass-manufacturing industry founded by him lasted until the early seventeenth century in this area. Richard Holmere and John de Alemayen, the immediate successors, continued making window-glass but also made "urynalls, bottles, bowles, cuppis to drink, and such like", to sell locally.

A patent was granted to John Colenet and Henry Holder of England who made claim to having invented glass bottles in 1662. They were allowed a fourteen year licence provided the bottles contained a full measure of liquid. In 1696, there were ninety glasshouses listed for England and Wales and forty-two of these are said to have produced bottles. Around 1650, a few of the wine bottles then produced began to be made with seals. A dollap of molten glass was dropped on the still hot bottle and impressed with a metal stamp bearing a coat of arms, a crest or other form of identification of the future owner of the bottle. Some of these bottles were dated and it is by these 'dated seals' the sequence of bottle shapes has been charted.

The first attempt at glass making in America was around 1608 at Jamestown. Other early efforts were made but it was not until 1739 that the first major glass-house was built in America, lasting to 1779 and operated by Caspar Wistar and later his son in Salem County, New Jersey.

The discovery of the earliest glass factory yet recorded in Canada is credited to Mr. Gerald Stevens. In further research on this factory by Mr. John Sheeler, it has been established that this factory was "opened" by Amasa Whitney Mallory in Mallorytown in 1839 and continued into 1840 when it was closed "owing to the unreliableness of the foreman".

Mr. William Parker started a glass factory at Caledonia Springs in 1844, (see section on Caledonia Springs). This factory was still manufacturing bottles in 1848 but more research is yet needed to establish its closing date. The Montreal Transcript, April 24, 1845, mentions in an article under 'Home Manufactures' that "Glass Works have recently been erected at St. Johns, by a Mr. Smith of Burlington, and in a few days we learn employment will be afforded to at least eighty hands in the manufacture of glass, etc.*". Other glass houses soon followed and happily for the bottle collector, some of these, at least, can be identified, as Hamilton and Erie.

Sir Kenelm Digby, an Englishman, is credited with the idea of using bottles for the storage and transporting of wine. He died in 1665. Many liquids were stored and shipped in the square shaped bottles generally known as case

1

* DISC. BY NEWT COBURN, MONT.

bottles or 'gins' during the eighteenth century.

Bottles were frequently advertised for sale as just off, or along side the boat until around 1844. "Just received per the Lapwing and for sale by the Subscribor - 200 boxes of window glass and 100 gross of Wine Bottles. W. Henderson & Co., Quebec, June 18, 1812." - "Sales by AUCTION - Coal, Medical Bottles, Windown glass Etc., - will be sold this morning, (Tues) the 4th inst., alongside the Brig Ormond, from Newcastle, lying at Cringen's Wharf: 100 chaldrons Newcastle Coals, 50 chaldrons Cinders, 500 boxes Window Glass, 126 crates of Bottles, consisting of Wine, Porter and a general assortment of Medical Bottles. Sale at 1 o'clock, James Young, 1838. Montreal."

Soda Water and Ginger Beer bottles were advertised as two distinct types as "SODA WATER AND GINGER BEER BOTTLES - just received and for sale by the Subscribors. 100 gross of Soda Water Bottles, and 400 Stone Ginger Bottles. Alfred Savage & Co., Montreal. June 4th, 1842."

Gullivier & Sons, Toronto, 1843, held an auction of Glass Ware at their store consisting of Tumblers, Phials, Confectioners and Covers, 50 crates of Bottles, Flat Octagons, Mustard, Winchester Pints, and half pints, Corlyn Qts., 22doz., Castor Oils, Soda Waters, and Wines in pints and quarts. The duty on imported bottles in 1844 was "Bottles - duty: 20% ad valorem on Foreign; 5% on British". This would certainly account for buying British.

Lyman Elliot & Co., Toronto, offered 40 crates of wine bottles to Brewers in 1860 and, for all bottles were frequently advertised, they never seemed to be in very good supply around Toronto until after the Hamilton Glass Works started. James Leask, a whisky dealer was among those who often asked for any quantity of wine and ale bottles and would pick them up if desired.

The old story about the 'Scotch' Doctor who instructed his assistant to always tell the patients to bring in a sample when they came because he needed the bottles, may have been based more on fact than fiction.

There is still much to learn about both bottles and their users in Canada and this book is intended, hopefully, to help the collector along the way. I include no price guide: After all, who knows better than you and your pocket-book just how much that bottle is really worth.

References

Munsey, Cecil - The Illustrated Guide to Collecting Bottles, Hawthorn Books, New York & Prentice Hall of Canada, Scarborough, 1970.

Sheeler, John - Mallorytown Glass Factory - 1839-1840, - 1967.

Wills, Geoffrey - English and Irish Glass, Doubleday Publishers, New York, 1968.

Wills, Geoffrey - Antique Glass for Pleasure and Investment, John Gifford Ltd., London WC2, 1971.

La Gazzette de Quebec - 1812.

Montreal Advertiser - 1838.

Montreal Pilot - 1843.

Montreal Transcript - 1842-44-45.

Toronto Globe - 1848-60-62.

Toronto Examiner - 1843.

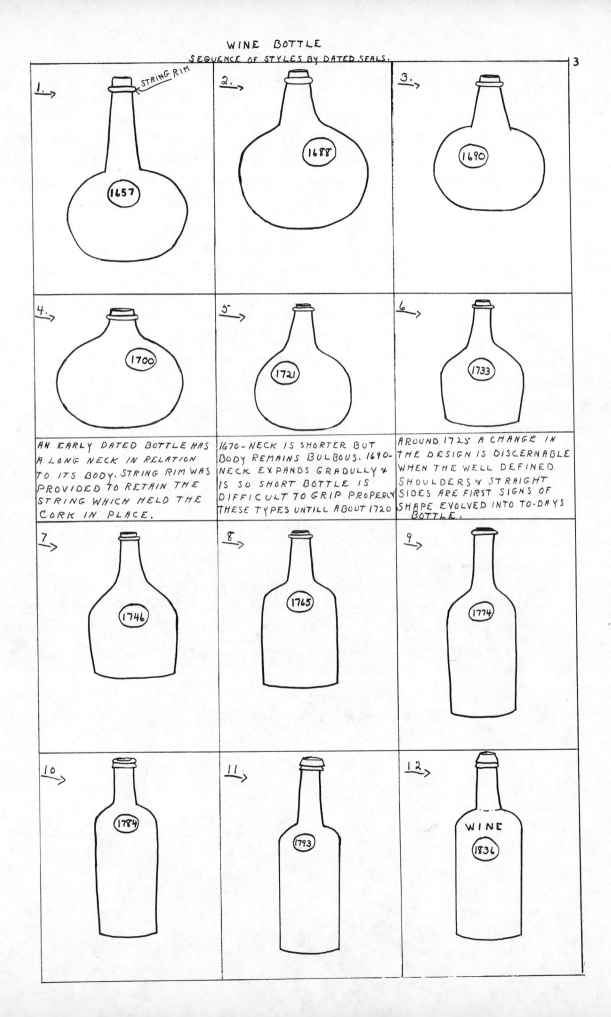

1. → STRING RIM

1657

2. → 1688

3. → 1690

4. → 1700

5. → 1721

6. → 1733

AN EARLY DATED BOTTLE HAS A LONG NECK IN RELATION TO ITS BODY. STRING RIM WAS PROVIDED TO RETAIN THE STRING WHICH HELD THE CORK IN PLACE.

1670-NECK IS SHORTER BUT BODY REMAINS BULBOUS. 1690-NECK EXPANDS GRADULLY & IS SO SHORT BOTTLE IS DIFFICULT TO GRIP PROPERLY THESE TYPES UNTILL ABOUT 1720

AROUND 1725 A CHANGE IN THE DESIGN IS DISCERNABLE WHEN THE WELL DEFINED SHOULDERS & STRAIGHT SIDES ARE FIRST SIGNS OF SHAPE EVOLVED INTO TO-DAYS BOTTLE.

7. → 1746

8. → 1765

9. → 1774

10. → 1784

11. → 1793

12. → WINE 1836

Early bottle glass was generally composed of soap-makers waste and sand. The following recipe was recommended by a Dr. Ure as producing a good dark green glass: - "Dry glauber salts, 11 pounds; soaper salts, 12 pounds; half a bushel of waste soap ashes; sand, 56 pounds; glass skimmings, 22 pounds; green broken glass, 1 cwt; and basalt, 25 pounds."

In England by 1863, the soap-makers waste (which contained soda-salts), fresh-water river-sand, brick-dust, calcined-lime, and marl (soil consisting of carbonate of lime and clay), was used and to this a quantity of cullet, or broken glass of the works, was always added. This was the mixture employed for the manufacture of black bottles used for wine, beer, etc. For some years light-green coloured glass had been preferred for soda water and medicine bottles, and this colour was commonly produced by adding a large proportion of the cullet of crown-glass, which by its light colour, diluted the darker material. If a still finer quality was desired it was made with a light coloured sand, containing only about two tenths percent of oxide of iron. To 50 parts of this sand was added 20 parts of heavy spar (sulphate of Baryta), 30 parts of soap-makers waste, and about two-tenths percent of oxide of manganese.

In France, kelp and wood-ashes were used to furnish the alkaline part of the mixture; in other respects the material used was essentially the same. In Germany, where a brown tint was in fashion for bottles to contain the light-coloured Rhine Wines, the materials consisted of light coloured clay; 16 parts, a light coloured-sand, 20 parts; kelp, 8 parts; wood-ashes, 38 parts; cullet, 15 parts; and oxide of manganese, 3 parts.

Preparation of the melting pots was one of the first essentials to the successful manufacture of glass. These pots were made up of clay and required to be as free as possible from lime and iron. This clay was dried and sifted and then mixed with hot water and worked into a paste, when it was transferred to the kneading-floor and there kneaded by men tramping it with their bare feet. It was then layed in large masses in a dark cellar to ripen. When required for forming the pots, a sufficient quantity was taken and again kneaded with one fourth its quantity of the material from old pots which were ground to a fine powder and sifted, making the finished pot less liable to be effected by heat. The open pot (Fig. 1) was the type used for melting common glass such as window and bottle. The pots were made carefully by hand, the bottom being first molded on a board, when the sides were built up

layer by layer until the pot was complete. The workmen did not work continuously as it was necessary to leave off from time to time to allow a certain amount of drying, else the weight of the clay would prevent the form from being kept. The pots made for bottle and window glass were three or four inches thick. They were then thoroughly dried and stored for from six to nine months before being used, at which time they were placed for four or five days in the annealing furnace and kept at a red-heat. They were then transferred to the main furnace from the annealing furnace by an immense pair of forceps placed horizontally upon an upright iron pillar about three feet in height which rose from a samll iron truck on four wheels, so the whole could be moved easily from place to

FIG. 1

place. By this means the pot was lifted and withdrawn from the oven and quickly transferred to its position in the main furnace while still red hot, that no sudden cooling would injure the pot. The pots were seated on a platform of fire-brick or stone, and each was opposite to a small arched opening, through which it could be filled or emptied. This entrance was then closed with a movable fire-brick door and covered with fireclay to prevent heat escapage. The pots were then filled with the prepared glass materials, now called 'frit', mixed with about a sixth or eighth part of broken glass, (cullet), and the openings closed for two or three hours, when the first charge of materials had melted down, leaving room for a further supply, and being repeated two or three times until the pot was full. The openings were then closed and the heat increased to the utmost for ten or twelve hours, this was called 'founding' and the result was to melt and vitrify the materials, when the heat was somewhat reduced, and the scum removed from the surface of the melted material now called metal, by a workman called the skimmer. The metal was now ready for the commencement of the journey, as the operation of working it up is called.

In the ground plan of a Bottle House the main furnace is (Fig. 2 - next page) A, and in this case is square, and made to hold four pots; at each corner is an opening which allows the fire to enter four small reverberatory furnaces: B, B, B, B, called arches; two are called the coarse arches and the other two the fine. In the first two, the soap-makers waste was calcined at a red heat for at least four hours, or while a set of pots were worked out - (one journey). The calcined material was then ground and sifted in the grinding and sifting house, H, after which it was mixed with the sand etc., and transferred to the fine arches, where for the term of another journey it was again calcined. At the end of that time, the now empty pots were refilled with this material.

When the furnaces were opened for a journey and the scum removed, the way was clear for the blower and moulder, who took his blow-pipe (of iron, about six foot in length), the part held in the hand being guarded by wood or other non-conducting materials. After heating the end of the blow-pipe in the furnace mouth, he dipped it in the pot and turning it around, gathered as much metal on the end as was needed to form a bottle of the size required. The operator then blew gently down the pipe, and having thus slightly distended the bulb of red-hot plastic glass (Fig. 3), took it to a plate of polished iron, forming a low bench called the 'maver', or mavering table. He turned it around on this, moulding the round lump of glass into a conical form, the change being represented in (Fig. 4). This operation(then called mavering), was performed in all cases where glass was blown; and as it was necessary that the glass be fairly firm before mavering, was often cooled by sprinkling with water, and even, as in the case of window glass, and other large blowings, turning it in a cavity containing water, which was made by hollowing out a block of wood, usually that of a pear tree, if obtainable, thought to be best for the purpose.

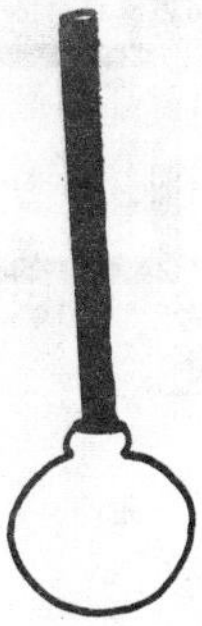

After being 'mavered', the glass was held to the mouth of the furnace and further distended by blowing. "Formerly he moulded it into the shape of a bottle with his shears, one arm of which was of charred wood, and the concave bottom was made by pushing a little piece of glass, called a 'punty', at the end of an iron rod called a pointel; the blow-pipe was then detached by a slight blow of the shears, and the partly formed bottle was

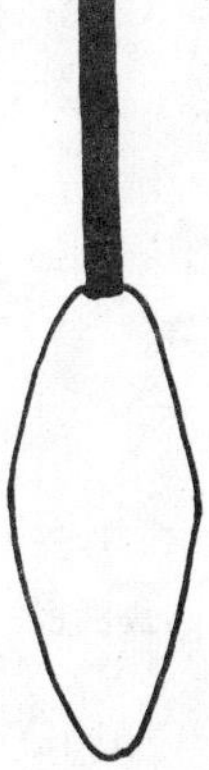

FIG. 3

FIG. 4

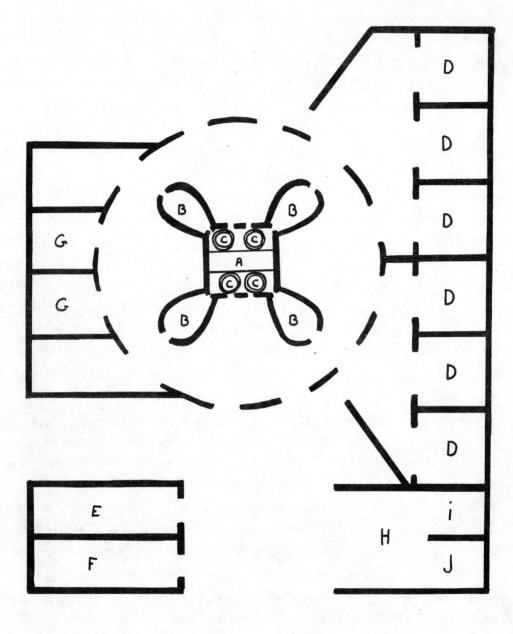

FIG. 2

left at the end of the pointel attached by the punty in the hands of a boy who attends upon the man, and brought and applied the punty. The man then took the pointel in one hand, and after softening the bottle in the mouth of the furnace moulded the neck by means of his shears, regulating the size of the opening by means of a small brass mould, the size and shape of a cork, attached to the middle of the shears; he formed with a small portion of metal from the pot the ring around the mouth of the bottle.

"Now, however, after mavering, and the first slight blowing, the operator inserts the glass into an iron or brass mould, which is formed in two pieces, opening or closing by the pressure of a foot on a lever. When the mould is closed he blows down the pipe, and the bottle is completed all but the neck, the ring of which has to be formed by the addition of a fresh piece of metal, as before described. By this process bottles are made with wonderful rapidity and exactness. At this stage of the manufacture, in either process, the bottles are taken from the workman by a little boy, who inserts the prongs of a fork into the necks, and carries them to one of the annealing arches, D, D, D, D, D, D, where they are carefully arranged in proper bins, until the arch, which usually holds 144 dozen, is full." The arch was then closed and the heat raised almost to the melting point, when it was allowed to subside gradually until cold when the bottles were removed for a fresh batch (charge).

In the plan (Fig.2), E and F are the sand and alkali stores; G, G, are stores for the prepared frit; and I and J are sifting-cribs in the sifting-house.

In an article printed some twenty years earlier the brass mould on the shears was mentioned thus - "on one of the blades of the shears, is a piece of brass resembling a cork, by which the inside of the neck is formed."

The "mavering table" was referred to as a "marver" and the "punty" and "pointel" were referred to jointly as a "punty-rod".

Bibliography

Chambers Encyclopaedia - 1870, (article written in 1863) Philadelphia: J.B. Lippincott & Co. - Edinburgh: W.& R. Chambers

Chambers Information for the People - Pub. by William & Robert Chambers, Edinburgh - 1842.

III BOTTLE COLLECTING

Bottle collectors are fast becoming more numerous in Canada and if you depend on your pocket-book and another's labours as your source it could be a rather expensive hobby. Bottles may be found at flea markets and the odd dealer may have a few at the antique show, but unless you have just been newly bitten by the bottle bug the best source is the bottle show. Here collectors and dealers gather to buy, sell, dicker, deal and chin wag. Toronto had its first bottle show in the fall of seventy-three, organised by Jon Delondrea of "Old York Bottles" and shows are also held in other cities. Collectors attend from near and far and a great day is had by all.

Many of the older farms had a spot where the owners disposed of their garbage for many years and these, if you can find them and they were not also used for a rock pile, are good hunting grounds. Ask the owners permission first please. A friend brought us some bottles from an old well they were cleaning out, another from a construction site. I have heard of bottles taken from an old 'privie'. We have bottles from an old wood-shed where a previous owner had lined them up on a ledge under the roof years ago. An old dump has other goodies than bottles, we have found glass lamps, unbroken crocks, salt shakers and a spittoon among other things.

A garden fork and hand trowel are better than a spade for digging; you will find too many broken bottles as it is. We carry a plastic jug filled with a mixture of water and javex for washing our hands; sure we wear gloves, but these often come off to grub around with bare fingers. A can of bug repellent - the kind you spray yourself with, can be a blessing. Wear sturdy shoes so you won't cut your feet, and don't forget something to carry the bottles back to the car in, you could have a bit of a hike. Watch out for hornets and snakes and consider the fresh air and exercise an added benefit.

Pine pitch, tar, goose grease, turpentine and your guess is as good as mine - seems to have been a mixture no-one could do without, and generally stored in a nicer bottle. Tri Sodium Phosphate (T.S.P.) from the hardware or drug store, is good to cut through this. Put a couple of tsp. in the bottle and fill with warm (not hot - old glass can be fragile) water and let it soak, shaking once in awhile. Most will clean in an hour or so but some may take a week and a change or so of solution. Full strength javel water is good for rust stains. For the ordinary dirty bottle - once you have disposed of any dead mice that might be in it, rinse and then clean with sink powder and a brush. Coat hanger wire is good for poking into corners and pipe cleaners help on very small bottles. A tooth brush and scouring powder or a fine steel wool pad are fine for the outside. For spots you cannot otherwise reach, drop a metal chain inside with some water and shake. It is simpler to remove than pebbles or shot and will not clog your drain as rice could. A very old method recommended for cleaning bottles is to soak with raw ground potato, salt and water. This is said to be good for stains in wine decanters. The streaked foggy stain sometimes left after the bottle is dry can be hidden with a coating of mineral oil if it bothers you, but cork to keep the dust out. Coat hangers or meat skewers bent to a hook will help remove corks.

You will not find labeled bottles in a dump, but they are available otherwise on occasion. Do not wash the label if it can be avoided, but rather see what you can do with a soft eraser to remove dirt. Some of the early inks were not indelible and will wash off. Usually a label with a glossy surface may be safely wiped with a damp cloth and the flat surface not. If you do wash, be sure it is thoroughly dry before using a preservative. A semi-gloss urethane or clear nail polish works well for this last, but make certain the label does not need reglueing before you apply.

A coat or so of clear nail polish will dull a sharp chip enough to prevent a cut finger and with time and patience will even fill it in. There are clear glues available at hobby shops that may be used for repairing broken bottles. Clean broken surfaces thoroughly before attempting any repair and follow instructions on the tube, using the least possible amount of glue. A bottle in good supply is not worth the time involved, but a repaired example of a scarce one is something else.

Old bottles are found by skin divers on the bottoms of lakes and rivers in Canada, in particular the resort areas. Before general garbage dumps came into use these were a favoured dumping ground of cottagers and fishermen. Bottles are where ever you find them. Enjoy them.

IV   COLOUR IN GLASS

The collector of old bottles finds the bubbles and crudeness in the glass fascinating, and the many shades of amber, blue, green and amethyst contribute their full share of pleasure, an added delight is when a beautiful black held to the light is discovered to be a dark rich ruby.

The 'Catalogue of Economic Minerals and Deposits of Canada, with localities' by W.E. Logan, Provincial Geologist, in Scobie's Canadian Almanac, 1848 - 55, listed - "Materials for glass making - White Quartz Sandstone - Lake Huron -

on the north shore and Islands near, in great abundance. Cayuga, lots 45 and 46, Town line, north of Talbot Road; Dunn, Vaudreuil Seigniory; Isle Perrot Seigniory; Beauharnois Seigniory - Pitchstone, Basalt and Allied Rocks (for black glass) - Lake Superior - North shore and Islands; Michipicoten Island and East Coast. Lake Huron - in the trap dykes of the north shore, and neighboring Islands; Rigaud Mountain; Montreal Mountain; Montarville Mountain."

The Caledonia Glass Works, (Caledonia Springs, Canada) were advertising for two men "acquainted with the manufactury of black bottles", in 1846. This was the desired colour for wine or other spirits. Purchasers were advised to store the water from the Springs in a cool dark place so here also the 'black Glass' would be deemed a desirable trait. In 1868 the Hamilton Glass Work's display at the Hamilton Provincial Exhibition was mentioned as being principally in green glass, but also "The firm confine themselves to the manufacture of descriptions from green, blue and amber glass and hitherto have".

The presence of iron in sand renders the glass batch green when untreated with other oxides and the shade of green depends upon the amount of iron present. This untreated bottle glass was the cheapest to produce, hence the commonest product of the bottle house for many years.

Very early glass-makers learned how to colour their glass by adding certain compounds to their basic mixture. Copper was the colouring agent for shades of greens and blue greens. The Romans used antimony to produce an opaque white, and in later years tin oxide was used for the same purpose. Violet, purple and brown were produced by using manganese in fairly large quantities, and in small amounts acted as a decolourizer by neutralizing the greenish tinge. It is this manganese that was used when clear bottles came into demand (by manufacturers wanting a better visual appearance of their product) that causes bottles left in the sun to become 'sun coloured'. The amount of manganese used in the batch determines the darkness or lightness of the 'purple'. Around 1916 manganese was discontinued, and the 'sun-yellow' colour results from the selenium used in its stead. This changing from clear to colour is caused by a chemical reaction with the ultra-violet rays from the sun and the decolourizing agent used.

The chart following is an example of materials frequently used and colours obtained:

Black glass	–	iron slag
Blues	–	copper or cobalt
Browns	–	carbon or nickle
Greens	–	copper or chromium
Greens & Yellows	–	iron
Pinks & Yellows	–	selenium
Purples	–	manganese or nickle
Milkglass (White)	–	tin or zinc
Reds	–	copper, gold, selenium

Some old bottles have a rainbow-like iridescence (something like the appearance of oil spilled on a wet road) that have been dug. The iridescence is caused by the interaction of the glass surface with certain acids in the soil, and the colours are in reality a reflection of broken light rays passing through layers of corrosion. Long burial is generally necessary for the development of this iridescence, but not slways so; I have seen some bottles made no earlier than 1910 that were taken from a swamp near Uxbridge, Ontario that are very colourful.

References

George Savage, "Glass - Pleasures and Treasures", Weidenfeld & Nicholson, 20 New Bond Strret, London, W1, 1965.

Cecil Munsey, "The Illustrated Guide to Collecting Bottles", Hawthorn Books Inc., N.Y., U.S.A. and Prentice-Hall of Canada Ltd., Scarborough, Ontario.

"Scobie's Canadian Almanac", Toronto, 1848 - 55.

"The Globe", Toronto, Sept. 22, 1868.

"Life at the Springs, and Visitors List", Caledonia Springs, Canada, Sept. 8, 1846.

V   MOLD SEAMS

Molds have been in use for centuries but the concern here is the seams on hand blown bottles mainly from the nineteenth centrury and later by machine. Geoffrey Wills (From Bottles to 1720, English and Irish Glass) mentions a London newspaper item in 1752 that referred to "one Brass Bottle-Mould stolen from a glass house" presuming it to be of a type that came together for making the bottle and fell apart to release it. The London Daily Register (Feb. 23, 1784) printed a letter of testimonial for some 'Drops' with the addition "These Drops are sold in the new moulded Bottles at 2s.6d, & One Guinea each".

"The junction of the separate pieces or parts of the composite mold leaves a surface mark on the glass that is blown within it no matter how carefully the molds are made and it is the position of these marks (Mold seams) that help determine the type of mold used". (Toulouse, "A Primer on Mold Seams".)

A bottle with no mold seams may be one of three kinds. It could be a Free Blown bottle, blown in a Tapered Dip Mold or Turned in a Mold.

Free Blown without Molds are initially blown in the globular or balloon shape that glass assumes when inflated and free from any restraint but the attachment to the blowpipe. This shape may be modified by tooling and manipulation of the blowpipe during the blowing process to lengthen or shorten the bottle. It could be rolled on a 'marvre', flattened, twisted or pressed to give a pattern, and in any case it will be a bit lop-sided. Free blown bottles have been made for centuries - and are still made today. (Fig. 1.)

A TAPERED DIP MOLD looks very much like a Free Blown, marver rolled bottle, but is tapered from the widest point near the shoulder down to the smallest diameter near the base. The neck and shoulders are Free Blown and hand finished. There may be a slight swelling or ridge at the point where the glass left the mold. The action of pressing the hot glass tipped pontil against the bottom to adhere and form the push-up, as well as setting the bottle upright act together to give the bell bottomed appearance of many of these bottles. (Fig. 2.)

In the TURN MOLD it is not the mold but the bottle that is turned. This rotating of the bottle erased the side seams while the glass was still in a plastic state. Because of this designs and lettering could not be used and the bottle had always to be circular, but could have any vertical contour. The molds were given a special surface treatment on parts coming into contact with the glass, such as sawdust paste, and were generally wetted between each blowing. This made a layer of steam that helped the rotation and polished the bottle. Aside from the lack of mold seams these

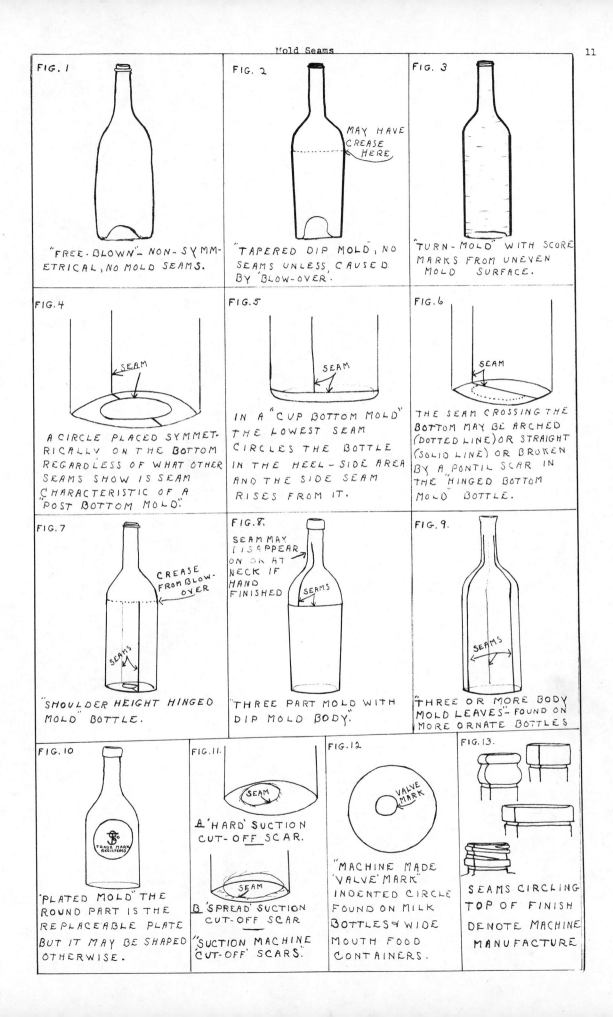

FIG. 1
"FREE·BLOWN"· NON·SYMM-ETRICAL, NO MOLD SEAMS.

FIG. 2
MAY HAVE CREASE HERE
"TAPERED DIP MOLD", NO SEAMS UNLESS CAUSED BY 'BLOW-OVER.'

FIG. 3
"TURN-MOLD" WITH SCORE MARKS FROM UNEVEN MOLD SURFACE.

FIG. 4
SEAM
A CIRCLE PLACED SYMMET-RICALLY ON THE BOTTOM REGARDLESS OF WHAT OTHER SEAMS SHOW IS SEAM CHARACTERISTIC OF A "POST BOTTOM MOLD".

FIG. 5
SEAM
IN A "CUP BOTTOM MOLD" THE LOWEST SEAM CIRCLES THE BOTTLE IN THE HEEL-SIDE AREA AND THE SIDE SEAM RISES FROM IT.

FIG. 6
SEAM
THE SEAM CROSSING THE BOTTOM MAY BE ARCHED (DOTTED LINE) OR STRAIGHT (SOLID LINE) OR BROKEN BY A PONTIL SCAR IN THE "HINGED BOTTOM MOLD" BOTTLE.

FIG. 7
CREASE FROM BLOW-OVER
SEAMS
"SHOULDER HEIGHT HINGED MOLD" BOTTLE.

FIG. 8
SEAM MAY DISAPPEAR ON OR AT NECK IF HAND FINISHED
SEAMS
"THREE PART MOLD WITH DIP MOLD BODY."

FIG. 9
SEAMS
"THREE OR MORE BODY MOLD LEAVES"· FOUND ON MORE ORNATE BOTTLES

FIG. 10
TRADE MARK REGISTERED
"PLATED MOLD" THE ROUND PART IS THE REPLACEABLE PLATE BUT IT MAY BE SHAPED OTHERWISE.

FIG. 11.
SEAM
A 'HARD' SUCTION CUT-OFF SCAR.
SEAM
B 'SPREAD' SUCTION CUT-OFF SCAR
"SUCTION MACHINE CUT-OFF' SCARS."

FIG. 12
VALVE MARK
"MACHINE MADE 'VALVE' MARK" INDENTED CIRCLE FOUND ON MILK BOTTLES & WIDE MOUTH FOOD CONTAINERS.

FIG. 13.
SEAMS CIRCLING TOP OF FINISH DENOTE MACHINE MANUFACTURE

bottles have horizontal lines; some heavy and easily seen and others visible only under reflected light. Turn Molds became popular in the 1870's for wine etc. They are generally dated to 1900 - 1905, but were used later. The 'Kirsch' bottle (Spirits, 101, p.12) produced and bottled in Switzerland, has a picture of a tractor drawing a binder through a field of wheat on the back part of the neck label from 1920 or later. (Turn Mold, Fig. 3.)

A POST BOTTOM MOLD has a circular seam, always centred, at the contact area on which the bottle stands. From this circle the two or more seams branch off, turn the heel and go on up the body. The raised platform in the centre of the bottom forming area is called the post. This construction was old when Mason used it in the fruit jar he patented in 1858. Post Bottoms may be used with any type of body mold. (Fig. 4.)

On the CUP BOTTOM MOLD the lowest bottle seam is a circle around the heel from which the side seam rises. "In contrast with the Post Bottom Mold, the part that shapes the bottom of the bottle is cut into the bottom plate as a small depression or cup. The construction requires some sort of limiting stops in order to centre the body mold halves over the cup without off-set." This is still a common machine type mold. (Fig. 5.)

In the HINGED BOTTOM MOLD the seam crosses the bottom of the bottle. It may be straight or it can take a half circle around a central push-up. Either way it turns the heel and goes up toward the finish and the seam crosses the bottom. This mold was in use by 1810. In the earlier period the seam is partly erased by the pontil scar. It may be found without a scar, so may be dated until 1890 or later, when held in a snap case. (Fig. 6.)

A HINGED SHOULDER HEIGHT MOLD is not necessarily tapered and differs from the Shoulder Height Dip Mold in that it may be decorated and lettered. In this the side seam disappears at or just above the widest diameter of the bottle. This mold opened at the shoulder to remove the bottle but the operator must still shape the shoulder with his own skill as in the Tapered Dip Mold. "A Shoulder Height Mold was not limited as to the number of leaves making up its girth". (Fig. 7.)

The THREE PART MOLD with DIP MOLD BODY was most popular from 1870 to 1910. The body was tapered and generally without decoration or lettering, although this was done (Spirits, Whyte & Mackay, 106, p.13, an example). These bottles are identified by the lowest seam encircling the bottle at its widest point and two seams from this point upward. (Fig. 8.)

THREE or MORE PART MOLDS with BODY MOLD LEAVES are found on the more ornate decorated bottle. Each part is a complete segment of the body mold from base to neck and may be used with any type base. Picture an orange peeled and separated, but with the bottom intact. (Fig. 9.)

BLOW-BACK and BLOW-OVER MOLDS are identified by a seam that goes all the way to the top of the bottle, which is sometimes left ragged but is usually ground or fired. This technique was used so long as hand made finishes were blown in a mold in order to standardise their forms, and included screw threads and other forms as external lugs or sharp cornered ledges for wire and other clips. The purpose of the Blow-Back was to provide a place where the glass would blow thinner and could easily be cracked off. The Blow-Back was a circular bulb like formation, above the finish in the mold.

In the Blow-Over a small fraction of an inch of straight metal was designed into the mold above the top of the finish. When the mold was blown full the operator would keep on blowing and balloon the glass above the top of the mold and "pop it free". You can not determine from the bottle which method was used.

In the PLATED MOLD the identifying seam characteristic is a circular or oblong seam on either or both sides of the bottle, the seam does not touch any other seams and is found in Round, Oblong and Panelled bottles. It is caused by a junction of a body mold part and a removable insert called a Plate. By this method personalised bottles could be made for many customers using the same body mold and inserting a Plate with their name, trade mark etc., at a lesser cost. Prescription and medicine bottles were commonly and are still made by this method. (Fig. 10.)

A SUCTION MACHINE 'CUT-OFF SCAR is made as the junction between the knife that severs the glass from the pot, and the side of the bottom opening of the blank mold. This formation dates from the development of the first suction machine in 1904 to the present time. Since this scar is formed as part of the 'blank' mold operation it is stretched by blowing after it is formed so is not usually centred. This Scar is identified as an irregular circle with ragged edges on the bottom of the bottle varying from small and strong (Hard Suction Cut-Off Scar) to a wider and fainter mark, which may extend around the curve of the heel to the lower sidewall, and be termed a Spread Suction Cut-Off Scar. (Fig. 11, A & B.)

The MACHINE MADE VALVE MARK is a circle generally from one half to seven-eighths of an inch in diameter formed as an indention into the surface of the glass on the base of the bottle. It is strongly marked, seldom centred and found most often on the wide mouthed food containers of the 1930's and 40's and common on milk bottles. (Fig. 12.)

SEAM DISAPPEARING IN THE NECK is caused by the Finishing Tool and has nothing to do with the type of mold used, it may be of any part construction with any type of bottom as long as the bottle has seams that go all the way to the finish as it is removed from the mold and prepared for hand finishing. The end of the neck seam is determined by the finishing tool used, not the time when the bottle was made. The glass worker could insert a cylindrical rod into the mouth of the bottle to keep the metal from collapsing under jaw pressure while fire curing. Reheating and turning the bottle would erase the seam. Generally a ring of glass was laid around the top part of the neck before using the tool. This 'laid on ring' is usually quite evident on the earlier bottles, but not always so. A laid on ring could also be used for decoration, or, as in the case of some decanters, to insure a better grip. The cruder finished rings can usually be dated pre the gas fired glory hole (late 1870's), when it fused the two glasses so well they appear as one. Bubbles add interest to a bottle and many of the older ones have plenty, but are not neccessarily a sign of age. Many machine made bottles are 'measled' with bubbles.

ONE or MORE SEAMS Circle Top of Finish - Almost all machines have a 'plunger' or 'tip' which merely defines the inner throat diameter of the finish in the narrow mouth, or presses the parison into shape in the wide mouth. In either case the tip has to contact glass. A collar also descends into contact with the glass to guide the tip, and the juncture between the tip and collar leaves a circular seam.

"Since the collar also contacts the neck rings, their junction also produces a seam that is circular, concentric with, but larger and outside of, the tip-collar seam. These two seams can be a mark of a machine made glass piece (container) with certainty. If they are smoothed over by firepolishing, other signs must be relied upon to indicate machine making for the bottle." The exception here are beer and beverage bottles with the crown finish and often firepolished to smooth the top of the finish. (Fig. 13.)

13

WHITTLE MARKS - Many older bottles have a wavy or hammered appearance on the surface of the glass, and early collectors assumed that these marks were caused by the glass being blown into a carved wooden mold, hence the terms 'Whittle' or 'Chip' marks still used to describe the marks on these bottles. With the growth of bottle collecting these "Whittle Marks" were found by competent researchers to be caused by the shrinkage of hot glass when blown into a cold mold. As bottles are a common article, the producers would be more interested in quantity than surface smoothness and not worry much about warming molds at the beginning of the day. (Munsey, p.46, "Whittle Marks".)

References

From Bottles to 1720, English and Irish Glass by Geoffrey Wills.

The London Daily Register, Feb. 23, 1784.

A Primer on Mold Seams by Dr. Julian Harrison Toulouse, Reprinted from the Western Collector, November, December, 1969.

The Illustrated Guide to Collecting Bottles by Cecil Munsey, published by Hawthorn Books, Inc., 70 Fifth Avenue, New York, New York 10011 and published simultaneously in Canada by Prentice Hall of Canada, Ltd., 1870 Birchmount Road, Scarborough, Ontario.

VI   PONTILS AND PUSH-UPS

The pontil is the rod used to hold the glass article after it has been separated from the blowpipe during the finishing process. A sharp tap on the rod detaches the pontil from the base leaving a scar which is called a pontil mark.

The "glass tipped" pontil mark is made by a solid iron bar slightly wider at the end which is dipped in molten glass (Fig. 1) and adheres to the glass of the base. The mark is generally fairly small but varies with the size of the vessel and is usually evident either by the excess glass left when the pontil was detached or because bits of glass have been torn out of the base. Sometimes it is smoothed off by polishing. This technique was used on flasks, medicine, toiletry bottles and tableware and still is, on hand manufactured articles. (Fig. 2.)

The sand glass-tipped pontil - "sand pontil" is a gather of glass on the pontil shaped to conform with the basal profile and then dipped in sand. (Fig. 3.)

The sand pontil mark consists of a thin line of glass chips encircling the push-up and enclosing a pebbled surface caused by the grains of sand. Some of the sand may also be embedded in the base. The mark is usually larger than the glass-tipped one, but here again varies with the size of the bottle. These marks are common on dark green English bottles found on Canadian sites dating from the 18th century and later. They are found on octagonal and occasionly on case bottles. Sand pontils are still used on articles manufactured by hand. (Figs. 4 and 5.)

The blow-pipe pontil technique consisted of using the glass left on the blow-pipe after the bottle was snapped off. (Fig. 6.) "The bottle was laid on a V-shaped structure while the glass-maker applied the blowpipe with its excess glass to the base of the bottle". (Fig. 7.) The action of removing the blowpipe from the base either tore glass out with it or left extra glass behind, leaving a distinct ring-shaped mark. (Fig. 8.)

French "flower pot" wine bottles made with this empontilling technique have been found "on a Canadian site occupied by the French between 1732 and 1745" and was still used in the nineteenth century in the United States. These ring-

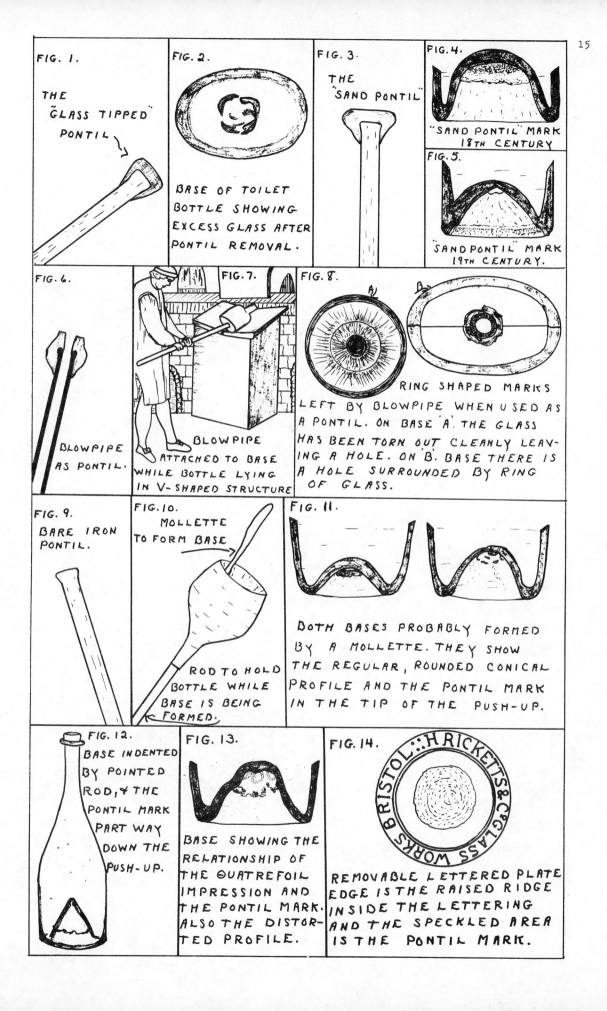

FIG. 1.

THE "GLASS TIPPED" PONTIL

FIG. 2.

BASE OF TOILET BOTTLE SHOWING EXCESS GLASS AFTER PONTIL REMOVAL.

FIG. 3.

THE "SAND PONTIL"

FIG. 4.

"SAND PONTIL" MARK 18TH CENTURY

FIG. 5.

"SAND PONTIL" MARK 19TH CENTURY.

FIG. 6.

BLOWPIPE AS PONTIL.

FIG. 7.

BLOWPIPE ATTACHED TO BASE WHILE BOTTLE LYING IN V-SHAPED STRUCTURE

FIG. 8.

RING SHAPED MARKS LEFT BY BLOWPIPE WHEN USED AS A PONTIL. ON BASE 'A' THE GLASS HAS BEEN TORN OUT CLEANLY LEAVING A HOLE. ON 'B' BASE THERE IS A HOLE SURROUNDED BY RING OF GLASS.

FIG. 9.
BARE IRON PONTIL.

FIG. 10.
MOLLETTE TO FORM BASE

ROD TO HOLD BOTTLE WHILE BASE IS BEING FORMED.

FIG. 11.

BOTH BASES PROBABLY FORMED BY A MOLLETTE. THEY SHOW THE REGULAR, ROUNDED CONICAL PROFILE AND THE PONTIL MARK IN THE TIP OF THE PUSH-UP.

FIG. 12.
BASE INDENTED BY POINTED ROD, & THE PONTIL MARK PART WAY DOWN THE PUSH-UP.

FIG. 13.

BASE SHOWING THE RELATIONSHIP OF THE QUATREFOIL IMPRESSION AND THE PONTIL MARK. ALSO THE DISTORTED PROFILE.

FIG. 14.

BRISTOL ∴ H.RICKETTS & C° GLASS WORKS

REMOVABLE LETTERED PLATE EDGE IS THE RAISED RIDGE INSIDE THE LETTERING AND THE SPECKLED AREA IS THE PONTIL MARK.

shaped marks are found on vials, flasks, medicine, champagne and case bottles.

The "bare iron" empontilling technique consisted of using the end of a suitably shaped bare iron pontil (usually a shallow arch, Fig. 10), heating it red hot and applying it directly to the base of the bottle. The resulting pontil mark is circular and covered with a reddish or black deposit. Tests on these marks have indicated the presence of ferric oxide, and sometimes ferrous oxide. This distinct form has been found in American flasks, fruit jars and carbonated beverage bottles dating from about 1845 to 1870.

Miss Jones mentions having seen 18th and early 19th century bottles in the National Historic Sites Service Collection (Ottawa), with iron oxide deposits spread unevenly over the pontil mark area. She offers several explanations for this deposit including possibly a bare iron pontil having been used and states "Obviously further investigations will have to be carried out on this technique".

The sabot and snap case were introduced between the late 1840's and 50's, and gradually replaced the pontil, and, "By the 1870's they had superceded the pontil for holding bottles during the finishing process".

A base that has been pushed up into the body cavity is called a "push-up" or "kick" and several explanations have been given for its presence.

1 - An indented base helped the glassmakers produce a bottle that would stand upright without wobbling.

2 - A push-up helped to make a stronger bottle. The bottle often rested on its base while being made allowing the glass to flow toward the basal area and the glass was redistributed and thinned by pushing up the base. The annealing process is less effective if the glass is concentrated too heavily in one place. The push-up could also help the bottle withstand more internal pressure as in sparkling wines.

3 - Others suggest deep push-ups were made deliberately in the dark bottles so they would appear larger than they actually were.

4 - Many people also believe that the push-up assists in the sedimentation of wines.

Various tools have been used to form the push-up. One type found on the French "flower pot" wines which have been excavated from many formerly French occupied Canadian sites seemed to have been formed by a 'mollette'. (Fig. 10.) These bases are normally very regular with evenly rounded conical profiles and a small pontil mark in the top of the push-up. (Fig. 11.)

A sharply pointed push-up appearing primarily on vials, medicine bottles and olive oil bottles, but never on a wine bottle appears to have been formed by a thin, sharply pointed rod of wood or metal. (Fig. 12.) As it was replaced by molding techniques, the use of this tool became less common during the 19th century.

A circular iron rod like a pontil with the working end split into quadrants appears to have been another tool used to form push-ups. A quatrefoil impression in the top of the kick was left by the separated quadrants. This mark can barely be felt on some push-ups while on others "it is unmistakeable even to the extent of distorting the profile". (Fig. 13.) The earliest bases in the National Historic Sites Service Collection with these marks date from the 1720's and continue through the eighteenth and into the nineteenth century, and appear almost exclusively in dark green "wine" bottles manufactured in the English shapes.

In 1821, the H. Ricketts Company of Bristol developed a specially designed mould part which fit into the body mould forming a fourth way of making the push-up. "The patent included a lettered ring which could be placed close to the circumference of the base and according to the thickness or thinness of the said ring is the body of the mould shortened or increased, and the various sizes of bottles produced. (Ricketts 1821: 3)". On the ring could be cut such information as the address of the manufacturer or the volume of the bottle.

The neck and finish was completed in a separate hand operation as only the base, body and shoulder were formed in the Ricketts "three-piece" mould. A pontil was attached to the base after the bottle was withdrawn from the mould while the neck was finished and these bottles negate a belief that basal lettering and pontil marks cannot be found on the same bottle.

The Ricketts Mould was originally an improvement used for Porter, Beer, Cyder and Wine bottles, but later in the 19th and early 20th century was widely used for other bottles including solids.

"The speckled area is the pontil mark and the raised ridge inside the lettering is the edge of the removable lettered plate. There is also a raised mould line on the resting surface which is not visable in the drawing." (Fig. 15.)

Miss Jones mentions other examples of base formations and the tools used in her discussion that have been here omitted. She also states "Obviously the above discussion does not include all the tools or moulds that have been used to form bases".

References

Jones, Olive - Glass Bottle Push-Ups and Pontil Marks, The National Historic Sites Service, Ottawa.

Historical Archaeology 1971 Annual Publication of the Society for Historical Archaeology, Volume V, Mackinac Island State Park Commission, Stevens T. Mason Building, Lansing, Mich.

Dr. Wheeler's Nerve Vitalizer
Slocum's Oxygenized Pure Codliver Oil Toronto Ont.
Dinneford's Magnesia
and Comstock's Vermifuge.

VII   MEDICAL

A.   Chemists and Apothecaries.

The business, or profession of an Apothecary, although neither regulated nor even fully recognised until the latter part of the eighteenth century, was the subject of several ancient statutes and is traceable to a remote period in the history of healing in England. Richard Fitznigel, who died Bishop of London, was said to have been apothecary to Henry II, and in 1345 King Edward III is said to have given a pension of sixpence a day to Coursus de Gangland, a London apothecary, for attending him during an illness in Scotland. It is doubtful that apothecaries were well known publicly at that time for in 1511 an Act of Parliament was passed regulating the admissions of persons practising physic or surgery, but with no mention of apothecaries. However in 1543, Parliament passed an act dealing severely with the ignorance and cupidity of the then London Surgeons, and as a remedy provided for the irregular practitioners, who later acquired the distinctive name of apothecaries as a body. This Act was the foundation of the Apothecary. The Act complained that the London surgeons were not only unskillful, but grasping, and they had "Sued, troubled, and vexed divers honest persons, as well men as women, whom God had endued with the knowledge of the nature, kind, and operation of certain herbs, roots and waters, and the using and ministering of them to such as had been pained with customable diseases, as women's breasts being sore, a pin and the web in the eye, uncomes of hands, burnings, scaldings, sore mouths, the stone, strangury, sauccelim, and morphew, and such other like diseases; and yet the said persons have not taken anything for their pains or cunning, but have ministered the same to poor people only for neighborhood and for God's sake, and of pity and charity". The Act went on to say that any King's subject having knowledge and experience of the nature of herbs, roots and waters could "practise, use and administer according to their own cunning and knowledge both inward and outward sores, without suit, vexation, trouble, penalty, or loss of their goods".

Apothecaries were however still not distinguishable from the grocers (as in the same way the surgeons were not apart from the barbers) until the thirteenth year of the reign of James I when under a charter from him they were formed into two distinct bodies. However it was not until 1815 (George III) that apothecaries were required to pass an examination for a certificate stating that they were duly qualified to act as such. This was not to be granted to any person under the age of twenty-one, nor to anyone who had not served at least five years as an apprentice to an apothecary. This Act of Parliament was passed on the 12th of July 1815, and provided for the exemption from its rule of such Apothecaries as had been in practise on or before the first day of August of that year.

In Canada, chemicals, patent medicines, wines, window glass, bottles, paints, dye-stuffs etc., were advertised as sold under one roof for some years and the medicines and drugs listed were generally mentioned as newly imported from England.

In 1764, Henry Taylor was advertising himself as Apothecary and Druggist in Quebec. Romeo Wadsworth, Montreal, carried a large stock of imported goods in 1810, as did Joseph Scott, Surgeon, of Kingston in 1817, and who, with McGee advertised themselves a year later as Surgeons, Chemists and Druggists. Lewis Lyman & Co. of Montreal were advertising in 1810, and the name Lyman was listed as druggist for many years in various cities. By a notice of Co-partnership posted in Toronto, 1846, it is probable they all stemmed from the same source. "The business heretofore conducted in Toronto, under the name of Lyman, Farr & Co., will now be known under the style of Lyman, Kneeshaw & Co. ... William Lyman & Co., Montreal and Richard Kneeshaw, Toronto." Mention had been made of the late Timothy Jones Farr in an earlier ad.

J. Winer, a Hamilton druggist was advertising his "J. Winer's Chemical Red Drop" for scrofula etc. in 1842. Winer's Canadian Vermifuge, prepared and sold by J. Winer, Chemist, was advertised 1843 along with other medicines of his own manufacture. By this time his products were for sale by various druggists in surrounding towns. Winer's Arcanium Extract for "Syphilis and those very disagreeable affections arising therefrom and which have been hitherfore considered incurable" - "is a complete antidote" etc. "Prepared by John Winer, Hamilton, C.W. and John Winer & Co., 83 Maiden Lane, N.Y., Sole Proprietors" was an ad. in 1846. Proffessor Mott's Febrifuge Wine, in quart bottles "make sure the name of the Proprietor John Winer, is on the engraved label on the bottle", another ad. in 1855.

Dalley's Magical Pain Extractor was advertised as "The wonder and blessing of the age" - "Next to the Bible let it be prized" - "Keeping a supply on hand is as 'having your lamps trimmed and full of oil' " - in 1844. In the same ad., Mr. Dalley of Hamilton mentioned that "Comstock now wantonly pretends that he knows how to make my Pain Extractor". He further offered to pay the sum of $5,000.00 to anyone who could prove the extractor was not made from his own recipe. "The falsehoods before the public in Comstock's publications, are fully rebutted by the Chanalloi's decision, (at Court of Chancery held at Albany), where he declared the pretended contract void, and his injunction dissolved. These facts will be sufficient to prove to the people, what credit any of Comstock's statements are entitled to; also, make him feel " 'tis hard to kick against the pricks", and on and on.   Dalley may have won his battle with Comstock but others were not always so fortunate.

W.H. Comstock, Brockville, started manufacturing in 1834, and by 1840 had quite a number of products on the market and was agent for others. Dr. Spohn's Remedy, E. Spohn, Inventor and Comstock & Co., Proprietor - Kolmstock's Vermifuge "Caution - Never buy this article unless it has 'Dr. Kolmstock's Vermifuge' handsomely engraved on the outside of the vial and the facsimile of Comstock & Co. on the label". Balm of Columbia - this was a hair tonic of which he accused others of counterfieting, claiming the distinctive wrapper "complete with the Falls of Niagara" had been copied, but not the name Comstock. Any type of medicine or cosmetic that was currently popular, Mr. Comstock had a counterpart for, including "Comstock's Magical Pain Extractor".

Comstock had established a base across the border by 1841, and seems to have run into troubles there also. A.J. White & Co., N.Y., complained that "One Comstock of the firm of Comstock & Co., is pretending that he has bought our recipe and accounts of Morse's Indian Root Pills. Such is not the case. We have never sold him a recipe or account, nor never shall. We give this notice that parties owing us may not be induced to pay him", etc., 1859. He must have won that round because from an article printed in 1892 - "W.H. COMSTOCK - Proprietor of Dr. Morse's Indian Root Pills, Dead Shot Worm Pellets, etc., etc., Brockville, Ont., are sold by Mr. Comstock, and his own production. The very fact that they have been before the public since 1834 being strong evidence of their reliability, and sterling worth." - "The Canadian Trade is an enormous one and keeps a small army of employees constantly engaged. His business is not confined to Canada, but extends to every one of the United States. The American Head Quarters being located at Morristown, N.Y." - "Mr. Comstock is genial and clever in business, but still finds time to enjoy driving his horses, or with a jolly party, which he well knows how to select, tripping through the Thousand Islands on his splendid yacht the Albani, one of the finest on the St. Lawrence..." - "...has filled the position of Councillor, School Trustee and Mayor of the town." - "Mr. Comstock lives in a magnificent residence..." (an engraving of this was in the same issue) - "...he has amassed a large fortune." - "...a very heavy holder of real estate in and around Brockville, and takes a lively interest in all that pertains to it." - "His social qualities, sterling integrity, and devotedness to the public make him a favorite with all who are fortunate enough to make his acquaintance. Mr. Comstock is one of Canada's representative citizens. Twice he has been a candidate for Parliamentary honors and other honors unsolicited, have been offered to him time and time again."

T.A. Slocum, M.D., 186 Adelaide St. W., Toronto, was advertising his positive cure for comsumption in 1884. "Indeed so strong is my faith in its efficiacy that I will send two bottles free with a valuable treatice on this disease to any sufferer who will send me their express and Post Office address. Thousands of cases of long standing of the worst kind have been cured." Various other products were put up by Slocum, and sample bottles offered but "PSYCHINE", pronounced "SI-KEEN" was the one he touted the most.

By 1900 he had moved to 179 King St. W., Toronto, and was calling himself T.A. Slocum Chemical Co. Around 1905 as the T.A. Slocum Co., Manf'g Chemist, he opened branch offices in New York and London. He used at least two different designs for his Psychine bottles, one has "Psychine for Consumption" with a large anchor in centre and "T.A. Slocum, M.D., Toronto, Ont." at bottom of bottle front. The other more familiar bottle has the name and address on the front with a figure of Hope clinging to an anchor circled by a belt and the words "Hope is the Anchor of the Soul" and the other lettering on the sides of the bottle.

The Warner Safe Cure bottle was used by H.H. Warner who had made a comfortable fortune selling safes in Rochester, when he went into the patent medicine business, advertising heavily. This did however pay off and he was soon selling in England, Germany, Australia and Canada. He sold out to an English firm in 1889, investing the money in Arizona mines and was bankrupt by 1893.

He was advertising in 1882 as H.H. Warner & Co., Toronto, Ont., Rochester, etc. In an ad. after 1900 was advice on how to test your own kidneys - "Let some morning urine stand for twenty-four hours in a glass or bottle - if it is then milky or cloudy in appearance - or contains a redish brick-dust sediment - or particles of germs float about in it, YOUR KIDNEYS ARE DISEASED". If such was the case, a sample was to be sent to the Medical Depot, Warners Safe Cure Co., 44 Lombard St., Toronto, for a free analysis. All letters from women would be read and answered by a woman doctor, or so the ad. claimed. (Hey Bill - it's your turn to be woman, you answer these.)

Anderson's Cough Drops prepared by James Mellen & Co., for ten years, were advertised by R.J. Chapman of Hollowell in 1831 with "Caution - beware of counterfeiters, see that the bottles are stamped in the glass 'Anderson's Cough Drops prepared by J. Mellen' ". The manufacturers of Perry Davis Pain Killer began using embossed bottles in 1854 when they stated that "owing to a miserable, filthy production, calculated to do great injury to those who might use it" they had been obliged to resort to a very expensive measure to protect the public from harm. "The Pain Killer will be put up in a new style panel bottle with the words 'Davis' Vegetable Pain Killer' blown in the glass". Radway & Co., New York, advertised in a Toronto paper in 1853, that not only their R.R.R. (Radway's Ready Relief) was counterfeited but "The BOTTLES of RADWAY'S READY RELIEF ARE ALSO COUNTERFEIT". They inserted a notice to glass makers cautioning them against using any mold "bearing our trade marks, or blowing any bottles bearing our name". They claimed these bottles were circulating through the Eastern and Western States and Canada and were furnished from some glass blowers from just outside the viscinity of Buffalo, N.Y.

Donald Kennedy of Roxbury, Mass., who started manufacturing his "Greatest Medical Discovery of the Age" in 1846, purchased some of his bottles in Canada. The following notice is on a label in my possession from a bottle of his medicine:
"NOTICE - Owing to the lateness of the season, I am not able to get bottles from my own moulds at the Canada Glass Works, but am compelled to take others of different shape, yet holding exactly the same quantity, just one pint. DONALD KENNEDY."
He, in all probability, would not have been the only one from the U.S.A. to use Canadian made bottles for their products.

The wild claims made by the advertisers of 'patent medicines' add to the interest of the bottles. They could (according to the ads.), cure everything from growing new flesh to softening of the brain.

The later dispencing bottles made in plated molds were a cheaper way for the druggist to advertise his own name, when he filled a prescription for practising physician, or used it for his own concoctions. These bottles are certainly of more interest to the bottle collector than the ones now commonly in use.

20

POISON BOTTLES like Bitters and Sarsaparilla are usually considered a category in themselves by collectors.

The British Parliament considered a law requiring all containers of poison to be identifiable by touch in the late 1850's and early 60's. This law was never passed but pharmacists soon began using 'rough to the hand' bottles of their own accord for holding poisons. This was done so that mistakes in handling poisons could be avoided even in the dark. These bottles are usually embossed with the word "poison" as well.

HOMOEOPATHY is a system of medicine introduced by a German physician named Hahnemann around the end of the 18th century and founded on the belief that medicines have the power to cure conditions similar to those they have the power to excite or 'like cures likes'. That diseases were curable by substances that gave the healthy person symptons of the disease, has been recognised by writers as far back as 404 B.C., and the oldest expression of it is ascribed by Athenaeus to Antiphanes, and translated in part to:

"Take the hair, it is well written,
Of the dog by which you're bitten;
Work off one wine by his brother,
And one labour with another."

In Austria, physicians were not allowed to use medicines of their own making even gratuitously; all medicines administered to the sick were prepared by the apothecaries, thus without some changes in the law it was impossible to carry on the homoeopathic business. In 1836 during an outbreak of cholera, a Dr. Fleishman used the system with some success.

From Germany as a centre where it was now extensively practised and taught, homoeopathy spread over Europe and America, and although it had some number of converts, the majority of physicians remained skeptical as to its effectiveness.

Dr. Campbell, Toronto, advertised himself as being president of the Homoeopathic Medical Board of Canada in 1864, and D.L. Thompson, 394 Yonge St., Toronto, advertised his Homoeopathic Pharmacy for some time, as did others.

VII   MEDICAL - cont'd

B.   Bitters.

Bitters were prepared from an infusian of herbs containing bitter principles, and the plant most generally used was the Angelica. The roots or seed, or both, were placed in water and left to simmer for several days, to make the infusion strong enough. By 1870, this method had been almost entirely replaced by the use of gentian etc., but was still in use as a household medicine in some places by elderly people.

The medicinal properties of Bitters were mainly those of a mild tonic and pungent aromatic stimulent, considered useful in cases of weakness of the digestive organs. Camomile flowers, coriander seeds, and other vegetable tonics were employed in the preparation of bitters, and stimulents. (These last in no small way contributing to their popularity in Canada, due to the swelling ranks of the Temperance Movement.)

In April 1808, a society was established at Moreau, in the State of New York and having forty-three members. One of their rules was - "No member shall drink rum, gin, whisky, wine, or any distilled spirits, or compositions of the same, except by the advice of a physician, or in cases of actual disease (also excepting at public dinners), under the penalty of twenty-five cents, provided this article shall not infringe on any religious rite". This society had similar rules regarding offering stimulents to others and continued for fourteen years, but other than stirring up a few clergymen, did not accomplish much else. After a series of sermons had been preached and published by a Dr. B.J. Clarke, against a vice that was threatening (according to him) to make the Americans a community of drunkards, a society was started at Boston in 1826, called the American Temperance Society to "Restrain and prevent the use of intoxicating liquors". In 1829, the New York Temperance Society was formed; and by the end of the year, 1000 local societies were in existance.

Reports of these societies soon spread across the sea to the 'Old World' and before the end of another year, sixty societies had been formed in Ireland with over three thousand, five hundred members, both Protestant and Catholic. The close of 1831 had about ten thousand members in England, and in Scotland there were 187 ministers lecturing on Temperance alone.

The more fervid members soon decided that the crusade against gin, rum, etc., was not enough, and that beer was the great cause of drunkenness in the country, and by September 1833, the work 'Teetotal' was the byword. According to the story, this word was derived from one Dicky Turner a 'lime-larry' or plasterer's helper who was heard to say at a lecture, "I'll hev nowt to do wi' this moderation-botheration-pledge: I'll be reet down tee-tee-total forever and ever". Whatever the origin, the word was taken to mean total abstinence from all intoxicating drinks. There was some disagreement between the two factions for a time, but by the end of 1842, they had united, forming the National Temperance Society.

In Canada by the end of 1843 the influence of Temperance was showing in the advertising of whisky, beer, etc., or in many cases, by the lack of it. "Best Wines for sacramental and medicinal purposes (but no more ardent spirits he hopes)", from a Yarmouth dealer. "In opposition to the spread of the Teetotal Principals, (with at the same time, a due regard for the sobriety of Her Majesty's liege subjects) having opened a tavern in Rideau St., informs his friends and the public, that he will keep a supply of the best MOUNTAIN DEW always on hand. Being of a generous disposition he will provide a little of the UNINEBRIATING BEVERAGE to treat his antagonists. James Black, Bytown." 1845.

By 1847, the names of people joining and attending Temperance meetings were published weekly in some newspapers. Included were articles on the horrors of drink and testimonials from various individuals telling of the hell they had lived in and still would be in, were it not for the Temperance Society. It was not only the men who had spent all their money on hooch while their families starved, many were the sad tales of women who had neglected their homes, beat the kids, and sunk to the depths of degradation for a drink, who had been redeemed by Temperance.

Bitters were now a very popular medicine and often advertised as being available in any quantity.

Stoughton's Bitters had been available at Henry Taylors, Quebec, in 1764 and were still around in 1848. Many of the advertised bitters in Canada were American or elsewhere, but Canada's medicine manufacturers were not behind in this respect. Lin's Temperance Bitters were a product of Comstock, Brockville, 1840. Two years later, Temperance Life Bitters - "Entered according to the Act of Congress" - "of the District Court of the United States" - "Messrs. Comstock & Co. are the sole Agents" were probably the same. J. Swain & Co., Toronto, advertised Bitters and other medicines in 1847. In a report from the 17th Annual Exhibition, 1862, Stomach Bitters were shown by Edward Corker, and W. Moore, both of Toronto. Hewlett's Strenthening Bitters, were prepared by John Hewlett, 95 York St., Toronto, 1848. Crowfoot Indian Bitters, from Meaford Ont., Golden Fruit Bitters, manufactured by Haswell & Co., Montreal, and Turner's Tonic Bitters, manufactured by Robert Turner, Brantford, Ont., were advertised in 1883. Some companies simply mentioned Bitters along with other products of their manufacture.

The label on a To-ni-ta Bitters bottle printed after 1906 lists the alcohol content at 23 percent, and claims to be an invigorating, stimulating tonic. Dose for adults one or two tablespoons before meals and on going to bed, or, AS OFTEN AS REQUIRED. Dose to be much reduced for children or delicate women. The "Old Ladies of the Home of the Friendless" were so built up with Hop Bitters they felt young again. A.D. Royce claimed "Gents - I have taken not quite one bottle of Bitters. I was a feeble old man of seventy-eight when I got it. Today I am as active and feel as well as I did at thirty". That was powerful medicine. It was no wonder that the most astonishing effects were claimed by the Superintendant of Soldiers Home, Cinci., with Plantation Bitters.

VII   MEDICAL - cont'd

C.   Sarsaparilla.

Sarsaparilla was a heavily employed medicine produced from shrubs native to the warm parts of America, and were found in South America and on the Mexican Andes. The part of the plant used was the dried root, and of the class of medicines called Diaphoretics. The British Pharmacopoeia contained three preparations of this drug - viz., the Decoctation, the Compound, and the Liquid Extract. The cases in which they were considered useful were chronic rheumatism, secondary syphilitic affections, chronic skin diseases, scrofula or King's Evil, etc. It was considered a medicine that had to be taken in large does, and often, to be of any use, as "The compound decoctation formerly known as the Decoctation of Sweet Woods, is the best preparation and should be taken in doses of four to six ounces three times a day". This no doubt accounted for some of the earlier advertisements playing on the size of their bottles, as Bristol's in 1850: "Larger bottle than ever offered by any vendor". Scrophula, or Scrofula, was until the latter part of the 1860's regarded as consisting essentially of indolent glandular tumours, occuring frequently in the neck, suppurating slowly and healing with difficulty. The word was derived from the Latin, 'scrofa', a sow, it being supposed that this animal was especially liable to tumours such as occur in this disease. The Greek and Arabic names for the disease were similarly taken from the word meaning swine in these languages, while scrofula was the popular term used by Celsus, Pliny, and other Latin writers, and considered the classical name for the disease.

The King's Evil, an English name for scrofula was derived from the long cherished belief that scrofulous tumours and abcesses could be cured by the royal touch. Multitudes of patients were submitted to this treatment, and the old historians assert, with perfect success, from the time of Edward the Confessor to the reign of Queen Anne. "The writer of the article 'Scrofula' in the English Cyclopoedia, mentions the curious historical facts that 'The old Jacobites considered that this power did not descend to Mary, William, or Anne, as they did not possess a full hereditary title, or in other words, did not reign by divine right. The kings of the House of Brunswick have, we believe, never put this power to the proof; and the office for the ceremony which appears in our Liturgy as late as 1719 has been silently omitted.' " The exiled Princes of the House of Stuart were supposed to have inherited this virtue and mention is made of the case of one Christopher Lowel who went to Avignon, where court was then held, in 1716, and received a temporary cure. In October of 1745, Prince Charles Edward, although but Prince of Wales, was said to have touched a female child who was completely cured in twenty-one days. Henry VII introduced the practise of giving a small silver or gold coin when he 'touched'. The French kings also touched for the 'Evil', the practise here being traced back to Clovis, 481 A.D. On Easter Sunday, 1686, Louis XIV is said to have touched 1600 people; and at the same time saying "Le roi te touche, Dieu te guérisse", ("The King touches thee, may Godd cure thee").

The 'small silver or gold coin' would undoubtedly be responsible for curing a good many who would not have had the disease otherwise.

Sarsaparilla was a widely advertised product. The earlier ads were usually accompanied with a long letter from someone who had been waiting for death to relieve their suffering. "After having exhausted all the remedies my husband could hear of to prolong my wretched life..." etc. (The remedies that had been tried would be named.) "I was reduced to my bed, where I lay for almost three years, perfectly helpless, an object of pity, abandoned by all doctors as in- curable..."etc. "The wings of my nose all gone leaving only a hole instead of nostrils, the roof of my mouth entirely eaten away..." etc., etc. "Before I had taken one bottle I got out of my bed without help and walked."

By 1860, Sarsaparilla advertising had toned down considerably and while still used as a cure for syphilis was more generally in use for cutaneous conditions and blood purifier. As more and more brands came on the market the extolling of their virtues lessened. By 1890, Ayer's and Hoods (American) were still heavy advertisers but Canadian were simply listed along with other products by the same company or similar to "Recamier Sarsaparilla, $1.00 per bottle, made by the Recamier Manufacturing Co., 374-376 St. Paul St., Montreal".

Alex Urquhart of Montreal was advertising his "Urquhart's Fluid Extract of Jamaica Sarsaparilla" in 1847, with letters from several Montreal Doctors giving their varied experiences with the product. They of course, agreed it was the best on the market.

"Masury's Compound Extract of Sarsaparilla, in two quart bottles - the largest bottle in the world - for $1.00, improved composition of Sarsaparilla and Wau-A-Hoo." An Advertisement by Winer & Sims, Hamilton, 1851. They claimed no danger of an over-dose, even in unskilled hands. In spite of other claims to the contrary this appears to have been the largest sized bottle used for Sarsaparilla.

References

Papers -

Brockville Recorder - 1835-40
Byetown Gazette - 1840-45
Chatham Journal - 1842
Chatham Weekly Planet - 1847
Evangelical Churchman - 1889
Grand River Satchem - 1850-55
Hollowell Free Press - 1831
Kingston Gazette - 1817-18
La Gazette de Quebec - 1764-1810
Montreal Transcript - 1847
St. Thomas Liberal - 1832
Toronto Examiner - 1846
Toronto Globe & changes - 1842-44-47-48-53-54-59-62-64-67-69-80-83-84-92-1903
Toronto Herald - 1843
Yarmouth Herald - 1833-48
Western Herald and Farmers Magazine - 1839

Books -

Chambers Information for the People - 1842, vol. II

Chambers Encyclopaedia - 1873, vol. VIII; 74, vol. V; 75, vol. I.

① M.S. GREEN GLASS, 4½" TALL BOTTLE HAS FOUR INDENTED PANELS. RIGHT SIDE EMBOSSED "CHAMBERLAIN MED. CO.

DES MOINES & TORONTO

CHAMBERLAIN'S COLIC CHOLERA AND DIARRHEA REMEDY

¾" BY 1¾"

② M.S. 495

PLEASANT WORM SYRUP

TORONTO

⅞" BY 1½"

③ M.S. BALSAM OF HONEY

PALE GREEN COLOR, 4" TALL

1¼ DIAM.

5" HIGH, AMETHYST COLOR, 4 INDENTED PANELS. RIGHT SIDE READS "DR. LOWS.

⑥ DR. S. PITCHER'S

16J

1" BY 2"

"CASTORIA" EMBOSSED ON OTHER SIDE PANEL. AQUA BLUE GLASS — 5¼" TALL

⑤ NERVILINE PREPARED BY THE CATARRHOZONE CO. KINGSTON ONT.

DARK AMETHYST GLASS FOUR INDENTED PANELS: 5¼" TALL.

⑦⅞" BY 1¾"

④ M.S. J.E. COMBAULT'S CAUSTIC BALSAM.

THE LAWRENCE WILLIAMS CO. SOLE PROPS FOR U.S. AND CANADA.

1½ BY 2½"

DARK GREEN GLASS, 6½" TALL. FOUR RAISED PANELS. BOTH SIDE PANELS HAVE SAME EMBOSSING.

⑦ M.S. PHILA, PA & TORONTO, ONT.

1½" BY 2¼"

DEEP AQUA BLUE COLOR. FOUR INDENTED PANELS. EMBOSSING ON SIDE PANELS ONLY. OTHER SIDE "ZOPESA CHEMICAL, CO."

⑧ M.S. GENUINE SANDFORDS GINGER A DELICIOUS COMBINATION OF GINGER FRENCH BRANDY AND CHOICE AROMATICS REG'D 1876

1½" BY 2¾"

DARK AQUA BLUE GLASS, 6¾" HIGH. FRONT & SIDE PANELS INDENTED. LEFT SIDE READS "BOSTON, MASS. U.S.A. & RIGHT SIDE "POTTER DRUG & CHEMICAL CORP." BACK SHOULDER "4 OZ.

⑨ M.S. DR. FISHER BRIGDON

STRAP SIDES

⅞" BY 1½"

GREY GLASS, 6" TALL. FRONT AND SIDE OF SAME BOTTLE

⑩ M.S. CHEMISTS The Clement Drug Co. SARNIA. ONT.

¾" BY 1½"

CLEAR GLASS 5½" HIGH.

⑪ M.S.

P.D.&CO. 208 C

2¾" DIAM.

LIGHT AMBER COLOR 7½" TALL

⑫ 2⅛ BY 1⅞"

12

DAVIS VEGETABLE

AQUA GLASS, 5¾" TALL 4 INDENTED PANELS LEFT SIDE READS "PAIN KILLER.

PAGE ONE

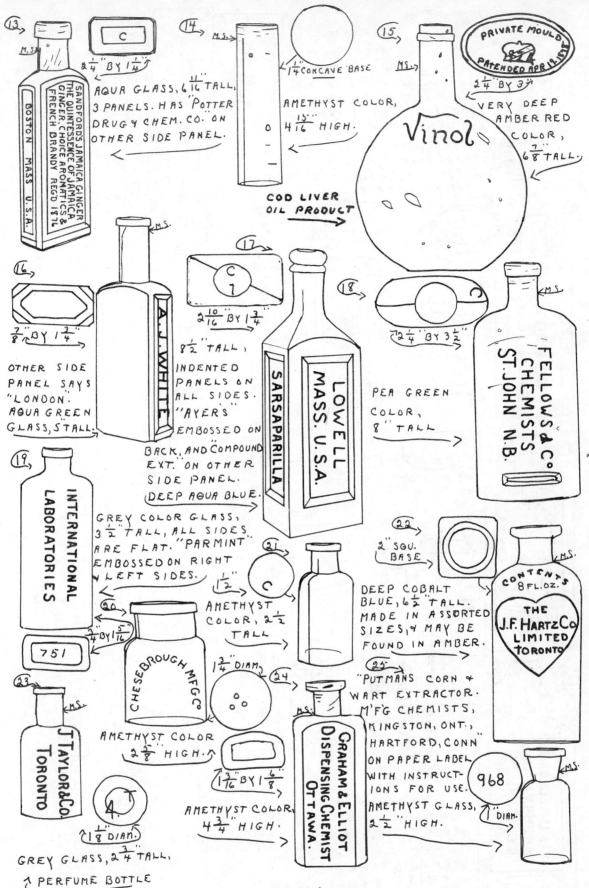

13

M.3"

2 1/4" BY 1 1/4"

AQUA GLASS, 6 1/16" TALL, 3 PANELS. HAS "POTTER DRUG & CHEM. CO." ON OTHER SIDE PANEL.

SANDFORD'S JAMAICA GINGER THE QUINTESSENCE OF JAMAICA GINGER, CHOICE AROMATICS & FRENCH BRANDY REG'D 1874

BOSTON MASS U.S.A.

14

M.S.

1 1/4" CONCAVE BASE

AMETHYST COLOR, 4 1/16" HIGH.

15

M.S.

2 1/4" BY 3"

PRIVATE MOULD PATENDED APR 14, 1896

VERY DEEP AMBER RED COLOR, 6 7/8" TALL.

Vinol

COD LIVER OIL PRODUCT

16

7/8" BY 1 3/4"

OTHER SIDE PANEL SAYS "LONDON". AQUA GREEN GLASS, 5" TALL.

17

C 7

2 10/16" BY 1 3/4"

A.J.WHITE

8 1/2" TALL, INDENTED PANELS ON ALL SIDES. "AYER'S" EMBOSSED ON BACK, AND "COMPOUND EXT." ON OTHER SIDE PANEL. DEEP AQUA BLUE.

SARSAPARILLA

LOWELL MASS. U.S.A.

18

2 1/4" BY 3 1/2"

PEA GREEN COLOR, 8" TALL

FELLOWS & Co. CHEMISTS ST. JOHN N.B.

19

INTERNATIONAL LABORATORIES

GREY COLOR GLASS, 3 1/2" TALL, ALL SIDES ARE FLAT. "PARMINT" EMBOSSED ON RIGHT & LEFT SIDES.

20

2 3/4" BY 5 5/16"

751

21

1/2"

C

AMETHYST COLOR, 2 1/2" TALL

22

2" SQU. BASE

DEEP COBALT BLUE, 6 1/2" TALL. MADE IN ASSORTED SIZES, & MAY BE FOUND IN AMBER.

M.S.

CONTENTS 8 FL. OZ.

THE J.F. Hartz Co LIMITED TORONTO

23

M.S.

J. TAYLOR & Co. TORONTO

CHESEBROUGH MFG Co

1 3/4" DIAM

AMETHYST COLOR 2 5/8" HIGH.

24

1 3/16" BY 1 6/8"

AMETHYST COLOR, 4 3/4" HIGH.

M.S.

GRAHAM & ELLIOT DISPENSING CHEMIST OTTAWA.

25

"PUTMANS CORN & WART EXTRACTOR. M'F'G CHEMISTS, KINGSTON, ONT., HARTFORD, CONN" ON PAPER LABEL WITH INSTRUCTIONS FOR USE. AMETHYST GLASS, 2 1/2" HIGH.

968

DIAM.

M.S.

4"

1 1/8" DIAM.

GREY GLASS, 2 3/4" TALL, PERFUME BOTTLE

PAGE TWO

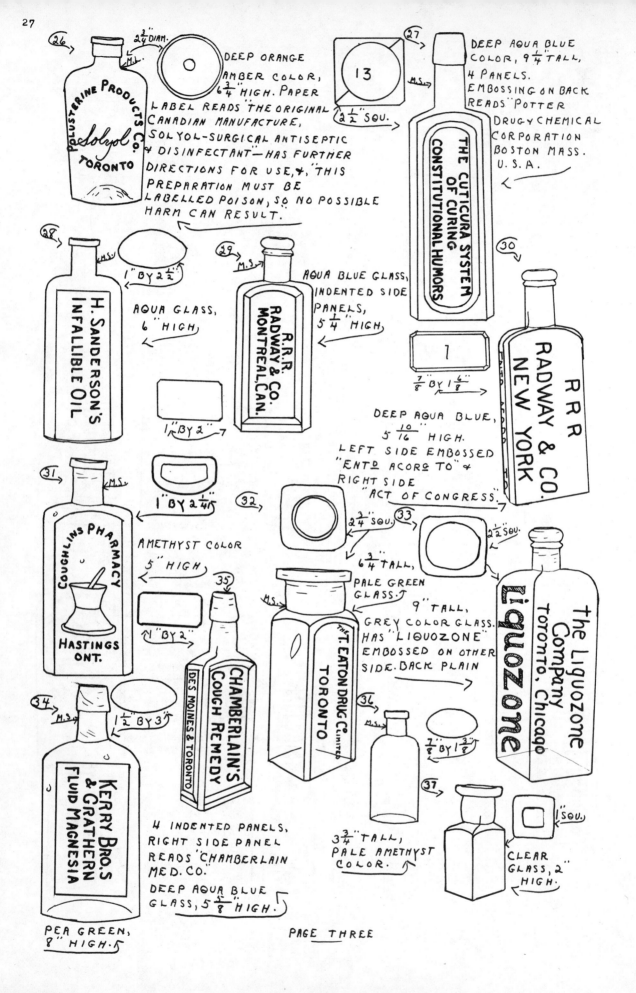

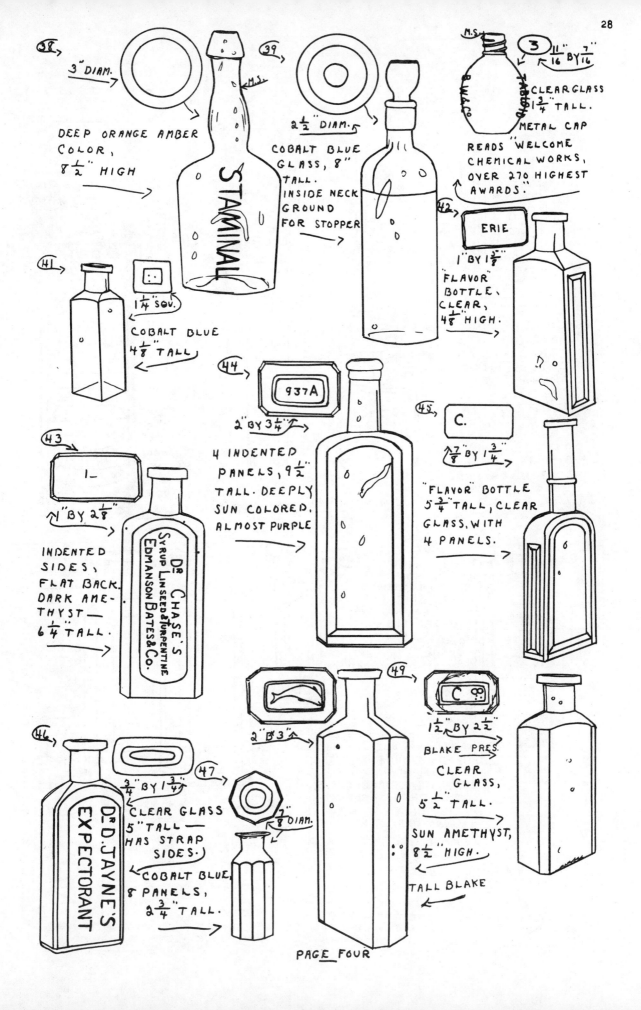

38
3" DIAM.
DEEP ORANGE AMBER COLOR, 8½" HIGH

STAMINAL

39
2½" DIAM.
COBALT BLUE GLASS, 8" TALL. INSIDE NECK GROUND FOR STOPPER

M.S.
3
$\frac{11}{16}$" BY $\frac{7}{16}$"
B.W.&Co.
CLEAR GLASS 1¾" TALL. METAL CAP READS "WELCOME CHEMICAL WORKS, OVER 270 HIGHEST AWARDS.

41
1¼" SQU.
COBALT BLUE 4⅛" TALL

44
937A
2" BY 3¼"
4 INDENTED PANELS, 9½" TALL. DEEPLY SUN COLORED. ALMOST PURPLE

42
ERIE
1" BY 1⅞"
"FLAVOR" BOTTLE, CLEAR, 4⅛" HIGH.

45
C.
$\frac{7}{8}$" BY 1¾"
"FLAVOR" BOTTLE 5¾" TALL, CLEAR GLASS, WITH 4 PANELS.

43
1-
1" BY 2⅛"
INDENTED SIDES, FLAT BACK. DARK AMETHYST 6¼" TALL.

Dr CHASE'S Syrup Linseed & Turpentine EDMANSON BATES & Co.

49
2" B 3"
1½" BY 2½"
BLAKE PRES
CLEAR GLASS, 5½" TALL. SUN AMETHYST, 8½" HIGH.
TALL BLAKE
C.

46
Dr D. JAYNE'S EXPECTORANT

47
¾" BY 1¾"
CLEAR GLASS 5" TALL — HAS STRAP SIDES.
$\frac{7}{8}$" DIAM.
COBALT BLUE, 8 PANELS, 2¾" TALL.

PAGE FOUR

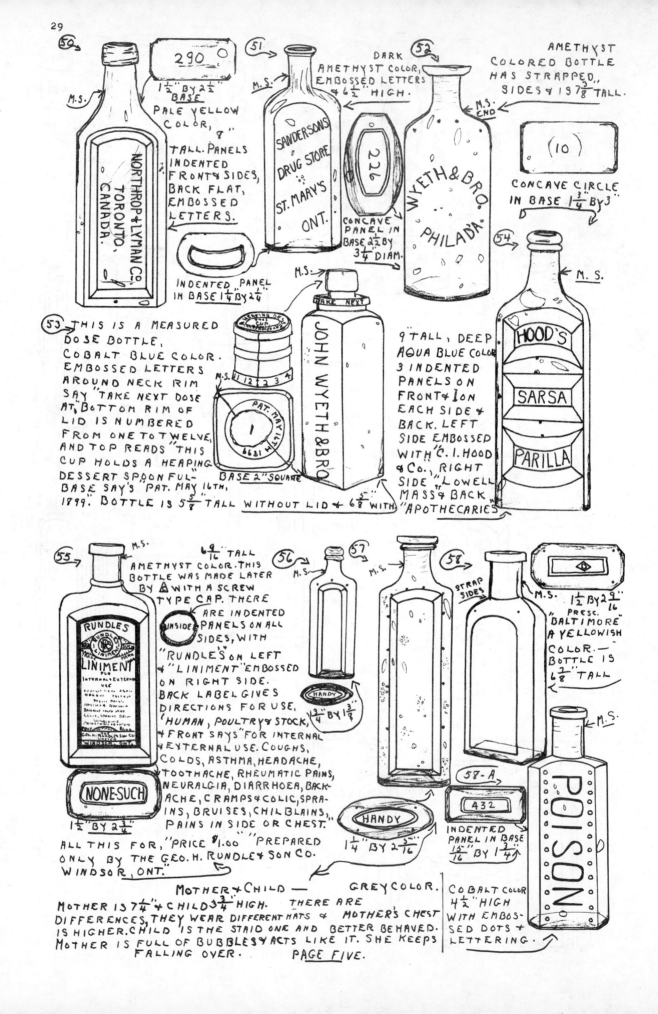

50

290

1½" BY 2½"
BASE

M.S.

PALE YELLOW
COLOR, 8"

TALL. PANELS
INDENTED
FRONT & SIDES,
BACK FLAT,
EMBOSSED
LETTERS.

NORTHROP & LYMAN CO.
TORONTO,
CANADA.

INDENTED PANEL
IN BASE 1¼ BY 2¼"

51

M.S.

DARK
AMETHYST COLOR,
EMBOSSED LETTERS
& 6½" HIGH.

SANDERSONS
DRUG STORE
ST. MARY'S
ONT.

52

226

CONCAVE
PANEL IN
BASE 2½ BY
3¾ DIAM.

WYETH & BRO.
PHILAD'A.

AMETHYST
COLORED BOTTLE
HAS STRAPPED
SIDES & 19⅞ TALL.

M.S.
END

(10)

CONCAVE CIRCLE
IN BASE 1¾ BY 3"

54

M.S.

HOOD'S
SARSA
PARILLA

53 THIS IS A MEASURED
DOSE BOTTLE,
COBALT BLUE COLOR.
EMBOSSED LETTERS
AROUND NECK RIM
SAY "TAKE NEXT DOSE
AT" BOTTOM RIM OF
LID IS NUMBERED
FROM ONE TO TWELVE,
AND TOP READS "THIS
CUP HOLDS A HEAPING
DESSERT SPOON FUL"
BASE SAY'S "PAT. MAY 16TH,
1899. BOTTLE IS 5⅝" TALL WITHOUT LID & 6⅝ WITH

M.S.

M.S. 11 12 1 2 3 4

PAT. MAY 16TH 1899

1

BASE 2" SQUARE

TAKE NEXT

JOHN WYETH & BRO.

9 TALL, DEEP
AQUA BLUE COLOR
3 INDENTED
PANELS ON
FRONT & 1 ON
EACH SIDE &
BACK. LEFT
SIDE EMBOSSED
WITH "C. I. HOOD
& CO.", RIGHT
SIDE "LOWELL
MASS & BACK"
"APOTHECARIES"

55

M.S.

6 9/16 TALL
AMETHYST COLOR. THIS
BOTTLE WAS MADE LATER
BY [A] WITH A SCREW
TYPE CAP. THERE
ARE INDENTED
PANELS ON ALL
SIDES, WITH
"RUNDLES" ON LEFT
& "LINIMENT" EMBOSSED
ON RIGHT SIDE.
BACK LABEL GIVES
DIRECTIONS FOR USE,
(HUMAN, POULTRY & STOCK,
& FRONT SAYS "FOR INTERNAL
& EXTERNAL USE. COUGHS,
COLDS, ASTHMA, HEADACHE,
TOOTHACHE, RHEUMATIC PAINS,
NEURALGIA, DIARRHOEA, BACK-
ACHE, CRAMPS & COLIC, SPRA-
INS, BRUISES, CHILBLAINS,
PAINS IN SIDE OR CHEST."
ALL THIS FOR, "PRICE $1.00" "PREPARED
ONLY BY THE GEO. H. RUNDLE & SON CO.
WINDSOR, ONT."

INSIDE

RUNDLES
LINIMENT
FOR
INTERNAL & EXTERNAL
USE

NONE-SUCH

1½" BY 2¾"

56

M.S.

HANDY

¾" BY 1⅜"

57

M.S.

58

STRAP
SIDES

HANDY

1¼" BY 2 5/16"

58-A

432

INDENTED
PANEL IN BASE
15/16" BY 1¾"

M.S. 1½ BY 2 9/16"
PRESC.
"BALTIMORE"
A YELLOWISH
COLOR.
BOTTLE IS
6⅛" TALL

M.S.

POISON.

COBALT COLOR
4½" HIGH
WITH EMBOS-
SED DOTS &
LETTERING.

MOTHER & CHILD —   GREY COLOR.
MOTHER IS 7¼" & CHILD 3¾" HIGH.   THERE ARE
DIFFERENCES, THEY WEAR DIFFERENT HATS &   MOTHER'S CHEST
IS HIGHER. CHILD IS THE STAID ONE AND   BETTER BEHAVED.
MOTHER IS FULL OF BUBBLES & ACTS LIKE IT. SHE KEEPS
FALLING OVER.   PAGE FIVE.

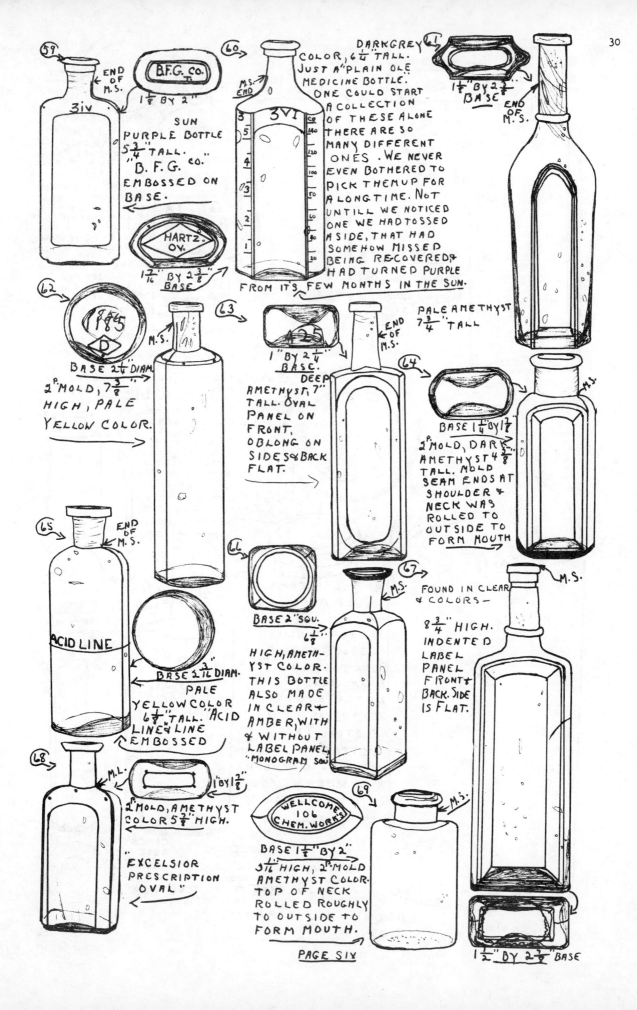

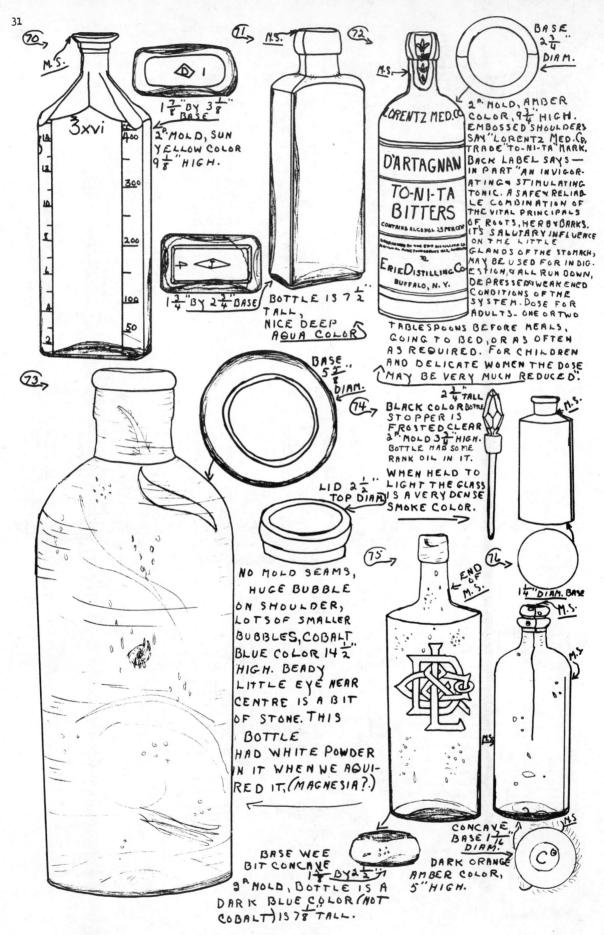

70 M.S.

3xVI

400
300
200
100
50

1 7/8" BY 3 1/8" BASE

2° MOLD, SUN YELLOW COLOR 9 1/8" HIGH.

71 M.S.

72

M.S.

1 3/4" BY 2 3/4" BASE

BOTTLE IS 7 1/2" TALL, NICE DEEP AQUA COLOR

LORENTZ MED. CO

D'ARTAGNAN TO-NI-TA BITTERS

CONTAINS ALCOHOL 23 PER CENT

ErieDistilling Co BUFFALO, N.Y.

BASE 2 3/4" DIAM.

2° MOLD, AMBER COLOR, 9 3/4" HIGH. EMBOSSED SHOULDERS SAY "LORENTZ MED. Co. TRADE "TO-NI-TA" MARK. BACK LABEL SAYS — IN PART "AN INVIGORATING & STIMULATING TONIC. A SAFE & RELIABLE COMBINATION OF THE VITAL PRINCIPALS OF ROOTS, HERB & BARKS. IT'S SALUTARY INFLUENCE ON THE LITTLE GLANDS OF THE STOMACH, MAY BE USED FOR INDIGESTION, & ALL RUN DOWN, DEPRESSED & WEAKENED CONDITIONS OF THE SYSTEM. DOSE FOR ADULTS. ONE OR TWO TABLESPOONS BEFORE MEALS, GOING TO BED, OR AS OFTEN AS REQUIRED. FOR CHILDREN AND DELICATE WOMEN THE DOSE MAY BE VERY MUCH REDUCED".

73

BASE 5 1/8" DIAM.

74

LID 2 1/2" TOP DIAM

NO MOLD SEAMS, HUGE BUBBLE ON SHOULDER, LOTS OF SMALLER BUBBLES, COBALT BLUE COLOR 14 1/2" HIGH. BEADY LITTLE EYE NEAR CENTRE IS A BIT OF STONE. THIS BOTTLE HAD WHITE POWDER IN IT WHEN WE AQUIRED IT, (MAGNESIA?.)

2 1/4" TALL BLACK COLOR BOTTLE STOPPER IS FROSTED CLEAR 2° MOLD 3 3/4" HIGH. BOTTLE HAD SOME RANK OIL IN IT. WHEN HELD TO LIGHT THE GLASS IS A VERY DENSE SMOKE COLOR.

M.S.

75

END OF M.S.

76

1 1/4" DIAM. BASE

M.S.

M.S.

BASE WEE BIT CONCAVE 1 1/4" BY 2 1/2" 2° MOLD, BOTTLE IS A DARK BLUE COLOR (NOT COBALT) IS 7 7/8 TALL.

CONCAVE BASE 1 7/16" DIAM. DARK ORANGE AMBER COLOR, 5" HIGH.

PAGE SEVEN

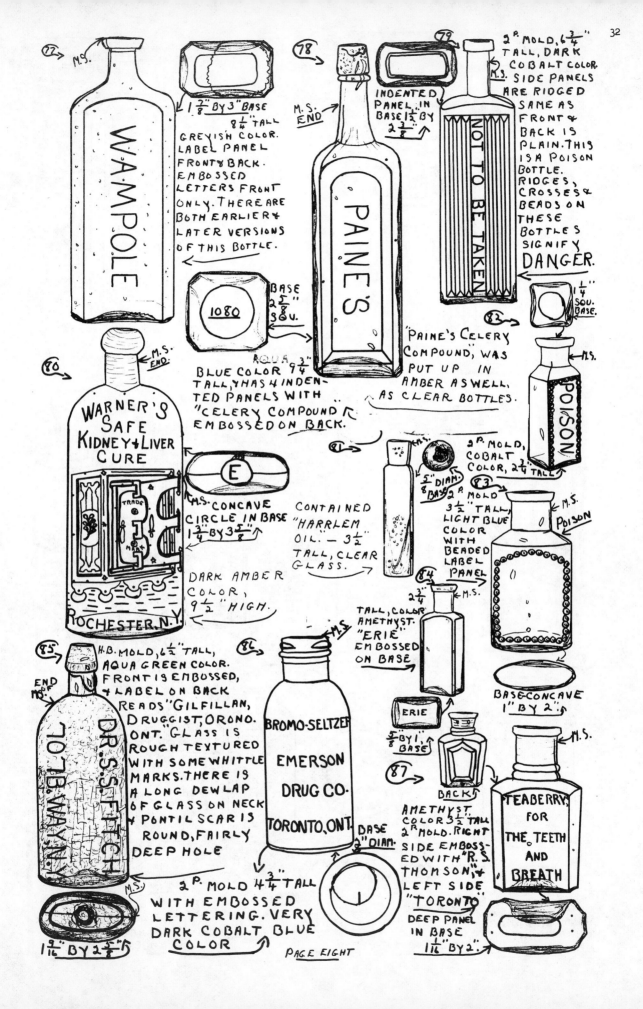

77 → M.S.

WAMPOLE

1 7/8" BY 3" BASE 8 1/4" TALL GREYISH COLOR. LABEL PANEL FRONT & BACK. EMBOSSED LETTERS FRONT ONLY. THERE ARE BOTH EARLIER & LATER VERSIONS OF THIS BOTTLE.

78 → M.S. END

PAINE'S

INDENTED PANEL IN BASE 1 1/2 BY 2 3/8

BASE 2 5/8" SQU. 1080

AQUA BLUE COLOR 9 3/4" TALL, Y HAS 4 INDENTED PANELS WITH "CELERY COMPOUND" EMBOSSED ON BACK.

'PAINE'S CELERY COMPOUND', WAS PUT UP IN AMBER AS WELL AS CLEAR BOTTLES.

79

NOT TO BE TAKEN

2 P. MOLD, 6 3/4" TALL, DARK COBALT COLOR. M.S. SIDE PANELS ARE RIDGED SAME AS FRONT & BACK IS PLAIN. THIS IS A POISON BOTTLE. RIDGES, CROSSES & BEADS ON THESE BOTTLES SIGNIFY DANGER.

1 1/4" SQU. BASE.

82 → POISON M.S. 2 P. MOLD, COBALT COLOR, 2 3/4" TALL

80 → M.S. END

WARNER'S SAFE KIDNEY & LIVER CURE ROCHESTER. N.Y.

E

M.S. CONCAVE CIRCLE IN BASE 1 3/4" BY 3 5/8"

DARK AMBER COLOR, 9 1/2" HIGH.

81 → M.S. CONTAINED "HARRLEM OIL. — 3 1/2" TALL, CLEAR GLASS.

5/8" DIAM. BASE 2 P.

83 → 2 P. MOLD 3 1/2" TALL, LIGHT BLUE COLOR WITH BEADED LABEL PANEL M.S. POISON

BASE CONCAVE 1" BY 2"

84 → 2 3/4" M.S. TALL, COLOR AMETHYST. "ERIE" EMBOSSED ON BASE

ERIE 5/8" BY 1" BASE

85 → END OF M.S.

DR. S. S. FITCH 707 B'WAY N.Y.

H.B. MOLD, 6 1/2" TALL, AQUA GREEN COLOR. FRONT IS EMBOSSED, & LABEL ON BACK READS "GILFILLAN, DRUGGIST, ORONO. ONT." GLASS IS ROUGH TEXTURED WITH SOME WHITTLE MARKS. THERE IS A LONG DEWLAP OF GLASS ON NECK & PONTIL SCAR IS ROUND, FAIRLY DEEP HOLE

M.S. 1 9/16" BY 2 5/8"

86 → M.S.

BROMO-SELTZER EMERSON DRUG CO. TORONTO, ONT.

BASE 2" DIAM.

2 P. MOLD 4 3/4" TALL WITH EMBOSSED LETTERING. VERY DARK COBALT BLUE COLOR

PAGE EIGHT

87 → BACK

TEABERRY, FOR THE TEETH AND BREATH M.S.

AMETHYST COLOR 3 1/2" TALL 2 P. MOLD. RIGHT SIDE EMBOSSED WITH "R.S. THOMSON" & LEFT SIDE "TORONTO" DEEP PANEL IN BASE 1 1/4" BY 2"

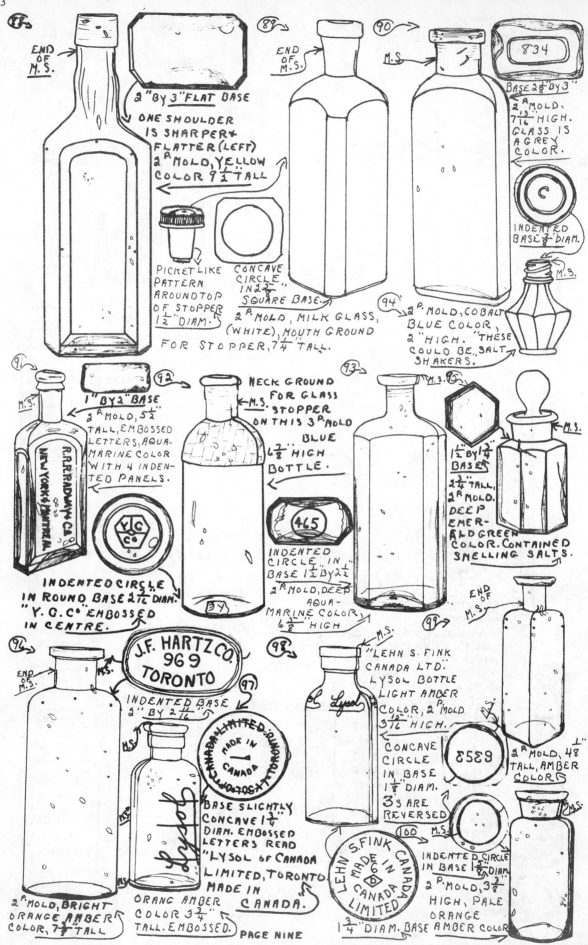

88

END OF M.S.

89 →

90 →

834

2" BY 3" FLAT BASE

ONE SHOULDER IS SHARPER + FLATTER (LEFT) 2 P. MOLD, YELLOW COLOR 9½" TALL

END OF M.S.

M.S.

BASE 2⅛" BY 3" 2 P. MOLD, 7 13/16" HIGH. GLASS IS A GREY COLOR.

C

INDENTED BASE 2⅜" DIAM.

M.S.

PICKET LIKE PATTERN AROUND TOP OF STOPPER 1½" DIAM.

CONCAVE CIRCLE IN 2⅝" SQUARE BASE. 2 P. MOLD, MILK GLASS, (WHITE), MOUTH GROUND FOR STOPPER, 7¼" TALL.

94

2 P. MOLD, COBALT BLUE COLOR, 2" HIGH. "THESE COULD BE SALT SHAKERS.

91

M.S.

1" BY 2" BASE 2 P. MOLD, 5½" TALL, EMBOSSED LETTERS, AQUA-MARINE COLOR WITH 4 INDENTED PANELS.

R.R.R.RADWAY & Co. NEW YORK & MONTREAL

92

M.S.

NECK GROUND FOR GLASS STOPPER ON THIS 3 P. MOLD BLUE 6⅞" HIGH BOTTLE.

93

M.S.

1½" BY 1¾" BASE. 2¾" TALL, 2 P. MOLD. DEEP EMER-ALD GREEN COLOR. CONTAINED SMELLING SALTS.

M.S.

Y G C Co

INDENTED CIRCLE IN ROUND BASE 2⅛" DIAM. "Y.G.C°" EMBOSSED IN CENTRE.

465

37

INDENTED CIRCLE IN BASE 1½" BY 2½". 2 P. MOLD, DEEP AQUA-MARINE COLOR, 6⅝" HIGH.

95

END OF M.S.

96 →

END OF M.S.

M.S.

J.F. HARTZ CO. 969 TORONTO

INDENTED BASE 2" BY 2¼"

97

98

M.S.

"LEHN S. FINK CANADA LTD." LYSOL BOTTLE LIGHT AMBER COLOR, 2 P. MOLD 3½" HIGH.

99

Lysol

MADE IN CANADA

CANADA LIMITED - TORONTO

BASE SLIGHTLY CONCAVE 1¾" DIAM. EMBOSSED LETTERS READ "LYSOL of CANADA LIMITED, TORONTO MADE IN CANADA.

Lysol

CONCAVE CIRCLE IN BASE 1⅛" DIAM. 3's ARE REVERSED

8363

2 P. MOLD, 4⅝" TALL, AMBER COLOR.

2 P. MOLD, BRIGHT ORANGE AMBER COLOR, 7⅞" TALL

ORANG AMBER COLOR 3¾" TALL. EMBOSSED.

100

M.S.

LEHN S. FINK CANADA MADE IN CANADA LIMITED 6 1¾" DIAM. BASE

INDENTED CIRCLE IN BASE 1⅝" DIAM. 2 P. MOLD, 3⅞" HIGH, PALE ORANGE AMBER COLOR

PAGE NINE

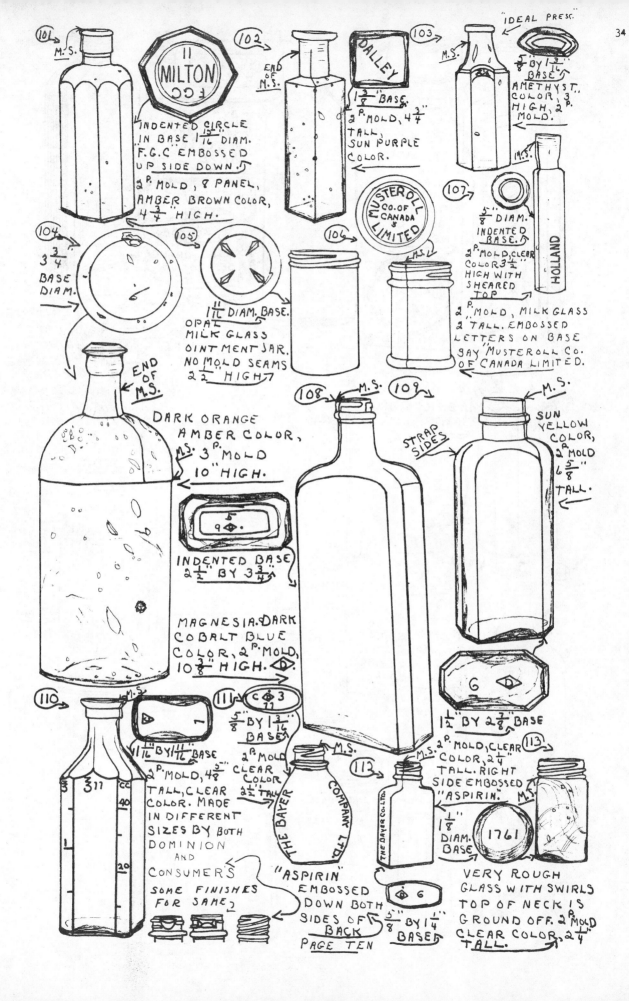

101 M.S.

102 END OF M.S.

103 DALLEY

"IDEAL PRESC."

M.S.

34

11 MILTON F.G.C

INDENTED CIRCLE IN BASE 1 15/16" DIAM. F.G.C EMBOSSED UP SIDE DOWN. 2 P. MOLD, 8 PANEL, AMBER BROWN COLOR, 4 3/4" HIGH.

1 3/8" BASE. 2 P. MOLD, 4 3/4" TALL. SUN PURPLE COLOR.

MUSTEROLL CO. OF CANADA LIMITED

5/8" BY 1 1/16" BASE. AMETHYST COLOR, 3 P. HIGH, 2 P. MOLD.

107

5/8" DIAM. INDENTED BASE. 2 P. MOLD, CLEAR COLOR 3 1/2" HIGH WITH SHEARED TOP

HOLLAND

M.S.

104 3 3/4" BASE DIAM.

105

106

2 P. MOLD, MILK GLASS 2" TALL. EMBOSSED LETTERS ON BASE SAY "MUSTEROLL CO. OF CANADA LIMITED.

1 1/4" DIAM. BASE. OPAL MILK GLASS OINTMENT JAR. NO MOLD SEAMS 2 1/2" HIGH

END OF M.S.

DARK ORANGE AMBER COLOR, M.S. 3 P. MOLD 10" HIGH.

108 M.S. 109 M.S.

STRAP SIDES

SUN YELLOW COLOR, 2 P. MOLD 6 5/8" TALL.

5 9 INDENTED BASE 2 1/2" BY 3 3/4"

MAGNESIA. DARK COBALT BLUE COLOR, 2 P. MOLD, 10 3/8" HIGH.

G

1 1/2" BY 2 7/8" BASE

110 M.S.

3 3 11 CC 40 20

A 1

111 C 3 11

5/8" BY 1 3/16" BASE

1 1/16" BY 1 11/16" BASE

2 P. MOLD, 4 3/8" TALL, CLEAR COLOR. MADE IN DIFFERENT SIZES BY BOTH DOMINION AND CONSUMER'S SOME FINISHES FOR SAME

2 P. MOLD CLEAR COLOR 2 1/2" TALL.

THE BAYER

112

COMPANY LTD.

THE BAYER CO. LTD.

6

5/8" BY 1 1/4" BASE.

M.S. 2 P. MOLD, CLEAR COLOR, 2 1/4" TALL. RIGHT SIDE EMBOSSED "ASPIRIN."

113

1 1/8" DIAM. BASE

M.S.

1761

VERY ROUGH GLASS WITH SWIRLS TOP OF NECK IS GROUND OFF. 2 P. MOLD CLEAR COLOR, 2 1/4" TALL.

"ASPIRIN" EMBOSSED DOWN BOTH SIDES OF BACK PAGE TEN

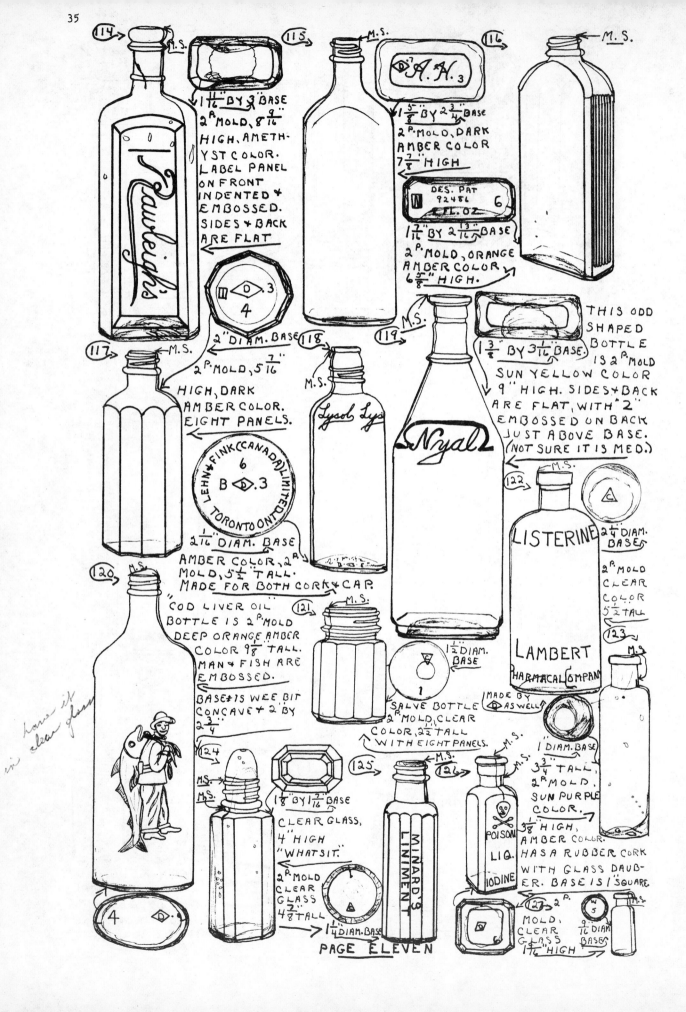

114 → M.S.

115 →

16 →

M.S.

D."A.H."3

1 1/16" BY 3" BASE
2P. MOLD, 8 9/16"
HIGH, AMETH-
YST COLOR.
LABEL PANEL
ON FRONT
INDENTED &
EMBOSSED.
SIDES & BACK
ARE FLAT

Rawleigh's

1 5/8" BY 2 3/4" BASE
2P. MOLD, DARK
AMBER COLOR
7 7/8" HIGH

DES. PAT
92486
FL. OZ.   6

1 7/16" BY 2 13/16" BASE
2P. MOLD, ORANGE
AMBER COLOR
6 5/8" HIGH.

II D 3 4

2" DIAM. BASE 118

117 →
M.S.
2P. MOLD, 5 7/16"
HIGH, DARK
AMBER COLOR.
EIGHT PANELS.

M.S.

119 → M.S.

1 3/8" BY 3 1/16" BASE.

THIS ODD
SHAPED
BOTTLE
IS 2P. MOLD
SUN YELLOW COLOR
9" HIGH. SIDES & BACK
ARE FLAT, WITH "2"
EMBOSSED ON BACK
JUST ABOVE BASE.
(NOT SURE IT IS MED.)

Lysol Lys

Nyal

M.S.

LEHN & FINK (CANADA) LIMITED
6
B D .3
TORONTO ONT.

2 1/16" DIAM. BASE
AMBER COLOR, 2P.
MOLD, 5 1/4" TALL.
MADE FOR BOTH CORK & CAP.

122 → M.S.

LISTERINE

2 1/4" DIAM.
BASE
2P. MOLD
CLEAR
COLOR
5 1/2" TALL

LAMBERT

PHARMACAL COMPANY

123 →

120 → M.S.
"COD LIVER OIL
BOTTLE IS 2P. MOLD
DEEP ORANGE AMBER
COLOR 9 1/8" TALL.
MAN & FISH ARE
EMBOSSED.

BASE # IS WEE BIT
CONCAVE & 2" BY
2 3/4".

121 → M.S.

1 1/2" DIAM.
BASE

C
1

SALVE BOTTLE
2P. MOLD, CLEAR
COLOR, 2 1/2" TALL
WITH EIGHT PANELS.

MADE BY D & S WELL

1" DIAM. BASE

3 3/4" TALL.
2P. MOLD.
SUN PURPLE
COLOR.

have it in clear glass

124 →

M.S.
M.S.

125 →

M.S.   M.S.
126 →

M.S.

1 7/8" BY 1 2/16" BASE
CLEAR GLASS,
4" HIGH
"WHATSIT."

2P. MOLD
CLEAR
GLASS
2"
4.8" TALL

A

1 1/4" DIAM. BASE

MINARD'S LINIMENT

POISON
LIQ.
IODINE

3 1/8" HIGH,
AMBER COLOR.
HAS A RUBBER CORK
WITH GLASS DAUB-
ER. BASE IS 1" SQUARE.

4 D

127 → 2P.
MOLD,
CLEAR GLASS
1 7/16" HIGH

W
5

9/16" DIAM.
BASE

PAGE ELEVEN

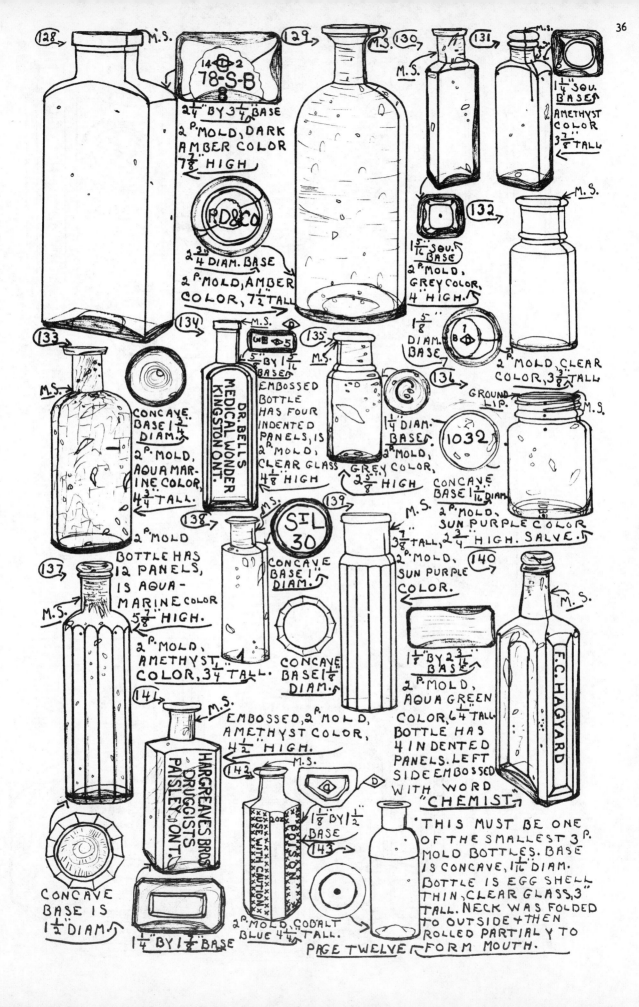

128 → M.S.

129 → M.S. 130 → M.S. 131 →

14 · 2 / 78-S-B / 8
2¼" BY 3¾" BASE
2 P. MOLD, DARK AMBER COLOR
7⅞" HIGH

R D & Co

2¾" DIAM. BASE
2 P. MOLD, AMBER COLOR, 7½" TALL

1¼" SQU. BASE
AMETHYST COLOR
3⅞" TALL

132 →
1 5/16" SQU. BASE
2 P. MOLD, GREY COLOR, 4" HIGH.
1⅝" DIAM. BASE

2 P. MOLD CLEAR COLOR, 3⅜" TALL

M.S.

133 →
M.S. →
CONCAVE BASE 1¼" DIAM.
2 P. MOLD, AQUA MARINE COLOR, 4¾" TALL.

134 → M.S.
5/8" BY 15/16" BASE
EMBOSSED BOTTLE HAS FOUR INDENTED PANELS, IS 2 P. MOLD, CLEAR GLASS 4⅛" HIGH.
DR. BELL'S MEDICAL WONDER KINGSTON ONT.

135 → M.S.
1¼" DIAM. BASE
2 P. MOLD, GREY COLOR, 2⅝" HIGH.

136 →
GROUND LIP.
1032
CONCAVE BASE 1 3/16" DIAM.
2 P. MOLD, SUN PURPLE COLOR 2¾" HIGH. SALVE.
M.S.

137 →
M.S. →
2 P. MOLD BOTTLE HAS 12 PANELS, IS AQUA-MARINE COLOR 5⅞" HIGH.

138 → M.S.

139 →
SIL 30
CONCAVE BASE 1" DIAM.
CONCAVE BASE 1⅛" DIAM.
EMBOSSED, 2 P. MOLD, AMETHYST COLOR, 4½" HIGH.

M.S.
3⅞" TALL, 2¾
2 P. MOLD, SUN PURPLE COLOR.

140 →
M.S. →
1⅛" BY 2 3/16" BASE
2 P. MOLD, AQUA GREEN COLOR, 6¼" TALL. BOTTLE HAS 4 INDENTED PANELS. LEFT SIDE EMBOSSED WITH WORD "CHEMIST"
F.C. HAGYARD

2 P. MOLD, AMETHYST, COLOR, 3¼" TALL.

141 →
M.S. →
CONCAVE BASE IS 1½" DIAM.

HARGREAVES BROS. DRUGGISTS PAISLEY, ONT.
1¼" BY 1⅞" BASE

142 →
M.S. →
USE WITH CAUTION 2 OZ. POISON
1⅛" BY 1½" BASE
143 →
2 P. MOLD, COBALT BLUE 4¼" TALL.

THIS MUST BE ONE OF THE SMALLEST 3 P. MOLD BOTTLES. BASE IS CONCAVE, 1½" DIAM. BOTTLE IS EGG SHELL THIN, CLEAR GLASS, 3" TALL. NECK WAS FOLDED TO OUTSIDE & THEN ROLLED PARTIALLY TO FORM MOUTH.

PAGE TWELVE

37

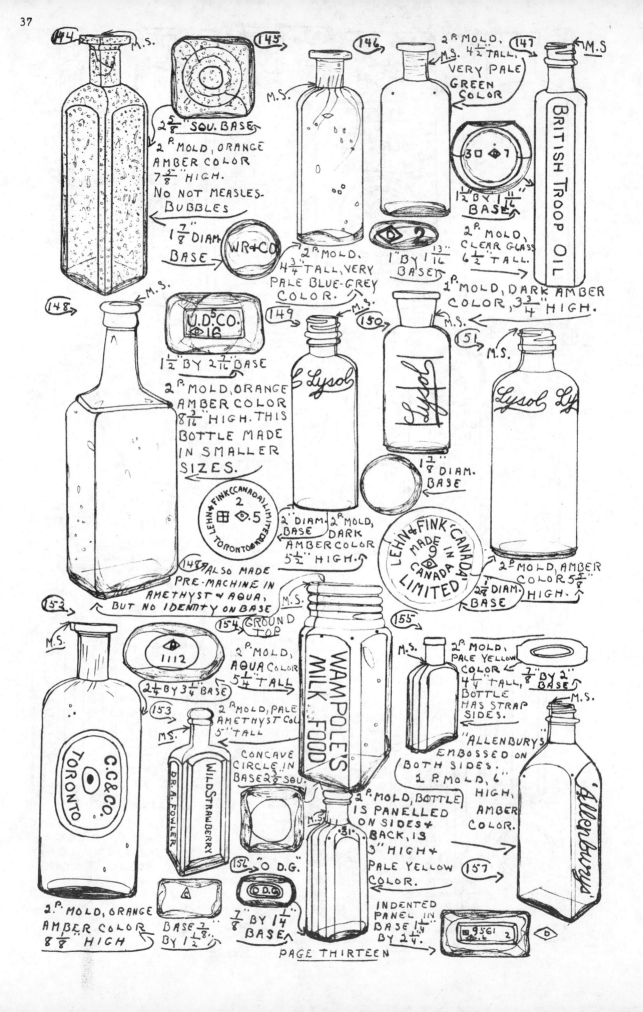

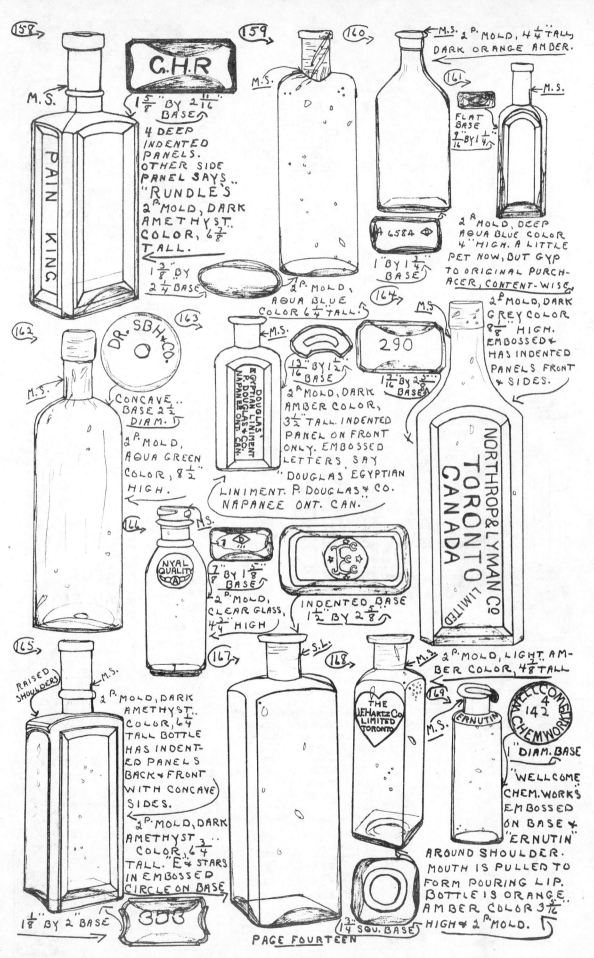

158 → M.S.

PAIN KING

G.H.R

1 5/8" BY 2 11/16" BASE

4 DEEP INDENTED PANELS. OTHER SIDE PANEL SAYS.. "RUNDLE'S" 2 P. MOLD, DARK AMETHYST. COLOR, 6 7/8" TALL.

1 3/8" BY 2 1/4" BASE

159   160 →

M.S.

M.S. 2 P. MOLD, 4 1/4" TALL DARK ORANGE AMBER.

161

FLAT BASE 9/16" BY 1 1/4"   M.S.

2 P MOLD, DEEP AQUA BLUE COLOR 4" HIGH. A LITTLE PET NOW, BUT GYP TO ORIGINAL PURCH-ACER, CONTENT-WISE.

A 6584

1" BY 1 3/4" BASE

2 P. MOLD, AQUA BLUE COLOR 6 1/4" TALL

162   DR. SBH & CO.   163

CONCAVE.. BASE 2 1/2" DIAM.

2 P. MOLD, AQUA GREEN COLOR, 8 1/2" HIGH.

M.S.

DOUGLAS' EGYPTIAN LINIMENT P. DOUGLAS & CO. NAPANEE ONT. CAN.

13/16" BY 1/2" BASE

2 P. MOLD, DARK AMBER COLOR, 3 1/2" TALL. INDENTED PANEL ON FRONT ONLY. EMBOSSED LETTERS, SAY "DOUGLAS EGYPTIAN LINIMENT. P. DOUGLAS & CO. NAPANEE ONT. CAN."

164 →   M.S.

290

1 7/16" BY 2 3/8" BASE

2 P. MOLD, DARK GREY COLOR 8 1/8" HIGH. EMBOSSED & HAS INDENTED PANELS FRONT & SIDES.

NORTHROP & LYMAN Co TORONTO CANADA LIMITED

166   M.S.

NYAL QUALITY A

7/8" BY 1 1/8" BASE

2 P. MOLD, CLEAR GLASS, 4 3/4" HIGH

INDENTED BASE 1 1/2" BY 2 5/8"

2 P. MOLD, LIGHT AMBER COLOR, 4 7/8 TALL

165 →   RAISED SHOULDERS   M.S.

2 P. MOLD, DARK AMETHYST.. COLOR, 6 1/4 TALL BOTTLE HAS INDENTED PANELS BACK & FRONT WITH CONCAVE SIDES.

2 P. MOLD, DARK AMETHYST 3.. COLOR, 6 3/4 TALL. "E" & STARS IN EMBOSSED CIRCLE ON BASE

1 1/8" BY 2" BASE

333

167   S.L.   168

THE J.E.Hartz Co LIMITED TORONTO

M.S.   169

ERNUTIN

WELLCOME CHEM WORKS 4 142

1" DIAM. BASE

"WELLCOME CHEM. WORKS" EMBOSSED ON BASE & "ERNUTIN" AROUND SHOULDER. MOUTH IS PULLED TO FORM POURING LIP. BOTTLE IS ORANGE AMBER COLOR 3 5/16" HIGH & 2 P. MOLD.

3/4" SQU. BASE

PAGE FOURTEEN

170

171

172

173 M.S.

1" BY 1¾" BASE
5⅝" TALL, 2ᴾ. MOLD, SUN YELLOW COLOR. "PINEX" EMBOSSED ON BOTH INDENTED SIDE PANELS.

1" BY 2" BASE

PINEX

NORTHROP & LYMAN CO. LIMITED TORONTO. ONT.

NORTHROP & LYMAN CO. LIMITED TORONTO. ONT.

1" BY 2" BASE

2ᴾ. MOLD, CLEAR GLASS, 5" TALL. RIGHT SIDE READS "INTERNAL" & LEFT "EXTERNAL" BACK "DR. S.N. THOMAS' NO. 5520 THE PROPIETARY OR PATENT MEDICINE ACT. ECLECTRIC OIL"

NORTHROP & LYMAN CO. LIMITED TORONTO. ONT.

AQUA GREEN COLOR, 2ᴾ. MOLD 5¼" TALL. SIDES & BACK SIMILAR TO 171.

15/16" BY 1⅛" BASE

178

174 M.S.

"DR SCHOLLS" MILK GLASS BOTTLE 2 1/16 TALL & 2ᴮ MOLD

2ᴾ. MOLD, AQUA BLUE COLOR, 5½" TALL. INDENTED PANEL ON FRONT ONLY BUT EMBOSSED ON ALL SIDES, RIGHT SIDE READS "INTERNAL", LEFT "EXTERNAL" & BACK "DR. S. N. THOMAS ECLECTRIC OIL" IN ROUGH LETTERING.

13 Dr Scholls

⅝" DIAM. BASE.

176

177

M.S.

2ᴾ. MOLD, 5¾" TALL, PALE AQUAMARINE COLOR, WITH 4 INDENTED PANELS. EMBOSSED LETTERS READ "CHAS H. FLETCHERS CASTORIA".

M.S.

1⅜" DIAM. BASE.

2ᴾ. MOLD GREY GLASS 3⅞" TALL, WITH EIGHT PANELS.

175

5

1" BY 1 1/16" BASE

2 OZ.

2ᴾ. MOLD, 4" TALL, COBALT BLUE "POISON" BOTTLE. ALSO MADE IN AMBER.

FRENCH MAGNETICOIL
J. W. BRAYLEY

Chas H Fletchers

1½" BY 2⅜" BASE

7

M.S.

SLIGHTLY CONCAVE BASE 1" BY 2"

1" BY 1⅛" BASE

m.s.

1

2ᴾ. MOLD, AQUA GREEN COLOR, 5 4/16" HIGH. EMBOSSED LETTERS ON RIGHT SIDE SAY "AGENT".

181 2ᴾ. MOLD AQUA-MARINE COLOR 7¾" TALL, WITH EMBOSSED LETTERS & DESIGN.

SCOTT'S EMULSION

TRADE MARK

COD LIVER OIL WITH LIME & SODA

CONCAVE CIRCLE IN BASE 2½" BY 3⅞"

2ᴾ. MOLD, AMBER COLOR 7½" HIGH.

RED SEAL ON TOP OF CORK READS "AWARDED ONLY GOLD MEDAL, INTERNATIONAL MEDICAL CONGRESS 1894.

179

M.S.

180

CORK

TRADE "ROBOPHOS" MARK

REED AND CARNRICK PHARMACISTS NEW YORK

PAPER LABEL HAS INSTUCTIONS FOR USE PLUS "LITERATURE AND SUPPLIES FROM MERVYN E. VANZANT, 732, YONGE STREET, TORONTO."

NO SEAMS ON BOTTLE, CLEAR GLASS 4" TALL. IT IS ENCASED IN WOODEN THREADED CONTAINER.

182 2ᴾ. MOLD, CLEAR COLOR, 3" HIGH.

1 3/16" DIAM. BASE

G

M.S.

CLARNICO

⅝" DIAM. BASE

PAGE FIFTEEN.

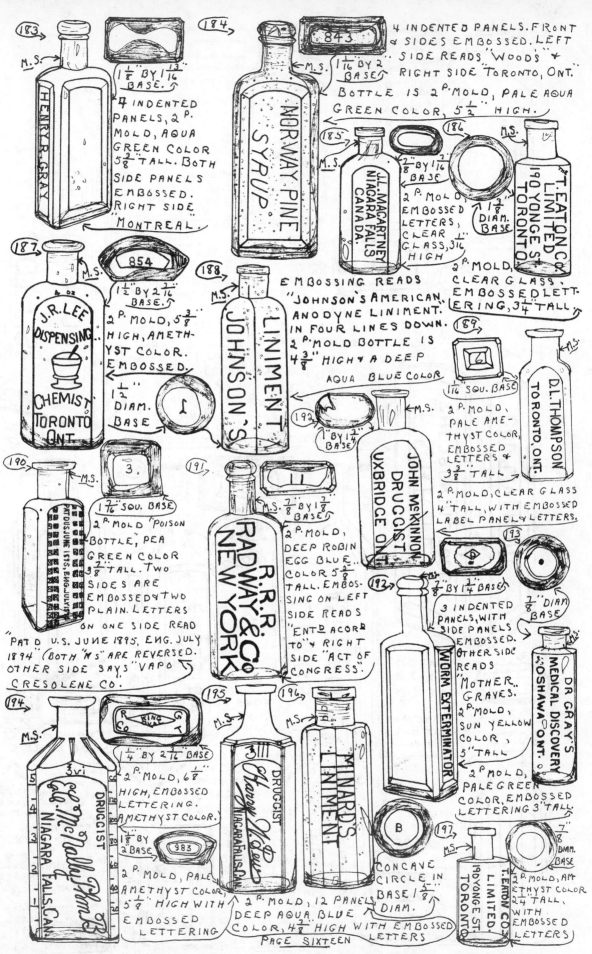

41

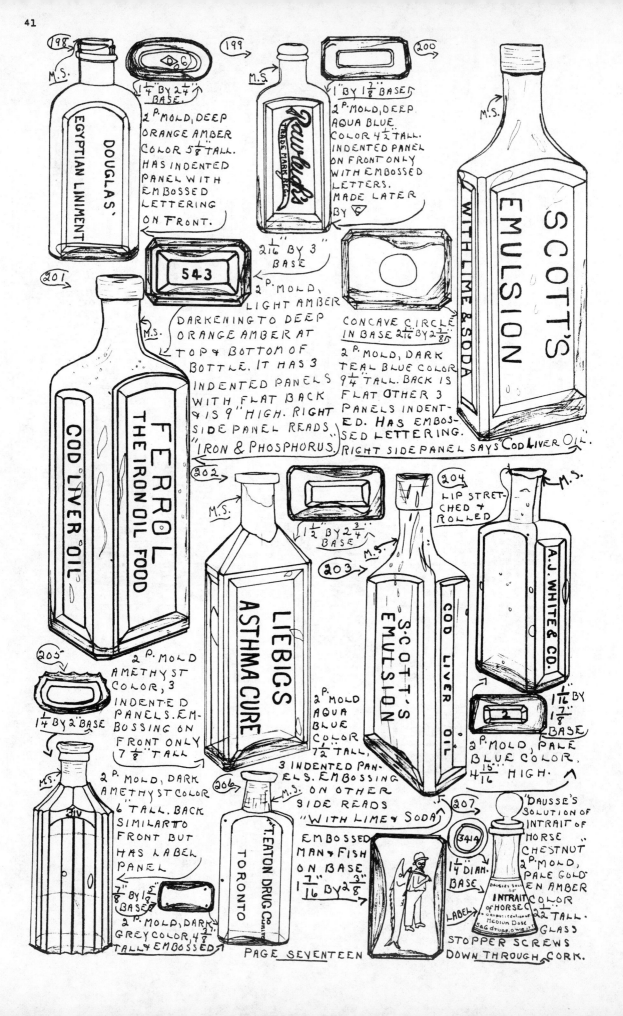

198

M.S.

DOUGLAS' EGYPTIAN LINIMENT

1¼" BY 2⅟₄"
BASE.

2 P. MOLD, DEEP
ORANGE AMBER
COLOR 5⅛ TALL.
HAS INDENTED
PANEL WITH
EMBOSSED
LETTERING
ON FRONT.

199

M.S.

Rawbud's
TRADE MARK REG.

1" BY 1⅞" BASE.

2 P. MOLD, DEEP
AQUA BLUE
COLOR 4½" TALL.
INDENTED PANEL
ON FRONT ONLY
WITH EMBOSSED
LETTERS.
MADE LATER
BY ◯

200

M.S.

SCOTT'S EMULSION WITH LIME & SODA

CONCAVE CIRCLE
IN BASE 2⁶⁄₁₆ BY 2⅝"

2 P. MOLD, DARK
TEAL BLUE COLOR
9¾" TALL. BACK IS
FLAT. OTHER 3
PANELS INDENT-
ED. HAS EMBOS-
SED LETTERING.
RIGHT SIDE PANEL SAYS "COD LIVER OIL"

201

M.S.

COD LIVER OIL

FERROL THE IRON OIL FOOD

543

2⁶⁄₁₆ BY 3"
BASE

2 P. MOLD,
LIGHT AMBER
DARKENING TO DEEP
ORANGE AMBER AT
TOP & BOTTOM OF
BOTTLE. IT HAS 3
INDENTED PANELS
WITH FLAT BACK
& IS 9" HIGH. RIGHT
SIDE PANEL READS
"IRON & PHOSPHORUS."

202

M.S.

1½" BY 2¾"
BASE

203

M.S.

LIEBIGS ASTHMA CURE

S.COTT'S EMULSION

COD LIVER OIL

204

LIP STRET-
CHED &
ROLLED

M.S.

A.J. WHITE & CO.

2 P. MOLD
AQUA
BLUE
COLOR
7½" TALL.

3 INDENTED PAN-
ELS. EMBOSSING
M.S. ON OTHER
SIDE READS
"WITH LIME & SODA"

EMBOSSED
MAN & FISH
ON BASE
1⁷⁄₁₆ BY 2⅜

2
1¹⁶⁄₁₆ BY
1⅞"
BASE

2 P. MOLD, PALE
BLUE COLOR,
4¹⁵⁄₁₆" HIGH.

205

M.S.

1¼ BY 2" BASE

2 P. MOLD
AMETHYST
COLOR, 3
INDENTED
PANELS. EM-
BOSSING ON
FRONT ONLY
7⅛" TALL

2 P. MOLD, DARK
AMETHYST COLOR
6" TALL. BACK
SIMILAR TO
FRONT BUT
HAS LABEL
PANEL

7⅞" BY 1⁵⁄₈"
BASE

2 P. MOLD, DARK
GREY COLOR 4½"
TALL & EMBOSSED

206

℥iv

T. EATON DRUG Co. TORONTO

207

341A

1¼ DIAM.
BASE

LABEL

"DAUSSE'S
SOLUTION OF
INTRAIT OF
HORSE
CHESTNUT."
2 P. MOLD,
PALE GOLD-
EN AMBER
COLOR
2⅖ TALL.
GLASS
STOPPER SCREWS
DOWN THROUGH CORK.

DAUSSE'S SOLN
OF
INTRAIT
of HORSE
MEDIUM DOSE
5 OR 6 drops, etc.

PAGE SEVENTEEN

208
M.S.
W.S. ROBINSON
DISPENSING
PRIME CURÆ NOBIS CANADA SIT
CHEMIST
YORKVILLE

2 1/8" SQU. BASE
2 P. MOLD,
CLEAR GLASS
6 3/4" HIGH.
EMBOSSED.

WRS
1 7/16" BY 2 9/16" BASE
2 P. MOLD, 6 7/8"
TALL, EMBOSSED
& AQUA BLUE COLOR.

209
M.S.
ENO'S
FRUIT SALT

210
M.S.
ENO'S
FRUIT SALT

1 9/16" BY 2 5/8"
BASE
2 P. MOLD,
GREEN COLOR,
EMBOSSED
LETTERING
& 7/8" TALL.

10
W
2 3/8" DIAM.
BASE

211
M.S.
SHOSHONEES
REMEDY OF

CONCAVE
OVAL PANEL
IN BASE
2 1/16" BY 3 4"
2 P. MOLD, 3 INDENTED PANELS.
EMBOSSED LETTERS ON RIGHT
SIDE READ "THE GREAT"
& LEFT "DR JOSEPHUS."
BOTTLE IS VERY DARK
AQUA BLUE COLOR,
& IS
9 1/4" HIGH.

212
M.S.
MERCURY
LYMAN BROTHERS & Co.
WHOLESALE DRUGGISTS & MANUFACTURERS
TORONTO

556
CONCAVE
CIRCLE ON
BASE 2 1/2" DIAM.
3 P. MOLD, BOTTLE
GREEN COLOR,
9" HIGH. LABEL
"LYMAN BROTHERS & Co.
WHOLESALE DRUGGISTS &
MANUFACTURERS, TORONTO
PAGE EIGHTEEN

213
1 5/16" BY 3 4"
BASE

LABEL
LABEL
STRAP
SIDES
2 P. MOLD, DARK BLUE
AQUA COLOR, 8 1/4" TALL.
HAS FRONT PANEL &
EMBOSSED LETTERS.

214
GROUND
FOR STOPPER
M.S.
MANLEY'S CELERY NERVE
COMPOUND

2 P. MOLD, COBALT
BLUE COLOR
6 5/8" HIGH
EMBOSSED, DARK
AMBER COLOR,
6 5/16" HIGH

M.S.

215
1 3/4" BY 2 1/2"
BASE

HORNER'S
M.S.

43

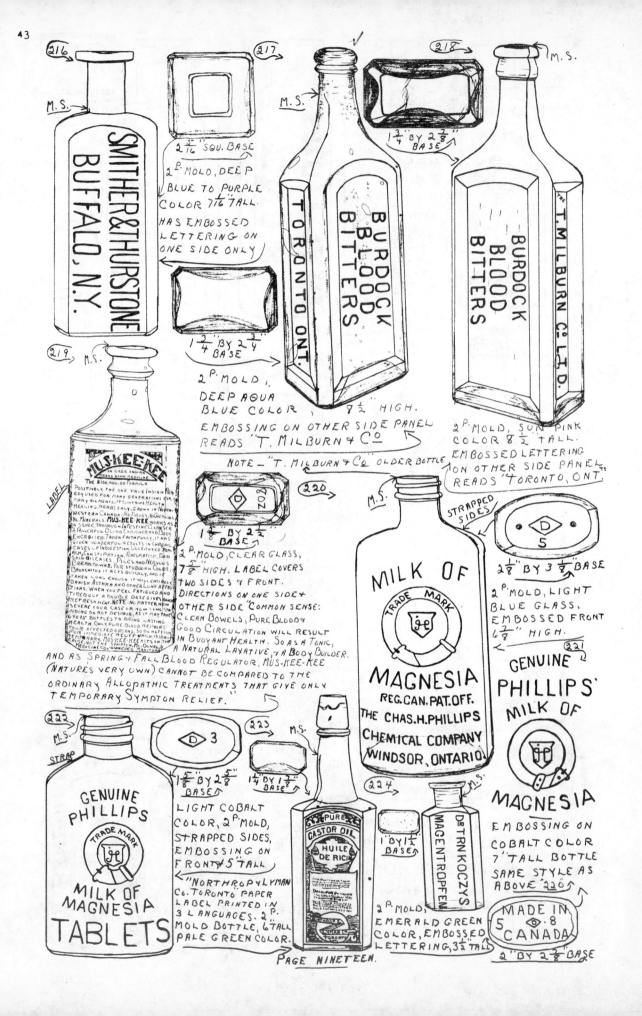

216

M.S.

SMITHER & THURSTONE
BUFFALO, N.Y.

217

2 1/16" SQU. BASE

2 P. MOLD, DEEP BLUE TO PURPLE COLOR 7 7/16" TALL.

HAS EMBOSSED LETTERING ON ONE SIDE ONLY

1 3/4" BY 2 3/4" BASE

✓

218

M.S.

1 3/4" BY 2 7/8" BASE

M.S.

BURDOCK BLOOD BITTERS

TORONTO ONT.

THE T. MILBURN C° LT'D.

BURDOCK BLOOD BITTERS

M.S.

2 P. MOLD, DEEP AQUA BLUE COLOR, 8 1/2" HIGH. EMBOSSING ON OTHER SIDE PANEL READS "T. MILBURN & C°"

NOTE — "T. MILBURN & C°" OLDER BOTTLE

2 P. MOLD, SUN PINK COLOR 8 1/2" TALL. EMBOSSED LETTERING ON OTHER SIDE PANEL READS "TORONTO, ONT."

219

M.S.

MUSKEEKEE

LABEL

Positively the one true Indian Remedy used for many generations for many ailments. It contains Health Healing Herbs only, grown in North-Western Canada. No Drugs, No Chemicals, No Minerals. MUS-KEE-KEE works as a sure, thorough Intestine Cleanser, a Powerful Blood Enricher and Body Energiser. Taken faithfully, it has given wonderful results in chronic cases of Indigestion, Ulcerated Stomach, Constipation, Rheumatism, Bad Skin Diseases, Piles and Nervous Breakdowns. For stubborn Colds, Bronchitis it acts quickly, and if taken long enough it will completely banish Asthma and other Lung affections. When you feel fatigued and tired out a double dose gives you refreshment. NOTE - No matter how severe your case or how long standing do not despair, as it may take 5 to 15 bottles to bring lasting health. Only pure blood repairs your affected organs, so do not look for immediate relief which is only temporary. MUS-KEE-KEE acts on the cause not the symptom. McDonald Medicine Co. Winacres, Manitoba.

AND AS A SPRING & FALL BLOOD REGULATOR, MUS-KEE-KEE (NATURE'S VERY OWN) CANNOT BE COMPARED TO THE ORDINARY, ALLOPATHIC TREATMENTS THAT GIVE ONLY TEMPORARY SYMPTOM RELIEF."

220

8 oz.

1 5/8" BY 2 1/2" BASE

2 P. MOLD, CLEAR GLASS, 7 5/8" HIGH. LABEL COVERS TWO SIDES & FRONT. DIRECTIONS ON ONE SIDE & OTHER SIDE "COMMON SENSE: CLEAN BOWELS, PURE BLOOD & GOOD CIRCULATION WILL RESULT IN BUOYANT HEALTH. SO AS A TONIC, A NATURAL LAXATIVE, & A BODY BUILDER.

M.S.

STRAPPED SIDES

5

2 1/8" BY 3 1/8" BASE

2 P. MOLD, LIGHT BLUE GLASS, EMBOSSED FRONT 6 7/8" HIGH.

MILK OF MAGNESIA

TRADE MARK

REG. CAN. PAT. OFF.
THE CHAS. H. PHILLIPS
CHEMICAL COMPANY
WINDSOR, ONTARIO

221

GENUINE PHILLIPS' MILK OF MAGNESIA

EMBOSSING ON COBALT COLOR 7" TALL BOTTLE SAME STYLE AS ABOVE "220"

222

M.S.

STRAP

GENUINE PHILLIPS

TRADE MARK

MILK OF MAGNESIA TABLETS

223

D 3

1 5/8" BY 2 5/8" BASE

M.S.

1 1/4" BY 1 3/8" BASE

LIGHT COBALT COLOR, 2 P. MOLD, STRAPPED SIDES, EMBOSSING ON FRONT & 5" TALL

"NORTHROP & LYMAN C° TORONTO" PAPER LABEL PRINTED IN 3 LANGUAGES. 2 P. MOLD BOTTLE, 6" TALL PALE GREEN COLOR.

224

6 1/2% PURE CASTOR OIL HUILE DE RICIN

1" BY 1 1/4" BASE

MAGENTROPFEN

Dr. TRNKOCZYS

2 P. MOLD, EMERALD GREEN COLOR, EMBOSSED LETTERING, 3 1/2" TALL

M.S.

MADE IN CANADA 5 8

2" BY 2 7/8" BASE

MAGNESIA

PAGE NINETEEN.

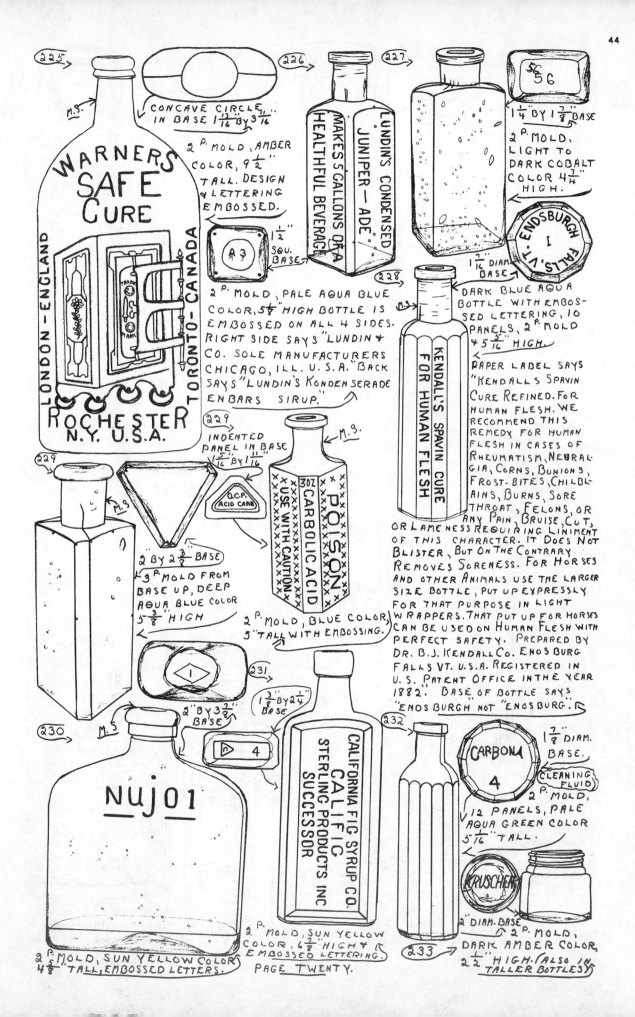

225 →

M.S.

WARNERS SAFE CURE

LONDON — ENGLAND

TORONTO — CANADA

ROCHESTER N.Y. U.S.A.

CONCAVE CIRCLE IN BASE 1 13/16 BY 3 3/16

2 P. MOLD, AMBER COLOR, 9 1/2" TALL. DESIGN & LETTERING EMBOSSED.

A 3 1 1/2" SQU. BASE

2 P. MOLD, PALE AQUA BLUE COLOR, 5 7/8" HIGH BOTTLE IS EMBOSSED ON ALL 4 SIDES. RIGHT SIDE SAYS "LUNDIN & CO. SOLE MANUFACTURERS CHICAGO, ILL. U.S.A." BACK SAYS "LUNDIN'S KONDEN SERADE EN BARS SIRUP."

226 →

MAKES 5 GALLONS OF A HEALTHFUL BEVERAGE

LUNDIN'S CONDENSED JUNIPER — ADE

227 →

56 1 1/4 BY 1 7/8 BASE

2 P. MOLD, LIGHT TO DARK COBALT COLOR 4 3/4" HIGH.

ENDSBURGH FALLS, VT. 1 1 7/16 DIAM. BASE

DARK BLUE AQUA BOTTLE WITH EMBOSSED LETTERING, 10 PANELS, 2 P. MOLD & 5 5/16 HIGH.

228 →

M.S.

KENDALL'S SPAVIN CURE FOR HUMAN FLESH

PAPER LABEL SAYS "KENDALL'S SPAVIN CURE REFINED. FOR HUMAN FLESH. WE RECOMMEND THIS REMEDY FOR HUMAN FLESH IN CASES OF RHEUMATISM, NEURALGIA, CORNS, BUNIONS, FROST-BITES, CHILBLAINS, BURNS, SORE THROAT, FELONS, OR ANY PAIN, BRUISE, CUT, OR LAMENESS REQUIRING LINIMENT OF THIS CHARACTER. IT DOES NOT BLISTER, BUT ON THE CONTRARY REMOVES SORENESS. FOR HORSES AND OTHER ANIMALS USE THE LARGER SIZE BOTTLE, PUT UP EXPRESSLY FOR THAT PURPOSE IN LIGHT WRAPPERS. THAT PUT UP FOR HORSES CAN BE USED ON HUMAN FLESH WITH PERFECT SAFETY. PREPARED BY DR. B.J. KENDALL CO. ENOSBURG FALLS VT. U.S.A. REGISTERED IN U.S. PATENT OFFICE IN THE YEAR 1882. BASE OF BOTTLE SAYS "ENOSBURGH" NOT "ENOSBURG."

229 →

INDENTED PANEL IN BASE 5/16 BY 1 11/16

M.S.

229 →

M.S.

O.C.P. ACID CARB.

3 OZ CARBOLIC ACID USE WITH CAUTION POISON

2 BY 2 3/8 BASE

3 P. MOLD FROM BASE UP, DEEP AQUA BLUE COLOR 5 3/8" HIGH

2 P. MOLD, BLUE COLOR, 5" TALL WITH EMBOSSING.

1

231 →

1 3/8" BY 2 1/4 BASE

2" BY 3 1/2" BASE

D 4

230 → M.S.

NUJOL

CALIFORNIA FIG SYRUP CO. CALIFIG STERLING PRODUCTS INC SUCCESSOR

232 →

CARBONA 4 1 7/8" DIAM. BASE.

CLEANING FLUID

2 P. MOLD, 12 PANELS, PALE AQUA GREEN COLOR 5 3/16" TALL.

KRUSCHEN

233 →

2 DIAM. BASE

2 P. MOLD, DARK AMBER COLOR, 2 1/2" HIGH. (ALSO IN TALLER BOTTLES)

2 P. MOLD, SUN YELLOW COLOR 4 3/8" TALL, EMBOSSED LETTERS.

2 P. MOLD, SUN YELLOW COLOR, 6 7/8" HIGH & EMBOSSED LETTERING. PAGE TWENTY.

45

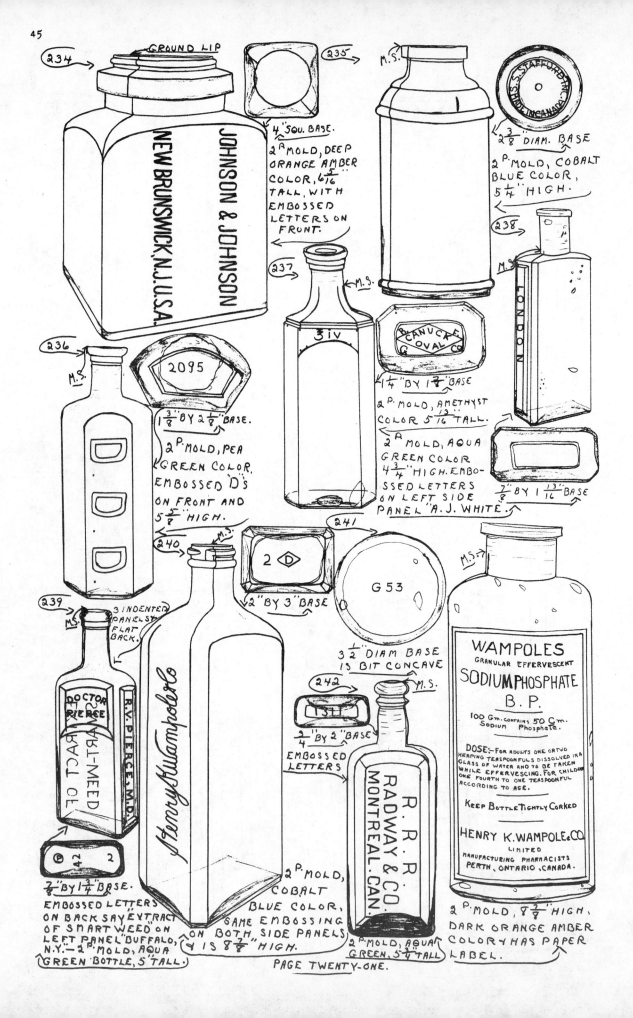

234 → GROUND LIP

JOHNSON & JOHNSON
NEW BRUNSWICK, N.J. U.S.A.

235 →

4" SQU. BASE.
2ᴬ MOLD, DEEP
ORANGE AMBER
COLOR, 6 5/16"
TALL, WITH
EMBOSSED
LETTERS ON
FRONT.

M.S.

S.S. STAFFORD INC.
MADE IN CANADA

2 3/8" DIAM. BASE
2ᴾ. MOLD, COBALT
BLUE COLOR,
5 1/4" HIGH.

238

M.S.

LONDON

237

M.S.

3 IV

CANUCK
OVAL
B G CO

1 1/4" BY 1 13/16" BASE
2ᴾ. MOLD, AMETHYST
COLOR 5 13/16" TALL.
2ᴬ MOLD, AQUA
GREEN COLOR
4 3/4" HIGH. EMBO-
SSED LETTERS
ON LEFT SIDE
PANEL "A.J. WHITE."

236

M.S.

2095

1 3/8" BY 2 1/8" BASE.

2ᴾ. MOLD, PEA
GREEN COLOR,
EMBOSSED "D'S
ON FRONT AND
5 5/8" HIGH.

7/8" BY 1 13/16" BASE

240

M.S.

241

2 ◇

2" BY 3" BASE

G 53

3 1/2" DIAM BASE
IS BIT CONCAVE

M.S.

242

3 II

2/4" BY 2" BASE

EMBOSSED
LETTERS

239

M.S.

3 INDENTED
PANELS,
FLAT
BACK.

DOCTOR
PIERCE

R.V. PIERCE. M.D.

TABLET TO

Stanley Drug Co.

R. R. R.
RADWAY & CO.
MONTREAL. CAN.

WAMPOLES
GRANULAR EFFERVESCENT
SODIUM PHOSPHATE
B. P.

100 Gm. CONTAINS 50 Gm.
Sodium Phosphate.

DOSE:- FOR ADULTS ONE OR TWO
HEAPING TEASPOONFULS DISSOLVED IN A
GLASS OF WATER AND TO BE TAKEN
WHILE EFFERVESCING. FOR CHILDREN
ONE FOURTH TO ONE TEASPOONFUL
ACCORDING TO AGE.

KEEP BOTTLE TIGHTLY CORKED

HENRY K. WAMPOLE & CO.
LIMITED
MANUFACTURING PHARMACISTS
PERTH, ONTARIO, CANADA.

7/8" BY 1 3/4" BASE.
EMBOSSED LETTERS
ON BACK SAY "EXTRACT
OF SMART WEED" ON
LEFT PANEL "BUFFALO,
N.Y.- 2ᴾ. MOLD, AQUA
GREEN BOTTLE, 5" TALL."

2ᴾ. MOLD,
COBALT
BLUE COLOR,
SAME EMBOSSING
ON BOTH SIDE PANELS
IS 8 7/8" HIGH.

2ᴾ. MOLD, AQUA
GREEN, 5 1/4" TALL.

2ᴾ. MOLD, 8 7/8" HIGH,
DARK ORANGE AMBER
COLOR, HAS PAPER
LABEL.

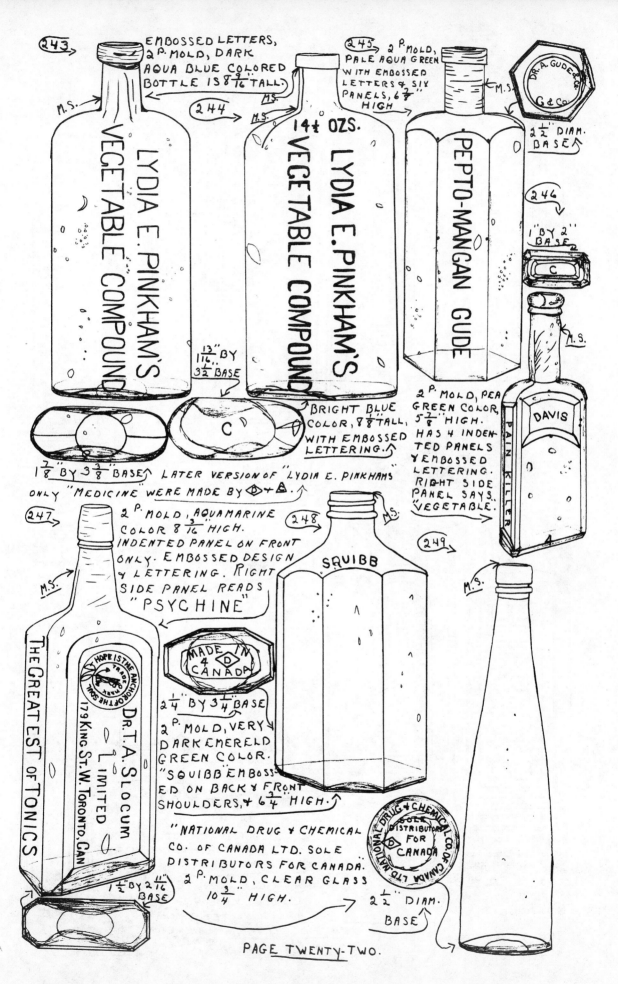

243 → EMBOSSED LETTERS, 2 P. MOLD, DARK AQUA BLUE COLORED BOTTLE IS 8 7/16" TALL.

M.S.

LYDIA E. PINKHAM'S VEGETABLE COMPOUND

244 → M.S.

13" BY 3 1/2" BASE

1 7/8" BY 3 3/8" BASE LATER VERSION OF "LYDIA E. PINKHAMS ONLY "MEDICINE" WERE MADE BY ◇ + △.

14 1/4 OZS.

LYDIA E. PINKHAM'S VEGETABLE COMPOUND

M.S.

BRIGHT BLUE COLOR, 8 7/8" TALL, WITH EMBOSSED LETTERING.

245 → 2 P. MOLD, PALE AQUA GREEN WITH EMBOSSED LETTERS & SIX PANELS, 6 7/8" HIGH

M.S.

PEPTO-MANGAN GUDE

DR. A. GUDE & CO. G & CO.

2 1/2" DIAM. BASE

246 →

1" BY 2" BASE

C

M.S.

DAVIS

PAIN KILLER

2 P. MOLD, PEA GREEN COLOR, 5 7/8" HIGH. HAS 4 INDENTED PANELS & EMBOSSED LETTERING. RIGHT SIDE PANEL SAYS "VEGETABLE."

247 →

M.S.

THE GREATEST OF TONICS

HOPE IS THE ANCHOR OF THE SOUL TRADE MARK

Dr. T. A. Slocum LIMITED 179 King St. W. Toronto. Can

1 1/2" BY 2 11/16" BASE

2 P. MOLD, AQUAMARINE COLOR 8 3/16" HIGH. INDENTED PANEL ON FRONT ONLY. EMBOSSED DESIGN & LETTERING. RIGHT SIDE PANEL READS "PSYCHINE"

248 → M.S.

SQUIBB

MADE IN CANADA 4 D

2 1/4" BY 3 1/4" BASE

2 P. MOLD, VERY DARK EMERELD GREEN COLOR. "SQUIBB" EMBOSSED ON BACK & FRONT SHOULDERS, & 6 3/4" HIGH.

"NATIONAL DRUG & CHEMICAL CO. OF CANADA LTD. SOLE DISTRIBUTORS FOR CANADA." 2 P. MOLD, CLEAR GLASS 10 3/4" HIGH.

249 → M.S.

SOLE DISTRIBUTORS FOR CANADA NATIONAL DRUG & CHEMICAL CO. OF CANADA LTD

2 1/2" DIAM. BASE

PAGE TWENTY-TWO.

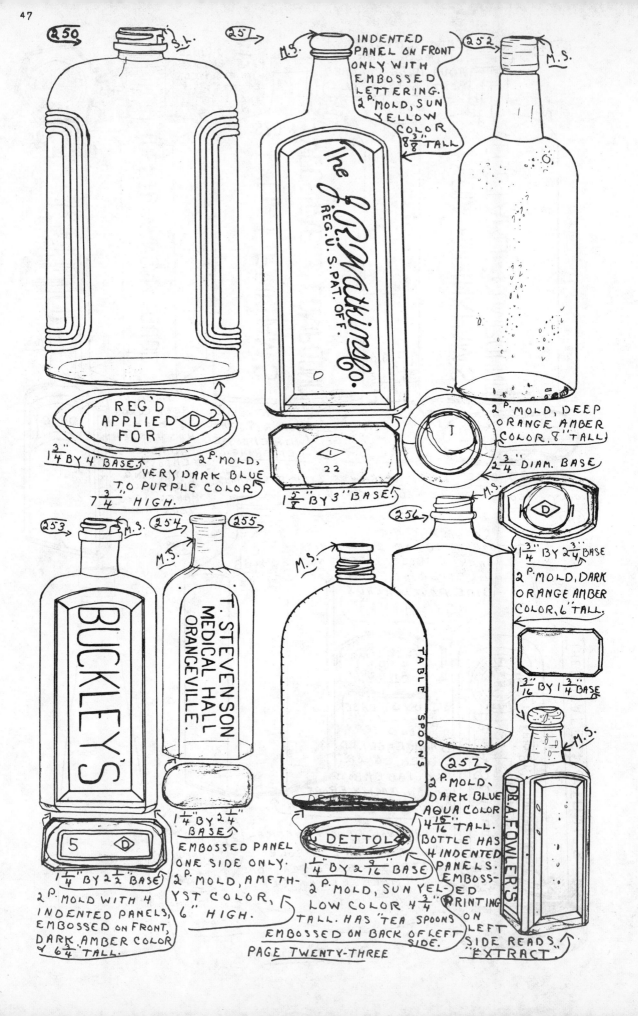

250

251

INDENTED PANEL ON FRONT ONLY WITH EMBOSSED LETTERING. 2 P. MOLD, SUN YELLOW COLOR 8 3/8" TALL

M.S.

252

M.S.

The J.R. Watkins Co.
REG. U.S. PAT. OFF.

REG'D APPLIED FOR

2 P. MOLD, DEEP ORANGE AMBER COLOR, 8" TALL

2 3/4" DIAM. BASE

3 1/4" BY 4" BASE.

2 P. MOLD, VERY DARK BLUE TO PURPLE COLOR 7 3/4" HIGH.

1 5/8" BY 3" BASE.

1 3/4" BY 2 3/4" BASE

2 P. MOLD, DARK ORANGE AMBER COLOR, 6" TALL.

253

M.S.

254

255

M.S.

256

M.S.

M.S.

1 3/16" BY 1 3/4" BASE

BUCKLEY'S

T. STEVENSON MEDICAL HALL ORANGEVILLE.

TABLE SPOONS

DR. A. FOWLER'S

M.S.

5

257

2 P. MOLD, DARK BLUE AQUA COLOR 4 15/16" TALL. BOTTLE HAS 4 INDENTED PANELS. EMBOSSED PRINTING ON LEFT SIDE READS "EXTRACT."

1 1/4" BY 2 2/4" BASE

1 1/4" BY 2 1/4" BASE

DETTOL

1 1/4" BY 2 9/16" BASE

2 P. MOLD WITH 4 INDENTED PANELS, EMBOSSED ON FRONT, DARK AMBER COLOR 6 1/4" TALL.

EMBOSSED PANEL ONE SIDE ONLY. 2 P. MOLD, AMETHYST COLOR, 6" HIGH.

2 P. MOLD, SUN YELLOW COLOR 4 3/4" TALL. HAS "TEA SPOONS EMBOSSED ON BACK OF LEFT SIDE.

PAGE TWENTY-THREE

48

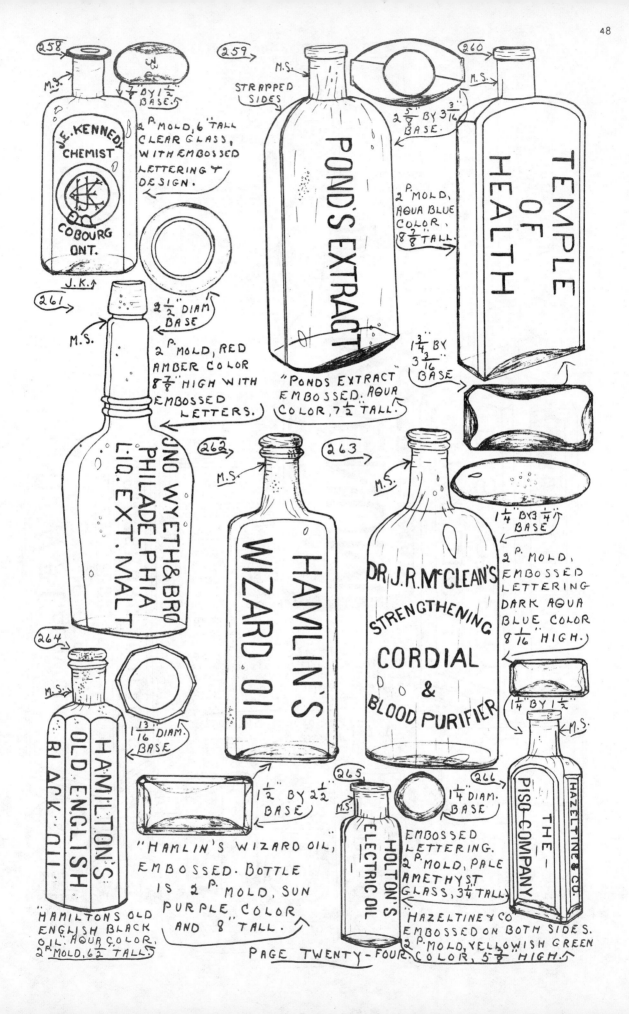

258

M.S.

3"

⌐ 7" BY 1½"
BASE 5

J.E. KENNEDY
CHEMIST
COBOURG
ONT.

J.K.

2 P. MOLD, 6" TALL
CLEAR GLASS,
WITH EMBOSSED
LETTERING & DESIGN.

259

M.S.

STRAPPED
SIDES

POND'S EXTRACT

2 ⅝" BY 3 ³⁄₁₆"
BASE.

2 P. MOLD,
AQUA BLUE
COLOR,
8 ⅞" TALL.

"PONDS EXTRACT"
EMBOSSED. AQUA
COLOR, 7½" TALL.

260

M.S.

TEMPLE
OF
HEALTH

1 ¾" BY
3 ³⁄₁₆"
BASE

261

M.S.

2 ½" DIAM
BASE

2 P. MOLD, RED
AMBER COLOR
8 ⅞" HIGH WITH
EMBOSSED
LETTERS.

JNO WYETH & BRO
PHILADELPHIA
LIQ. EXT. MALT

262

M.S.

HAMLIN'S
WIZARD OIL

263

M.S.

DR. J.R. McCLEAN'S
STRENGTHENING
CORDIAL
&
BLOOD PURIFIER

1 ¼" BY 3 ⁴⁄₁"
BASE

2 P. MOLD,
EMBOSSED
LETTERING
DARK AQUA
BLUE COLOR
8 ⁵⁄₁₆" HIGH.

264

M.S.

HAMILTON'S
OLD ENGLISH
BLACK OIL

1 ¹³⁄₁₆" DIAM.
BASE

1½" BY 2½"
BASE

"HAMLIN'S WIZARD OIL,
EMBOSSED. BOTTLE
IS 2 P. MOLD, SUN
PURPLE COLOR
AND 8" TALL.

"HAMILTONS OLD
ENGLISH BLACK
OIL", AQUA COLOR.
2 P. MOLD, 6½" TALL.

265

M.S.

HOLTON'S
ELECTRIC OIL

1 ¼" DIAM.
BASE

EMBOSSED
LETTERING.
2 P. MOLD, PALE
AMETHYST
GLASS, 3 ¾" TALL.

266

1 ¼" BY 1½"

M.S.

THE
PISO COMPANY

HAZELTINE & CO.

"HAZELTINE & CO"
EMBOSSED ON BOTH SIDES.
2 P. MOLD, YELLOWISH GREEN
COLOR, 5 ⅞" HIGH.

PAGE TWENTY-FOUR

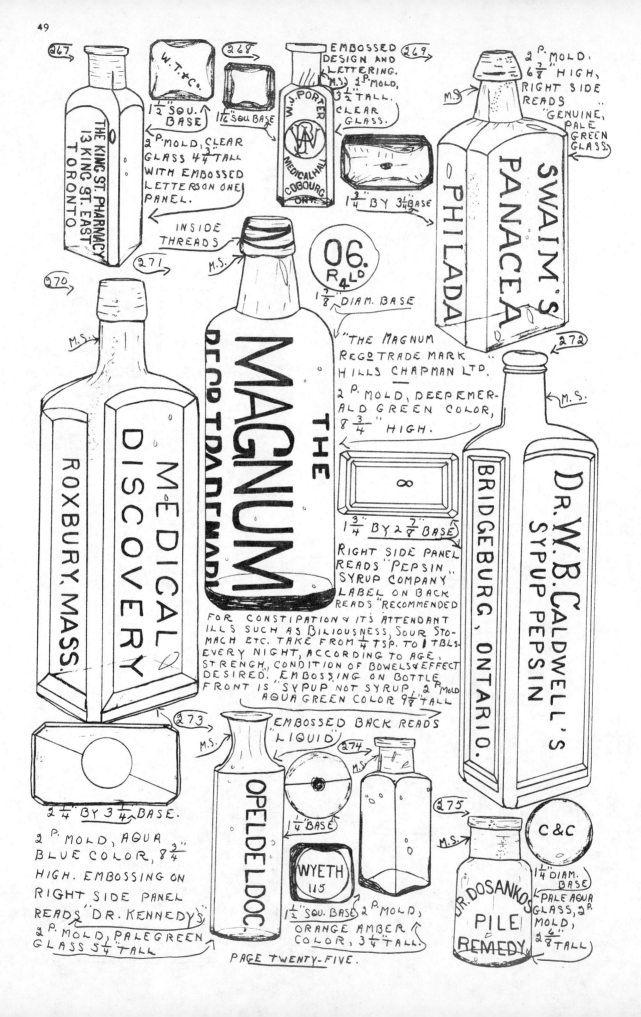

276 →

D.J. →

HOOPER & CO
CHEMISTS
HONI SOIT QUI MAL Y PENSE
MCHC
43 KING ST. W.
444 SPADINA AVE
TORONTO

DO NOT HAVE
HEIGHT ETC.
FOR THIS
BOTTLE.
2 P. MOLD,
CLEAR GLASS.

4

1 7/8 BASE

277 →

M.S. →

DR. WISTAR'S
BALSAM OF
WILD CHERRY PHILAD A.

DR. WISTAR'S BALSAM OF
WILD CHERRY PHILAD A.
2 P. MOLD, 8 PANEL, AGUA
BLUE GLASS, 5" TALL.
HAS I B. EMBOSSED ON
CENTRE BACK PANEL.

278 →

M.S.

MALTOPEPSYN
HAZEN MORSE
TORONTO

1 1/8 BY 1 7/8
2 P. MOLD, AMETHYST
COLOR, 4" TALL.

279 →

M.S. →

Mrs WINSLOW'S
SOOTHING SYRUP
THE ANGLO AMERICAN DRUG CO.

1 1/4 DIAM.

2 P. MOLD, AGUA
GLASS, 5 1/2 TALL,
HAS "SUCCESSORS
TO CURTIS &
PERKINS PROP-
RIETORS" EMBOSSED
ON THE BACK.

280 →

M.S. →

Ozone is Life

The Ozone Co.
Of Toronto
Limited

2 5/8" SQUARE
2 P. MOLD, CLEAR
GLASS, 8 5/8" HIGH.
"OZONE IS LIFE"
EMBOSSED ON OTHER
SIDE & BACK IS
BLANK.

281 →

M.S. →

FELLOWS
SYRUP OF
HYPOPHOSPHITES

284 →

10.

2" BY 3 1/2"
2 P. MOLD, DEEP AGUA
BLUE GLASS, 7 3/4" TALL.

282 →

M.S. →

283 →

M.S. →

SYR HYPOPHOS COMP
FELLOWS

1 1/2 BASE
2 P. MOLD, CLEAR
THIN GLASS,
3 7/8" TALL.

TEA SPOONS

2 P. MOLD,
5" TALL,
CLEAR GLASS.

1 1/8" BASE

M.S. →

POLUSTERINE PRODUCTS Co.
Solyol
TORONTO

1 7/8 DIAM.

2 P. MOLD,
3 1/2" HIGH,
AMBER
GLASS.

PAGE TWENTY-SIX

51

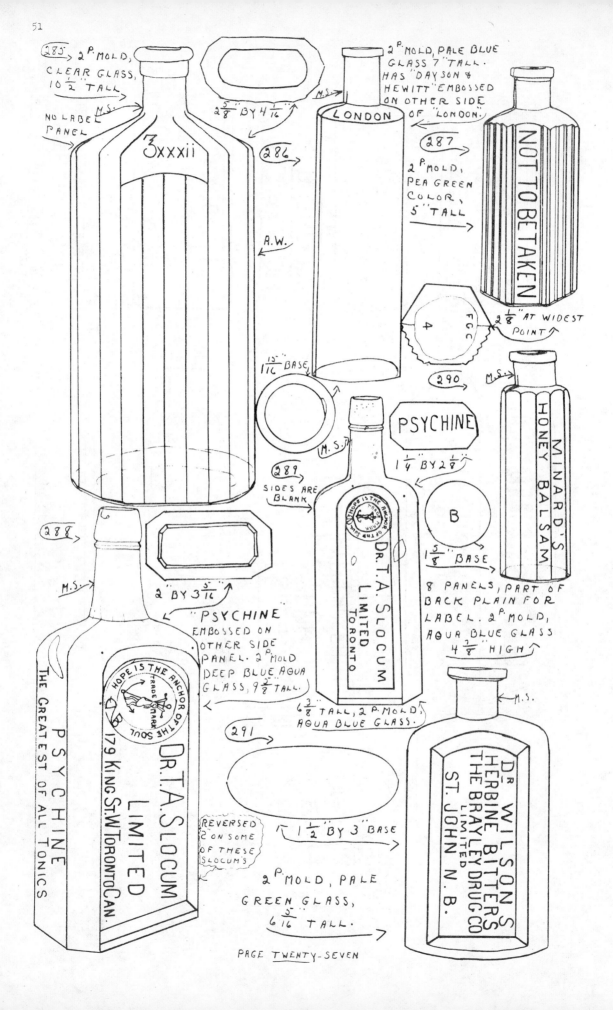

285 2 P. MOLD, CLEAR GLASS, 10½" TALL

NO LABEL PANEL

M.S.

Ʒxxxii

2 ⅝" BY 4 1/16"

286

A.W.

2 P. MOLD, PALE BLUE GLASS 7" TALL. HAS "DAYSON & HEWITT" EMBOSSED ON OTHER SIDE OF "LONDON".

LONDON

M.S.

287

2 P. MOLD, PEA GREEN COLOR, 5" TALL

NOT TO BE TAKEN

2 ⅛" AT WIDEST POINT

15/16" BASE

4   F.G.C.

290

M.S.

M.S.

289

SIDES ARE BLANK

PSYCHINE

1¼" BY 2⅛"

B

1⅝" BASE

8 PANELS, PART OF BACK PLAIN FOR LABEL. 2 P. MOLD, AQUA BLUE GLASS 4⅞" HIGH

MINARD'S HONEY BALSAM

288

M.S.

2" BY 3 5/16"

"PSYCHINE EMBOSSED ON OTHER SIDE PANEL. 2 P. MOLD DEEP BLUE AQUA GLASS, 9⅞" TALL.

HOPE IS THE ANCHOR OF THE SOUL   TRADE MARK

DR. T. A. SLOCUM LIMITED TORONTO

6⅜" TALL, 2 P. MOLD, AQUA BLUE GLASS.

M.S.

291

REVERSED 2 ON SOME OF THESE SLOCUM'S

1½" BY 3" BASE

2 P. MOLD, PALE GREEN GLASS, 6 5/16" TALL.

PSYCHINE THE GREATEST OF ALL TONICS

HOPE IS THE ANCHOR OF THE SOUL   TRADE MARK

DR. T. A. SLOCUM LIMITED 179 KING ST. W. TORONTO CAN.

DR WILSONS HERBINE BITTERS THE BRAYLEY DRUG CO LIMITED ST. JOHN N. B.

PAGE TWENTY-SEVEN

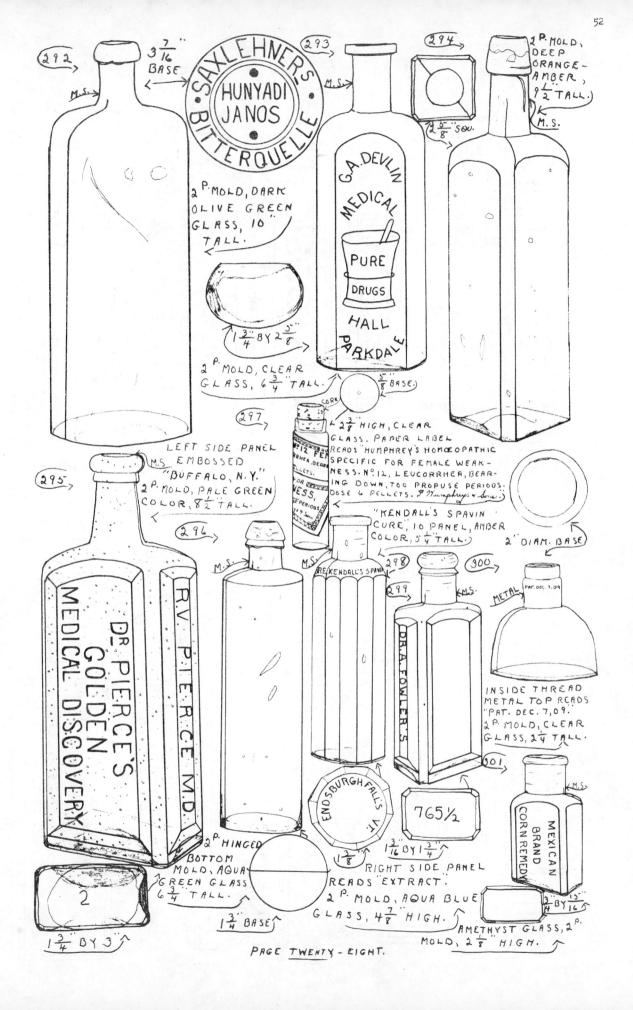

292→

M.S.

3 7/16" BASE

293→

M.S.

294→

2 5/8" SQU.

2 P. MOLD, DEEP ORANGE-AMBER, 9 1/2" TALL. M.S.

SAXLEHNER'S • BITTERQUELLE

HUNYADI JANOS

2 P. MOLD, DARK OLIVE GREEN GLASS, 10" TALL.

1 3/4" BY 2 5/8"

2 P. MOLD, CLEAR GLASS, 6 3/4" TALL.

G.A. DEVLIN MEDICAL PURE DRUGS HALL PARKDALE

5/8" BASE.

297→

CORK

N°12 FEM ...RHEA, BEAR... ...ELLETS. ...NESS, OF PERIODS.

2 3/8" HIGH, CLEAR GLASS. PAPER LABEL READS "HUMPHREY'S HOMŒOPATHIC SPECIFIC FOR FEMALE WEAK-NESS. N°. 12, LEUCORRHŒA, BEAR-ING DOWN, TOO PROPUSE PERIODS. DOSE 6 PELLETS. F. Humphreys & Sons."

LEFT SIDE PANEL M.S. EMBOSSED "BUFFALO, N.Y." 2 P. MOLD, PALE GREEN COLOR, 8 1/2" TALL.

295→

296→

M.S.

M.S.

"KENDALL'S SPAVIN CURE, 10 PANEL, AMBER COLOR, 5 1/4" TALL.

2" DIAM. BASE

DR. PIERCE'S GOLDEN MEDICAL DISCOVERY.

R.V. PIERCE M.D.

RE KENDALL'S SPAVIN

298→

299→

M.S.

300→

DR. A. FOWLER'S

METAL PAT. DEC. 7,09

INSIDE THREAD METAL TOP READS "PAT. DEC. 7, 09. 2 P. MOLD, CLEAR GLASS, 2 1/4" TALL.

301→

M.S.

2

1 3/4" BY 3"

2 P. HINGED BOTTOM MOLD, AQUA GREEN GLASS 6 3/4" TALL.

1 3/4" BASE

ENDSBURGH FALLS, VT.

1 3/8"

765 1/2

1 3/16" BY 1 3/4"

RIGHT SIDE PANEL READS "EXTRACT. 2 P. MOLD, AQUA BLUE GLASS, 4 7/8" HIGH.

MEXICAN BRAND CORN REMEDY

3/4" BY 1 5/16"

AMETHYST GLASS, 2 P. MOLD, 2 1/8" HIGH.

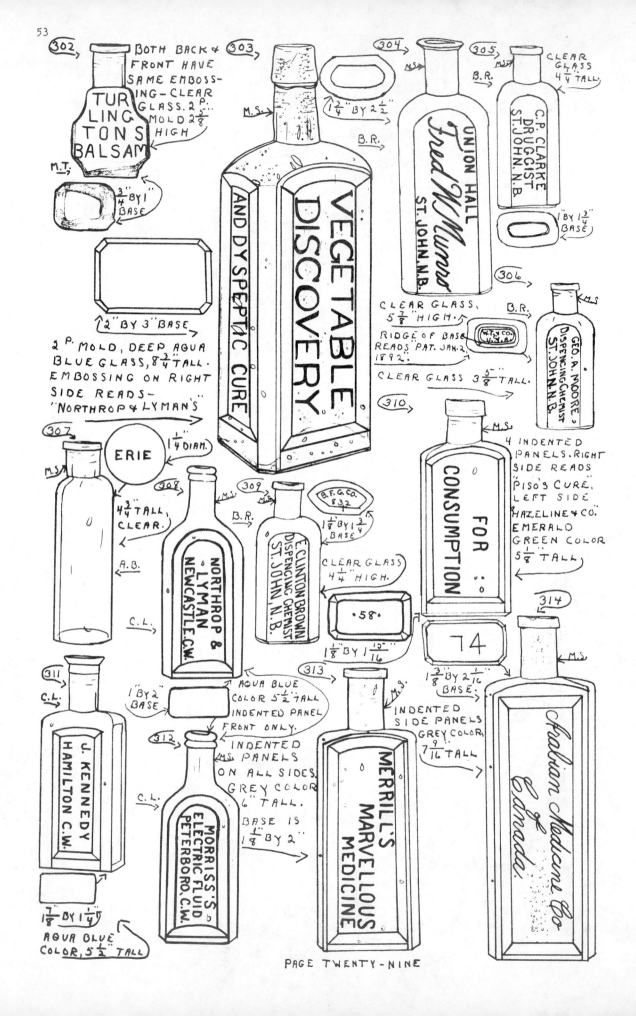

53

302 BOTH BACK & FRONT HAVE SAME EMBOSS-ING-CLEAR GLASS. 2 P. MOLD 2⅝ HIGH

TUR LING TON S BALSAM

M.T.

¾ BY 1 BASE

303

M.S.

B.R.

VEGETABLE DISCOVERY

AND DYSPEPTIC CURE

2" BY 3" BASE

2 P. MOLD, DEEP AGUA BLUE GLASS, 8¾ TALL. EMBOSSING ON RIGHT SIDE READS— "NORTHROP & LYMAN'S

1¼ DIAM.

ERIE

307 M.S.

4¾ TALL, CLEAR.

A.B.

C.L.

304 M.S. B.R.

UNION HALL Fred W. Munro ST. JOHN, N.B.

305 M.S. B.R. CLEAR GLASS 4¼ TALL.

C.P. CLARKE DRUGGIST ST. JOHN, N.B.

1" BY 1¾ BASE

306 M.S.

B.R.

CLEAR GLASS, 5⅞ HIGH. RIDGE OF BASE READS PAT. JAN. 2 1892.

·M.T. & CO U.S.A.

CLEAR GLASS 3⅝ TALL.

GEO. A. MOORE DISPENCING CHEMIST ST. JOHN, N.B.

310 M.S.

FOR CONSUMPTION

4 INDENTED PANELS. RIGHT SIDE READS PISO'S CURE, LEFT SIDE HAZELINE & CO. EMERALD GREEN COLOR 5⅛ TALL

308 M.T. 309 M.S. B.R.

·B.F.G. CO. 832

1⅛ BY 1¾ BASE

NORTHROP & LYMAN NEWCASTLE. C.W.

E. CLINTON BROWN DISPENCING CHEMIST ST. JOHN, N.B.

CLEAR GLASS 4¼ HIGH.

·58·

1⅛ BY 1 15/16

74

1⅛ BY 2 1/16 BASE

314 M.S.

Arabian Medicine Co of Canada.

311 C.L.

J. KENNEDY HAMILTON C.W.

1" BY 2 BASE

AGUA BLUE COLOR 5½ TALL INDENTED PANEL FRONT ONLY.

312 M.S. C.L.

INDENTED PANELS ON ALL SIDES. GREY COLOR 6" TALL. BASE IS 1⅛ BY 2"

313 M.S.

MERRILL'S MARVELLOUS MEDICINE

INDENTED SIDE PANELS GREY COLOR 7 9/16 TALL

MORRISS'S ELECTRIC FLUID PETERBORO. C.W.

7/8 BY 1¼

AGUA BLUE COLOR, 5½ TALL

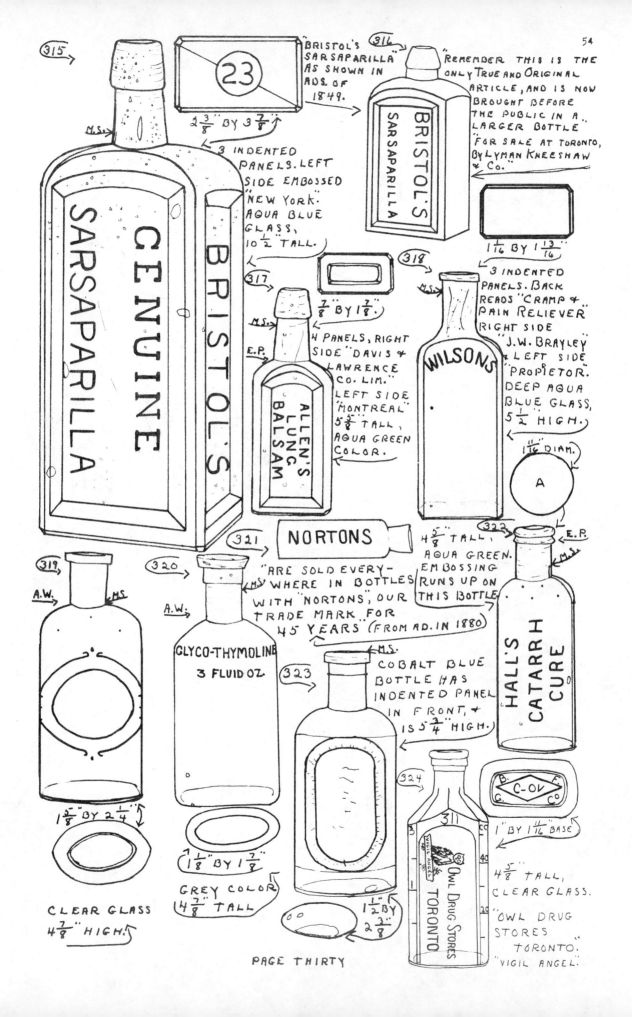

315

23

$2\frac{3}{8}$ BY $3\frac{7}{8}$

316

"BRISTOL'S SARSAPARILLA" AS SHOWN IN ADS OF 1849.

"REMEMBER THIS IS THE ONLY TRUE AND ORIGINAL ARTICLE, AND IS NOW BROUGHT BEFORE THE PUBLIC IN A LARGER BOTTLE FOR SALE AT TORONTO, BY LYMAN KNEESHAW & CO."

M.S.

GENUINE SARSAPARILLA

BRISTOL'S

BRISTOL'S SARSAPARILLA

3 INDENTED PANELS. LEFT SIDE EMBOSSED "NEW YORK". AQUA BLUE GLASS, $10\frac{1}{2}$ TALL.

$1\frac{1}{16}$ BY $1\frac{13}{16}$

317

M.S.

E.P.

$\frac{7}{8}$ BY $1\frac{7}{8}$.

ALLEN'S LUNG BALSAM

H PANELS, RIGHT SIDE "DAVIS & LAWRENCE CO. LIM." LEFT SIDE "MONTREAL" $5\frac{5}{8}$ TALL, AQUA GREEN COLOR.

318

WILSONS

3 INDENTED PANELS. BACK READS "CRAMP & PAIN RELIEVER" RIGHT SIDE "J.W. BRAYLEY" LEFT SIDE "PROPRIETOR. DEEP AQUA BLUE GLASS, $5\frac{1}{2}$ HIGH.

M.S.

$1\frac{11}{16}$ DIAM.

A

322

NORTONS

321

"ARE SOLD EVERYWHERE IN BOTTLES WITH "NORTONS", OUR TRADE MARK FOR 45 YEARS (FROM AD. IN 1880)

$4\frac{5}{8}$ TALL, AQUA GREEN. EMBOSSING RUNS UP ON THIS BOTTLE

E.P.

M.S.

HALL'S CATARRH CURE

319

A.W.

MS

320

A.W.

GLYCO-THYMOLINE

3 FLUID OZ.

MS

323

COBALT BLUE BOTTLE HAS INDENTED PANEL IN FRONT, & IS $5\frac{3}{4}$ HIGH.

324

C-OV

B. F. G. Co.

1" BY $1\frac{4}{16}$ BASE

$4\frac{5}{8}$ TALL, CLEAR GLASS.

"OWL DRUG STORES TORONTO. "VIGIL ANGEL.

OWL DRUG STORES TORONTO

311

VIGIL ANGEL

$1\frac{5}{8}$" BY $2\frac{1}{4}$"

CLEAR GLASS $4\frac{7}{8}$" HIGH.

$1\frac{1}{8}$" BY $1\frac{7}{8}$"

GREY COLOR $4\frac{7}{8}$" TALL

$1\frac{1}{2}$ BY $2\frac{3}{8}$

PAGE THIRTY

54

55

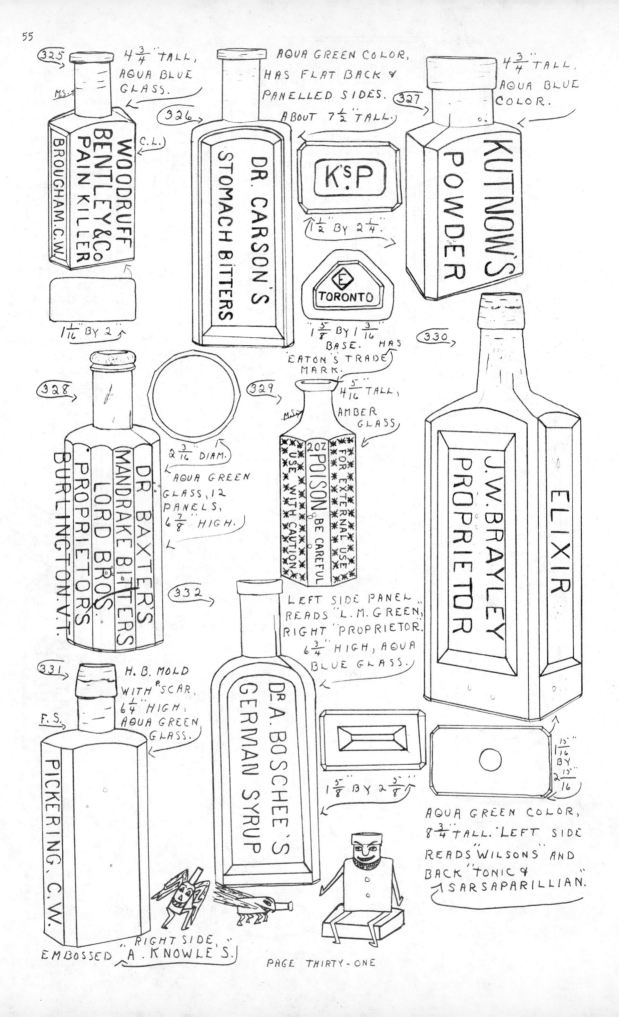

325 · $4\frac{3}{4}$" TALL, AQUA BLUE GLASS.

M.S.

C.L.

WOODRUFF BENTLEY & Co. PAIN KILLER

BROUGHAM. C.W.

$1\frac{1}{16}$" BY 2

326 · AQUA GREEN COLOR, HAS FLAT BACK & PANELLED SIDES. ABOUT $7\frac{1}{2}$" TALL.

DR. CARSON'S STOMACH BITTERS

K·S·P

$1\frac{1}{2}$" BY $2\frac{1}{4}$"

E TORONTO

$1\frac{5}{8}$" BY $1\frac{3}{16}$" BASE. HAS EATON'S TRADE MARK.

327 · $4\frac{3}{4}$" TALL, AQUA BLUE COLOR.

KUTNOW'S POWDER

328

$2\frac{3}{16}$" DIAM.

DR. BAXTER'S MANDRAKE BITTERS LORD BROS. PROPRIETORS

BURLINGTON. V.T.

AQUA GREEN GLASS, 12 PANELS, $6\frac{7}{8}$" HIGH.

329 · $4\frac{5}{16}$" TALL, AMBER GLASS.

M.S.

2OZ POISON BE CAREFUL USE WITH CAUTION FOR EXTERNAL USE

LEFT SIDE PANEL READS "L.M. GREEN", RIGHT "PROPRIETOR. $6\frac{3}{4}$" HIGH, AQUA BLUE GLASS.

330

J.W. BRAYLEY PROPRIETOR

ELIXIR

331 · H.B. MOLD WITH SCAR, $6\frac{1}{4}$" HIGH, AQUA GREEN GLASS.

F.S.

PICKERING. C.W.

332

DR A. BOSCHEE'S GERMAN SYRUP

$1\frac{5}{8}$" BY $2\frac{5}{8}$"

$1\frac{15}{16}$" BY $2\frac{15}{16}$"

AQUA GREEN COLOR, $8\frac{3}{4}$" TALL. LEFT SIDE READS "WILSONS" AND BACK "TONIC & SARSAPARILLIAN."

RIGHT SIDE, "A. KNOWLE'S." EMBOSSED

PAGE THIRTY-ONE

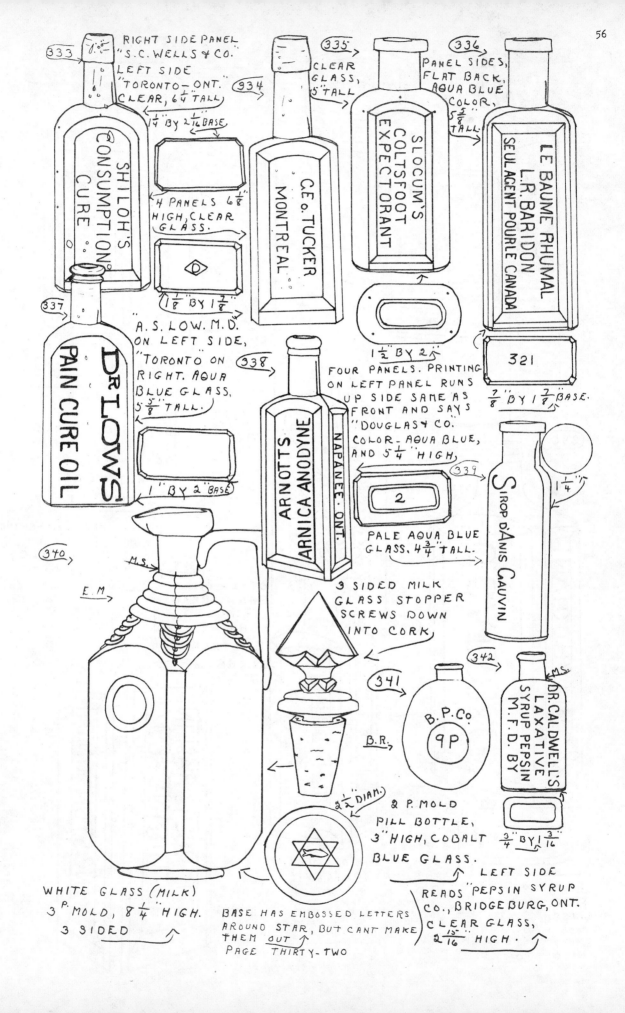

333 — RIGHT SIDE PANEL "S.C. WELLS & CO." LEFT SIDE "TORONTO — ONT." CLEAR, 6¼" TALL

1¼" BY 2 1/16" BASE

SHILOH'S CONSUMPTION CURE

4 PANELS 6⅛" HIGH, CLEAR GLASS.

1⅛" BY 1⅞"

934 —

335 — CLEAR GLASS, 5" TALL

C. EO. TUCKER MONTREAL

336 — PANEL SIDES, FLAT BACK, AQUA BLUE COLOR, 5⅝" TALL

SLOCUM'S COLTSFOOT EXPECTORANT

LE BAUME RHUMAL L.R. BARIDON SEUL AGENT POUR LE CANADA

321

2⅞" BY 1⅞" BASE.

1½" BY 2"

337 — A.S. LOW. M.D. ON LEFT SIDE, "TORONTO ON RIGHT. AQUA BLUE GLASS, 5⅝" TALL.

Dr LOWS PAIN CURE OIL

1" BY 2" BASE

338 — FOUR PANELS. PRINTING ON LEFT PANEL RUNS UP SIDE SAME AS FRONT AND SAYS "DOUGLAS & CO. COLOR — AQUA BLUE, AND 5¼" HIGH.

ARNOTT'S ARNICA ANODYNE

NAPANEE · ONT.

2

PALE AQUA BLUE GLASS, 4¾" TALL.

339 —

Sirop d'Anis Gauvin

1¼"

340 —

M.S.

E.M

3 SIDED MILK GLASS STOPPER SCREWS DOWN INTO CORK

341 —

B.R.

B.P.Co. 9P

342 —

M.S.

Dr. CALDWELL'S LAXATIVE SYRUP PEPSIN M.F.D. BY

¾" BY 1 3/16"

2¼" DIAM.

2 P. MOLD PILL BOTTLE, 3" HIGH, COBALT BLUE GLASS.

WHITE GLASS (MILK) 3 P. MOLD, 8¼" HIGH. 3 SIDED

BASE HAS EMBOSSED LETTERS AROUND STAR, BUT CANT MAKE THEM OUT
PAGE THIRTY-TWO

LEFT SIDE READS "PEPSIN SYRUP CO., BRIDGEBURG, ONT. CLEAR GLASS, 2 15/16" HIGH.

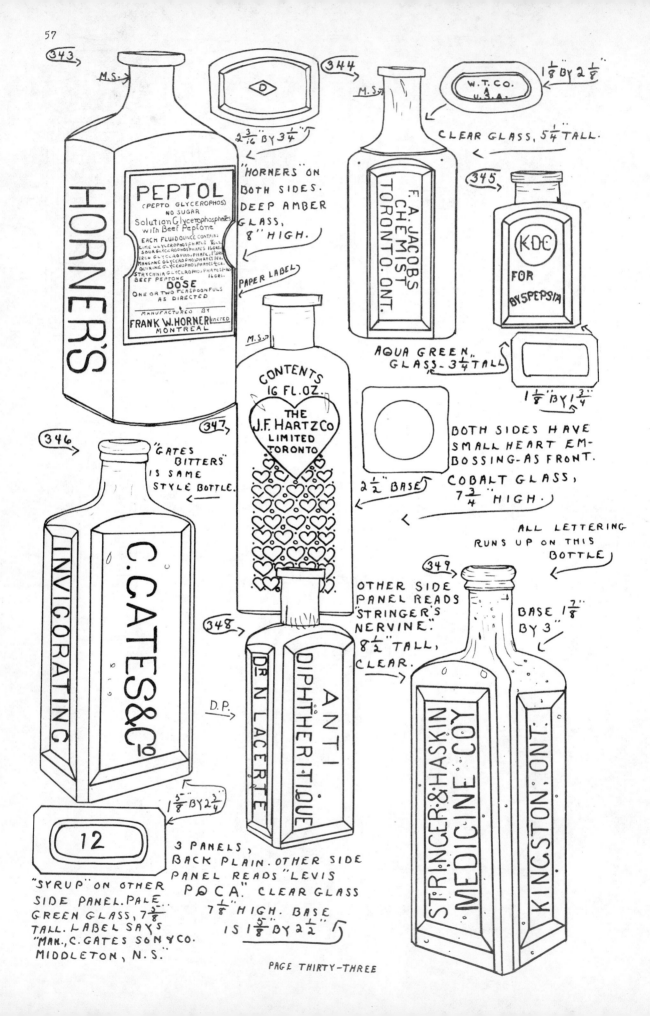

57

343

M.S.

344

M.S.

$2\frac{3}{16}$ BY $3\frac{1}{4}$

"HORNER'S" ON BOTH SIDES. DEEP AMBER GLASS, 8" HIGH.

$1\frac{1}{8}$ BY $2\frac{1}{8}$

CLEAR GLASS, $5\frac{1}{4}$" TALL.

W.T.CO. U.S.A.

345

PEPTOL
(PEPTO GLYCEROPHOS)
NO SUGAR
Solution Glycerophosphates
with Beef Peptone
EACH FLUID OUNCE CONTAINS
LIME GLYCEROPHOSPHATE 8grs.
SODA GLYCEROPHOSPHATES 1grs.
IRON GLYCEROPHOSPHATE 1grs.
MANGANE GLYCEROPHOSPHATE 1gr.
QUININE GLYCEROPHOSPHATE 1gr.
STRYCHNIA GLYCEROPHOSPHATES 1gr.
BEEF PEPTONE 16grs.
DOSE
ONE OR TWO TEASPOONFULS
AS DIRECTED
MANUFACTURED BY
FRANK W. HORNER LIMITED
MONTREAL

PAPER LABEL

F. A. JACOBS CHEMIST TORONTO. ONT.

KDC FOR DYSPEPSIA

M.S.

AQUA GREEN GLASS - $3\frac{1}{4}$ TALL

$1\frac{1}{8}$ BY $1\frac{3}{4}$

CONTENTS 16 FL. OZ.
THE J.F. Hartz Co LIMITED TORONTO

$2\frac{1}{2}$" BASE

BOTH SIDES HAVE SMALL HEART EM- BOSSING - AS FRONT. COBALT GLASS, $7\frac{3}{4}$" HIGH.

346

"GATES BITTERS" IS SAME STYLE BOTTLE.

ALL LETTERING RUNS UP ON THIS BOTTLE

349

BASE $1\frac{7}{8}$" BY 3"

INVIGORATING

C. CATES & Cº

347

348

D.P.

OTHER SIDE PANEL READS "STRINGER'S NERVINE". $8\frac{1}{2}$" TALL, CLEAR.

ANTI DIPHTHERITIQUE

DR N LACERTE

STRINGER & HASKIN MEDICINE COY

KINGSTON ONT.

$1\frac{5}{8}$ BY $2\frac{3}{4}$

12

"SYRUP" ON OTHER SIDE PANEL. PALE GREEN GLASS, $7\frac{3}{8}$ TALL. LABEL SAYS "MAN., C. GATES SON & CO. MIDDLETON, N.S."

3 PANELS, BACK PLAIN. OTHER SIDE PANEL READS "LEVIS P.Q.CA." CLEAR GLASS $7\frac{1}{8}$" HIGH. BASE IS $1\frac{5}{8}$" BY $2\frac{1}{2}$"

PAGE THIRTY-THREE

VIII   BREWERS AND DISTILLERS

A.   Beer.

The word Ale was introduced by the Danes and other Scandinavians to England. Ol is the name for malt liquor in

Scandinavian tongues. The name Ale was used in England for malt liquor in general before the introduction of hops,

taking place during the reign of Henry VIII, about the year 1524. The use of hops was derived from Germany and the

German name for malt liquor (bier), beer, was at first used to distinguish the hopped liquor from ale the unhopped.

South American Indians had a beer obtained from Indian Corn, (Chica), long before the Spanish conquest. The Abyssi-

nians, Arabians and many African tribes used millet seed and teft to make beer. The Russians have a rye beer called

'quass', and in some parts of the world an intoxicating liquor results from fermented buttermilk. The Upper Canada

Gazette published a recipe in 1799, calling for the use of green pea shells, claiming it to be superior to molasses beer

and if distilled yielded spirit "not unlike the tafte and colour of whifkey".

Beer-money was a payment to private soldiers in the English army and established in 1800 at the suggestion of the

Duke of York. It consisted of one penny per day for troups when on home service, as a substitute for an issue of beer

or spirits and continued as an addition to the daily pay.

From the time of England's Cromwell, who was a brewer, many brewers have played an important part in their commun-

ity and Canada's brewers were no exception. Edward Drewry, proprietor of Drewry's Red Brewery was known as a man who

took a leading part in the welfare of Winnepeg and development of the Northwest. As a member of the Winnepeg Trade

Council he was a prime mover in starting and developing the Manitoba Industrial Exhibition. Robert Bowie, Brockville

Brewery started in the brewing business in 1872 and by 1892 was President of the Board of Trade. After some years as

Yonge St. Brewers, Thomas and Nathaniel Davies dissolved their partnership and Thomas bought the Don Bridge Brewery in

1849. Some years later his was a well known name on the Toronto city council. Doel's Brewery, Toronto, 1827-1847, was

used a meeting place by leaders of the Reform Party preceding the Rebellion of 1837. Enoc Turner, another early brewer,

is remembered in Toronto as the man who erected the city's first free school on Trinity Street, in 1848. John Molson

was referred to in the Bytown Gazette, 1836 - as having been the father of Steam Navigation on the St. Lawrence River.

Jean Talon, 1625-1694, known as the Great Intendant of New France - is said to have started the first Brewery in Canada

in 1668 to combat intemperate drinking of Brandy and other Strong Liquors.

The Cape Diamond Brewery, Quebec, was advertising its products in 1791 with J.M. Goddard as proprietor. In 1801

beer from the same place would be "packed for the country" and in 1806 he mentions having "reduced from this day" the

price of his bottled beer. Mr. Goddard sold the Cape Diamond Brewery to a Mr. Brehaut in 1816. Less than a year later

Mrs. Brehaut announced that she would be running the business under her late husband's plans. In October of the same

year however, a notice of Co-partnership was posted between Mrs. Brehaut and John and Benjamin Racey, and it was not long

until the Cape Diamond Brewery became known as the Racey Brewery. In 1844 Boswell's Ale from "that long celebrated Racy

Brewery, Quebec" was being advertised.

The Dow Brewery was started in 1790 by a young Scotsman named Thomas Dunn at La Prairie, a few miles outside of

Montreal. Mr. Dunn moved his brewery to Notre Dame St. in Montreal in 1808, where ten years later another Scottish brewer named William Dow joined the firm as Head Brewer. He later became a partner, with the firm then being known as Dunn & Dow.

William's brother, Andrew, came into the brewery in 1830 and after the death of Thomas Dunn the business continued as William Dow & Co. Andrew died in 1853 and William, by now a prominent figure and noted philanthropist died in 1868, but the Dow operation continued to grow over the years.

In 1909, National Breweries Limited was formed - this being an amalgamation of fourteen breweries. The largest units among these were the Dow Brewery and Dawes Brewery, the latter having been started at Lachine by Thomas Dawes in the year of 1814. The other breweries were Boswell Brewery, Quebec; Montreal Brewing Co.; Union Brewery (Atkin Brewery had been incorporated into Union Brewery in 1898) ; Royal Brewery, Quebec; Canadian Breweries Ltd., (Ekers Brewery, est. 1840 and the Canadian Brewing Co. had combined to form C.B.L.); the Charles Reinhardt Brewery, Montreal: Imperial Brewery; the Ste. Therese Brewery, Ste. Therese; Beauport Brewery; Geo. E. Amyot Brewing Co., Fox Head; Proteau & Carignan, Quebec; and Michel Gauvin & Co., Quebec. The National Breweries had a separate charter and controlling interest in the Frontenac Brewery of Montreal but it was not one of the fourteen. In 1916 the locale of the business was moved to Montreal. Principal brands were Dow Ale and Black Horse Ale.

In 1952 Canadian Breweries Ltd. obtained control of National Breweries, and, in a major reorganization, the Dawes name and brands were removed from the market, with the emphasis being placed on the Dow corporate name and the Dow products, the brands being produced at the Montreal and Quebec City Breweries. The Montreal plant was expanded in 1968 and the Quebec City operations transferred there.

In Quebec City the Talon Vaults, operated by Dow as a tourist attraction, are situated on the site of the first brewery established by the then Intendent, Jean Talon in 1668. The Vaults serve as a reminder of the tradition of brewing and the company's identification with the Quebec scene.

In July 1964, Dow Brewery financed the construction of a Planetarium in Montreal. The completed project was donated to the City of Montreal in 1966 and is operated by the Parks Department.

Some of our early brewers offered a "Small Beer" for sale but it apparently had nothing to do with the bottle size as the following is a typical advertisement:

"The Subscribers have for sale at their Brewery the different sorts of Beer herein specified, at the following rates, viz:

Beer in Casks

Burton Ale,	at	100s.	per Hogshead		
Porter "	"	80s.	"	ditto	
Mild "	"	80s.	"	"	Exclusive of Casks
Table Beer "		60s.	"	"	
Small "	"	30s.	"	"	

Beer in Bottles

Burton Ale,	at	10s.	per Dozen	
Porter "	"	7s.6d.	per do	Exclusive of Bottles
Mild "	"	7s.6d.	" do	
Table Beer "		6s.	" do	

John Molson and Sons
Montreal, 8th March, 1817."

Thomas Molson took over a brewery in Kingston in 1824 and announced that he would have the different kinds of bottled beer for sale at a cheaper rate than any imported into the Province. His ad., like others, quoted one price only per kind so we can assume this would be for quart bottles, with pints not coming into general use in Canada until around 1839, when pints also began to be listed along with the quart bottles in Montreal under "Wholesale Prices Current" for beer bottles.

In any case - "Bourne's Ale from the Laprairie Brewery, Quarts - 3s.6d. per doz., Pints 2s.6d. per doz." was advertised in June, 1842. Gorrie's Brewery had a similar ad shortly, and, "Bottled Ales from this establishment are particularly recommended to the notice of Private Families".

The Pabst Brewing Company of Milwaukee opened a branch establishment in Montreal on M'Gill St. in 1896. They soon found this too small and moved to larger quarters on St. Paul St. At that time the beer was imported from Milwaukee in wood and bottled in Montreal.

The earlier beer bottles, if glass, would be 'black' and not identified as to user unless you are fortunate enough to find one with the label still intact. Black bottles are worthy of any collection and a assortment of them against a light coloured wall make an interesting decorating touch. As to the later ones, they offer plenty of variety in the embossed names and a few companies used bottles that were an exception to the general form.

VIII BREWERS AND DISTILLERS - cont'd

B. Cider.

The Bottled Cider mentioned in the early advertisements was an alcoholic drink and a big business for many apple growers. After the ripe apples were shaken from the trees they were left in heaps on the ground for a month to 'mellow' when they were then squashed, strained through several layers of horse-hair cloth and poured into casks placed either out of doors or in sheds with a free current of air. In about three or four days (according to the heat of the weather), this mixture started fermenting, the sediment sinking to the bottom and the rest becoming clear cider, which was wracked off into clean barrels. During the fermenting period it had to be watched closely, and the remedies used in the case of the cider not clearing were either yeast or the addition of other cider in a fermenting state, eggs, isinglass, or a quart of fresh blood stirred into the liquor, in which last case it had to be wracked the following day. At the beginning of the new year the cider was moved into cellars where, by large growers it was frequently stored in casks containing 1000, 1500 or even 2000 gallons. It was bunged down in March and could be sold soon after although it was improved by keeping.

If the cider was to be bottled it was thought best to keep until September or October after it had been bunged, but, "As some persons prefer an earlier time, the end of April or beginning of May, a greater degree of effervescence is thus attained, but a considerable loss accrues from the number of bottles that will burst".

Canada seems to have plenty of Cider Manufacturers but the later ones apparently did not advertise their product unless as Henry Calcutt, Peterborough, along with his brewery products.

VIII   BREWERS AND DISTILLERS - cont'd

C.   Gin.

Gin, or Geneva is distilled from malt, or from unmalted barley or other grain, and then rectified and flavoured. The gin which formed the common drink of the poorer people of earlier days in London and vicinity was flavoured with oil of turpentine and salt; each rectifier having his own recipe, but it was usually about five fluid ounces of spirit of turpentine, and 3¾ pounds of salt mixed in ten gallons of water. "These are placed in the rectifying still, with 80 gallons of proof corn spirit and distilled until the feints begin to come over. It is then used sweetened or unsweetened with sugar." The terms 'Gin' and 'Geneva' are derived from the Dutch where it is largely manufactured. In 1870, in Schiedam alone there were 175 distilleries, Gouda had 30 and Amsterdam 17, with many others scattered throughout the country. The largest part of this was exported to other countries, "in particular to North America and Northern Europe. It was formerly always exported in bottles, but casks are now much used as well". The casks would simplify shipping when the bottles were available here to put the gin in after landing. "Perhaps nothing used by man is liable to greater and more injurious adulteration than gin. Almost every gin-shop keeper has some vile recipe for increasing the pungency and giving a facticious strength to the much diluted sweetened spirit sold under this name; roach alum, salt of tartar", (carbonate of potash), "oil of juniper, cassia nutmeg, lemons, sweet fennel, caraway and corriander seeds, caramoms and capsicums;" (hot spice seeds), "and worse than all, creosote. It is said that sulphuric acid is even used, but this is by no means probable".

VIII   BREWERS AND DISTILLERS - cont'd

D.   Other Intoxicants.

The intoxicating drinks used in ancient times seem to have been produced by fermenting only. Distilling was first mentioned by an Arabian physician of the eleventh century called Abulkasen, although the invention has been attributed to some of the northern nations. It was highly regarded by Alchemists and Physicians, whoever did discover the process. Spirits were first distilled from wine and so called 'spirits of wine'.

A workman named Adam of Montpellier is credited with a great improvement in distilling in 1801. By making vapours from the still pass through a series of winding passages, he obtained from wine a spirit of any desired cleanness and strength at one operation. By 1817 this process had been adapted by Pistorious of Berlin to the distillation of the coarser washes of grain and other materials.

"GROG - the origin of this word was in this wise; a planter of Jamaica, wishing to send a puncheon of real good stuff to George Second, marked upon the head 'G.R.O.G.' - for George Rex - Old Gemakee."
(According to the Montreal Transcript, Sept. 22, 1836.)

VIII   BREWERS AND DISTILLERS - cont'd

E.   Wine.

The manufacture of wine has been carried on from the very earliest periods of history. From what has been written it is doubtful the early wines would be much appreciated by the modern palate. The following extract will given an idea of the way the ancients 'cooked' their wines. "The principal materials used as seasonings were 1 - sea-water; 2 - turpentine, (either pure or in the form of pitch, tar or resin); 3 - lime in the form of gypsum, burnt marble or calcined shells; 4 - inspissated must; 5 - aromatic herbs, spices and gums." These were used singly or cooked up together for a variety of complicated confections. It was also the custom to line the interiors of the wine containers with a coating of pitch. This last substance, or powdered resin was also added to the must during the fermenting period to render the wine more full bodied.

PORT - or the wine of Portugal became a favoured drink in England around 1750, and at a sale in 1870, 17£10s. per gallon was realised for some port, vintage 1820.

Wine was considered by many to be necessary for dietetic and medical reasons, and were prescribed for women because their delicate constitutions would not digest beer, for children with bad appetites, for literary persons and all those whose occupations taxed the brain more than the muscle.

VIII   BREWERS AND DISTILLERS - cont'd

F.   Whiskey.

Whiskey is made by distillation from grain of any sort, and other materials, as potatoes or even turnips.

Around the beginning of the eighteenth century, a duty of 20s per gallon was imposed by Parliament, besides a heavy tax on the retail dealers on ardent spirits in an attempt to put a stop to its heavy consumption, except by way of cordials or medicine. The effect however was not as anticipated, respectable dealers withdrew from the no longer profitable trade and were replaced by the unscrupulous who had no compunctions about breaking the law, and smuggling flourished. In 1742, this act was repealed and a more moderate duty imposed in England.

In Ireland this repressive system was carried to a still greater extent, with an additional fine imposed on the district in which illicit distilling was detected, and the culprits were subject to transportation for seven years. Smuggling flourished, the common people were generally in sympathy with the smugglers and officers of justice were assaulted, and prevented from doing their duty. A reward was offered to informers, and suspects were hunted down as enemies to the community.

Scotland's history was very similar in this respect and parts of both these countries were almost in a state of rebellion, with frequent and murderous conflicts with the smugglers and their sympathizers on one hand and excise officers and the military on the other. In 1823 these difficulties led to the adoption of a considerably lower duty in Scotland and Ireland than in England, with the result that more than ever from these two countries was smuggled into England. This state prevailed until 1858, when the duty was equalised in the three countries.

Mr. Gladstone, intending to lower the consumption of spirits in the United Kingdom, again raised the duty to 10s. per imperial gallon, where it still remained in 1871. Although it did not do much to stop consumption, neither did it increase illicit distilling to any great amount. Instead the drinks for the poorer population were watered down and otherwise flavoured.

An item in the Bytown Gazette in 1845 regarding intemperance said - "Two hundred years ago the voice of drunkenness was even more prevalent than it is now. In a discussion on the subject in British Parliament, the Bishop of Salisbury stated that in one street in London a board was put up with the following inscription : 'You may get drunk here for one penny, dead drunk for two pence, and have clean straw for nothing.' "

Canada was not without some troubles with Revenue laws and smuggling, mentioned were a "better product than any smuggled across the border", and the following was printed: "NOTICE - whereas some villainous disposed Poltroon, has asserted (and has been received by many as a fact) that the undersigned was the Informer against Ansel Crosby, and Benjamin Porter, for the violation of the Revenue Laws; I do declare, In the Presence of God, Angels and Man that I did not know either of the persons above mentioned, were absent from Yarmouth, nor had I any conversation by Word, Letter or any other Conveyance, with the Collector Warehouse Keeper, or any other person. I received instructions to assist the Warehouse Keeper, in the execution of his duties, which I attended to. I have ever held an Informer as a character utterly unworthy of any respect and do so to the present. I submit my opinion to the generous Public. William C. Williams, Yarmouth, July 15, 1833."

On Feb. 7, 1769, the Receivor General's Office issued a public notice from St. Lewis Street, Quebec, that they were proposing to demand and collect from all vessels arriving in Port the ensuing season the following Duty. "Ten Shillings Sterling per hogshead upon Wine; Twenty Shillings Sterling per hogshead upon Rum; One Shilling per Velte, or measure of two gallons of Brandy; One Half-penny Sterling per Bottle of ordinary Wine; Five Pence Sterling per Gallon upon Eau de Vie de Liqueur"; etc. "But upon all British Brandies and other Spirits imported in vessels from Great Briton and being of the manufacture thereof, only one half of the aforesaid Duty, which was levied by the French Government, in the year 1757, of Brandies and Spirits of the like Quality imported into Canada, is to be demanded and Collected; His Majesty being Graciously Pleased to remit one Mority of the Duties on British Brandies and Spirits, and the whole of the Duties on Dry Goods imported and exported, except the Duty on Tobacco and Snuff imported, as well in Tenderness to his Subjects in the Province of Quebec, as in favour of the Manufactures of Great Britain".

Even with lesser duties on alcoholic beverages throughout the years, brewers and distillers were plentiful in Canada and their products much cheaper. From the United Empire Loyalist, 1826, "The manufacture of iron and hollow ware is carried on extensively at Marmosa", etc. etc. "Distilleries and Breweries are to be found in every part of the Province".

An emigrant recently arrived in 1835 wrote to his friends to be sure to come over to Canada at the first opportunity, "For" said he, "you can get a glass of rum for three cents, and be drunk all day for ten". - an added inducement. In an article under 'Immigration to British America' another thought on the subject - "We cannot sufficiently impress on the minds of emigrants the necessity they will be under of adhereing to temperate habits. In the Canadas, whisky is much cheaper than in Britain, hence this advice becomes of double importance. Mr. Ferguson, in his 'Practical Notes' made in 1831 says 'Returning to the St. Lawrence, we find numerous settlers, and thousands of acres well adapted to the farmers. The language, customs and habits of their Celtic Sires still distinguish the clan, though at the same time accompanied by some of the less profitable traits, which stamp the highlander as more at home wielding a claymore or extracting 'mountain dew' than in guiding the ploughshare.'—These of course would not be your ancestors, nor mine - but other peoples .

Distillery products were commonly shipped to the retailors in barrels where some at least were bottled for resale. Samuel Sills offered bottled wares for sale at his Cellars in Lower Town, Quebec, in 1764, where "N.B. the bottles to be paid for or returned". The same year the Three Gun Tavern offered red wine for sale by the dozen at 8s. or a single bottle at 6d., returning the empty bottles or drinking the wine in the house. "Likewise good English Cyder at 12s. per doz., bottles included, New England Cyder, 12s. per doz., returning the bottles."

A Quebec Distiller, R. Quirouet, advertised his products for sale by cask or single case of twelve bottles each in 1815, with no mention of returning the bottles. The St. Dennis Distillery, Montreal had bottled malt whisky for sale in 1837, and P. Wallace's Toddy Whiskey (Cobourg) sold with liberal allowance to trade "Price 2s.6d. per bottle" in 1843.

Imported products were sometimes bottled after arrival too. "Just arrived in the Brig Earl St. Vincent, Thomas J. Brehout's Supercargo", etc., "and sold on their wharf, 111 Pipes of Spanish Wine", etc., "All the above Wines have been fined and wracked, are of the best quality, and will be fit to bottle a few days after landing." The bottles would require special packing and take up more room. Space would often be of prime consideration when loading the cargo.

James F. Smith of York advertised various brands of liquors in 1831, as being available in quart, pint, and half-pint bottles. Superior Scotch Whiskey in Bottles was mentioned along with other items for sale at the Sandwhich Cash Store in 1841.

January 1st, 1885, Hiram Walker & Sons mentioned in an advertisement that the Inland Revenue Department's newly adopted regulations for Distillers to "Bottle in Bond" with each bottle bearing the Excise Officers Certificate was an "indisputable guarantee" as to age of contents. The labels on bottles that mention this stamp could be a help in dating the bottle. The bottle was frequently pictured with the advertisement of the 1890's and later. These were mostly the tall round style still commonly used. Many of the later prohibition bottles are interesting because the designs were so elaborate.

References

Brockville Recorder - 1835
Bytown Gazette - 1844
The Globe, (Toronto) - 1849-58-85-90-91-92-98
Kingston Gazette - 1824
La Gazette de Quebec - 1764-69-91-92-95; 1801-05-06-10-13-15-17
Montreal Herald - 1817
Montreal Pilot - 1844-47
Montreal Transcript - 1836-39-40-42
Toronto Star -1974
United Empire Loyalist, (York) - 1826
Upper Canada Gazette, (York) - 1799
Western Herald & Farmers Magazine, (Sandwhich) - 1841
Yarmouth Herald, N.S. - 1833
York Gazette - 1831

"The Dow Story" - Canadian Breweries Ltd., Toronto

Chambers Information for the People, 1842 - Vol. I and II, William and Robert Chambers, Edinburgh

Chambers' Encyclopaedia, 1873 - Vol. II, IV and VIII; 1874 - Vol. I, II, IV and X; 1875 - Vol. I. W.& R. Chambers, Edinburgh and J.B. Lippincott & Co., Philadelphia.

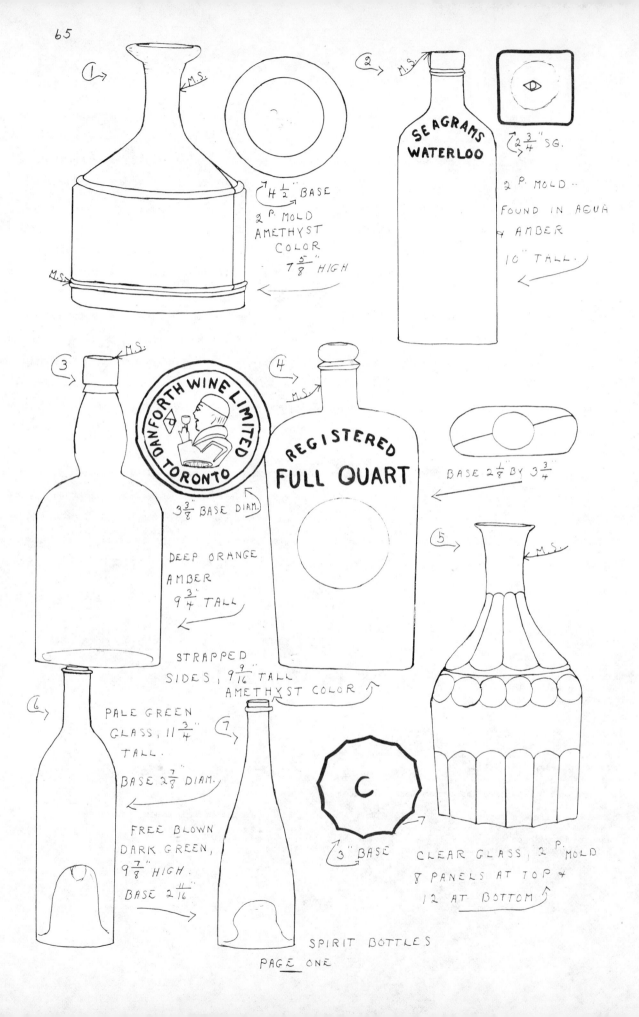

65

1.
M.S.
M.S.
H $\frac{1}{2}$" BASE
2 P. MOLD
AMETHYST
COLOR
7 $\frac{5}{8}$" HIGH

2.
M.S.
SEAGRAMS
WATERLOO
2 $\frac{3}{4}$" SG.
2 P. MOLD ..
FOUND IN AGUA
& AMBER
10" TALL.

3.
M.S.
DANFORTH WINE LIMITED
TORONTO
3 $\frac{3}{8}$" BASE DIAM.
DEEP ORANGE
AMBER
9 $\frac{3}{4}$" TALL

4.
M.S.
REGISTERED
FULL QUART
BASE 2 $\frac{1}{8}$" BY 3 $\frac{3}{4}$"
STRAPPED
SIDES, 9 $\frac{9}{16}$" TALL
AMETHYST COLOR

5.
M.S.

6.
PALE GREEN
GLASS, 11 $\frac{3}{4}$"
TALL.
BASE 2 $\frac{7}{8}$" DIAM.
FREE BLOWN
DARK GREEN,
9 $\frac{7}{8}$" HIGH.
BASE 2 $\frac{11}{16}$

7.
C
3" BASE
CLEAR GLASS, 2 P. MOLD
8 PANELS AT TOP &
12 AT BOTTOM

SPIRIT BOTTLES
PAGE ONE

8 → END OF M.S.

9

1 1/16 BY 3" BASE & 297 INSIDE INDENTED PAN.

AMETHYST COLOR, 2ⁿ MOLD FLASK 7 3/4 TALL. "OVAL"

2ⁿ MOLD FLASK 7 1/4 TALL. DEEP ORANGE AMBER SHADING ALMOST TO RED AT CENTRE. "COFFIN OR SHOO-FLY"

4641

1 2/8" BY 2 3/4 BASE INDENTED PANEL & 4641

FINISHED FOR GLASS STOPPER

79

M.S. END

PANELED BASE 1 1/4" BY 2 15/16

10 → END OF M.S.

COFFIN FLASK 2ⁿ MOLD, AMETHYST COLOR, WITH VERY SLIGHT CONCAVE LABEL PANEL FRONT & BACK. 7 1/2 TALL

11 GROUND MOUTH / END OF M.S.

2" BY 3 1/2 BASE WITH SHALLOW PANEL

AMETHYST BOTTLE. 2ⁿ MOLD, SCREW TOP, 8 1/2 TALL, WITH EMBOSSED DIAMOND ON BASE

TRADE & M MARK REGISTERED

END OF M.S.

"G & W TRADE MARK REGISTERED" ON BASE 1 3/8 BY 3 3/8

2ⁿ MOLD MACHINE MADE BOTTLE, 8" TALL, CLEAR GLASS ALSO IN AMBER.

12

4919

BASE 1 1/2 BY 3

14 → BASE A BIT CONCAVE 3 3/4 DIAM.

DARK GREEN 2ⁿ MOLD 12" TALL. DEEP WRINKLES IN GLASS

13 / BASE 3 1/4 DIAM.

DARK GREEN

END OF M.S.

2ⁿ MOLD, AQUA COLOR, 7 1/2 TALL. LABEL READS "THE VERY PUREST CANADA RYE WHISKEY. AGE STRENGH AND QUALITY GUARANTEED. DOMINION OF CANADA. R.H. HOWARD & CO. TORONTO"

15 → M.S. END

THE VERY PUREST CANADA RYE WHISKEY AGE STRENGH AND QUALITY GUARANTEED DOMINION OF CANADA R.H. HOWARD Co. Toronto

TURN MOLD BOTTLE 11 3/4" TALL

16 →

DEEP GREEN, TURN MOLD 9 3/8 TALL. BASE SLIGHTLY CONCAVE.

BASE 2 1/4 DIAM.

INDENTED BASE 5/8" SQUARE

BRIGHT OLIVE GREEN, 2ⁿ MOLD, A.B.M. 8" TALL

17 / M.S. END

18 →

M.S.

1 35 ◇ D

2 1/4 BY 3 3/4 BASE

AMBER TO RED COLORED BOTTLE 8 3/4 HIGH. 2ⁿ MOLD

PAGE TWO

(19) M.S. END

BASE HAS SHALLOW CONCAVE CIRCLE 3¼" DIAM. CLEAR GRAY COLOR, 3 MOLD, 9¼" TALL. NECK RINGS ARE 4 THE 3 MOLD LINES RUN FROM BOTTOM UP. THERE ARE 15 PLEATS & PANELS AROUND BODY

(20) END OF M.L. — SO S — CONCAVE BASE 3½" BY 2¼ DIAM. 2 MOLD, BRIGHT GREEN COLOR, 9¼" TALL.

(21) M.L. — BASE 2 6/8" DIAM. WITH INDENTED CIRCLE. 2 MOLD, 14" TALL, COVERED WITH SILVER CRIZZLE MARKS. THIS BOTTLE APPEARS BLACK BUT WHEN HELD TO LIGHT IS DARK RUBY RED.

(22) END OF M.S. — SHALLOW PANEL IN BASE 2 9/16 BY 4½. 2 MOLD, CLEAR COLOR. 11" TALL — Seagrams

(23) M.S. — B.C. DISTILLERY CO. LTD — B C D G — TRADE MARK — REGISTERED NEW-WESTMINSTER — B.C. DISTILLERY COMPANY LIMITED — 2⅛" BY 4" BASE CLEAR COLOR, 2 MOLD, 8½" TALL. OTHER SIDE HAS LABEL PANEL, BUT IS MARKED SIMILAR TO FRONT. "B.C. DISTILLERY CO. LTD. TRADE MARK REGISTERED NEW-WESTMINSTER."

(24) END OF M.S. — 2 MOLD, 12⅛" TALL. LOOKS BLACK, BUT IS VERY DARK GREEN. NOT OLIVE GREEN AS ARE MOST, JUST GREEN.

(25) 692 B — 2 3/4 BY 4¼ BASE. 2 MOLD, DARK GRAY COLOR, 10¾" HIGH. LOTS OF BUBBLES — TALL MONARCH — END OF M.S.

(26) M.S. — O'KEEFE'S BEVERAGES BOTTLE DESIGN REG'D 40 96 LIMITED — O'Keefes — BASE 2½" DIAM. 2 MOLD, AMBER COLOR, 7⅞ TALL. SO I BLOOPED AGAIN, "BEVERAGES DO NOT BELONG IN THIS SECTION. SORRY." — DEEP CONCAVE BASE 2¾" DIAM.

(27) END OF M.S. — 1" BY 2¼ BASE — PICNIC SHAPE CENTRE BACK & FRONT ARE SLIGHTLY CONCAVE. FLASK IS 2 MOLD & PALE GREEN COLOR. IT IS 4⅞" AT WIDEST PART & 5⅞" TALL

28

29

DEEP CONCAVE BASE 3 3/16" DIAM.

BASE CONCAVE 3" DIAM.

OLIVE GREEN BOTTLE WITH PRONOUNCED TURN MOLD LINES 10 1/2" TALL.

LONG SLIM NECKED POLISHED BLACK BEAUTY. MOLD BOTTLE 11 7/8" TALL. DEEP RUBY WHEN HELD TO LIGHT.

30 M.S.

TURN

A.B.M. 10 7/8" TALL.

DARK AMBER RED COLOR

31 M.S.

3 3/16" DIAMETER BASE.

INDENTED PANEL IN SQUARE BASE 2 5/16" ACROSS

32 M.S.

33

OLIVE GREEN CASE GIN, 9 1/4" HIGH. THE ONLY DISCERNIBLE MOLD SEAMS ARE OVER CENTRE SHOULDER ON EACH SIDE. LABEL IS BADLY WORN SO AM NOT SURE OF CO. NAME   AS FAR AS CAN MAKE OUT SAYS "GENUINE HOLLAND GENEVA, GOLDEN PRIZE MEDALS PORTO? 1865, PHILADELPHIA 1876 & AMSTERDAM 1883. A PUTMAN? & CO. CHIEDAM"

VERY PEBBLEY

TAPERED DIP MOLD MED. GREEN COLOR, 12" TALL. DEEP KICK UP BASE IS 2 13/16" DIAM.

3 2/16" DIAM. BASE

2" MOLD, MACHINE MADE, COMMON TYPE AMBER BOTTLE, 11 1/16" HIGH.

MOUTH FINISHED FOR GLASS STOPPER

END OF M.S.

CONCAVE CIRCLE IN 3" SQUARE BASE

LONDON DRY GIN GORDON'S ENGLAND

2" MOLD AQUA BLUE BOTTLE 8 7/8" HIGH. BACK READS SAME AS FRONT "GORDON'S DRY GIN, LONDON ENGLAND"

34 END OF M.S.

CONCAVE CIRCLE IN BASE 1 9/16" BY 3 2/16"

CORN FLOWER BLUE, 2" MOLD FLASK WITH HEAVY STRAPPED SIDES. NECK IS SCROOTCHED DOWN INTO SHOULDERS & IT IS 7 7/8" TALL.

35

36 END OF M.S.

38 IMPERIAL THE "OLD BUSHMILLS" DISTILLERY CO. TRADE PURE MALT MARK EST. 1784

39 M.S. END OF M.S.

BASE 2" DIAM.

BLACK (OLIVE GREEN) 3" MOLD 10 1/4" TALL

37 END OF M.S.

CONCAVE BASE 3" DIAMETER

3" MOLD BLACK BOTTLE 12" TALL. HAS BUBBLES UP TO 2 1/2" LONG. LABEL SAYS "LONDON DOCK" JAMAICA RUM.

JAMAICA RUM

DEEP BASE 2 3/8" DIAM.

3" MOLD BLACK (DARK OLIVE GREEN) BOTTLE 9 7/8" TALL

J.L. & CO. L? 3120

INDENTED PANEL IN BASE 2 5/7" BY 4 1/8"

AQUAMARINE COLOR, 2" MOLD 10 3/4" TALL. BACK SHOULDER SAYS "QUART. OLD BUSHMILLS DISTILLERY"

PAGE FOUR

69

40 → FINISHED FOR GLASS STOPPER

END OF M.S.

ENGLAND GORDONS DRY GIN

CONCAVE CIRCLE IN BASE 2½" BY 3½" BRIGHT AQUA GREEN COLOR,
9" TALL.

OTHER SIDES ALSO EMBOSSED; RIGHT SIDE SAYS LONDON & BACK SHOULDER HAS "REGᴰ 610617.

41 →
KICK UP, BASE 2½" DIAMETER

3" MOLD AQUA COLOR, 11½" TALL. NECK OF THIS BOTTLE HAS CREASES & M.S. APPEARS TWISTED. SHOULDER IS WHITTLE MARKED.

M.S.

42 → SIDE MOLD SEAM GO'S UP TO HERE

IMPERIAL

F + S Lᵀᴰ STH
CONCAVE BASE 2⅝" BY 4⅜"

OTHER SIDE SAYS "QUART"

AQUA GREEN COLOR, 11¼" HIGH

43

24" BASE HAS INDENTED SQUARE PANEL

44 →
DEEP KICK & BASE LOP SIDED
END OF M.S.

BASE 4¼" DIAM. BOTTLE 12½" TALL 3" MOLD, BLACK, HEAVY GLASS. FOOT RIM SAGS IN ON THIS ONE.

ROUGH SIDE PANELS & AN ALL OVER RIBBED EFFECT
M.S.
10¼" HIGH
DARK OLIVE AMBER

47 →
MOLD SEAM ENDS AT SHOULDER
M.S.
SCAR

45
END OF M.L.
VERY NARROW FOOT RIM, KICK UP BASE 2½" DIAM.

WILSONS INVALIDS' PORT WINE

SCAR

GROUND LIP

46 →

ON BASE IS A SCAR

KICK UP BASE 4⅛" DIAM

BOTTLE LEANS TO ONE SIDE & BASE RIM SWELLS, SO IT DOES NOT SIT LEVEL. 3" MOLD BLACK (DEEP OLIVE GREEN) 12¼" TALL.

DARK OLIVE GREEN BOTTLE, 11¾" HIGH. DEEP SCAR RUNS ALMOST ALL THE WAY AROUND BODY

EMBOSSED LETTERS SAY "WILSONS INVALIDS PORT WINE".

BASE FLAT 2¼" DIAM.

DARK GREY COLOR, 6" TALL. SWIRLED RIBS ARE VERY PRONOUNCED AT TOP, BUT THIN OUT AS THEY GO DOWN

PAGE FIVE

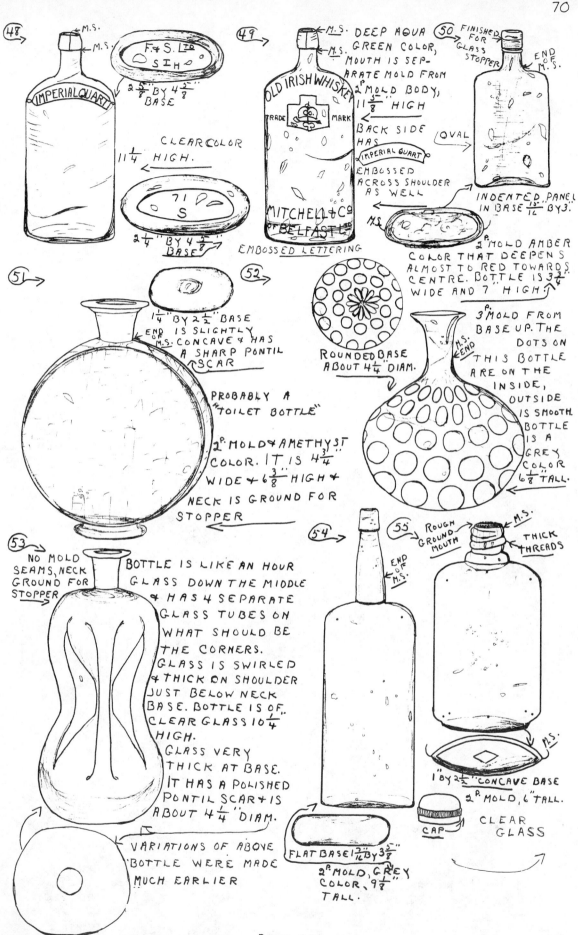

48 → M.S. M.S. F. & S. LTD S IH 2 5/8 BY 4 5/8 BASE

IMPERIAL QUART

CLEAR COLOR 11 1/4 HIGH.

71 S 2 1/4 BY 4 5/8 BASE

49 → M.S. M.S. DEEP AQUA GREEN COLOR, MOUTH IS SEPARATE MOLD FROM 2 MOLD BODY, 11 5/8 HIGH

OLD IRISH WHISKEY TRADE MARK

BACK SIDE HAS IMPERIAL QUART EMBOSSED ACROSS SHOULDER AS WELL

MITCHELL & CO OF BELFAST

EMBOSSED LETTERING

50 → FINISHED FOR GLASS STOPPER END OF M.S.

OVAL

INDENTED PANEL IN BASE 15/16 BY 3.

2 MOLD AMBER COLOR THAT DEEPENS ALMOST TO RED TOWARDS CENTRE. BOTTLE IS 3 3/4 WIDE AND 7 HIGH.

51 → 1 1/4 BY 2 1/2 BASE END OF M.S. IS SLIGHTLY CONCAVE & HAS A SHARP PONTIL SCAR

PROBABLY A "TOILET BOTTLE"

2 MOLD & AMETHYST COLOR. IT IS 4 3/4 WIDE & 6 3/8 HIGH & NECK IS GROUND FOR STOPPER

52 → ROUNDED BASE ABOUT 4 1/4 DIAM.

M.S. END

3 MOLD FROM BASE UP. THE DOTS ON THIS BOTTLE ARE ON THE INSIDE, OUTSIDE IS SMOOTH BOTTLE IS A GREY COLOR 6 7/8 TALL.

53 → NO MOLD SEAMS, NECK GROUND FOR STOPPER

BOTTLE IS LIKE AN HOUR GLASS DOWN THE MIDDLE & HAS 4 SEPARATE GLASS TUBES ON WHAT SHOULD BE THE CORNERS. GLASS IS SWIRLED & THICK ON SHOULDER JUST BELOW NECK BASE. BOTTLE IS OF CLEAR GLASS 10 1/4 HIGH. GLASS VERY THICK AT BASE. IT HAS A POLISHED PONTIL SCAR & IS ABOUT 4 1/4 DIAM.

VARIATIONS OF ABOVE BOTTLE WERE MADE MUCH EARLIER

54 → END OF M.S.

FLAT BASE 1 7/16 BY 3 5/8 2 MOLD, GREY COLOR, 9 1/8 TALL.

55 → ROUGH GROUND MOUTH M.S. THICK THREADS

M.S. 1 BY 2 1/2 CONCAVE BASE 2 MOLD, 6 TALL.

CAP CLEAR GLASS

71

56

M.S.

LABEL LINE ON BACK

ROBT DAVIES "LAGER BEER" DOMINION BREWERY TORONTO

M.S. RARE THICK & STAND OUT

CONCAVE CIRCLE IN BASE 2¾" DIAMETER. 2 P. MOLD, 9¼" HIGH, LETTERS ARE EMBOSSED & IT IS AQUA BLUE COLOR

L.G.C°
1⅞" BY 3½" BASE

57

M.S.

2 P. MOLD AMBER BROWN COLOR 7¾" HIGH

58

M.S.

CONCAVE CIRCLE IN BASE 3" DIAM.

HUEBNER TOLEDO
TOLEDO OHIO BREWERIES CO.
REGISTERED
PURE AND WITHOUT DRUGS OR POISON

M.S.

2 P. MOLD, YELLOW AMBER COLOR, WITH EMBOSSED LETTERS. BASE LINE READS "PURE AND WITHOUT DRUGS OR POISON." BOTTLE IS 11" TALL.

YES WE DO FIND SOME OF THESE IN "CANADIAN DUMPS."

59

M.S. END

M.S.

+BÉNÉDICTINE+

DEEP BASE 4" DIAM.

BOTTLE 10½" TALL, DARK GREEN TO BROWN COLOR, 3 P. MOLD. NECK RING WAS LAYED ON & FLATTEND WITH SOMETHING ON BOTH FRONT & BACK, & IT HAS AN EMBOSSED HORSE SHOE ON BACK SHOULDER.

60

M.S.

INDENTED CIRCLE IN BASE 3" DIAM.

STEGMAIER WILKES-BARRE PA.

M.S.

M.S. BOTTLE IS 8 1/16" HIGH, 2 P. MOLD, EMBOSSED LETTERS AND IS DARK YELLOW AMBER COLOR.

61

M.S.

GLUEK BREWING Co. C TRADE MARK MINNEAPOLIS, MINN.
THIS BOTTLE NOT TO BE SOLD

BEER BOTTLE 9½" HIGH, 2 P. MOLD, PALE AQUA GREEN COLOR. "1652" EMBOSSED ON SIDE ABOVE BASE.

62

M.S.

D 15

BASE 2" BY 3½" & BIT CONCAVE. 2 P. MOLD, 10" TALL, AMBER COLOR

G&W
25 OZ.
EMBOSSED ON BACK SAME AS FRONT.

63

M.S.

2 5647A D
2½" BY 3⅝" BASE

2 P. MOLD, ORANGE AMBER COLOR 10" HIGH.

NUMBERS 62 & 63 ARE NIETHER OLD NOR SCARCE BUT COLOR IS MUCH NICER THAN BROWN AMBERS OF TO-DAY.

M.S.

INDENTED CIRCLE IN BASE 2⅝" DIAMETER.

PAGE SEVEN

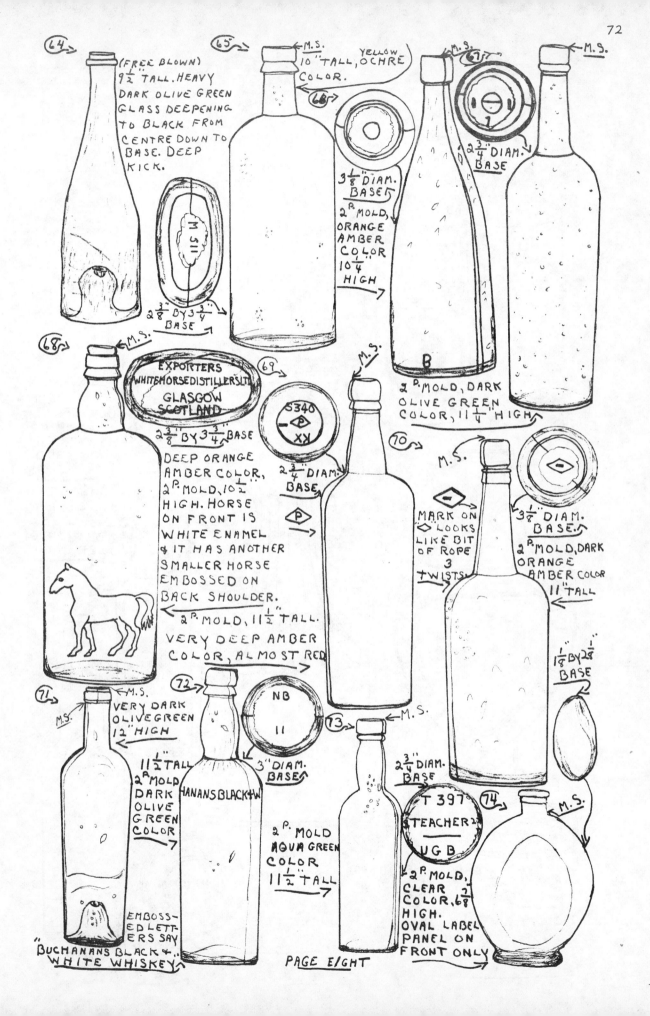

64
(FREE BLOWN)
9½" TALL. HEAVY
DARK OLIVE GREEN
GLASS DEEPENING
TO BLACK FROM
CENTRE DOWN TO
BASE. DEEP
KICK.

M 511

2⅜" BY 3¾"
BASE

65
M.S.
10" TALL, OCHRE
COLOR.

66

3⅛" DIAM.
BASE

2ᴾ. MOLD,
ORANGE
AMBER
COLOR
10¼"
HIGH

67
M.S.

2¾" DIAM.
BASE

M.S.

B

2ᴾ. MOLD, DARK
OLIVE GREEN
COLOR, 11¼" HIGH

68
M.S.

69
EXPORTERS
WHITE HORSE DISTILLERS LTD
GLASGOW
SCOTLAND

2⅜" BY 3¾" BASE

DEEP ORANGE
AMBER COLOR,
2ᴾ. MOLD, 10½"
HIGH. HORSE
ON FRONT IS
WHITE ENAMEL
& IT HAS ANOTHER
SMALLER HORSE
EMBOSSED ON
BACK SHOULDER.

5340
XX

2¾" DIAM.
BASE

P

2ᴾ. MOLD, 11½" TALL.
VERY DEEP AMBER
COLOR, ALMOST RED

M.S.

70

M.S.

MARK ON
LOOKS
LIKE BIT
OF ROPE
3
TWISTS.

3⅛" DIAM.
BASE.

2ᴾ. MOLD, DARK
ORANGE COLOR
11" TALL

71
M.S.
M.S.

VERY DARK
OLIVE GREEN
12" HIGH

11½" TALL
2ᴾ. MOLD
DARK
OLIVE
GREEN
COLOR

72
CHANANS BLACK+W

NB
11

3" DIAM.
BASE

2ᴾ. MOLD
AQUA GREEN
COLOR
11½" TALL

73
M.S.

2¾" DIAM.
BASE

T 397
TEACHERS
U G B

2ᴾ. MOLD,
CLEAR
COLOR, 6⅞"
HIGH.
OVAL LABEL
PANEL ON
FRONT ONLY

1⅛" BY 2⅝"
BASE

74
M.S.

EMBOSS-
ED LETT-
ERS SAY
"BUCHANANS BLACK +
WHITE WHISKEY"

PAGE EIGHT

73

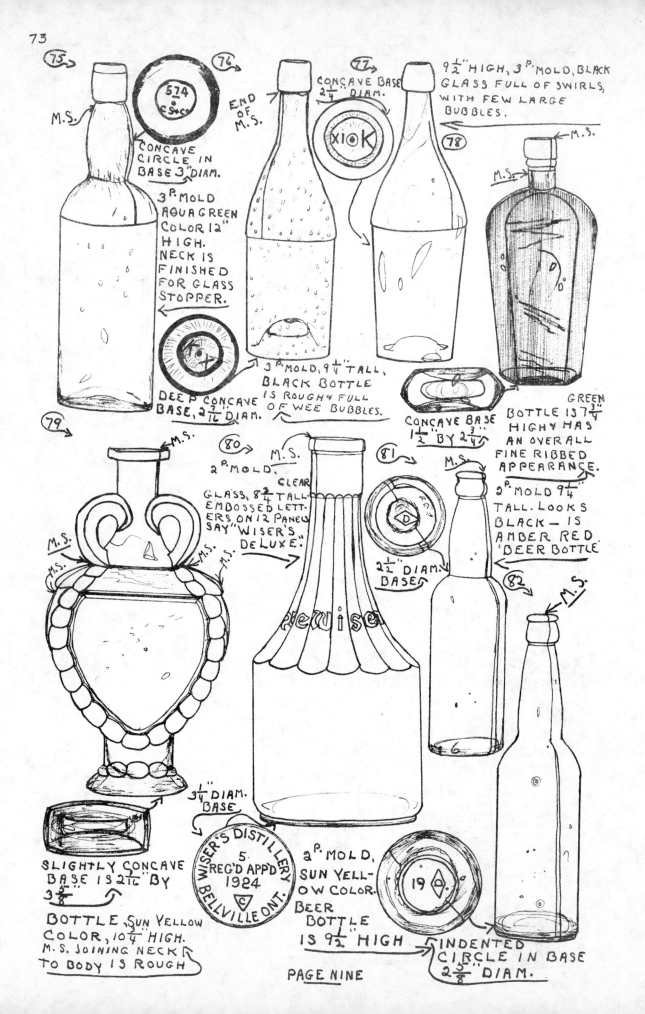

75 →

M.S.

574
C.S.&Co.

CONCAVE
CIRCLE IN
BASE 3" DIAM.

3ᴾ MOLD
AQUA GREEN
COLOR 12"
HIGH.
NECK IS
FINISHED
FOR GLASS
STOPPER.

X

DEEP CONCAVE
BASE 2 7/16" DIAM.

76 →

END OF
M.S.

CONCAVE BASE
2 1/4" DIAM.

X10K

3ᴾ MOLD, 9 1/4" TALL,
BLACK BOTTLE
IS ROUGHY FULL
OF WEE BUBBLES.

77 →

CONCAVE BASE
1 1/2" BY 2 3/4"

9 1/2" HIGH, 3ᴾ MOLD, BLACK
GLASS FULL OF SWIRLS,
WITH FEW LARGE
BUBBLES.

78 ←

M.S.

M.S.

GREEN
BOTTLE IS 7 3/4"
HIGH Y HAS
AN OVERALL
FINE RIBBED
APPEARANCE.

79 →

M.S.

M.S.

M.S.

M.S.

M.S.

SLIGHTLY CONCAVE
BASE IS 2 1/16" BY
3 5/8"

BOTTLE, SUN YELLOW
COLOR, 10 1/4" HIGH.
M.S. JOINING NECK
TO BODY IS ROUGH

80 →

M.S.

2ᴾ MOLD.

CLEAR
GLASS, 8 3/4" TALL.
EMBOSSED LETT-
ERS ON 12 PANELS
SAY "WISER'S
DELUXE."

eWise

3 1/4" DIAM.
BASE

WISER'S DISTILLERY
5.
REG'D APP'D
1924
BELLVILLE ONT.

81 →

M.S.

2 1/2" DIAM.
BASE

2ᴾ MOLD, 9 1/4"
TALL. LOOKS
BLACK — IS
AMBER RED
BEER BOTTLE

82 →

M.S.

2ᴾ MOLD,
SUN YELL-
OW COLOR.
BEER
BOTTLE
IS 9 1/2" HIGH

19

INDENTED
CIRCLE IN BASE
2 5/8" DIAM.

PAGE NINE

83→

←M.S.

←M.S.

GLASS STOPPER FINISH

7/8" BY 2 3/4" BASE

84→

INDENTED CIRCLE 3 3/4" DIAM

85→

CANADIAN SCHENLEY

BOTTLE MADE IN CANADA

←M.S.

2 3/4" BY 3 1/2" BASE

MACHINE MADE. 2 P. MOLD, DEEP ORANGE AMBER COLOR, 7" TALL.

CREST ON TOP SIMILIAR TO ONE ON BOTTLE BELOW 88

86→

←M.S.

For Connoisseur

2 P. MOLD BOTTLE HAS 2 LIDS AS SHOWN. IT IS CLEAR GLASS, 8 3/4" HIGH. BACK & FRONT ARE EMBOSSED, BUT MOST OF BACK HAS LARGE LABEL PANEL & BOTTOM SAYS.. "MADE IN CANADA, JUST ABOVE BASE LINE.

2 P. MOLD, DEEP ORANGE AMBER COLOR 9 1/2" TALL

SPUN IN MOLD, DARK OLIVE GREEN BOTTLE, 10 1/2" HIGH.

2 1/4" BY 4" BASE

UNITED DISTILLERS LIMITED GRIMSBY ONTARIO

87→

3" BY 2" BY 3 1/16" BASE

M.S. END

2 P. MOLD, MILK GLASS, 8 1/16" HIGH. FRONT IS EMBOSSED "BELLE OF ANDERSON, OLD FASHION, HAND MADE, SOUR MASH", & BACK IS PLAIN.

88→

←M.S.

UNITED DISTILLERS G LIMITED VANCOUVER CANADA

2 3/8" BY 4 1/2" BASE

2 P. MOLD, SUN YELLOW COLOR 10 1/2" HIGH. BACK EMBOSSED SAME AS FRONT BUT NO CREST.

UDL UNITED DISTILLERS LIMITED

OLD MASH BELLE OF ANDERSON FASHION HAND SOUR MADE

89→

M.S.

BASE IS SLIGHTLY CONCAVE & 2 1/2" DIAM.

2 P. MOLD, BEER BOTTLE. OLIVE GREEN COLOR, 9 1/4" HIGH.

PAGE TEN

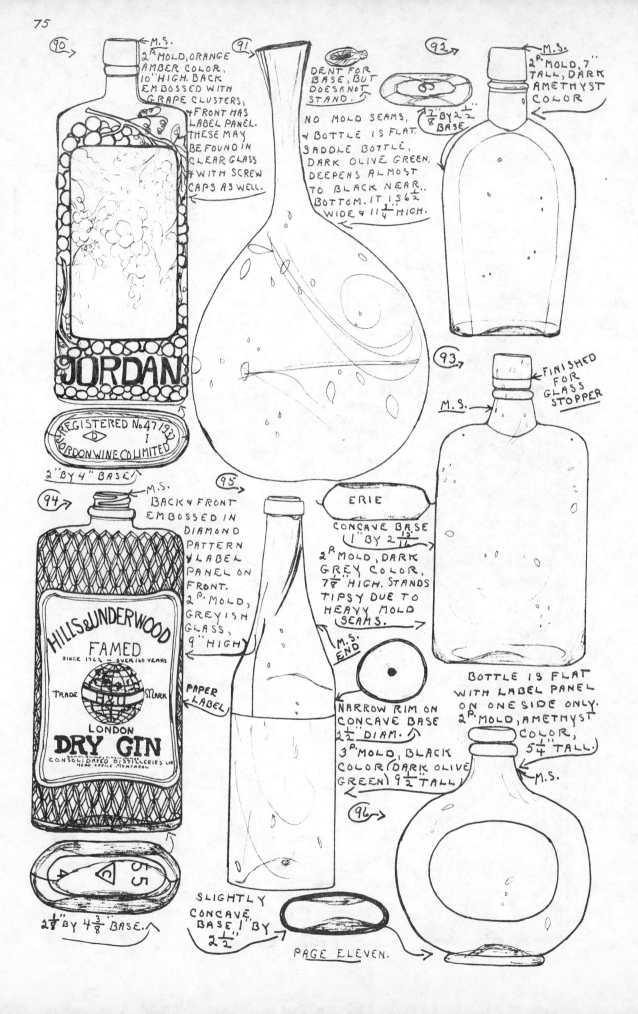

90 →

M.S.
2"P. MOLD, ORANGE
AMBER COLOR,
10" HIGH. BACK
EMBOSSED WITH
GRAPE CLUSTERS,
+ FRONT HAS
LABEL PANEL.
THESE MAY
BE FOUND IN
CLEAR GLASS
+ WITH SCREW
CAPS AS WELL.

JORDAN

REGISTERED No 47/93
D   I
JORDAN WINE CO. LIMITED

2" BY 4" BASE.

91

DENT FOR
BASE, BUT
DOES NOT
STAND.

1⅞" BY 2½"
BASE

NO MOLD SEAMS,
+ BOTTLE IS FLAT.
SADDLE BOTTLE.
DARK OLIVE GREEN,
DEEPENS ALMOST
TO BLACK NEAR
BOTTOM. IT IS 6½"
WIDE + 11¾" HIGH.

92 →

M.S.
2 P. MOLD, 7"
TALL, DARK
AMETHYST
COLOR

93 →

FINISHED
FOR
GLASS
STOPPER

M.S.

94 →

M.S.

BACK + FRONT
EMBOSSED IN
DIAMOND
PATTERN
+ LABEL
PANEL ON
FRONT.
2 P. MOLD,
GREYISH
GLASS,
9" HIGH.

HILLS & UNDERWOOD
FAMED
SINCE 1762 — OVER 160 YEARS
TRADE   Mark
LONDON
DRY GIN
CONSOLIDATED DISTILLERIES LTD
HEAD OFFICE MONTREAL.

PAPER
LABEL

2⅞" BY 4⅜" BASE.

95 →

ERIE

CONCAVE BASE
1" BY 2 13/16"

2 P. MOLD, DARK
GREY COLOR,
7⅞" HIGH. STANDS
TIPSY DUE TO
HEAVY MOLD
SEAMS.

M.S.
END

NARROW RIM ON
CONCAVE BASE
2½" DIAM.

3 P. MOLD, BLACK
COLOR (DARK OLIVE
GREEN) 9½" TALL.

96 →

SLIGHTLY
CONCAVE
BASE 1" BY
2½"

PAGE ELEVEN.

BOTTLE IS FLAT
WITH LABEL PANEL
ON ONE SIDE ONLY.
2 P. MOLD, AMETHYST
COLOR,
5¼" TALL.

M.S.

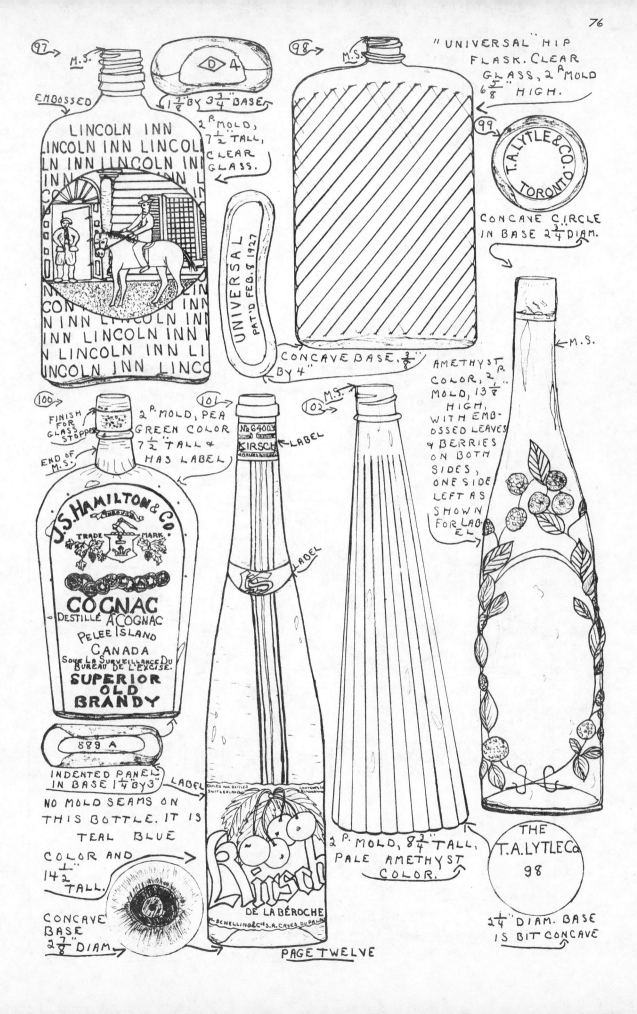

97 → M.S.
EMBOSSED
LINCOLN INN
LINCOLN INN LINCOL
LN INN LINCOLN INN
INN LINCOLN INN

D 4
1 7/8 BY 3 3/4 BASE
2 P. MOLD, 7 1/2 TALL, CLEAR GLASS.

UNIVERSAL PAT'D FEB. 8 1927

98 → M.S.
"UNIVERSAL" HIP FLASK. CLEAR GLASS, 2 P. MOLD 6 5/8 HIGH.

99
T.A. LYTLE & CO. TORONTO
CONCAVE CIRCLE IN BASE 2 3/4 DIAM.

CONCAVE BASE, 3/8 BY 4"

100 →
FINISH FOR GLASS STOPPER
END OF M.S.
2 P. MOLD, PEA GREEN COLOR 7 1/2 TALL & HAS LABEL

J.S. HAMILTON & CO.
TRADE MARK
COGNAC
DESTILLÉ A COGNAC
PELEE ISLAND
CANADA
SOUS LA SURVEILLANCE DU BUREAU DE L'EXCISE.
SUPERIOR OLD BRANDY
889 A
INDENTED PANEL IN BASE 1 1/4 BY 3"
NO MOLD SEAMS ON THIS BOTTLE. IT IS TEAL BLUE COLOR AND 14 1/2 TALL.
CONCAVE BASE 2 7/8 DIAM →

101 →
N° 64003
KIRSCH ← LABEL
LABEL
Kirsch DE LA BÉROCHE

102 → M.S.
2 P. MOLD, 8 3/4 TALL, PALE AMETHYST COLOR.

M.S.
AMETHYST COLOR, 2 P. MOLD, 13 1/8 HIGH, WITH EMBOSSED LEAVES & BERRIES ON BOTH SIDES, ONE SIDE LEFT AS SHOWN FOR LABEL

THE T.A. LYTLE Co 98
2 3/4 DIAM. BASE IS BIT CONCAVE

PAGE TWELVE

77

103 →

M.S.

104

SIX TO GALLON

127A

2 3/4" DIAM.
BASE

1 1/2" SQU. BASE

GLASS
SEAL

LABEL "ASCHINO
FABRICA
P. GARNIER
ENGHIEN"

PALE AQUAMARINE
COLOR, 12 1/4" TALL,
2 P. MOLD.

CORNER OF LABEL
TORN, REST READS
"ARASCHINO - DELLA
FABRRICA - DEL Signor
P. GARNIER - ENGHIEN.

"MARACHINO"
IMPRESSED ON SEAL.

3 P. MOLD, AQUA
GREEN COLOR
11 3/4" HIGH, WITH
PAPER LABEL.
BOTTOM LINE ON LABEL
READS "THE NAME, SEAL,
BOTTLE AND LABEL ARE
REGISTERED TRADE
MARKS."

M.S.

M.S.

105

3 P. MOLD,
SKY BLUE
COLOR,
6 9/16"
TALL

← M.S.

TEACHER'S
HIGHLAND CREAM
TRADE MARK
Perfection of OLd Scotch
WHISKY
Wm TEACHER & SONS
GLASGOW.

107
CONCAVE
CIRCLE
IN BASE
3 3/16" SQU.

ED

1 3/8" DIAM.
BASE

106
P. MOLD,
3 P. MOLD,
AQUA GREEN
DARK COLOR,
9 3/4" TALL.
EMBOSSED
LETTERS.
M.S.
BACK HAS
EMBOSSED
CIRCLE AROUND
W&M

32

M.S.

3 1/2" DIAM. BASE
WITH FAIRLY
DEEP CONCAVE
CIRCLE

EMBOSSED
STAR ON
FOUR CORNERS

2 P. MOLD, DEEP EMER-
ELD GREEN COLOR,
9 7/8" HIGH. 2 EMBOSSED
SIDES & 2 PLAIN
WITH LABEL ON ONE.
"GREEN STAR
PEPPERMINT"

M.S. 3 1/2" BASE
DIAM. 5

108

WHYTE & MACKAY
GLASGOW

GREEN STAR
Peppermint

P. BARDINET
BORDEAUX

ICE
PEPPERMINT

BARDINET
BORDEAUX

PAPER LABEL

INDENTED STAR ON
TWO SIDES WITH EMBO-
SSED LETTERS. SIDE NOT
SHOWN READS "BARDINET
BORDEAUX FRANCE"
PAGE THIRTEEN

2 P. MOLD, DARK ORANGE
AMBER COLOR, 8 1/2"
HIGH.

(109)

METAL RING

M.S. $1\frac{5}{16}$" BY $3\frac{1}{16}$" BASE

CORK

DOSE CAP

(110)

M.S.

2" BY $4\frac{1}{4}$" BASE

2 P. MOLD, SUN YELLOW COLOR, $10\frac{1}{8}$" HIGH. FRONT IS EMBOSSED AS SHOWN + EMBOSSED LETTERING ON BACK READS "H. ROBINSON CORPORATION LIMITED HAMILTON CANADA."

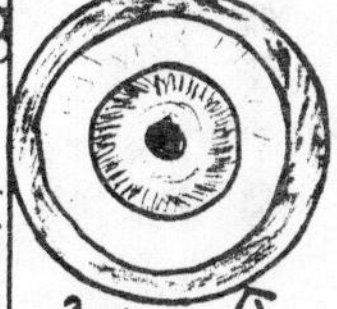

2 P. MOLD, ORANGE AMBER COLOR, $7\frac{3}{4}$" HIGH. BACK IS EMBOSSED SAME AS FRONT, BUT WITH SINGLE LARGER LABEL PANEL. DOSE CAP IS METAL PAINTED BROWN. EMBOSSED PRINTING ON TOP OF CAP READS "MONTREAL CANADA, CONSOLIDATED DISTILLERIES LIMITED. CAP MADE IN U.S.A."

$2\frac{3}{8}$" DIAM BASE

(111)

(112) M.S.

(113) CONCAVE CIRCLE IN BASE $3\frac{5}{8}$" DIAM.

DARK AQUA GREEN COLOR, $12\frac{1}{2}$" HIGH.

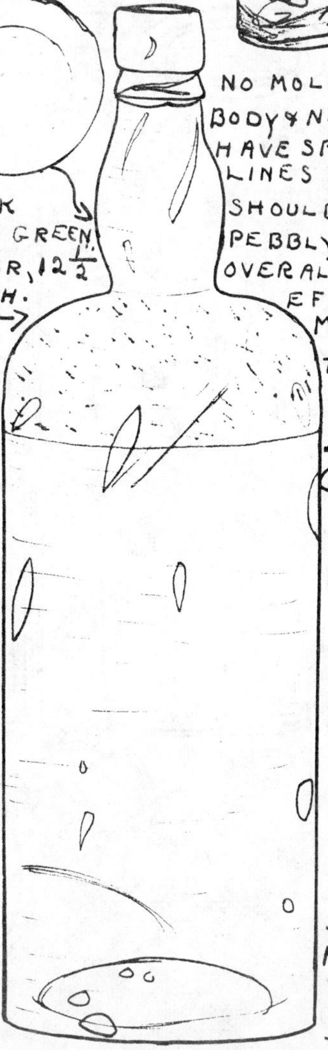

NO MOLD SEAMS, BODY & NECK HAVE SPIN LINES BUT SHOULDER PEBBLY & OVERALL EFFECT MUCH ROUGHER THAN IS USUAL IN SPUN IN MOLD BOTTLE

SPUN IN MOLD, DARK TEAL BLUE COLOR, $11\frac{1}{2}$" HIGH

Bright's

DESIGN REGISTERED

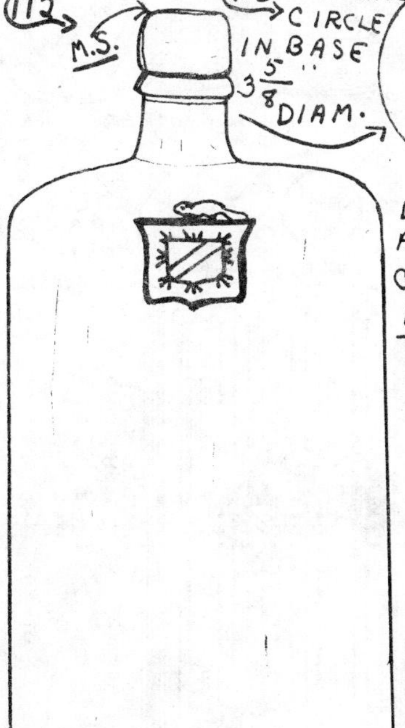

$1\frac{7}{8}$" BY $4\frac{1}{4}$" BASE

2 P. MOLD, DARK GREEN COLOR, $10\frac{1}{8}$" TALL. BOTH SIDES HAVE SAME EMBOSSING.

(114)

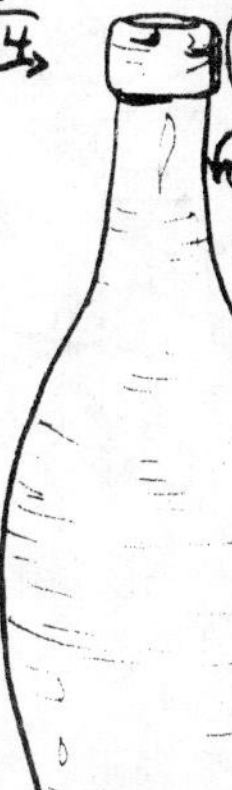

CONCAVE BASE $1\frac{1}{4}$" DIAM

SPUN IN MOLD AMETHYST COLOR $6\frac{1}{4}$" HIGH

PAGE FOURTEEN.

79

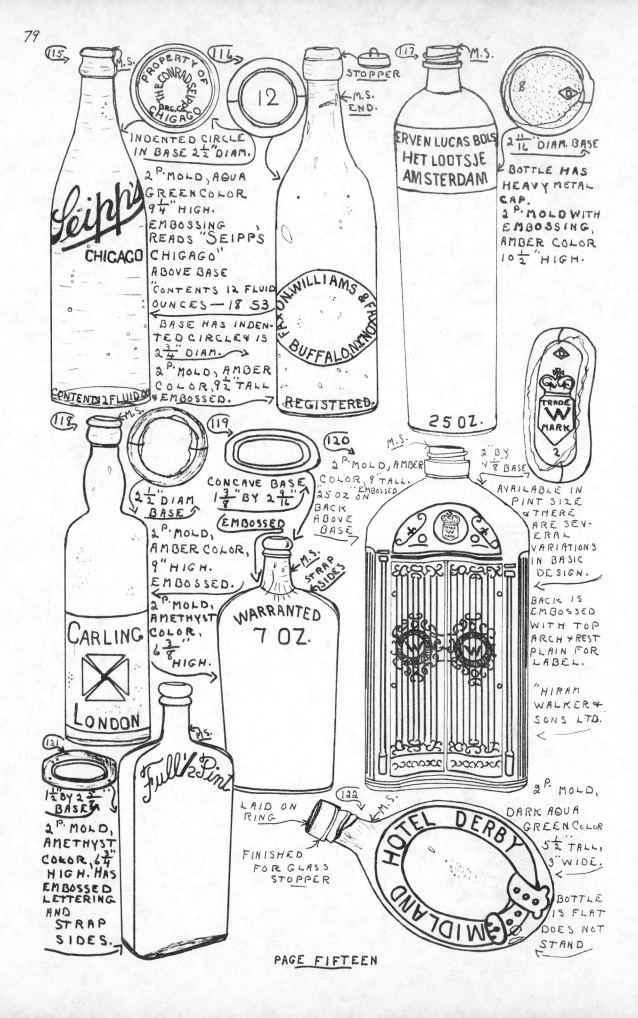

115 → M.S.

116 →
PROPERTY OF THE CONRAD SEIPP BRG. CO. CHIGAGO

12

INDENTED CIRCLE IN BASE 2½" DIAM.

2 P. MOLD, AQUA GREEN COLOR 9¼" HIGH. EMBOSSING READS "SEIPP'S CHIGAGO" ABOVE BASE "CONTENTS 12 FLUID OUNCES — 1853

BASE HAS INDENTED CIRCLE & IS 2¾" DIAM.

2 P. MOLD, AMBER COLOR, 9½" TALL & EMBOSSED.

Seipp's CHICAGO

CONTENTS 12 FLUID O

F. FIXON. WILLIAMS & FAXON BUFFALO. N.Y.
REGISTERED.

117 → M.S.

STOPPER

M.S. END.

ERVEN LUCAS BOLS HET LOOTSJE AMSTERDAM

25 OZ.

8

2 11/16" DIAM. BASE

BOTTLE HAS HEAVY METAL CAP. 2 P. MOLD WITH EMBOSSING, AMBER COLOR 10½" HIGH.

TRADE W MARK
2

2" BY 4⅛ BASE

AVAILABLE IN PINT SIZE & THERE ARE SEVERAL VARIATIONS IN BASIC DESIGN.

BACK IS EMBOSSED WITH TOP ARCH & REST PLAIN FOR LABEL.

"HIRAM WALKER & SONS LTD.

2 P. MOLD, DARK AQUA GREEN COLOR 5½ TALL, 3" WIDE.

BOTTLE IS FLAT DOES NOT STAND

118 → M.S.

119

2½" DIAM BASE

CONCAVE BASE 1⅜" BY 2 9/16"
EMBOSSED

120

2 P. MOLD, AMBER COLOR, 9 TALL. EMBOSSED 25 OZ ON BACK ABOVE BASE

M.S.

2 P. MOLD, AMBER COLOR, 9" HIGH. EMBOSSED.

2 P. MOLD, AMETHYST COLOR, 6⅜" HIGH.

CARLING

LONDON

M.S. STRAP SIDES

WARRANTED 7 OZ.

121

1½ BY 2½" BASE

2 P. MOLD, AMETHYST COLOR, 6¾" HIGH. HAS EMBOSSED LETTERING AND STRAP SIDES.

Full ½ Pint

M.S.

LAID ON RING

FINISHED FOR GLASS STOPPER

122 → M.S.

HOTEL DERBY MIDLAND

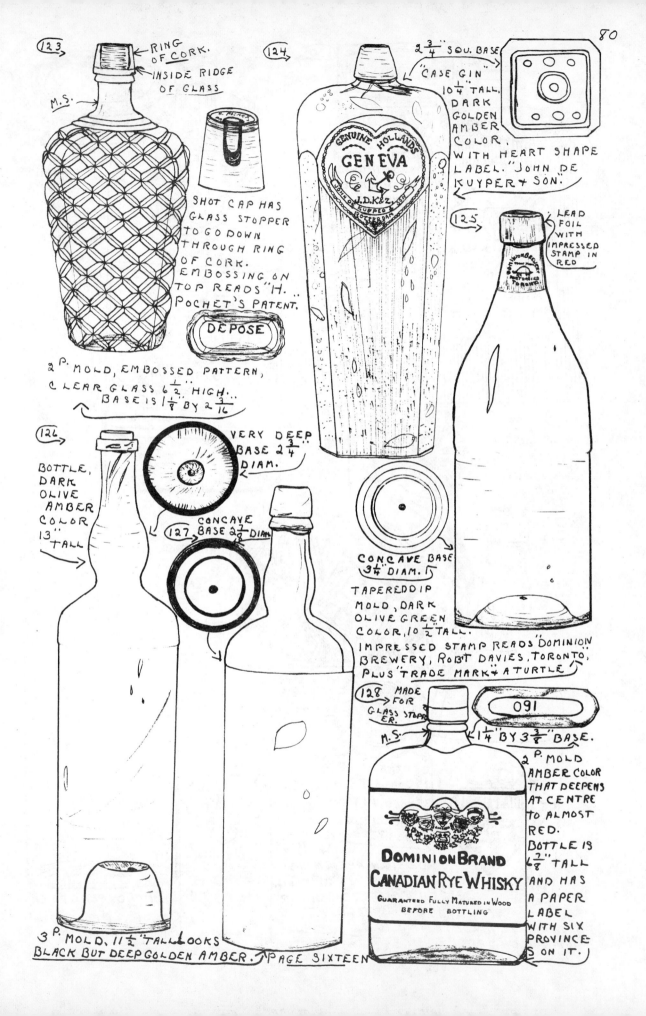

123
RING OF CORK.
INSIDE RIDGE OF GLASS
M.S.

SHOT CAP HAS GLASS STOPPER TO GO DOWN THROUGH RING OF CORK. EMBOSSING ON TOP READS "H. POCHET'S PATENT.

DEPOSE

2 P. MOLD, EMBOSSED PATTERN, CLEAR GLASS 6½" HIGH. BASE IS 1⅛" BY 2 3/16"

124
GENUINE HOLLANDS
GENEVA
JOHN DE KUYPER
J.D.K&Z.
ROTTERDAM

2¾" SQU. BASE
"CASE GIN" 10¼" TALL. DARK GOLDEN AMBER COLOR. WITH HEART SHAPE LABEL. "JOHN DE KUYPER & SON."

VERY DEEP BASE 2¾" DIAM.

CONCAVE BASE 2⅞" DIAM.

125
LEAD FOIL WITH IMPRESSED STAMP IN RED

CONCAVE BASE 3¾" DIAM.

TAPERED DIP MOLD, DARK OLIVE GREEN COLOR, 10½" TALL. IMPRESSED STAMP READS "DOMINION BREWERY, ROB'T DAVIES, TORONTO, PLUS "TRADE MARK & A TURTLE"

126
BOTTLE, DARK OLIVE AMBER COLOR 13" TALL

127
CONCAVE BASE 2⅞" DIAM.

128 MADE FOR GLASS STOPPER.
M.S.
091
1¼" BY 3⅜" BASE.

DOMINION BRAND CANADIAN RYE WHISKY
GUARANTEED FULLY MATURED IN WOOD BEFORE BOTTLING

2 P. MOLD AMBER COLOR THAT DEEPENS AT CENTRE TO ALMOST RED. BOTTLE IS 6⅞" TALL AND HAS A PAPER LABEL WITH SIX PROVINCES ON IT.

3 P. MOLD, 11½" TALL LOOKS BLACK BUT DEEP GOLDEN AMBER. PAGE SIXTEEN

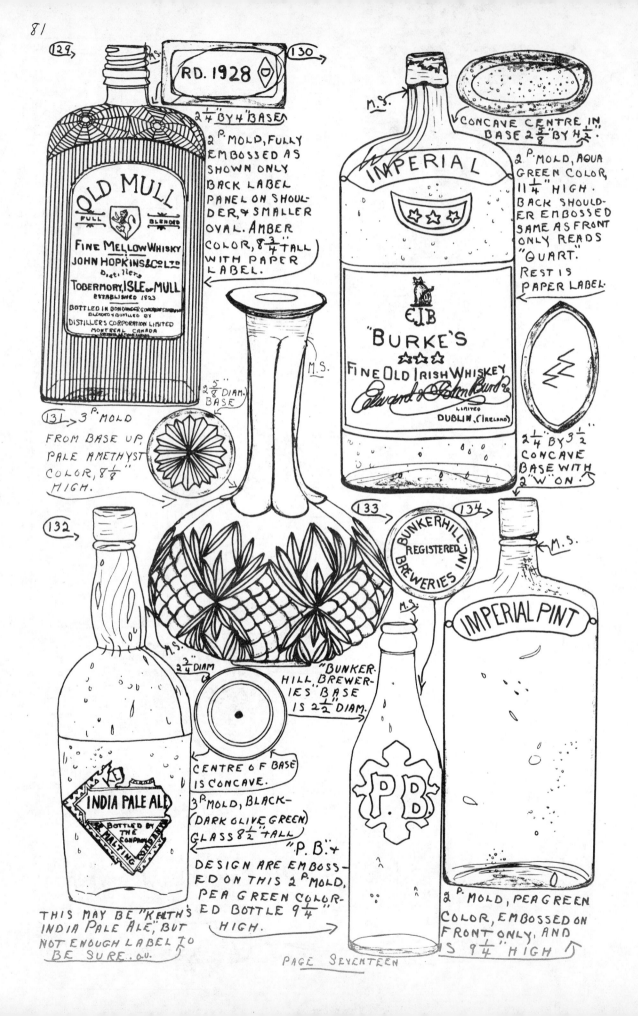

129

130

RD. 1928 ◇

2¼" BY 4" BASE

2 P. MOLD, FULLY EMBOSSED AS SHOWN ONLY BACK LABEL PANEL ON SHOULDER, & SMALLER OVAL. AMBER COLOR, 8¾" TALL WITH PAPER LABEL.

OLD MULL
FULL · BLENDED
FINE MELLOW WHISKY
JOHN HOPKINS & Co Ltd
Distillers
TOBERMORY, ISLE OF MULL
ESTABLISHED 1823
BOTTLED IN BOND UNDER GOVERNMENT SUPERVISION
BLENDED & BOTTLED BY
DISTILLERS CORPORATION LIMITED
MONTREAL CANADA

M.S.

CONCAVE CENTRE IN BASE 2⅝" BY 4½".

IMPERIAL
★★★

2 P. MOLD, AQUA GREEN COLOR, 11¼" HIGH. BACK SHOULDER EMBOSSED SAME AS FRONT ONLY READS "QUART". REST IS PAPER LABEL.

EJB
"BURKE'S"
★★★
FINE OLD IRISH WHISKEY
Edward & John Burke
LIMITED
DUBLIN, (IRELAND)

M.S.

2⅝" DIAM. BASE

131 3 P. MOLD FROM BASE UP, PALE AMETHYST COLOR, 8⅛" HIGH.

2¼" BY 3½" CONCAVE BASE WITH 2 "W" ON.

133

134

BUNKERHILL REGISTERED BREWERIES INC.

132

M.S.

IMPERIAL PINT

M.S.

2¾" DIAM

M.S.

"BUNKER-HILL BREWER-IES" BASE IS 2½" DIAM.

CENTRE OF BASE IS CONCAVE.

3 P. MOLD, BLACK (DARK OLIVE GREEN) GLASS 8½" TALL

P.B

INDIA PALE ALE
BOTTLED BY THE COMPANY
MALTING

"P.B." & DESIGN ARE EMBOSSED ON THIS 2 P. MOLD, PEA GREEN COLORED BOTTLE 9¼" HIGH.

THIS MAY BE "KEITH'S INDIA PALE ALE", BUT NOT ENOUGH LABEL TO BE SURE. o.u.

2 P. MOLD, PEA GREEN COLOR, EMBOSSED ON FRONT ONLY, AND IS 9¼" HIGH

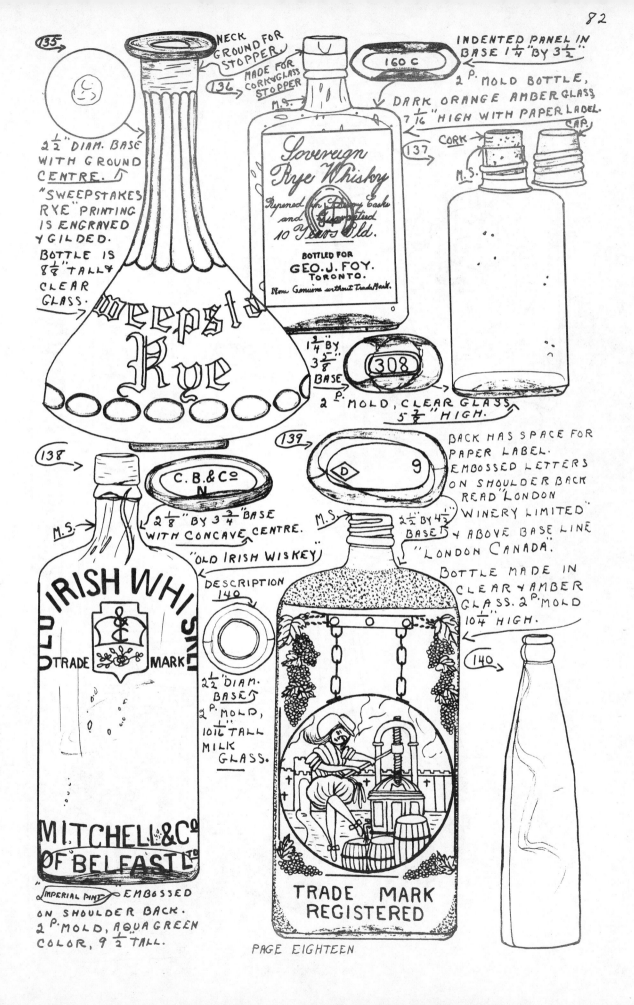

135

2½" DIAM. BASE WITH GROUND CENTRE.

NECK GROUND FOR STOPPER.

136 → MADE FOR CORK & GLASS STOPPER

"SWEEPSTAKES RYE" PRINTING IS ENGRAVED & GILDED. BOTTLE IS 8⅛" TALL & CLEAR GLASS.

Sweepstakes Rye

INDENTED PANEL IN BASE 1¼" BY 3½"

160 C

2 P. MOLD BOTTLE, DARK ORANGE AMBER GLASS 7 1/16" HIGH WITH PAPER LABEL.

137 → CORK → CAP.

M.S.

M.S.

Sovereign Rye Whisky
Ripened in Sherry Casks and Guaranteed
10 Years Old.
BOTTLED FOR
GEO. J. FOY.
TORONTO.
None Genuine without Trade Mark.

1 3/8" BY 3 5/8" BASE

308

2 P. MOLD, CLEAR GLASS 5 7/8" HIGH.

138 →

C.B.& Co N

2⅛" BY 3¾" BASE WITH CONCAVE CENTRE.

M.S.

"OLD IRISH WISKEY"

DESCRIPTION 140

2½" DIAM. BASE 2 P. MOLD, 10 1/16" TALL MILK GLASS.

OLD IRISH WHISKEY

TRADE   MARK

MITCHELL & Co OF BELFAST Ltd

IMPERIAL PINT EMBOSSED ON SHOULDER BACK. 2 P. MOLD, AQUA GREEN COLOR, 9½" TALL.

139 →

D   9

M.S.

2½" BY 4½" BASE

BACK HAS SPACE FOR PAPER LABEL. EMBOSSED LETTERS ON SHOULDER BACK READ "LONDON WINERY LIMITED" & ABOVE BASE LINE "LONDON CANADA".

BOTTLE MADE IN CLEAR & AMBER GLASS. 2 P. MOLD 10¼" HIGH.

140 →

TRADE   MARK
REGISTERED

83

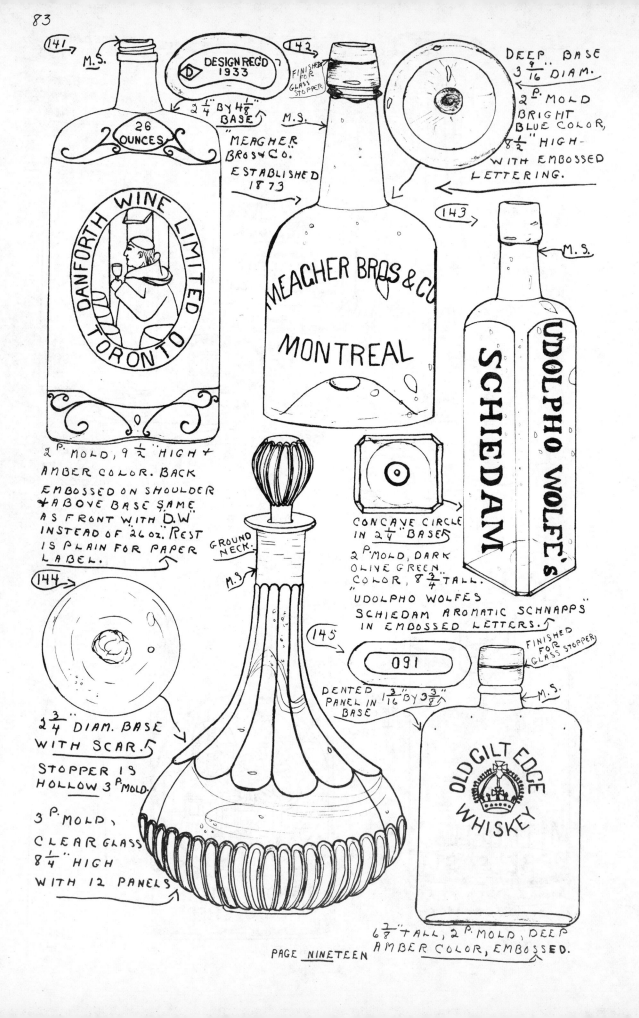

141
M.S.

DESIGN REG'D
1933

2¼" BY 4⅛"
BASE

142

FINISHED
FOR
GLASS
STOPPER

M.S.

26
OUNCES

DANFORTH WINE LIMITED

TORONTO

"MEAGHER
BROS & CO.
ESTABLISHED
1873

MEAGHER BROS & CO

MONTREAL

DEEP BASE
3 9/16" DIAM.

2 P. MOLD
BRIGHT
BLUE COLOR,
8½" HIGH
WITH EMBOSSED
LETTERING.

143

M.S.

UDOLPHO WOLFE'S

SCHIEDAM

2 P. MOLD, 9½" HIGH ↑
AMBER COLOR. BACK
EMBOSSED ON SHOULDER
↑ ABOVE BASE SAME
AS FRONT WITH "D.W"
INSTEAD OF "26 OZ." REST
IS PLAIN FOR PAPER
LABEL.

144

2¾" DIAM. BASE
WITH SCAR.

STOPPER IS
HOLLOW 3 P. MOLD.

3 P. MOLD,
CLEAR GLASS
8¼" HIGH
WITH 12 PANELS

GROUND
NECK.

M.S.

CONCAVE CIRCLE
IN 2¼" BASE

2 P. MOLD, DARK
OLIVE GREEN
COLOR, 8¾" TALL.
"UDOLPHO WOLFES
SCHIEDAM AROMATIC SCHNAPPS"
IN EMBOSSED LETTERS.

145

091

DENTED
PANEL IN 1 3/16" BY 3 3/8"
BASE

FINISHED
FOR GLASS STOPPER

M.S.

OLD GILT EDGE

WHISKEY

6⅞" TALL, 2 P. MOLD, DEEP
AMBER COLOR, EMBOSSED.

PAGE NINETEEN

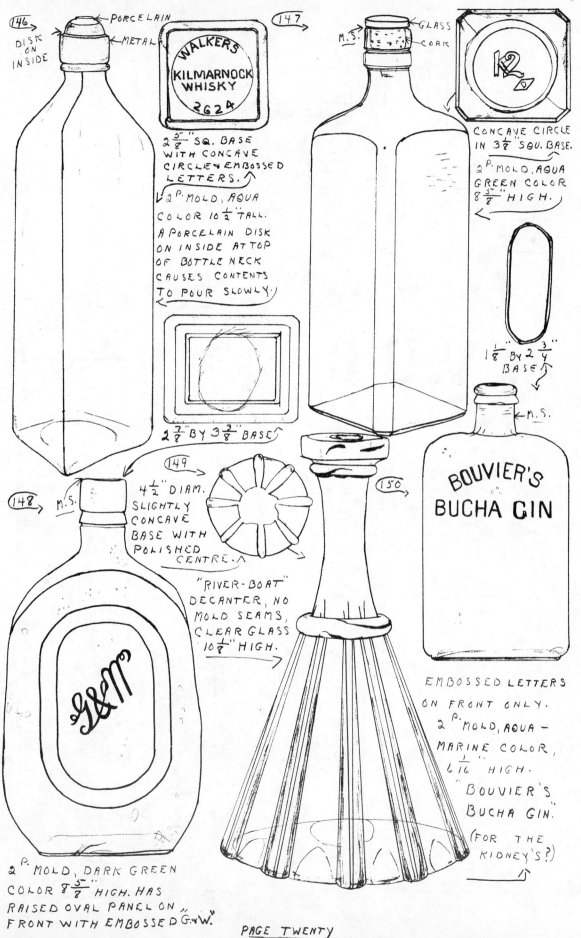

146 → PORCELAIN
DISK ON INSIDE — METAL

WALKERS
KILMARNOCK
WHISKY
2624

2 5/8" SQ. BASE WITH CONCAVE CIRCLE & EMBOSSED LETTERS.

2 P. MOLD, AQUA COLOR 10½" TALL. A PORCELAIN DISK ON INSIDE AT TOP OF BOTTLE NECK CAUSES CONTENTS TO POUR SLOWLY.

147 →

GLASS
M.S. — CORK

K2

CONCAVE CIRCLE IN 3⅜" SQU. BASE.

2 P. MOLD, AQUA GREEN COLOR 8 5/8" HIGH.

1⅛" BY 2¾" BASE

2 7/8" BY 3⅜" BASE

148 → M.S.

149 → 4½" DIAM. SLIGHTLY CONCAVE BASE WITH POLISHED CENTRE.

"RIVER-BOAT" DECANTER, NO MOLD SEAMS, CLEAR GLASS 10⅛" HIGH.

150 →

G&W

M.S.

BOUVIER'S BUCHA GIN

2 P. MOLD, DARK GREEN COLOR 8 5/8" HIGH. HAS RAISED OVAL PANEL ON FRONT WITH EMBOSSED "G&W."

EMBOSSED LETTERS ON FRONT ONLY. 2 P. MOLD, AQUA-MARINE COLOR, 6 1/16" HIGH. "BOUVIER'S BUCHA GIN." (FOR THE KIDNEY'S?)

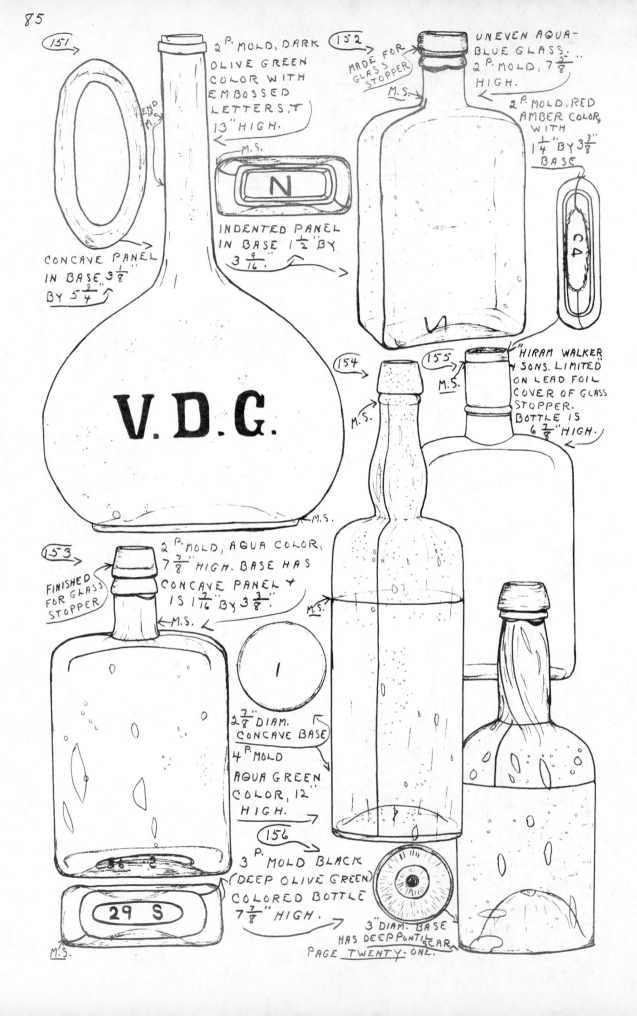

151

CONCAVE PANEL
IN BASE 3⅛"
BY 5¾"

2 P. MOLD, DARK
OLIVE GREEN
COLOR WITH
EMBOSSED
LETTERS, &
13" HIGH.

M.S.

N

INDENTED PANEL
IN BASE 1½" BY
3 9/16".

152

MADE FOR
GLASS
STOPPER

M.S.

UNEVEN AQUA-
BLUE GLASS. ..
2 P. MOLD, 7⅝"
HIGH.

2 P. MOLD, RED
AMBER COLOR,
WITH
1¼" BY 3⅜"
BASE

C4

V.D.C.

153

FINISHED
FOR GLASS
STOPPER

2 P. MOLD, AQUA COLOR,
7⅞" HIGH. BASE HAS
CONCAVE PANEL &
IS 1 7/16" BY 3⅜".

M.S.

I

2⅞" DIAM.
CONCAVE BASE

4 P. MOLD
AQUA GREEN
COLOR, 12"
HIGH.

156

3 MOLD BLACK
(DEEP OLIVE GREEN)
COLORED BOTTLE
7⅞" HIGH.

3" DIAM. BASE
HAS DEEP PONTIL SCAR.

29 S

M.S.

154

M.S.

155

M.S.

"HIRAM WALKER
& SONS. LIMITED"
ON LEAD FOIL
COVER OF GLASS
STOPPER.
BOTTLE IS
6⅞" HIGH.

M.S.

PAGE TWENTY-ONE.

157 →

158 → "CASE GIN"
DARK GREEN
COLOR, 10⅛"
TALL.

M.S

159 →

2¾" SQU.
BASE

M.S
2 P. MOLD, 7¾"
HIGH, DARK
ORANGE
AMBER
COLOR

ROUNDED BASE
3½" ACROSS
WIDEST POINT.

K×K

"CASE GIN" 10¾"
TALL. DEEP
HONEY AMBER
COLOR.

2¾" SQUARE.

2½" DIAM.
CONCAVE
BASE.

K○K

3 P. MOLD, BLACK
161 GLASS, 9½"
HIGH.

747

1¼" BY 3⅝" BASE

160 →

2⅜" BY 3¾" BASE

2 P. MOLD, AQUA
BLUE COLOR,
9¾" TALL.

M.S

M.S

162 →

GLASS
STOPPER

M.S

DARK AMBER AT CENTRE
LIGHTENS TO EDGES. 2 P.
MOLD 8" HIGH.

PAGE TWENTY-TWO.

87

163

M.S.

ROB! DAVIES
LAGER BEER
DOMINION BREWERY
TORONTO

2 7/8" DIAM. BASE
WITH SLIGHTLY
CONCAVE CENTRE.

2 P. MOLD, AQUA
BLUE COLOR
9 1/2" TALL.

DEEP BASE,
3" DIAM.

3 P. MOLD, PALE
AMBER COLOR
10 1/4" TALL,
EMBOSSED.

164
3 P MOLD,
DARK OLIVE
GREEN
GLASS
11 1/4" TALL.
HEAVY
MOLD SEAMS

165
2 P MOLD, 5 9/16"
HIGH, DARK
ORANGE
AMBER
COLOR.
5 OZ. SIZE

PAPER
LABEL

GLASS
STOPPER

M.S.

SEAGRAM'S
CANADIAN WHISKY
SEALED AND BOTTLED IN BOND AT
WATERLOO, ONTARIO, CANADA.
CONTAINS 5 IMPERIAL OUNCES
FULLY RIPENED IN WOOD, BOTTLED AND SEALED IN BOND AT AGE
UNDER THE DOMINION GOVERNMENT EXCISE SUPERVISION. THE AGE
OF THIS BOTTLE IS GUARANTEED BY THE DOMINION GOVERNMENT, WITH THEIR AFFIXED SEAL OVER
EACH CAPSULE, SHOWING DATE OF MANUFACTURE

1" BY 2 5/8" BASE.

3 1/4" BY 3 1/4" BASE.

166
CONCAVE BASE
3 1/2" DIAM.

QUAKER CLUB
OLD R RYE
S.B. ROTHENBERG

167
FINISHED
FOR GLASS
STOPPER

2 P. MOLD, CLEAR
GLASS 6 1/4" TALL

PAPER
LABEL

ROGER
&
FILS
COGNAC

4 A

1" BY 2 3/8"

TWENTY-THREE

168
LEFT
PANEL READS
"ENGLAND" &
BACK SHOULDER
"REGD 610617"

M.S.

FINISHED
FOR
GLASS
STOPPER.

M.S.

RDON'S
RY GIN
LONDON

2 P. MOLD, 8 3/4" HIGH, GREEN GLASS.

169

M.S.

ROUGH THICK
M.S. AROUND
BASE = $3\frac{3}{4}$ IN
DIAM.

CONCAVE

M.S.

170

$2\frac{1}{4}$ BASE

3 P. MOLD, $8\frac{1}{2}$
TALL, CLEAR
GLASS

171

AMETHYST
COLOR
$6\frac{5}{8}$
TALL,
8 CUT
PANELS

BOTTLE DOES NOT STAND
IS 2 P. MOLD, 6" HIGH,
OF CLEAR GLASS
WITH MULTI-
COLORED
FLECKS

174

2 P. MOLD, DEEP
ORANGE AMBER
COLOR, 9" TALL

M.S.

$2\frac{11}{16}$ BASE
DIAM.

LANCASTER CO-OPERATIVE
N.Y.
GLASS WK'S

Simon

172

MADE
IN
FRANCE

$3\frac{1}{2}$ DIAM.
BASE

4 WELL
BOTTLE,
AMETHYST
COLOR $10\frac{1}{2}$
TALL.

SEVERAL VARI-
ATIONS IN STYLE
& FINISH OF THIS
BOTTLE, AS WELL
AS COLOR, & THEY
ARE STILL
BEING MADE.

$1\frac{7}{8}$ DIAM.
BASE

173

MILKY TO CLEAR
GLASS WITH OPAL
PALE BLUE DESIGN.
2 P. MOLD, 8" TALL
WITH GROUND
MOUTH.

PAGE TWENTY-FOUR.

89

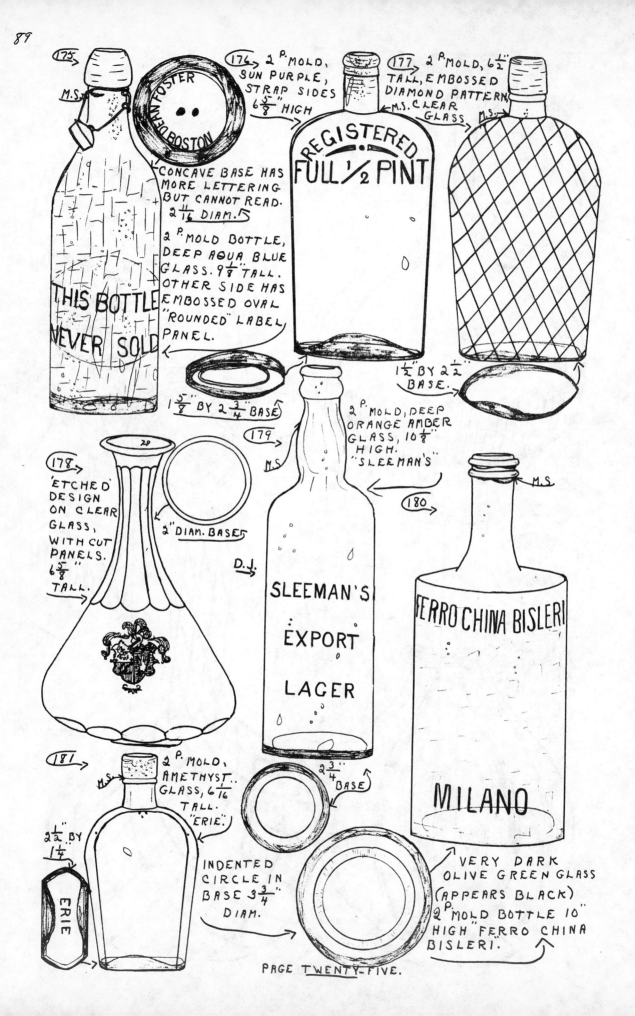

175 → M.S.

DEAN FOSTER BOSTON

176 → 2 P. MOLD, SUN PURPLE, STRAP SIDES 6⅜" HIGH

CONCAVE BASE HAS MORE LETTERING BUT CANNOT READ. 2¹¹⁄₁₆ DIAM.

2 P. MOLD BOTTLE, DEEP AQUA BLUE GLASS. 9⅛" TALL. OTHER SIDE HAS EMBOSSED OVAL "ROUNDED" LABEL PANEL.

THIS BOTTLE NEVER SOLD

1⅝" BY 2¾" BASE

177 → 2 P. MOLD, 6½ TALL, EMBOSSED DIAMOND PATTERN. M.S. CLEAR GLASS

M.S.

REGISTERED FULL ½ PINT

1½" BY 2½" BASE.

178 → 'ETCHED' DESIGN ON CLEAR GLASS, WITH CUT PANELS. 6⅝" TALL.

29

2" DIAM. BASE

179 → M.S.

2 P. MOLD, DEEP ORANGE AMBER GLASS, 10⅛" HIGH. "SLEEMAN'S"

180 →

M.S.

D.J. →

SLEEMAN'S EXPORT LAGER

2¾" BASE

FERRO CHINA BISLERI

MILANO

VERY DARK OLIVE GREEN GLASS (APPEARS BLACK) 2 P. MOLD BOTTLE 10" HIGH "FERRO CHINA BISLERI.

181 → M.S.

2 P. MOLD, AMETHYST GLASS, 6⁵⁄₁₆ TALL. "ERIE."

2½ BY 1¼

ERIE

INDENTED CIRCLE IN BASE 3¾" DIAM.

PAGE TWENTY-FIVE.

182 →

3 P. MOLD, CLEAR GLASS 8¾" TALL →

M.S.

2¾" BASE

183 →

M.S.

BACK IS EMBOSSED SIMILAR TO FRONT BUT LABEL PANEL IS LARGER AND BLANK.

2 P. MOLD, AMBER BROWN COLOR, 10¼" TALL →

E.P. ←

TRADE W MARK

2⅝" BY 4½" BASE

184 →

M.S.

CONCAVE CENTRE ON BASE 3" DIAM.

185 → M.S.

186 →

2 P. MOLD, DEEP AMBER GLASS 10 3/16" HIGH →

M.S.

P. B. & Co.

2¾" BASE →

2 P. MOLD, DEEP ORANGE AMBER COLORED GLASS 10⅛" TALL "THE O'KEEFE BREWERY CO. OF TORONTO LIMITED."

T. DAVIES & CO LAGER BEER TORONTO

M.S.

2 P. MOLD, AQUA GREEN GLASS, 9⅛" HIGH.

2⅝" BASE →

The O'Keefe Brewery Co of Toronto Limited

D.J. →

The O'Keefe Brewery Co Toronto Limited

"THE O'KEEFE BREWERY CO. TORONTO LIMITED.

PAGE TWENTY-SIX.

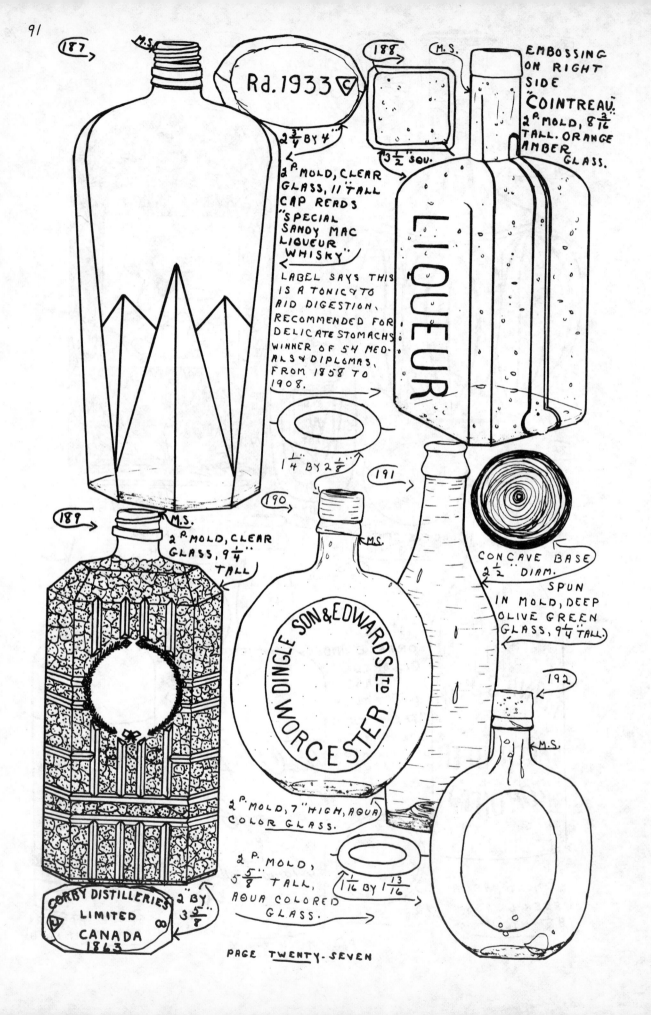

91

187 →

M.S.

Rd. 1933 ©

$2\frac{3}{4}$ BY 4"

2 P. MOLD, CLEAR GLASS, 11" TALL CAP READS "SPECIAL SANDY MAC LIQUEUR WHISKY"

LABEL SAYS THIS IS A TONIC & TO AID DIGESTION, RECOMMENDED FOR DELICATE STOMACHS. WINNER OF 54 MEDALS & DIPLOMAS FROM 1858 TO 1908. →

$1\frac{1}{4}$ BY $2\frac{1}{8}$"

188 →   M.S.

$3\frac{1}{2}$ SQU.

EMBOSSING ON RIGHT SIDE "COINTREAU". 2 P. MOLD, $8\frac{3}{16}$ TALL. ORANGE AMBER GLASS.

LIQUEUR

189 →

M.S.

2 P. MOLD, CLEAR GLASS, $9\frac{1}{4}$" TALL

CORBY DISTILLERIES LIMITED CANADA 1843

2" BY $3\frac{5}{8}$

190 →

M.S.

WM DINGLE SON & EDWARDS LTD WORCESTER

2 P. MOLD, 7" HIGH, AQUA COLOR GLASS.

2 P. MOLD, $5\frac{5}{8}$" TALL, AQUA COLORED GLASS.

$1\frac{1}{16}$ BY $1\frac{13}{16}$

191 →

CONCAVE BASE $2\frac{1}{2}$" DIAM.

SPUN IN MOLD, DEEP OLIVE GREEN GLASS, $9\frac{1}{4}$" TALL

192 →

M.S.

PAGE TWENTY-SEVEN

193 → PAPER LABEL, TAPERED DIP MOLD, QT., DARK OLIVE GREEN GLASS

A.B. →

WILLIAM DOW & COMPANY
INDIA PALE
L
MONTREAL

194 →

3 P. MOLD, DARK GREEN GLASS 8¾" TALL.

M.S.

COCA MARIANI

PARIS

195 →

M.S. →

COCA MARIANI FRANCE PARIS
E

CONCAVE BASE HAS RAISED SEAL WITH "E". BASE IS 3⅜" DIAM.

2 P. MOLD, VERY DARK OLIVE GREEN, 9½" TALL.

2¼" BASE
.B

196 →

M.S.

Catto's Whisky

197 →

2 P. MOLD, VERY DARK AMBER COLOR GLASS, 6½" TALL.

M.S. →

1.
1¼" BY 2¼"

198 →

M.S.

REINHARDT & CO'S

LAGER

TORONTO

A.B. →

2 P. MOLD, AMBER COLOR GLASS, 11" TALL.

3¾" DIAM.

2 P. MOLD, DARK GREEN GLASS, 10¼" TALL

2 6/16" BY 3¼"

PAGE TWENTY-EIGHT.

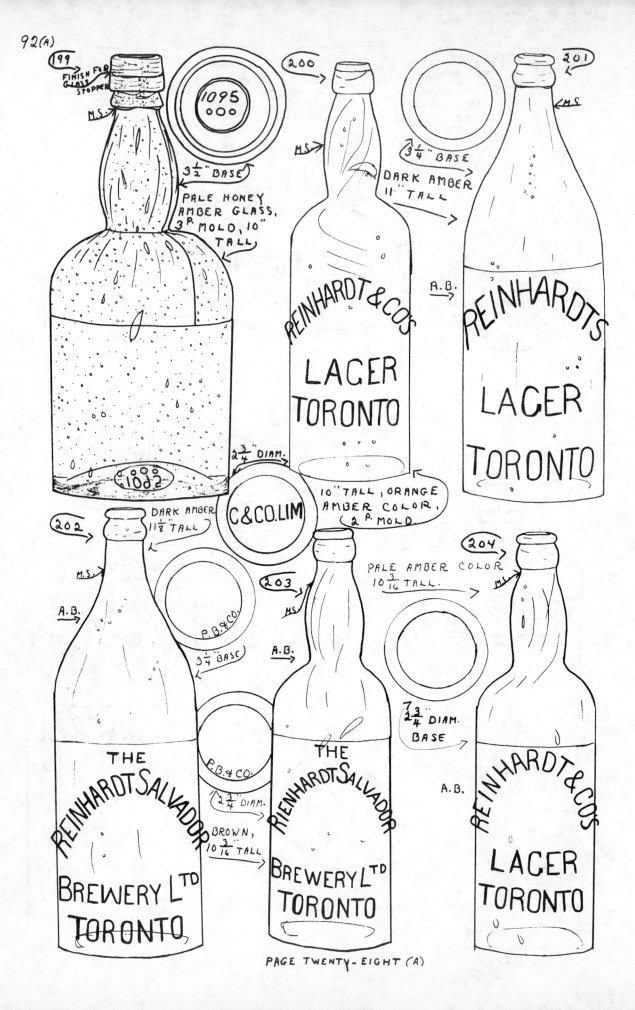

199 FINISH FOR GLASS STOPPER
M.S.
3½" BASE
1095 OOO
PALE HONEY AMBER GLASS, 3 P. MOLD, 10" TALL

200 MS
3¾" BASE
DARK AMBER 11" TALL
REINHARDT & CO'S LAGER TORONTO

201 MS
REINHARDTS LAGER TORONTO
A.B.

1002
2¾" DIAM.
C & CO. LIM
10" TALL, ORANGE AMBER COLOR, 2 P. MOLD

202 M.S. A.B.
DARK AMBER 11⅛" TALL
P.B.&CO.
3¾" BASE
THE REINHARDT SALVADOR BREWERY LTD TORONTO
P.B.&CO.
2¾" DIAM.
BROWN, 10 3/16 TALL

203 MS A.B.
THE REINHARDT SALVADOR BREWERY LTD TORONTO

204 M.
PALE AMBER COLOR 10 3/16 TALL
2¾" DIAM. BASE
A.B.
REINHARDT & CO'S LAGER TORONTO

205

OTHER SIDE SAYS
"B. GRANT & SONS
LAGER BEER
HAMILTON."

2 P. MOLD, AQUA
GLASS 9¼" TALL)

M.S.

C.L.

P G & SONS

2¾" DIAM.

2 P. MOLD,
ORANGE
AMBER C.
10¾" TALL

206

M.S.

GRANT'S SPRING BREWERY
Limited
HAMILTON

207

M.S.

2¾" DIAM.

AMBER COLOR
10" HIGH

C.L.

SLEEMAN'S
TRADE   MARK
EXPORT LAGER

2¾" BASE

208

M.S.

C.L.

2¾" DIAM.

AQUA GREEN
GLASS, 2 P. MOLD,
10" HIGH.

209

M.S.

PALE GREEN
GLASS,
10" HIGH

C.N. HEUTHER
BERLIN
LION BREWERY

2¾" DIAM.

210

M.S.

2 13/16" DIAM

GREY
GLASS
10" TALL

BERLIN
LION BREWERY.
C.N. HEUTHER PROP.
BERLIN ONT.

THE BIXEL BREWING & MALTING CO.
LIMITED.
BRANTFORD ONT.

94

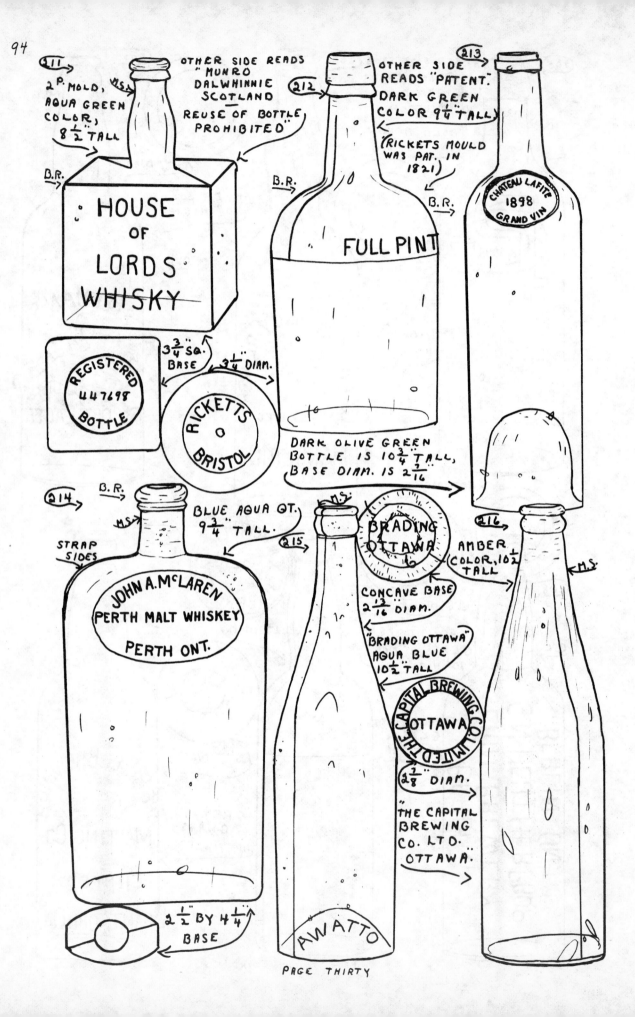

211
2 P. MOLD, V.S.?
AQUA GREEN
COLOR,
8½" TALL

OTHER SIDE READS
"MUNRO
DALWHINNIE
SCOTLAND

REUSE OF BOTTLE
PROHIBITED"

B.R.

HOUSE
OF
LORDS
WHISKY

REGISTERED
447698
BOTTLE

3¾" SQ.
BASE

3¼" DIAM.

RICKETTS
O
BRISTOL

212

B.R.

FULL PINT

B.R.

OTHER SIDE
READS "PATENT.
DARK GREEN
COLOR 9¼" TALL)

(RICKETTS MOULD
WAS PAT. IN
1821)

B.R.

213

CHATEAU LAFITE
1898
GRAND VIN

DARK OLIVE GREEN
BOTTLE IS 10¾" TALL,
BASE DIAM. IS 2 7/16"

214
B.R.
M.S.

STRAP
SIDES

BLUE AQUA QT.
9¾" TALL.

JOHN A. McLAREN
PERTH MALT WHISKEY
PERTH ONT.

2½" BY 4¼"
BASE

M.S.

215

BRADING
OTTAWA

CONCAVE BASE
2 13/16" DIAM.

"BRADING OTTAWA"
AQUA BLUE
10½" TALL

THE CAPITAL BREWING CO. LIMITED
OTTAWA

2⅞" DIAM.

"THE CAPITAL
BREWING
CO. LTD.
OTTAWA."

AWATTO

216

AMBER
COLOR, 10½"
TALL

M.S.

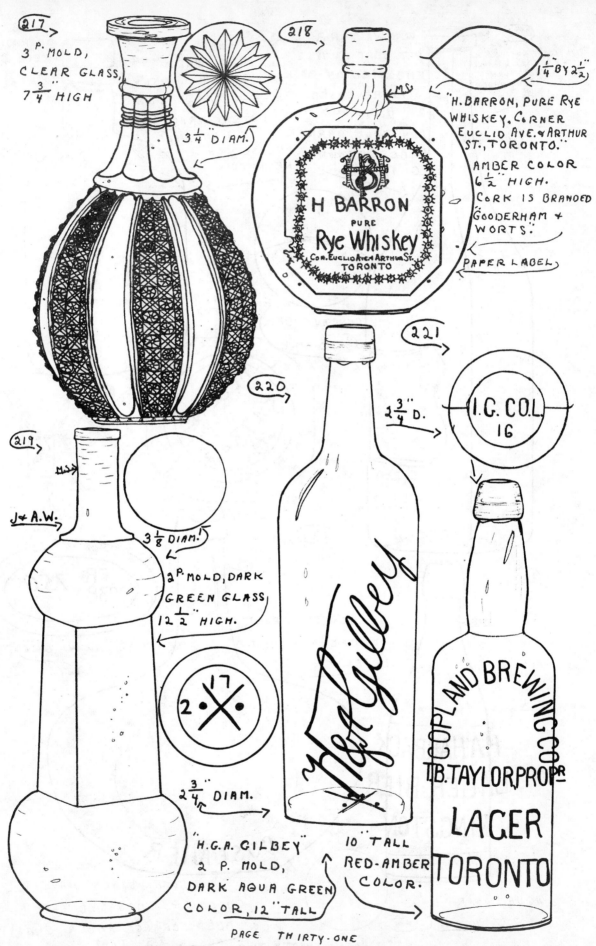

217 →
3 P. MOLD,
CLEAR GLASS,
7 3/4" HIGH

3 1/4" DIAM.

218 →

1 1/4 BY 2 1/2"

M.S.

"H. BARRON, PURE RYE
WHISKEY, CORNER
EUCLID AVE. & ARTHUR
ST., TORONTO."

AMBER COLOR
6 1/2" HIGH.
CORK IS BRANDED
GOODERHAM +
WORTS.

PAPER LABEL

H BARRON
PURE
Rye Whiskey
COR. EUCLID AVE. & ARTHUR ST.
TORONTO

221 →

I. G. CO.L.
16

220 →

2 3/4" D.

219 →

M.S.

J. & A.W.

3 1/8" DIAM.

2 P. MOLD, DARK
GREEN GLASS,
12 1/2" HIGH.

2 • 17 ✕

2 3/4" DIAM.

"H.G.A. GILBEY"
2 P. MOLD,
DARK AQUA GREEN
COLOR, 12" TALL

10" TALL
RED-AMBER
COLOR.

COPLAND BREWING CO.
T.B. TAYLOR, PROPR.
LAGER
TORONTO

PAGE THIRTY-ONE

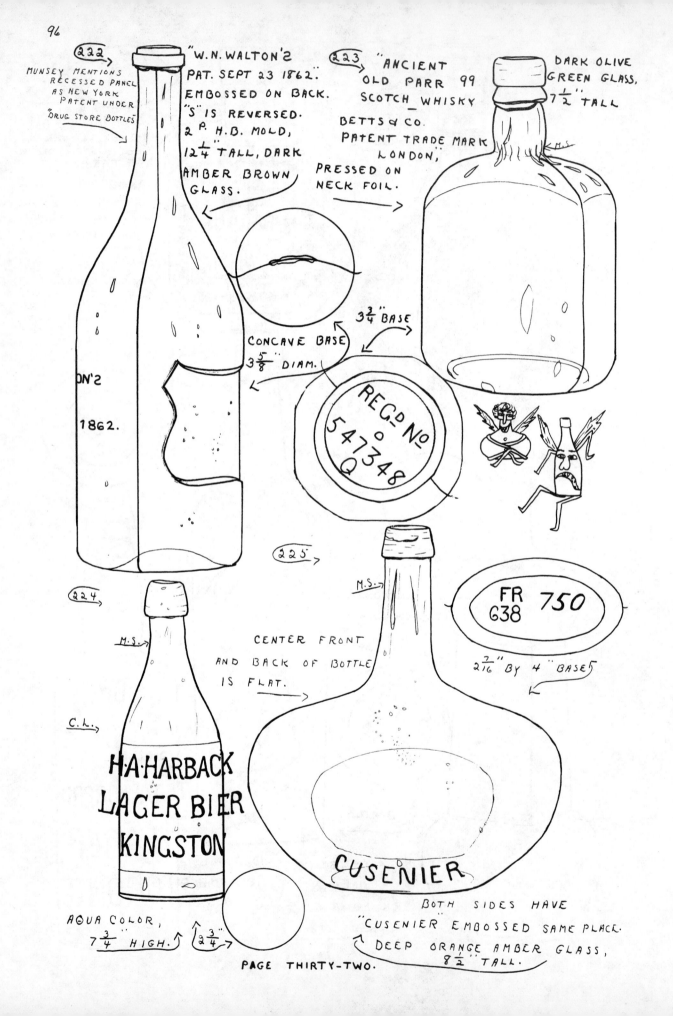

96

222 →
MUNSEY MENTIONS
RECESSED PANEL
AS NEW YORK
PATENT UNDER
"DRUG STORE BOTTLES"

"W.N. WALTON'S
PAT. SEPT 23 1862."
EMBOSSED ON BACK.
"S" IS REVERSED.
2 P. H.B. MOLD,
12¼" TALL, DARK
AMBER BROWN
GLASS.

223 →
"ANCIENT
OLD PARR 99
SCOTCH WHISKY
BETTS & CO.
PATENT TRADE MARK
LONDON,"
PRESSED ON
NECK FOIL.

DARK OLIVE
GREEN GLASS,
7½" TALL

ON'S
1862.

CONCAVE BASE
3⅝" DIAM.

3¾" BASE

REG.D N.O
547348
Q

225 →

224 →

M.S. →

C.L. →

H·A·HARBACK
LAGER BIER
KINGSTON

M.S. →

CENTER FRONT
AND BACK OF BOTTLE
IS FLAT. →

FR 750
638

2⁷⁄₁₆" BY 4" BASE

CUSENIER

AQUA COLOR,
7¾" HIGH.

2¾"

BOTH SIDES HAVE
"CUSENIER" EMBOSSED SAME PLACE.
DEEP ORANGE AMBER GLASS,
8½" TALL.

PAGE THIRTY-TWO.

226.

OLIVE GREEN
GLASS,
9½" TALL.

3 7/16" DIAM.

227.

BASE IS BIT CONCAVE
3 7/16" DIAM.

TURNED IN MOLD
BOTTLE, DARK
GREEN GLASS
12½" HIGH.

"King George IV"
Liqueur Whisky

The Distillers Company Ltd.
Edinburgh.

REGISTERED   TRADE MARK

Very Extra Special
A blend of the choicest Scotch Whiskies thoroughly
matured in Sherry Casks before being bottled

PRODUCE OF SCOTLAND

PAPER LABEL.

2 3/4" DIAM.
BASE.

230.

END OF
M.S.

228.

J. & A. W.   M.S.

OLD IRISH WHISKY

OLD
TRADE   MARK

MITCHELL & Co
OF BELFAST LTD.

F
6 X 9
B

15/16" BY 2"

AQUA COLOR,
6 1/8" HIGH.

1 1/4" BY 2 1/4"

ERIE

229.

M.S.

2 P. MOLD, CLEAR
GLASS, 10" HIGH.

J. & A. W.

AQUA COLORED GLASS
6½" HIGH. 2 P. MOLD.

C. N. HUETHER.
LION BREWERY
BERLIN ONT.

THIRTY-THREE

232 M.S.

J&A.W.

233

METAL BAND

L.D.L. Design Reg'd 1929

7 3/8" TALL, CLEAR GLASS. BOTH BOTTLES HAVE INDENTED CIRCLES AT SIDES.

234 M.S.

J&A.W.

10 1/4" TALL, CLEAR GLASS

Lindsay Distilleries Limited

Lindsay Distilleries Limited

RETURN THIS BOTTLE TO L.KUNTZ PARK BREWERY WATERLOO

2 1/2" BY 4" BASE

2 P. MOLD, DARK GREEN GLASS, 8 5/8" HIGH.

"SAUCE".

2 1/4" BY 3 1/2"

2 3/4" DIAM. BASE.

WATERLOO

AMBER GLASS 9 1/2" TALL

235

4

CONCAVE CIRCLE ON BASE 2 3/4" SQU.

AGUA GREEN GLASS, 11" HIGH.

2 5/8" BASE NO.236

R.G.&B CO 6

2 5/8" BASE NO.237

O·T

REGISTERED TRADE MARK THE PROPERTY OF O·T COY LONDON.N

236 M.S.

UNION BREWING CO. SHARON. PA.

237 M.S.

9 3/8" HIGH- AMBER YELLOW GLASS

Huebner TOLEDO

BEER

CONTENTS 12 FLUID

PURE AND WITHOUT DRUGS OR POISON

"UNION BREWING CO."

THIRTY-FOUR

IX   COSMETICS AND PERFUMES

A.   Cosmetics.

Cosmetics have been used from the time of the Queen of Sheba by women and there have been times in history when one would be hard pressed to decide just which sex used the most.

White Chio Paste to cover blemishes and a Vegetable Liquid Rouge "giving a colour so nearly resembling nature, as not to be distinguished by the most curious observer", were products of the late eighteenth century. A Protective Lotion to apply before going to bed with lousy people was said to offer no offence as it was odourless and invisable. Scott and McGee of Kingston sold Warren's Preventive to the Itch. "No matter how much a person may be exposed to unclean beds, or to people afflicted with the Itch, by applying a small quantity to the skin upon going to bed, they will be thoroughly guarded against infection." Who says 'the good old days'.

" 'Long hair is a glory to women' says Paul; and all feel the truth of this pious quotation" - in an advertisement that claimed many who had been bald for twenty years had restored their hair by using Balm of Columbia, a product of Comstock, Brockville. Oldridges Balm of Columbia was another hair product. East India Hair Dye would cover red or grey hair and was warranted by the gentleman who manufactured it "who is the celebrated Dr. Comstock, author of Comstock's Chemistry, Philosophy and many other works, well known and widely celebrated by the public".

Burnett's Cocaine produced noticeable results in one week to a man who had shaved his head because of illness. Mrs. S.A. Allen in offereing her Zylobalsamum to the public of Yarmouth, claimed it would not only colour and curl the hair but would also cure bad eye sight. "By its use Wigs, Spectacles and Grey Hair will soon be extinct." (1863)

Another popular product for the hair in the fourties and later was Bears Grease. Ross & Sons (England) claimed to fat and kill their own bears. They said that the length of hair obtained from some of the North American Indians was a sufficient answer to its effectiveness. It was declaimed by another source as being nothing else but perfumed beef-marrow, "in most cases creating a scurf on the head requiring considerable trouble to get rid of".

Hugh Miller, Toronto, manufactured creams and lotions. Atkinsons, also Toronto, recommended their cold cream for chapped hands and said it would 'keep good' for a long time, but because of its extensive sale it had to be made fresh every week anyway, (in 1863).

Recamier Toilet Preparations by Harriet Hubbard Ayers were advertised in 1890 - "Order direct of the Recamier Manufacturing Co., St. Paul St. Montreal", this if the druggist did not carry them. Sanitol tooth and toilet preparations were available in 1910, when by this time also were others - some still familiar.

IX   COSMETICS AND PERFUMES - cont'd

B.   Perfumes.

Perfumes are of four distinct classes, three from plants and the fourth of animal origin.

Class 1: The most ancient and in use from the earliest recorded period, consist of the various odoriferous gum-resins from trees, as myrrh and camphor, and used for incense and pastilles.

Class 2: Are those perfumes procured by distillation, adopted by the Greeks and Romans. Long before that time however fragrant waters were in use in Arabia. The old names for these pure odoriferous principles was Quintessence. Later they were termed Essential Oils, but by the 1850's were pretty much referred to as Otto's, from the Turkish word attar - familiar to us as 'Attar of Roses'. These are the oils used mainly for soaps, powders, flavourings etc.

Class 3: Are the perfumes proper, such as colognes. Most perfumes derived from flowers are not made from distillation, but by a process of enfleurage and maceration. It was a publication on the "Art of Perfumery" in the late 1860's that made this method generally known, although it had been in practise for over two centuries in the south of France. By placing fragrant flowers in grease the odour is absorbed by the fat, and by putting the fat in alcohol the odours leave the fat and enter the alcohol.

The method as described is more complicated however, as the flowers have to be changed frequently, the grease being worked each time; being enfleurée in this way for three weeks or more, generally for as long as the flowering season of the particular flower being used.

Maceration is the process of infusion of the flowers in oil or melted fat for several hours, when they are removed by straining and new flowers added, the oil in the meantime kept warm but not hot. This process is also repeated for the duration of the flowering season of the flowers used. The solid fat is chopped fine, put in alcohol and left about a month to extract the odour. In the case of the scented oil, it has to be agitated frequently with the alcohol.

Class 4: Are the perfumes of animal origin: Musk, Ambergris, Civet and Castor - the order of their importance.

Perfumes were used not only because of their pleasant odour, but also to mask the unpleasant. As late as 1890 washing the skin with ammonia and water was the recommended advice of a physician. He said that this was a better way of removing the unpleasant odour of perspiration than the application of costly unguents and perfumes so generally in use.

Smelling Salts were a popular item used to cover air odours as well as for ladies 'coming over with the vapours'. The manufacture of ornamental bottles to contain this preparation was an important branch of the glass and silver-smiths trade for many years.

Smelling Bottles of all sorts were for sale by Henry Taylor, Quebec, in 1764. Fine Cut Glass Ware from the Waterford Glass Works including Toilet Bottles were available at Wm. Rourke's of York in 1824. Lavender Bottles were among other bottle types listed by Budden & Vennor, Pointe-d-Calliere in 1839. Adam Reid, Toronto, offered an endless variety of shapes and styles in Toilette and Scent Bottles in 1857. "Direct from Bohemia and to which the attention of the ladies is respectfully directed."

Ryrie Bros., Toronto, 1897, advertised:
"SCENT BOTTLES - We are showing hundreds, literally hundreds of the choicest perfume bottles ever seen. They include all that is nice in cut glass, with sterling and gold mountings, ranging in price from 65¢ to $12.00 each. Some of the tops are set with choice miniatures - others with Turquoise, Jade and other stones. We have gold serpents entwined around the cut glass, whilst others again show 'dogsheads' in artistic enameling. Fancy a genuine cut glass perfume bottle 2¼" long, with a sterling top at 65¢".

Some perfume brands offered for sale in the 1850 and '60 era were - Spring Flowers, The Toronto and Collingwood Bouquets, Jockey Club, Bouquet de La Reine, Moussiline, Bouquet Caroline and others no stranger sounding than those of today. These were Lubin Perfumes "prepared only by H. Peareath Brumill (late F. Richardson), King St. E., Toronto".

John Maria Farina claimed to be the oldest distiller of cologne in 1844 and was offering his products for export to the British Empire in short or long bottles by the dozen and long green bottles in cases from 25 to 50 dozen.

The Davis & Lawrence Company of Montreal advertised their "Lotus of the Nile" as one of the most powerful and permanent perfumes ever prepared. "A single drop will be found sufficient to perfume a handkerchief or even a room. It is put up in the new style of glass stoppered bottle and sold." A bit overpowering should several choose the same for a party in 1885.

John A. Taylor, Chemist and Druggist, 45 Yonge St., Toronto, had soaps and perfumes of Gosnell & Co., England, for sale in 1855. In 1895, a John Taylor & Co. were advertising themselves as manufacturers of soaps and perfumes.

Scent bottles offer a wide range of styles and colours to the bottle collector, as do the barber bottles (on the preferred list of many). The embossed bottles that held various kinds of lotions are interesting; many of these products have disappeared from the market to be replaced with newer brands. Some of the cream jars were manufactured in styles that are different from the plain round in common use in milk glass today and are not exactly to be sneezed at.

References

Belleville Phoenix - 1833
Byetown Gazette - 1840
East Kent Plaindealer - 1890
Kingston Gasette - 1818
La Gazette de Quebec - 1764
London Daily Register - (England) 1784
London Times - (England) 1842
Montreal Transcript - 1839
Musical Visitor, The - (Duart, Ont.) 1887
Toronto Globe - 1855-57-59-63-85-90-95-97- 1910
Toronto Star - 1844
Upper Canada Gazette - (York) 1824
Yarmouth Herald - 1863

References re Food & Dairies

Chambers Information for the People, 1842

Papers -

Weekly Register - (York) 1822
The Globe - (Toronto) 1845, 46, 48, 57, 59, 67, 68, 74, 80, 92, 96, 98, 1900, 06
Toronto Examiner - 1843
Cobourg Star - 1846.

References re Miscellaneous

Grand River Satchem - 1867; Hamilton Gazette - 1853; La Gazette de Quebec - 1765; Montreal Transcript - 1839; Toronto Examiner - 1840, 45; Toronto Globe - 1870, 84; Toronto Herald - 1844; Toronto Morning Star & Toronto Transcript - 1843; Upper Canada Gazette, (York) - 1822; Yarmouth Herald, N.S. - 1848.

COKE DANDRUFF CURE
MADE IN U.S.A 3
DIP THE COMB IN THE BOTTLE
DR ELLIS SPECIAL QUICK DRY WAVING FLUID WAVESET
24
HAIR BALSAM
PARKER'S
4
HAIR HEALTH
HAY'S
HOUBICANT 1
87
HOYT'S GERMAN COLOGNE E.W. HOYT & CO LOWELL MASS.
MADE IN CANADA 3
7
7000 7
8 1
POND'S 3 11 MADE IN CANADA
3083 C 3 4
3083 8
MADE IN CANADA MUM 7
77

1. M.S. 1" BY 3" BASE. 2P. MOLD, CLEAR COLOR, 6¼" TALL.

2. M.S. 1½" BY 2¼" BASE. 2P. MOLD, SUN YELLOW, 6⅛" HIGH. IT'S NOT OLD, BUT IT SURE IS FANCILY EMBOSSED.

3. 1⅜" BY 2⅜" BASE. M.S. DEEP AMBER COLOR, 2P. MOLD 6¾" HIGH. 4 INDENTED PANELS, FRONT & SIDES WITH EMBOSSING. LEFT SIDE SAYS "NEW YORK".

4. M.S. 1⅛" BY 2½" BASE. 2P. MOLD, 7½" TALL, 4 INDENTED PANELS, 2 WITH EMBOSSED LETTERS. AMBER BROWN COLOR.

5. M.S. BRASS LID 1 3/16" DIAM. SIDE TAB SAYS "PUSH ON BOTH ENDS" & "PAT. 8-2-21". LID NOT SUPPOSED TO COME OFF, BUT I TOOK IT OFF TO WASH THIS POWDER BOTTLE 5⅞" TALL. CLEAR GLASS, 2P. MOLD, WITH 3 FRONT, 3 BACK & 2 SIDE PANELS. 1⅛" BY 1⅞" BASE.

6. CONCAVE CIRCLE IN BASE 1¼" DIAM. END OF M.S. 2P. MOLD CLEAR COLOR 3 9/16" TALL. EMBOSSED LETTERS SAY "HOYT'S GERMAN COLOGNE E.W. HOYT & CO. LOWELL, MASS." THIS PRODUCT CAME IN 3 SIZES & WAS ADVERTIZED IN AN EARLY 'EATON' CATALOGUE TO BE USED IN THE BATH, ON HANDKERCHIEF & CLOTHES ETC. PRICE 25¢, 50¢, $1.00

7. M.S. 2" DIAM. BASE WITH INDENTED CIRCLE. 2⅞" HIGH, 2P. MOLD, WHITE (MILK GLASS) MADE LARGER & SMALLER, CONTAINED "LADY ESTHER" FACE CREAM.

8. M.S. 1¾" DIAM. BASE. SPICE. 2P. MOLD, MILK GLASS 4⅞" TALL.

9. M.S. INDENTED CIRCLE IN BASE 2¾" DIAMETER. CREAM JAR 3 9/16" HIGH, 2P. MOLD, MILK GLASS.

10. M.S. 1¾" SQUARE BASE. 2P. MOLD 3" TALL, MILK GLASS.

11. M.S. 3⅛" BY 3½" BASE. MADE IN OTHER SIZES. 2P. MOLD, MILK GLASS, VERY HEAVY, 3" TALL.

12. BASE 2¼" DIAM. M.S. 2P. MOLD, MILK GLASS 2" TALL.

13. M.S. BASE 2⅛" DIAM. SAME AS 12 BUT DIFFERENT TOP.

14. BASE 1¾" DIAM. 2P. MOLD, MILK GLASS, 1" TALL.

15. 1 11/16" DIAM. ¾" HIGH. 2P. MOLD, MILK GLASS.

BEAUTY AIDS
PAGE ONE

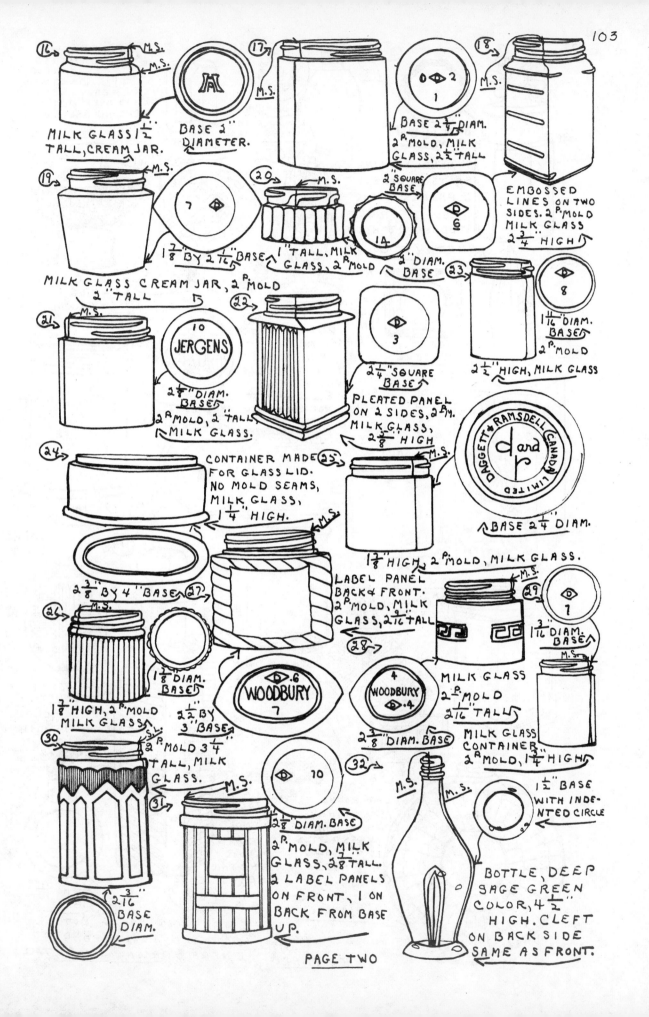

33 → M.S.

BASE 1¼ BY 1½ FLAT

2 P. MOLD, SMELLING SALTS BOTTLE. 6 PANELS, NECK GROUND FOR GLASS STOPPER. 2¾ HIGH AMETHYST COLOR.

34 → M.S.

DESIGN PAT. 135236

DIAM. BASE 2 P. MOLD, CLEAR GLASS 2¼ TALL

35 →

THIS WEE BOTTLE IS 2" HIGH & RUBY LINED WITH VERY HEAVY CLEAR GLASS OVER IT. HELD SMELLING SALTS WHEN I FOUND IT.

½ BY ¾ BASE

36 → END OF M.S.

A.S. Hinds — Portland Me.

CONCAVE CIRCLE IN BASE 2½ SQU.

2 P. MOLD, CLEAR COLOR 6¼ TALL EMBOSSED LETTERS SAY "A.S. HINDS, PORTLAND ME."

37 →

2 P. MOLD GREEN SATIN GLASS, 4" TALL INCLUDING BAKELITE LID. (STAND) LILY'S HAVE TRACES OF WHITE PAINT.

38 →

NECK GROUND FOR STOPPER — M.S. FOR STOPPER

2 P. MOLD, BRIGHT GREEN COLOR, 2 1/16 TALL

1" BY 2 1/16 BASE

39 → M.S.

1¼ BY 1½ BASE

2 P. MOLD, YELLOW COLOR, 2" HIGH. NECK GROUND FOR STOPPER

40 →

OLA JEN "REGISTERED"

NOT COSMETIC – "TONIC" EMBOSSED ON TIN LID

DEEP INDENTED CIRCLE 3 1/8 DIAM BASE

2 P. MOLD, 3 5/8 TALL, MILK GLASS.

M.S.

41 →

2" DIAM. BASE

2 P. MOLD, MILK GLASS, 3¼ TALL.

42 → M.S.

2 3/8 BASE WITH INDENTED CIRCLE

89

2 P. MOLD, DARK AMETHYST COLOR 3½ HIGH.

43 → M.S.

2 1/8 BY 2¾ BASE

2 P. MOLD, AMETHYST COLOR VERY THICK & HEAVY GLASS 6 5/16 HIGH

44 → M.S. — GROUND MOUTH

7/16 BY 5/8 BASE

2 P. MOLD, CLEAR GLASS 1 7/8 HIGH

GLASS CROWN STOPPER

45 → M.S.

1¼ BY 1 7/8 BASE

FLAT ROUND FLASK-LIKE WHITE CAMPHOR GLASS BOTTLE IS 2 P. MOLD, 4 9/16 HIGH. IT IS 1" WIDE FRONT TO BACK & 4" DIAMETER.

NOT OLD BUT NICE BOTTLE.

46 → M.S.

½ BY 11/16 BASE

"SMELLING SALTS" BOTTLE. 2 P. MOLD, POLISHED, DEEP EMERALD GREEN COLOR 2¼ TALL

PAGE THREE

47 END OF M.S. 4-2 3/8 BY 7/16 BASE. 2 P. MOLD, CLEAR COLOR, 2 1/4 HIGH. EMBOSSED LETTERS SAY "C&Co." THREADING IS IMPRESSION ONLY.

48 7/16 BY 5/8 BASE

49 2 P. MOLD, CLEAR GLASS, 3 1/16 TALL. LABEL ON FRONT READS "CRAB APPLE BLOSSOM. JOHN TAYLOR & Co. TORONTO." BACK HAS EMBOSSED LETTERS SAYING "TAYLOR'S PERFUMES." M.S.

M.S. 2 P. MOLD, 2 3/8" HIGH. PALE GOLDEN AMBER AT TOP DEEPENING ALMOST TO RED NEAR BASE. PAPER LABEL SAYS "WHITE ROSE, JACOBI PERFUMES, TORONTO. END 3/16 DIAM. BASE

50 M.S. 1/4 BY 5/8 BASE. 2 P. MOLD, CLEAR GLASS, 1 7/8 TALL

51 M.S. 3/4 DIAM. BASE. 2 P. MOLD CLEAR GLASS, 2 1/4 TALL. LABEL READS "NEW HORIZONS CIRO." HAS GLASS DOBBER ON STOPPER

52 Lotus by Yardley 7/16 DIAM. BASE "LOTUS" BY YARDLEY 2 P. MOLD CLEAR GLASS 7/8 HIGH

53 T.C.W Co 3/4 DIAM. BASE GOLD CORD M.S. GARDENIA MOUNARD BRASSE PARIS 2 P. MOLD, CLEAR GLASS 2" HIGH. LABEL READS "GARDENIA, MOUNARD BRASSE, PARIS."

54 GROUND TOP M.S.

LUCIEN LELONG MADE IN FRANCE 2 P. MOLD, 1 7/8 TALL, DARK BLUE COLOR. 7/16 BY 5/8 BASE

55 M.S. T.C.W Co 1 USA 2 P. MOLD, CLEAR GLASS, 2" TALL. 1 1/8 DIAM. BASE

56 1/2 SQU. BASE 2 P. MOLD, CLEAR COLOR, 1 1/2 TALL. LABEL READS "REFLEXIONS, CIRO."

57 3/8 BY 3/4 M.S. BASE CAMPHOR STOPPER 2 P. MOLD, CLEAR GLASS, 2" HIGH. LABEL SAYS "DU BARRY." RICHARD HUDNUT NEW YORK

SCREW TOP IS GROUND FOR STOPPER UNDER HEAVY METAL CAP BOTTLE IS M.S. 2 P. MOLD, CLEAR GLASS, 1 1/2 HIGH

59 M.S. 7/16 BY 3/4 BASE 2 P. MOLD, CLEAR COLOR, 2" TALL. GLASS STOPPER HAS THREADED BASE & GOES THROUGH CORK.

60 2 P. MOLD, CLEAR GLASS, 2 7/8 TALL & HAS WHITE ENAMEL DOTS ON IT. LABEL READS "LILIANELLE, PINAUD." STICKER ON BACK SAYS "WILKENSON, DEPOT FOR TORONTO" 3/4 DIAM. BASE 61-5.4

61 M.S. 1/4 BY 5/8 BASE 2 P. MOLD, AMETHYST COLOR 1 3/4 HIGH

63 2 P. MOLD CANARY M.S. YELLOW COLOR 1 1/2 TALL 9/16 SQU. BASE

63 M.S. 7/8 DIAM. BASE

64 M.S. 3/8 BY 7/8 BASE 2 P. MOLD, 1 13/16 HIGH, APPLE GREEN COLOR

65 2 P. MOLD, EMERELD GREEN COLOR 3 1/4 TALL NECK M.S. GROUND FOR STOPPER

66 2 P. MOLD, ORANG AMBER COLOR, 1 3/8 HIGH. LABEL READS "WOOD VIOLET, JACOBI PERFUMES TORONTO." 5/16 BY 3/8 BASE

2 P. MOLD, SUN PURPLE COLOR 2 1/16 HIGH

67 M.S. 7/8 DIAM. BASE 2 P. MOLD, AMETHYST COLOR, 2 1/16 HIGH. EMBOSSING ON BACK READS "TAYLORS PERFUMES."

68 M.S. MADE IN FRANCE 3/4 DIAM. BASE. 2 P. MOLD, CLEAR GLASS, 1 5/8" HIGH. TOP OF NECK IS GROUND, AS IS INSIDE FOR STOPPER.

69 M.S. 2 P. MOLD, AMETHYST COLOR, 2 1/4 HIGH. 3/4 DIAM. BASE

70 M.S. 5/8 DIAM. BASE 2 P. MOLD, CLEAR GLASS 1 5/8 HIGH

71 M.S. 1/4 BY 5/8 BASE 2 P. MOLD, 1 1/4 TALL, AMETHYST COLOR.

SPACE SHORTAGE? NO PROBLEM WITH MINIATURES. TAKE A NICE DEEP FRAME, CUT BACK TO FIT FROM PLY-WOOD, PAD WELL WITH QUILT BATT, COVER WITH VELVET. DITTO THE FRAME. EDGE WITH TRIM, FASTEN BACK IN. ARRANGE BOTTLES & HOLD IN PLACE WITH MATCHING ELASTIC THREAD. NOW HANG IT ON THE WALL.

106

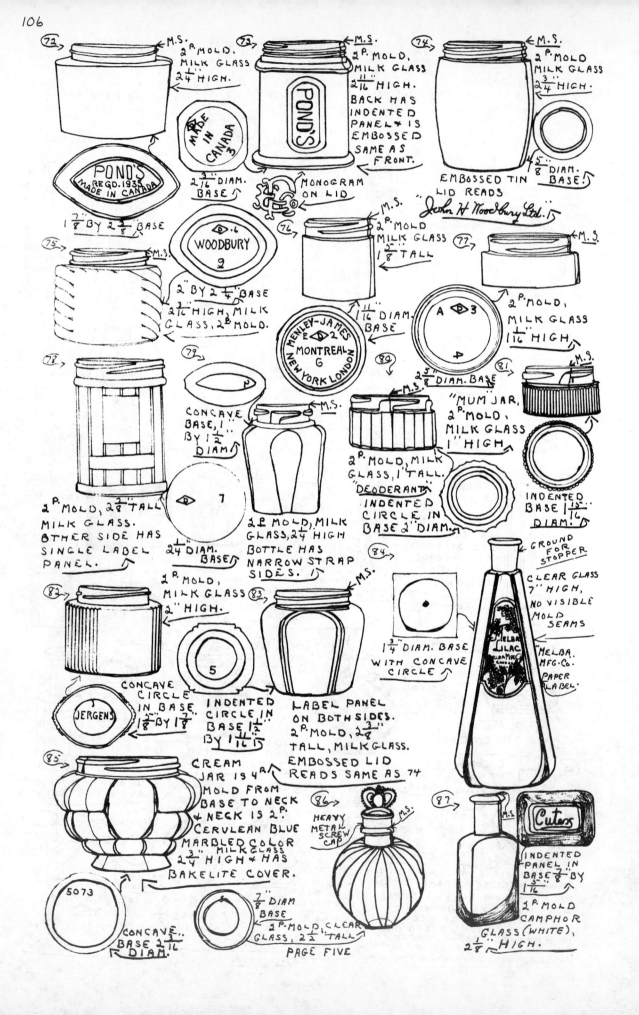

72 → M.S. 2 P. MOLD, MILK GLASS 2 1/4" HIGH.

POND'S REGD. 1935 MADE IN CANADA
1 7/8 BY 2 7/8" BASE

MADE IN CANADA 3
2 3/16" DIAM. BASE

73 → M.S. 2 P. MOLD, MILK GLASS 2 11/16" HIGH. BACK HAS INDENTED PANEL & IS EMBOSSED SAME AS FRONT.

POND'S

MONOGRAM ON LID

74 → M.S. 2 P. MOLD MILK GLASS 2 3/4" HIGH.

EMBOSSED TIN LID READS
John H. Woodbury Ltd.

5/8" DIAM. BASE

75 → M.S.
2" BY 2 1/4" BASE 2 3/16" HIGH, MILK GLASS, 2 P. MOLD.

WOODBURY 9

76 → M.S. 2 P. MOLD MILK GLASS 2 5/8" TALL
1 11/16" DIAM. BASE

MENLEY-JAMES MONTREAL NEW YORK LONDON

77 → M.S. 2 P. MOLD, MILK GLASS 1 11/16" HIGH

A ◇ 3 4

78 → 2 P. MOLD, 2 7/8" TALL MILK GLASS. OTHER SIDE HAS SINGLE LABEL PANEL.

79 → CONCAVE BASE, 1" BY 1 1/2" DIAM
◇ 7
2 1/4" DIAM. BASES

2 P. MOLD, MILK GLASS, 2 1/4" HIGH BOTTLE HAS NARROW STRAP SIDES. 1"

M.S.
2 P. MOLD, MILK GLASS, 1" TALL. "DEODERANT" INDENTED CIRCLE IN BASE 2" DIAM.
2 5/8" DIAM. BASE
80

81 → M.S. "MUM JAR, 2 P. MOLD, MILK GLASS 1" HIGH INDENTED BASE 1 15/16" DIAM.

82 → 2 P. MOLD, MILK GLASS 2" HIGH.
5
CONCAVE CIRCLE IN BASE 1 7/8" BY 1 7/8"
JERGENS

83 → M.S.
INDENTED CIRCLE IN BASE 1 1/2" BY 1 11/16"
LABEL PANEL ON BOTH SIDES. 2 P. MOLD, 2 3/8" TALL, MILK GLASS. EMBOSSED LID READS SAME AS 74.

84 → 1 3/4" DIAM. BASE WITH CONCAVE CIRCLE

GROUND FOR STOPPER
CLEAR GLASS 7" HIGH, NO VISIBLE MOLD SEAMS
MELBA LILAC MELBA MFG. CO.
"MELBA MFG. CO. PAPER LABEL.

85 → CREAM JAR 1 P. MOLD FROM BASE TO NECK & NECK IS 2 P. CERULEAN BLUE MARBLED COLOR MILK GLASS 2 1/4" HIGH & HAS BAKELITE COVER.
5073
CONCAVE BASE 2 1/16" DIAM.

7/8" DIAM BASE 2 P. MOLD, CLEAR GLASS, 2 1/2" TALL
PAGE FIVE

86 → HEAVY METAL SCREW CAP M.S.

87 → Cutex M.S.
INDENTED PANEL IN BASE 7/8" BY 3/16"
2 P. MOLD CAMPHOR GLASS (WHITE), 2 7/8" HIGH.

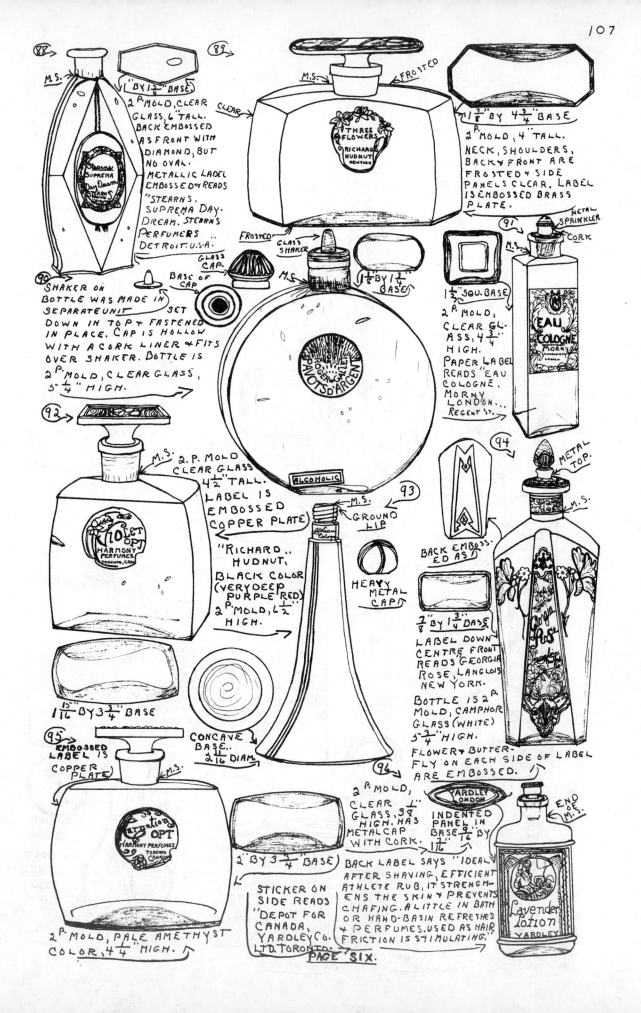

88 →
M.S.
1" BY 1 1/4" BASE
2 P. MOLD, CLEAR GLASS, 6" TALL. BACK EMBOSSED AS FRONT WITH DIAMOND, BUT NO OVAL. METALLIC LABEL EMBOSSED & READS "STEARNS. SUPREMA DAY-DREAM. STEARNS PERFUMERS .. DETROIT. U.S.A.

Stearns SUPREMA Day Dream STEARNS

89 →
CLEAR
CLEAR
FROSTED
THREE FLOWERS RICHARD HUDNUT NEW YORK

FROSTED
1 2/8" BY 4 3/4" BASE
2 P. MOLD, 4" TALL. NECK, SHOULDERS, BACK & FRONT ARE FROSTED & SIDE PANELS CLEAR. LABEL IS EMBOSSED BRASS PLATE.

90 SHAKER ON BOTTLE WAS MADE IN SEPARATE UNIT. SET DOWN IN TOP & FASTENED IN PLACE. CAP IS HOLLOW WITH A CORK LINER & FITS OVER SHAKER. BOTTLE IS 2 P. MOLD, CLEAR GLASS, 5 1/4" HIGH.

FROSTED
GLASS SHAKER
GLASS CAP.
BASE OF CAP
M.S.
1 1/8" BY 1 3/4" BASE

ROGER & GALLET PAVOTS D'ARGEN
ALCOHOLIC

91
METAL SPRINKLER
CORK
M.S.
1 1/2" SQU. BASE
2 P. MOLD, CLEAR GLASS, 4 3/4" HIGH. PAPER LABEL READS "EAU COLOGNE. MORNY LONDON .. REGENT ST.

EAU COLOGNE MORNY

92 →
M.S. 2.P. MOLD CLEAR GLASS 4 1/2" TALL. LABEL IS EMBOSSED COPPER PLATE "RICHARD .. HUDNUT, BLACK COLOR (VERY DEEP PURPLE RED) 2 P. MOLD, 6 1/2" HIGH.

VIOLET OPT HARMONY PERFUMES TORONTO, CAN.

1 15/16" BY 3 3/4" BASE

93
M.S.
GROUND LIP
HEAVY METAL CAPS
CONCAVE BASE.. 2 1/16 DIAM

96 →
2 P. MOLD, CLEAR GLASS, 3 1/8" HIGH. HAS METAL CAP WITH CORK.

94 →
METAL TOP.
M.S.
BACK EMBOSSED AS 1
2/8" BY 1 3/4" BASE
LABEL DOWN CENTRE FRONT READS GEORGIA ROSE, LANGLOIS NEW YORK. BOTTLE IS 2 P. MOLD, CAMPHOR GLASS (WHITE) 5 3/4" HIGH. FLOWER & BUTTERFLY ON EACH SIDE OF LABEL ARE EMBOSSED.

Georgia Rose Langlois

95
EMBOSSED LABEL IS COPPER PLATE
M.S.

Carnation OPT HARMONY PERFUMES TORONTO CANADA

2 P. MOLD, PALE AMETHYST COLOR, 4 1/4" HIGH.

2" BY 3 3/4" BASE
STICKER ON SIDE READS "DEPOT FOR CANADA, YARDLEY Co. LTD. TORONTO.

YARDLEY LONDON
INDENTED PANEL IN BASE 9/16" BY 1 1/16".
BACK LABEL SAYS "IDEAL AFTER SHAVING, EFFICIENT ATHLETE RUB, IT STRENGTHENS THE SKIN & PREVENTS CHAFING. A LITTLE IN BATH OR HAND-BASIN REFRESHES & PERFUMES. USED AS HAIR FRICTION IS STIMULATING.

END OF M.S.
Lavender Lotion YARDLEY

PAGE SIX.

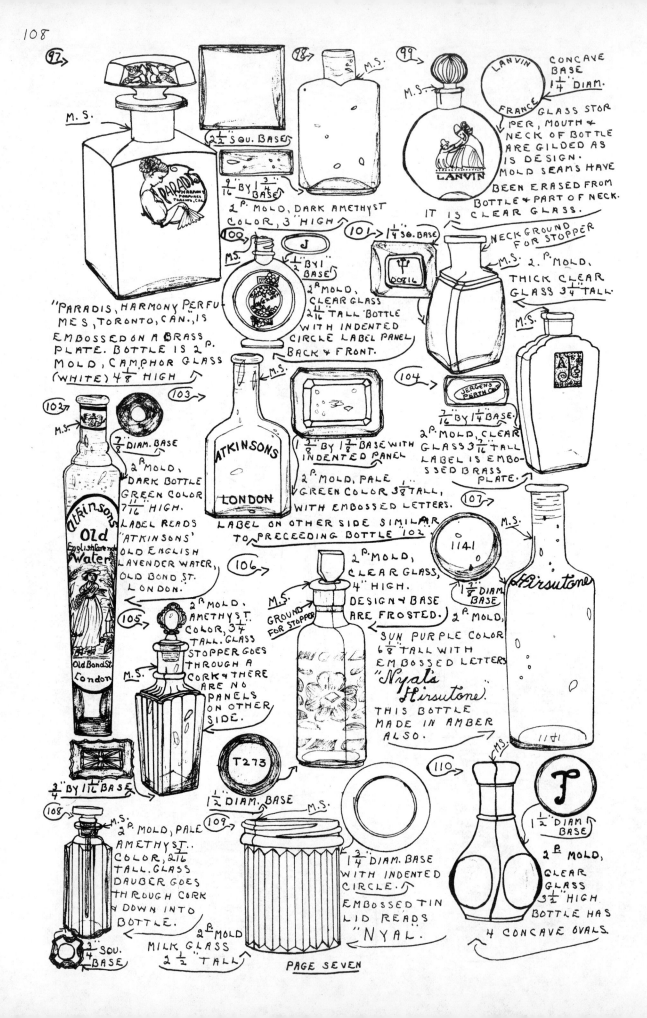

111 M.S. G.P. GLYCERINE

1 5/8" DIAM. BASE

HIGH SHOULDERS ON THIS 3 P. MOLD, AMETHYST COLOR, 5 12/16" HIGH BOTTLE. EMBOSSING ON SHOULDER READS "LARKIN SOAP CO."

GLYCERINE CO.

112 SLIGHTLY CONCAVE BASE 1 3/4" DIAM

49

113 2 P. MOLD, CLEAR GLASS 8" TALL & INDENTED LABEL PANEL ON ONE SIDE

FLORIDA WATER MURRAY & LANMAN DRUGGISTS NEW YORK

2 P. MOLD, AQUA BLUE COLOR 5 15/16" TALL WITH EMBOSSED LETTERS.

M.S. 2 1/2" DIAM. BASE

EMBOSSED LETTERS ON OTHER SIDE SAY "THIS BOTTLE IS OWNED BY JONES BROS & CO, LTD. TORONTO, ONT. CANADA.

THIS B IS OWNE JONES BRO TORONTO CANAD

116 M.S. M.S. M.S.

PALM OLIVE

2 1/8" DIAM. BASE 2 3/4" TALL, SKIM MILK BLUE COLOR. (MILK GLASS)

2 P. MOLD, WHITE (MILK GLASS) 2 3/16" TALL WITH INDENTED PANEL & EMBOSSED LETTERS.

114 M.S. EMBOSSED

Penslabs

1 5/8" DIAM. BASE

115 P. P.64

1 3/4" BY 2 7/8" BASE

2 P. MOLD, AMETHYST, 7 3/8" TALL

ROGER & GALLET R.G. PARIS

2 P. MOLD, 3 1/2" TALL, CLEAR GLASS WITH EMBOSSED LETTERING.

117 1 3/4" SQ. BASE

EL CAYA 1541

2 P. MOLD, CLEAR GLASS 6 15/16" TALL

121 34

1 1/4" BY 1 7/8" BASE

119 2 3/16" DIAM. BASE 357

120 M.S.

8 FL. OZ. NEWBRO'S HERPICIDE FOR THE SCALP

M.S.

CAMPANA'S ITALIAN BALM

M.S.

Danderine THE HAIR

2 P. MOLD, CLEAR GLASS, 4 1/2" HIGH. LABEL ON BOTH SIDES WITH FURTHER DIRECTIONS FOR USE ON BACK.

118 M.S. METAL SHAKER THROUGH CORK STOPPER

1181

1 1/2" BY 2 1/4" BASE 2 P. MOLD, SUN PURPLE COLOR, 7" HIGH

M.S. M.S.

NOX ZEMA

2" HIGH, COBALT BLUE, 8 PANELS. HAVE SEEN ONE IN CLEAR GLASS

1 5/8" DIAM. BASE 1" BY 1 7/8" BASE

2 P. MOLD, PALE AMETHYST COLOR EMBOSSED LABEL PANEL ON FRONT ONLY.

PAGE EIGHT

122 123 M.S. M.S.

5/8" BY 1 7/16" BASE

7/8" DIAM. BASE

NECK IS ROLLED TO FORM MOUTH. 3 P. MOLD FROM BASE UP, WHITE COLOR (MILK GLASS) BOTTLE 8 1/16" HIGH

2 P. MOLD, GROUND FOR STOPPER, CLEAR GLASS 3 5/16" TALL. LABEL READS "IDEAL R'G'D. ORCHID PERFUME. SOVEREIGN PERFUMES, LTD. TORONTO."

LABEL LABEL

124

4 P. MOLD PERFUME BOTTLE. 2" HIGH CLEAR GLASS M.S.

1 1/16" SQU. BASE

METAL SHAKER CAP

125 1 1/2" DIAM. BASE

126 MOUTH & SEAMS POLISHED. EMERALD GREEN COLOR. 3/4" HIGH.

Ed Pinaud
A

2 1/4" DIAM. BASE

2 P. MOLD, CLEAR GLASS, 6 3/4" HIGH WITH EMBOSSED DESIGN & LETTERING. HAS LABEL IN FRENCH & ENGLISH LABEL SAYS "A LITTLE OF THIS DELIGHTFUL AND REFRESHING PREPARATION APPLIED DAILY TO THE ROOTS OF THE HAIR AND THOROUGHLY MASSAGED INTO THE SCALP WILL BE FOUND MOST EXCELLENT IN REMOVING DANDRUFF, BEAUTIFYING THE HAIR AND PREVENTING IT FROM FALLING OUT."

E.D. PINAUD PARIS

127 SPUN IN MOLD DRESSER BOTTLE. HAS WHITE ENAMEL DAISIES WITH COLOR'D CENTER.

2 3/8" CONCAVE BASE.

GROUND LIP. CLEAR GLASS 4 1/2" TALL

2 3/8" BY 3/4" BASE

128 M.S. M.S.

Witch Hazel

GOB OF GLASS 4 P. MOLD, CLEAR GLASS 4" TALL. LETTERING & DECORATION DONE IN ENAMELS.

129 NECK IS FOLDED TO INSIDE TO FORM MOUTH
M.S.

DEEP INDENTED BASE 2" DIAM.

6 P. MOLD, CLEAR & OPALESCENT DRESSER BOTTLE IS 4 3/4" HIGH

130 M.S.

AYER

1 7/16" BY 3 1/8" BASE

2 P. MOLD, AQUA BLUE COLOR. 9 7/16" HIGH.

"AYER'S HAIR VIGOR" BOTTLE WAS SOLD WRAPPED RATHER THAN LABELED. DIRECTIONS WERE PRINTED IN FOUR LANGUAGES & PART AS FOLLOWS — "THIS REMEDY CLEANS THE PORES OF THE SCALP, PREVENTS FALLOUT OF HAIR & PROMOTES A GENTLE SOFT HAIR GROWTH. IT RESTORES THE NATURAL COLOR OF GREYING AND FADING HAIR AND LOST HAIR OFTEN GROWS BACK FROM USE OF SAME. IT CONTAINS NEITHER OIL NOR DYE & WILL NOT SOIL WHITE CLOTH IN RETAINING THE COLOR. SHAKE THE BOTTLE THEN DAMP AND RUB HAIR DAILY WITH IT, TO HINDER FALLOUT & PROMOTE GROWTH. FOR HAIR DRESSING SHAKE" ETC. PRINTED ON BASE— "ENTERED ACCORDING TO ACT OF CONGRESS IN THE YEAR OF 1867, BY J.C. AYER Co. TO THE CLERK'S OFFICE OF THE DISTRICT COURT OF THE DISTRICT OF MASSACHUSETTS."

PAGE NINE

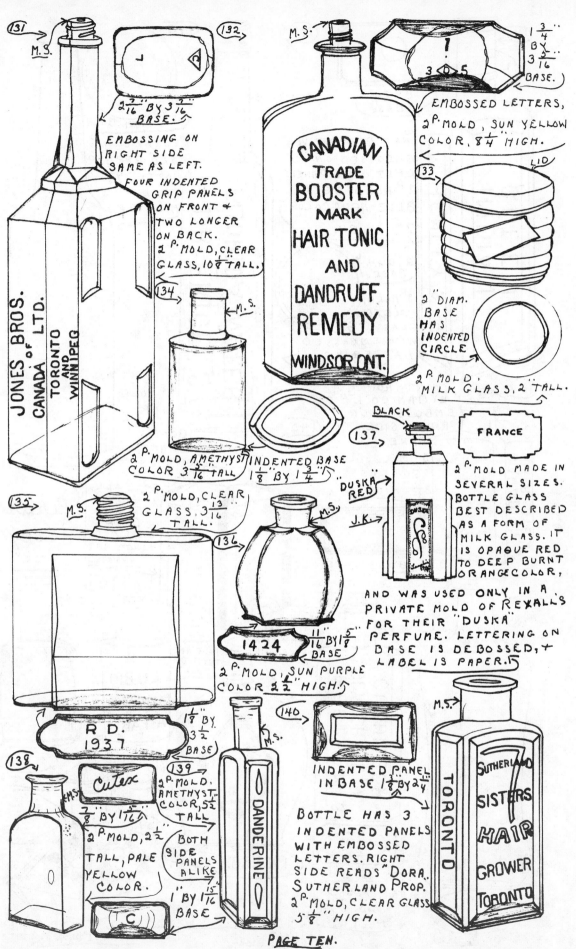

131 — M.S.

132

M.S.

1 3/4 BY 3 5/16 BASE.

2 7/16" BY 3 9/16 BASE.

EMBOSSING ON RIGHT SIDE SAME AS LEFT. FOUR INDENTED GRIP PANELS ON FRONT & TWO LONGER ON BACK. 2 P. MOLD, CLEAR GLASS, 10 1/8" TALL.

EMBOSSED LETTERS, 2 P. MOLD, SUN YELLOW COLOR, 8 1/4" HIGH.

133 — LID

CANADIAN TRADE BOOSTER MARK HAIR TONIC AND DANDRUFF REMEDY WINDSOR ONT.

JONES BROS. of CANADA LTD. TORONTO AND WINNIPEG

134 — M.S.

2" DIAM. BASE HAS INDENTED CIRCLE

2 P. MOLD, MILK GLASS, 2" TALL.

BLACK

FRANCE

2 P. MOLD, AMETHYST COLOR 3 5/16 TALL — INDENTED BASE 1 1/8" BY 1 3/4"

137

DUSKA RED

J.K.

2 P. MOLD MADE IN SEVERAL SIZES. BOTTLE GLASS BEST DESCRIBED AS A FORM OF MILK GLASS. IT IS OPAQUE RED TO DEEP BURNT ORANGE COLOR, AND WAS USED ONLY IN A PRIVATE MOLD OF REXALLS FOR THEIR "DUSKA" PERFUME. LETTERING ON BASE IS DEBOSSED, & LABEL IS PAPER.

135 — M.S.

2 P. MOLD, CLEAR GLASS, 3 13/16" TALL.

136

1424

11/16" BY 1 5/8" BASE

2 P. MOLD, SUN PURPLE COLOR 2 1/2" HIGH.

R.D. 1937

1/8" BY 3 1/2 BASE

138 — M.S.

Cutex

139

2 P. MOLD, AMETHYST COLOR, 5 1/2 TALL

7/8" BY 1 1/16"

2 P. MOLD, 2 1/2 TALL, PALE YELLOW COLOR.

BOTH SIDE PANELS ALIKE

1" BY 1 1/16 BASE

DANDERINE

140

INDENTED PANEL IN BASE 1 1/8 BY 2 1/4

BOTTLE HAS 3 INDENTED PANELS WITH EMBOSSED LETTERS. RIGHT SIDE READS "DORA SUTHERLAND PROP." 2 P. MOLD, CLEAR GLASS 5 1/8" HIGH.

M.S.

TORONTO

SUTHERLAND SISTERS HAIR GROWER TORONTO

112

141 → M.S.

1½" BY 2 9/16" BASE

142 →

M.S. →

143

9/16" 2¼" DIAM. BASE

"TURNED IN MOLD" BARBER BOTTLE 9⅛" TALL. MILK GLASS.

"HAIR RESTORATIVE" EMBOSSED ON LEFT SIDE PANEL. 2 P. MOLD, DEEP BLUE AQUA COLOR, 7⅝" HIGH.

INDIAN QUEEN

HENLEY'S

2" DIAM. BASE.

2 P. MOLD, PALE AQUA GLASS, 8" TALL WITH EMBOSSED LETTERING.

DR. PRICE'S FLORIDA WATER

2 P. MOLD, MILK GLASS BOTTLE PAINTED ORANGE & BLACK DESIGN 3¾" TALL

2¼" SQ. BASE "Girard Design" IS PAINTED

Girard Design

144

M.S. →

CANADIAN HAIR DYE

"NORTHROP & LYMAN CO LTD" EMBOSSED ON RIGHT SIDE PANEL. 2 P. MOLD, BLUE AQUA GLASS, 3 11/16" HIGH

1⅛" BY 1⅞" BASE

145 →

146 →

MS

2 P. MOLD, CLEAR GLASS, 6⅝" TALL

147 → MS

148

LABEL HAS COACH & FOUR IN CENTRE

PALE AMETHYST, 3" TALL

149

BEETHAM'S GLYCERINE & CUCUMBER

Mouson Lavendel

Mit der Postkutsche

LUBIN PARFUMEUR A PARIS

150 → CLEAR, 3½" TALL M.S.

1⅜"

11/16" BY 1½"

1⅞"

MOUSON

15/16" BY 2⅛"

151

1⅛" BY 2⅝" BASE

Alix

15/16" BY 11/16" BASE

DARK AQUA GLASS 2 P. MOLD 4 13/16" TALL

DARK AMBER YELLOW GLASS. 2 P. MOLD, 4¼" TALL

2 P. MOLD, CLEAR GLASS BLACK & ORANGE DESIGN, 2¾" TALL

1½" BY 2" BASE

PAGE ELEVEN

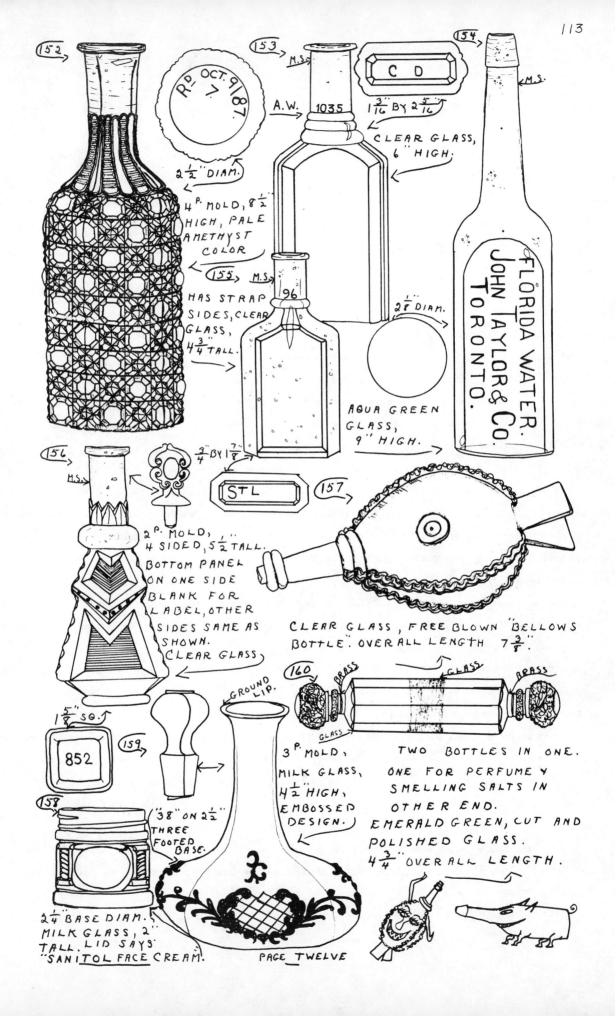

152

Rᴰ. OCT. 9 '87
7
2½" DIAM.

4ᴾ. MOLD, 8½"
HIGH, PALE
AMETHYST
COLOR

153   M.S.

A.W.   1035

155   M.S.

HAS STRAP
SIDES, CLEAR
GLASS,
4¾" TALL.

96

154   M.S.

C D

1 3/16 BY 2 5/16"

CLEAR GLASS,
6" HIGH.

2⅛" DIAM.

AQUA GREEN
GLASS,
9" HIGH.

FLORIDA WATER.
JOHN TAYLOR & CO.
TORONTO.

156   M.S.

¾ BY 1⅞

STL   157

2ᴾ. MOLD,
4 SIDED, 5½ TALL.
BOTTOM PANEL
ON ONE SIDE
BLANK FOR
LABEL, OTHER
SIDES SAME AS
SHOWN.
CLEAR GLASS.

CLEAR GLASS, FREE BLOWN "BELLOWS
BOTTLE". OVERALL LENGTH 7⅜".

GROUND
LIP.

160   BRASS   GLASS   BRASS

GLASS

1⅝" SQ.

852   159

3ᴾ. MOLD,
MILK GLASS,
4½" HIGH,
EMBOSSED
DESIGN.

TWO BOTTLES IN ONE.
ONE FOR PERFUME Y
SMELLING SALTS IN
OTHER END.
EMERALD GREEN, CUT AND
POLISHED GLASS.
4¾" OVER ALL LENGTH.

158

"38" ON 2½"
THREE
FOOTED
BASE.

2¼" BASE DIAM.
MILK GLASS, 2"
TALL. LID SAYS
"SANITOL FACE CREAM.

PAGE TWELVE

X FOOD AND DAIRIES

A. Food.

Nicholas Appert, a Frenchman, is credited with the basics of food preservation through heat and air elimination. During the Napoleonic Wars the French government offered a substantial award for the development of a method to preserve foods and fourteen years later, (1809), Appert claimed the prize. The idea was to enclose the food in a glass container, seal it and then boil the container.

The Weekly Register, York, 1822, printed directions to preserve cherries, plums, etc. "Fill large necked bottles with the fruit, put the corks in loose; let them be put in a kettle of water, increasing the heat to scalding, when of proper degree keep it for some half hour longer, fill up with boiling water, cork down tight; lay them on the side till wanted for use." It would seem that wines and soda waters were not the only things where it was needed to 'keep the cork wet', and may perhaps account for the flat-sided food bottle.

Emigrants to Canada from Scotland and Ireland were still providing their own food on the voyage in the 1830's, although by this time it was generally discouraged in England by the ship owners because of the mistakes passengers made in this matter. Those wishing to supply their own provisions were warned to be sure to bring enough for at least fifty days and it was thought better to prepare for seventy-five.

A cement "strong and cheap and particularly good for articles that are carried to sea" was made of a mixture of beeswax, rosin and brick dust plastered around the covers of food jars. Bottles to be corked tight and then dipped in the hot cement. Milk boiled with a pound of loaf sugar per quart and bottled when cool, was said to keep sweet for the journey. A bottle of vinegar to use in the water for drinking, a large bottle of castor oil and a good supply of old bottled beer, "which has less chance of flying, than if new," were listed along with potatoes, dried fish, etc., as necessities on the trip.

Various types of closures for food bottles were tried but it was not until Mason patented his tin lid for jars in 1858 that home preserving met with much success for anything other than pickles, jams or jellies, where, the vinegar in the first and sugar in the second helped in their preservation.

Mrs. Elizabeth Dunlop was offering her bottled preserves to the public of Toronto as early as 1846, continuing for some years, and Ely, Blain & Co., of the same city, had assorted jams etc. for sale in the 1890's.

Fellows Co., St. John, N.B., advertised their superior extracts for flavouring cakes and pies in 1848 in Toronto. Carlington Extracts of Ottawa and their wide array of flavouring in bottles were mentioned in notes on the Ottawa Industrial Exhibition, 1880, and where the J.F. Lyon & Co., Toronto, had an elaborate show of the same class of goods. The Pure Gold Manufacturing Co., had been in business at 31 Front St., Toronto, for nearly eight years by 1892 and were then known as the largest factory of the kind in the Dominion. An article of the time about this company said, "In the extract rooms some thirty different flavours are made and put up in their well known style of bottles".

English pickles and sauces were in good supply at most grocers and were generally mentioned as to maker. "Battby's London Pickles", "Crosse and Blackwell" pickles and their "Lea and Perrin", (pictured in the familiar embossed bottle), and "Lazenby's", some of these.

Holbrook's Sauce, 23 Scott St., Toronto, were offering a silver plated tea set as first prize for a soup recipe using their product in 1906. H. Mills of Cobourg, C.W., was "induced to offer" his Mill's Mandarine Sauce for fish, game, poultry, chops etc. to the public in 1846, and Rowland & Co., Toronto, had pickles, sauces, etc. for sale in 1859.

A.ıı. BOVRIL: J. Lawson Johnston introduced his patent preparation, 'Johnston's Fluid Beef' to Montreal in 1872. After working up an extensive demand for his product he sold his Canadian business and went to England. Once there he made arrangements for securing direct shipments of beef extracts from the Argentine Republic and Australia and with these aids soon had an improved preparation on the English market. He named this new product "BOVRIL" after reading a book by Lord Lytton, "The Coming Race", in which the ox is known as "Bo", and the "Vril" as almighty power, capable of endowing health, strength, longevity, etc.

Business prospered and in 1897 the London office extended to the American continent. They commenced by buying out the older Johnston's Fluid Beef Company, thereby taking back the parent business of the present concern. In advertisements of the time the public was invited to visit the Montreal plant any week day but Saturday between seven A.M. and five P.M., and look around should they wish to.

A.ııı.   Pickle and sauce bottles were advertised for sale by John Mulholland of Toronto in 1845. Francis Cundhill, Montreal, was Agent for the Aire & Caulder Bottle Co., Castleford, with glass bottles of every description in 1859. Food bottles made by the Kilner Brothers, London, are not uncommon in Canada. They were advertising all kinds of glass bottles in 1874, and Cannington Shaw was another English supplier. In 1867, the Hamilton Glass Co. were "now prepared to supply Canada West, East, and the Lower Provinces, with a better and cheaper fruit jar - both cork and self sealer".

Foods have been put up in a variety of bottle styles and your choice is wide. The ordinary wide mouthed bottle was also used for things other than food - as druggist's powders. Small candy bottles, made in shapes to please the children and some not so small, could form a specialized collection. The flowering pickles, made to be used as vases when empty, come in a variety of designs, and the earlier fancy sauce bottles are on the preferred list of many.

X   FOODS AND DAIRIES - cont'd

B. Dairies.

At the early dairy as such, the principal food for the cattle was grain or malt after it had been used by the brewer or distiller. The seasons for these were mainly spring and autumn and a stock was laid in at these times. Grass, turnips, mangels and dried hay were also given. Cow houses were frequently mentioned in connection with Canadian Distilleries when offered for sale or rent. Public establishments were usually supplied directly from the dairy by contract, but private families were mainly supplied by dealers, who had what were called milk walks (a certain number of customers on whom they called daily). The dairy owner calculated the number of cows needed to supply the dealer, and these cows were left for the dealer to milk. As supply and demand varied from day to day the surplus was placed in shallow vessels to 'throw up' cream, which was churned into butter. In an article printed in 1840, the author's idea was that if you wanted to enjoy drinking milk it was better if you did not see the inside of the general run of dairies.

"Genuine Grass Fed Milk" - "a very superior type" was for sale at Laidlaws, King St., John Pardy's Queen St., and Mr. Pelson's, shoemaker, Yonge St., in Toronto, and supplied by Arch Cameron, farmer in 1862.

In 1868, J. & J.L. Burney of 70½ Queen St. W., Toronto, patented an arrangement for cooling milk. It consisted of two vats, one of them double. The outer was made of wood and the inner of zinc with a four inch space between the two. This space was filled with cold water from pipes fed by means of a force pump connected with a water wheel, kept in motion by the current of a nearby stream and ending in a cistern in the milk building.

When the cows were milked, each pail was poured through a strainer extended across one end of the vat, the milk running by a gentle slope down to the other end and out through a tap into ten gallon cans. The second vat was built of brick and filled with water, into which the cans were placed, cooling them further until morning when they were taken to town and again put in ice water. A Mr. Campbell & Brothers were Toronto suppliers using the system, and another dairy in the Township of Nelson - M.T.D. Harrison - supplied Hamilton.

B.11. THE CITY DAIRY CO. LTD. was formed in Toronto in 1900. W.E.H. Massey, (President of the Massey Harris Co.), was the president and A.E. Ames, (of A.E. Ames & Co.), was vice-president. This company was formed with the idea of establishing sanitary conditions for the delivery of milk. It was stated that the conditions of barns, milk houses, transportation, handling and delivery of milk was almost unregulated and that only a small portion of farmers delivering milk to the city had ever been visited by Board of Health Inspectors.

At that time, there were around three hundred milk dealers in Toronto with an average delivery of five cans each per day, requiring about seven hundred and fifty wagons for the purpose and it was pointed out that less than one quarter the amount would do for the delivery under a proper system. The milk for the most part was delivered from the can by dipping from it into the various containers of the householder. Where the bottle system was used, the bottles were filled at the store or a private home and sometimes in the wagons on the street. The bottles were not properly cleaned as there were only two or three dealers with sterilizing equipment.

Under the new system, a large central plant with sufficient apparatus for aerating, cooling, sterilizing the bottles, etc., and with a cold storage plant, was to be erected. The company would buy directly from the farmers, each of whom were required to sign contracts regarding sanitary surroundings, feeding, watering, etc., and all of whom must be inspected by veterinarians and special officers of the company.

With the routes already secured the company would start out with 16,000 quarts delivery daily to retail customers. The City Dairy Co. Ltd. was incorporated under the Ontario Companies Act with Share Capital $950,000. The public was offered subscriptions for one share and upward, with allotment preference given to small subscribers who were bonafide residents of Toronto or Suburbs and Farmers in the vicinity.

Milk bottles, although they had a short life, are plentiful, and pretty much standard as to shape. Bottles like the Alex Bryce, Toronto, dug by Al Wilson, are more desirable than those with the paper disk finish. Most were made in clear glass but amber, although fairly scarce, may be found. The Caulfield's dark green milk bottle found by Claude Lunau, would be a most desirable one if whole - to my husband's mind anyway, as he likes milk bottles.

(For References re. Food & Dairies see page 101.)

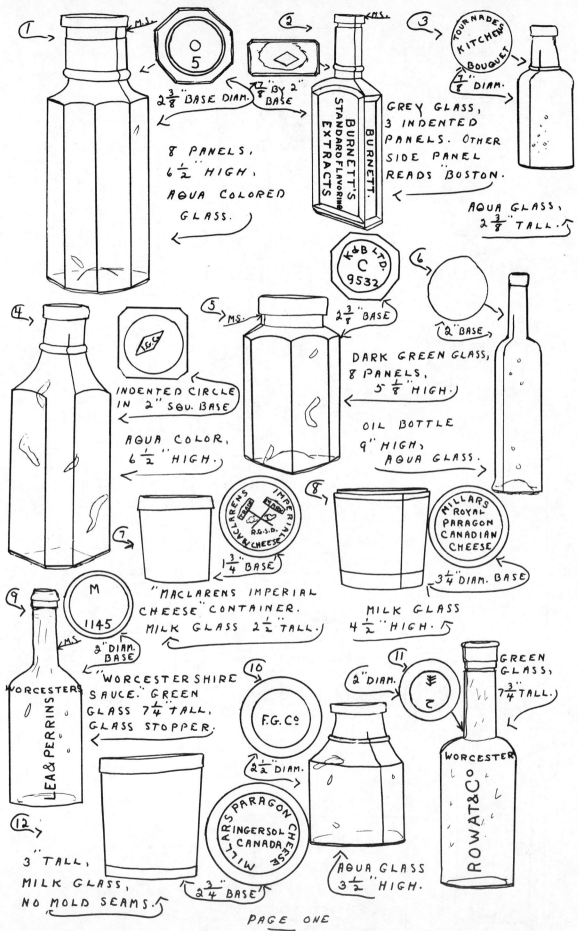

1 → M.S.

2 3/8" BASE DIAM.   7/8" BY 2" BASE   2 →   M.S.

8 PANELS, 6 1/2" HIGH, AQUA COLORED GLASS.

BURNETT'S STANDARD FLAVORING EXTRACTS

BURNETT.

3 →   TOURNADES KITCHEN BOUQUET   7/8" DIAM.

GREY GLASS, 3 INDENTED PANELS. OTHER SIDE PANEL READS "BOSTON".

AQUA GLASS, 2 3/8" TALL.

K&B LTD. C 9532

6 →   2" BASE   2 3/8" BASE

4 →   5 →   M.S.

I.G.Co

INDENTED CIRCLE IN 2" SQU. BASE

AQUA COLOR, 6 1/2" HIGH.

DARK GREEN GLASS, 8 PANELS, 5 1/8" HIGH.

OIL BOTTLE 9" HIGH, AQUA GLASS.

7 →   MACLARENS IMPERIAL CHEESE   TRADE   R.G.S.D.   1 3/4" BASE

8 →   MILLARS ROYAL PARAGON CANADIAN CHEESE   3 1/4" DIAM. BASE

"MACLARENS IMPERIAL CHEESE" CONTAINER. MILK GLASS 2 1/2" TALL.

MILK GLASS 4 1/2" HIGH.

9 →   M 1145   M.S.   2" DIAM. BASE

"WORCESTERSHIRE SAUCE". GREEN GLASS 7 1/4" TALL, GLASS STOPPER.

WORCESTERS LEA & PERRINS

10 →   F.G.Co   2 1/2" DIAM.

11 →   2" DIAM.

12 →

3" TALL, MILK GLASS, NO MOLD SEAMS.

MILLARS PARAGON CHEESE INGERSOL CANADA   2 3/4" BASE

AQUA GLASS 3 1/2" HIGH.

GREEN GLASS, 7 3/4" TALL.

WORCESTER ROWAT&Co

PAGE ONE

119

MAY BE COLOGNE

13

M.S. END

1578°

1½" DIAM. BASE.

J.K.&S. W 1773

3" SQU. BASE

14

3 P. MOLD, GREY GLASS, 6⅞" TALL.

CONCAVE BASE, DEEP AQUA GREEN COLOR, 7¼" HIGH.

ERIE

15

CONCAVE BASE 2⅞" DIAM.

AQUA BLUE GLASS, 7¾" HIGH. "ERIE" BOTTLE

BASE CONCAVE AND 4¾" DIAM.

16

12

2⅜" SQU. BASE

ROUGH BITS OF GLASS ON BASE OF THIS, GREY COLOR 13½" TALL

17

3" DIAM. BASE

2

19

M.S.

2⅜" DIAM. CONCAVE BASE

M.S.

18

DARK GREEN, 7" TALL.

IN USE AROUND 1940, CLEAR GLASS, 11¾" HIGH

TIGER CATSUP

THE GENUINE SMALL'S SYRUP CANADA

AQUA BLUE, DEEP COLOR, 11½" TALL.

20

239

2¾" BASE

AQUA GREEN BOTTLE, 8" HIGH.

21

1" DIAM. BASE

RED SNA

3" TALL, CLEAR GLASS BOTTLE HAS "RED SNAPPER SAUCE" EMBOSSED AROUND SHOULDER.)

PAGE TWO

22 M.S.

LEA BROS

23
2¼" BASE
GROUND LIP, AMETHYST GLASS, 6 PANEL, 5⅜" HIGH.

ESTERSHIR
LEA & PERRINS

24
2½" BASE
DARK GREEN, 8½" HIGH.

2½ DIAM.
C A Co ⬜
12
8 PANELS, 'CATSUP' CLEAR, 9¼" TALL.

25
2½ BASE
H.J. HIENZ Co. 49 PITTSBURGH U.S.A.
"H.J. HIENZ Co." AMETHYST GLASS, 7¼" TALL

26
3¼" BASE
3
AMETHYST COLOR, 8 PANELS, 6⅞" HIGH

27
ERIE
2⅛" DIAM.
GREY GLASS, 8" TALL. "ERIE."
2¼" SQU.

28
DARK BLUE-GREEN GLASS— 9 1/16" HIGH.
DARK AMETHYST COLOR, 8" TALL.

29
2⅜" BASE

30
1¼" BY 2"
DARK AMETHYST COLOR— 5⅜" TALL.

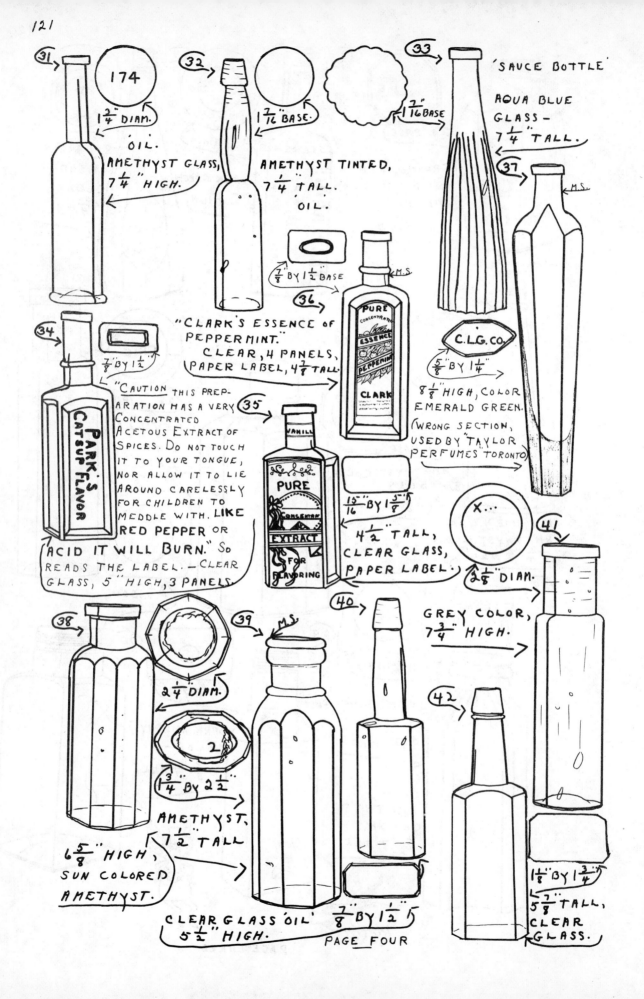

31

174

1¾" DIAM.

OIL.
AMETHYST GLASS,
7¼" HIGH.

32

1 7/16" BASE.

AMETHYST TINTED,
7¼" TALL.
OIL.

1 7/16" BASE

33

'SAUCE BOTTLE'

AQUA BLUE
GLASS -
7¼" TALL.

37

M.S.

7/8" BY 1½" BASE

36

PURE
CONCENTRATED
ESSENCE
OF
PEPPERMINT
CLARK

"CLARK'S ESSENCE of
PEPPERMINT."
CLEAR, 4 PANELS,
PAPER LABEL, 4 7/8" TALL.

C.L.G. Co.

5/8" BY 1¼"

8 1/8" HIGH, COLOR
EMERALD GREEN.
(WRONG SECTION,
USED BY "TAYLOR
PERFUMES TORONTO)

34

7/8" BY 1½"

PARK'S CATSUP FLAVOR

"CAUTION THIS PREP-
ARATION HAS A VERY
CONCENTRATED
ACETOUS EXTRACT OF
SPICES. DO NOT TOUCH
IT TO YOUR TONGUE,
NOR ALLOW IT TO LIE
AROUND CARELESSLY
FOR CHILDREN TO
MEDDLE WITH. LIKE
RED PEPPER OR
ACID IT WILL BURN." So
READS THE LABEL. — CLEAR
GLASS, 5" HIGH, 3 PANELS.

35

VANILLA
PURE
CONCENTRATED
EXTRACT
FOR
FLAVORING

1 15/16" BY 1 5/8"

4½" TALL,
CLEAR GLASS,
PAPER LABEL.

X...

2 1/8" DIAM.

41

GREY COLOR,
7¾" HIGH.

38

2¼" DIAM.

2

1¾" BY 2½"

AMETHYST,
7½" TALL

6 5/8" HIGH,
SUN COLORED
AMETHYST.

39

M.S.

40

CLEAR GLASS 'OIL'
5½" HIGH.

7/8" BY 1½"

42

1 1/8" BY 1¾"

5 7/8" TALL,
CLEAR
GLASS.

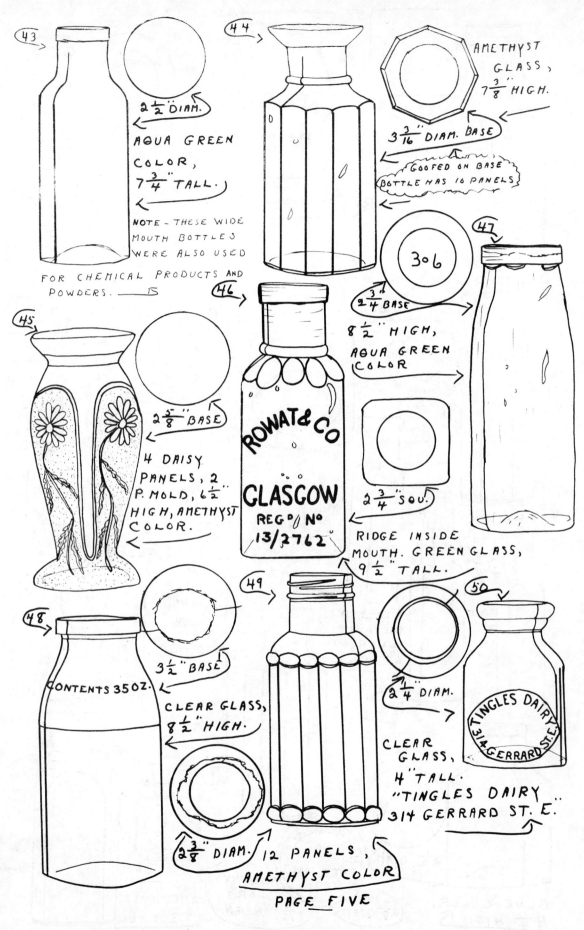

43
2½" DIAM.
AQUA GREEN COLOR, 7¾" TALL.
NOTE - THESE WIDE MOUTH BOTTLES WERE ALSO USED FOR CHEMICAL PRODUCTS AND POWDERS. ⬝

44
AMETHYST GLASS, 7⅜" HIGH.
3 3/16" DIAM. BASE
GOOFED ON BASE BOTTLE HAS 10 PANELS

47
306
2¾" BASE
8½" HIGH, AQUA GREEN COLOR

45
2⅝" BASE
4 DAISY PANELS, 2 P. MOLD, 6½" HIGH, AMETHYST COLOR.

46
ROWAT & CO
GLASGOW
REG⁰ N⁰ 13/2762

2¾" SQU.
RIDGE INSIDE MOUTH. GREEN GLASS, 9½" TALL.

48
CONTENTS 35 OZ.

49
3½" BASE
CLEAR GLASS, 8½" HIGH.

2⅜" DIAM.
12 PANELS, AMETHYST COLOR

50
2¼" DIAM.
CLEAR GLASS, 4" TALL. "TINGLES DAIRY 314 GERRARD ST. E."
TINGLES DAIRY 314 GERRARD ST. E.

PAGE FIVE

123

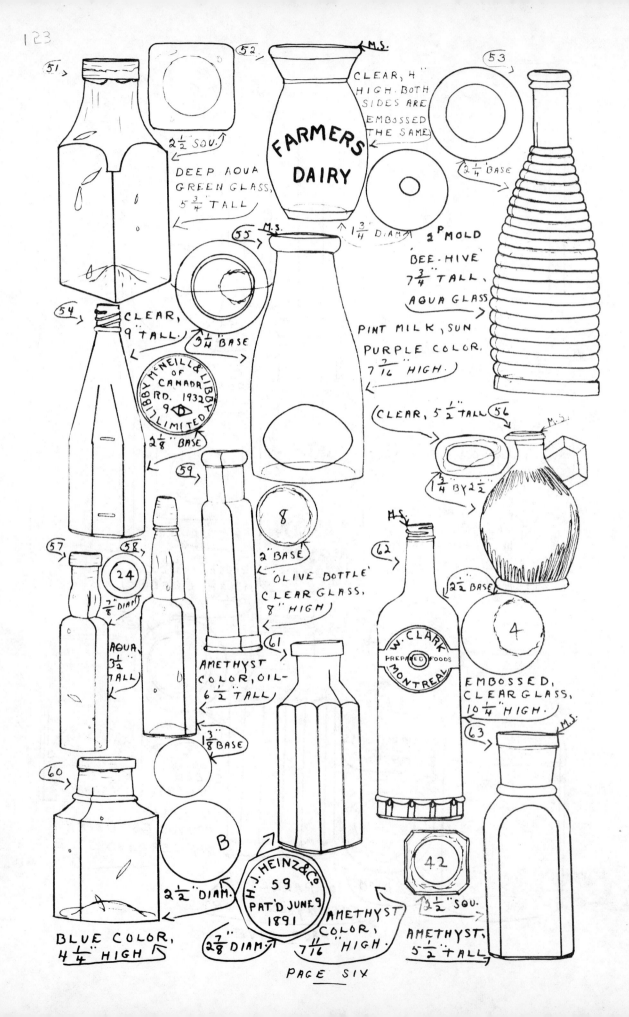

51

52

DEEP AQUA
GREEN GLASS,
5 3/4" TALL

2 1/2" SQU.

M.S.

CLEAR, 4"
HIGH. BOTH
SIDES ARE
EMBOSSED
THE SAME.

FARMERS
DAIRY

1 3/4" DIAM.

2 P. MOLD

53

2 1/4" BASE

'BEE-HIVE'
7 3/4" TALL,
AQUA GLASS

55 M.S.

54

CLEAR,
9" TALL.

3 1/4" BASE

LIBBY McNEILL & LIBBY
OF
CANADA
RD. 1932
9
LIMITED

2 1/8" BASE

PINT MILK, SUN
PURPLE COLOR,
7 7/16" HIGH.

CLEAR, 5 1/2" TALL 56

M.S.

1 3/4" BY 2 1/2"

59

8

2" BASE

'OLIVE BOTTLE'
CLEAR GLASS,
8" HIGH

M.S.

62

2 1/2" BASE

4

57

58

24

7/8" DIAM.

AQUA,
3 1/2"
TALL.

AMETHYST
COLOR, OIL-
6 1/2" TALL

61

W. CLARK
PREPARED FOODS
MONTREAL

EMBOSSED,
CLEAR GLASS,
10 1/4" HIGH.

63 M.S.

1 3/8" BASE

60

B

2 1/2" DIAM.

H. J. HEINZ & CO
59
PAT'D JUNE 9
1891

2 7/8" DIAM.

AMETHYST
COLOR,
7 1/16" HIGH.

42

2 1/2" SQU.

AMETHYST,
5 1/2" TALL.

BLUE COLOR,
4 1/4" HIGH

PAGE SIX

124

64 → M.S.

M.S.

BASE 3⅛″ DIAM.

..NT MILK, CLEAR COLOR, EMBOSSED CIRCLE & LETTERING. 2ᴾ. MOLD 8″ HIGH

Newmarket Dairy

67 → M.S.

BASE 3¼″ DIAM.

EMBOSSED LETTERS, 2ᴾ. MOLD, AMETHYST COLOR, 7½″ TALL.

The Queens Own Dairy

70 → M.S. TORONTO

7⅛″ BY 1⅞″ BASE. 4ᴾ. MOLD FROM BOTTOM UP, CLEAR COLOR 2⅝″ HIGH. HAT IS LID.

"MOON MULLINS"

4 PART MOLD 9½″ TALL CLEAR GLASS

65 M.S.

1½″ BY 2½″ BASE

AMETHYST COLOR, 7⅛″ TALL IS 2ᴾ. MOLD & HAS A FLAT PANEL UP EACH SIDE WITH 3 EACH FRONT & BACK.

CONCAVE CIRCLE IN BASE 2½″ DIAM.

SHALLOW RIM ON INSIDE

68 → END OF M.S.

THIS BOTTLE IS 3ᴾ. MOLD FROM THE BOTTOM UP. IT IS 8⅛″ HIGH, YELLOW (PALE) COLOR & SPECKLED WITH TINY BUBBLES.

CONCAVE CIRCLE IN BASE 2⅛″ ACROSS

71

BASE 3″ DIA.

GROUND RIM

PAGE SEVEN

66 → M.S.

2ᴾ. MOLD, DARK AGUA GREEN BIMAL 6″ TALL.

NECK FINISHED FOR GLASS LID.

69 → BASE 2¾″ SQU. END OF M.S.

RED CROSS K.J. PICKLES THE DYSON CO WINNEPEG

2ᴾ. MOLD, DARK GREY COLOR, 7⅞″ HIGH. LABEL PANELS ON ALL FOUR SIDES. EMBOSSED LETTERS ON FRONT PANEL ONLY. THEY READ "RED CROSS PICKLES, THE DYSON CO. WINNEPEG."

GLASS LID LOOKS SOMETHING LIKE

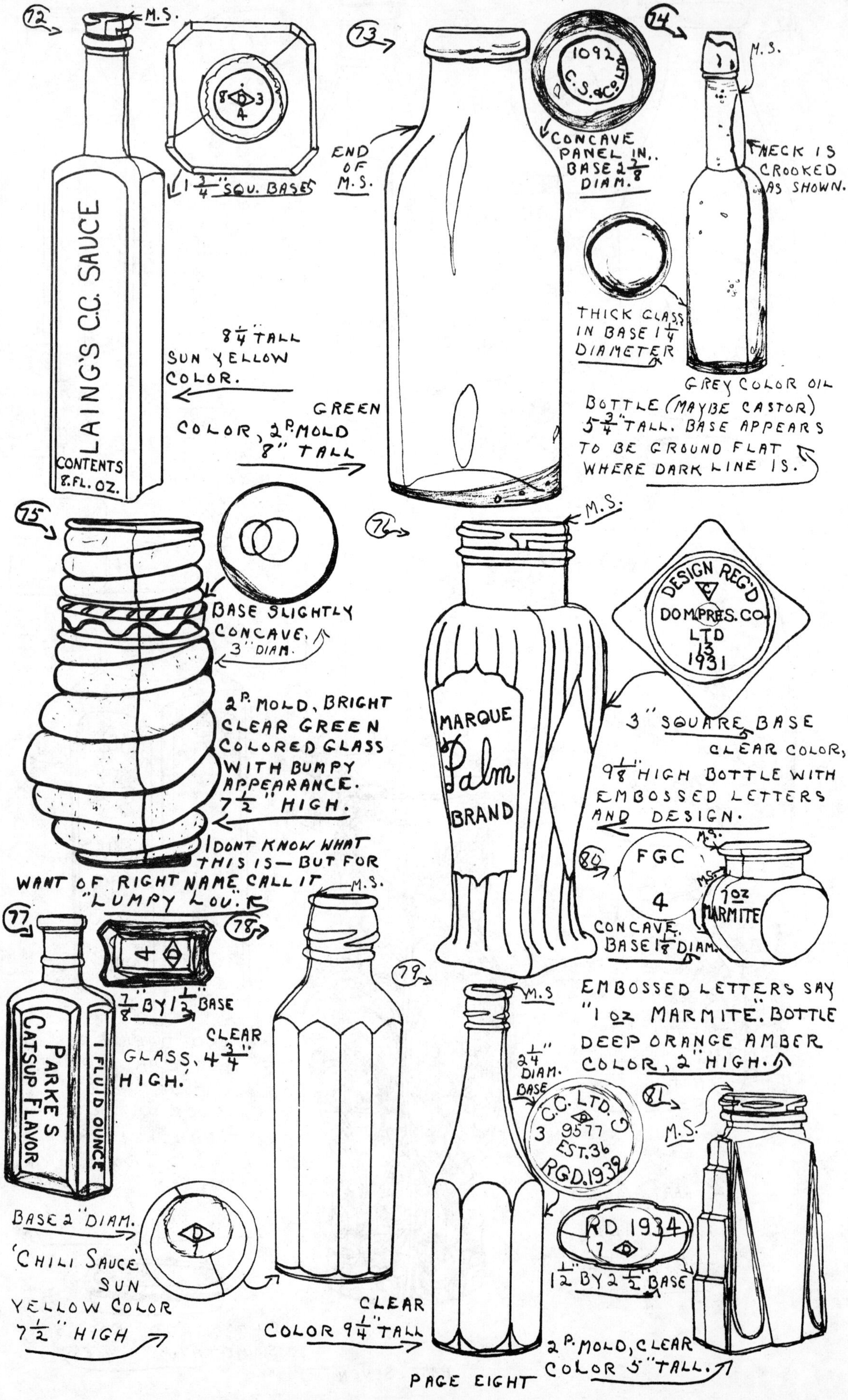

125

72

M.S.

1 3/4" SQU. BASE

LAING'S C.C. SAUCE

CONTENTS 8. FL. OZ.

8 1/4" TALL
SUN YELLOW
COLOR.

GREEN
COLOR, 2 P. MOLD
8" TALL

73

END OF M.S.

74

M.S.

1092
C. S. & Co Ltd

CONCAVE PANEL IN BASE 2 7/8 DIAM.

THICK GLASS IN BASE 1 1/4 DIAMETER

NECK IS CROOKED AS SHOWN.

GREY COLOR OIL BOTTLE (MAYBE CASTOR) 5 3/4" TALL. BASE APPEARS TO BE GROUND FLAT WHERE DARK LINE IS.

75

BASE SLIGHTLY CONCAVE, 3" DIAM.

2 P. MOLD, BRIGHT CLEAR GREEN COLORED GLASS WITH BUMPY APPEARANCE. 7 1/2" HIGH.

I DONT KNOW WHAT THIS IS — BUT FOR WANT OF RIGHT NAME CALL IT "LUMPY LOU".

76

M.S.

MARQUE Palm BRAND

DESIGN REG'D DOM PRES. CO. LTD 13 1931

3" SQUARE BASE CLEAR COLOR, 9 1/8" HIGH BOTTLE WITH EMBOSSED LETTERS AND DESIGN.

80

FGC 4

CONCAVE BASE 1 7/8 DIAM.

M.S.

1 OZ MARMITE

EMBOSSED LETTERS SAY "1 OZ MARMITE". BOTTLE DEEP ORANGE AMBER COLOR, 2" HIGH.

77

4

7/8" BY 1/2" BASE

CLEAR GLASS, 4 3/4" HIGH.

PARKE'S CATSUP FLAVOR
1 FLUID OUNCE

BASE 2" DIAM.

'CHILI SAUCE' SUN YELLOW COLOR 7 1/2" HIGH

78

M.S.

79

M.S.

2 1/4" DIAM. BASE

C.C. LTD. G 3 9577 EST. 36 RGD. 1939

RD 1934 7

1 1/2 BY 2 1/2" BASE

81

M.S.

CLEAR COLOR 9 1/4" TALL

2 P. MOLD, CLEAR COLOR 5" TALL.

PAGE EIGHT

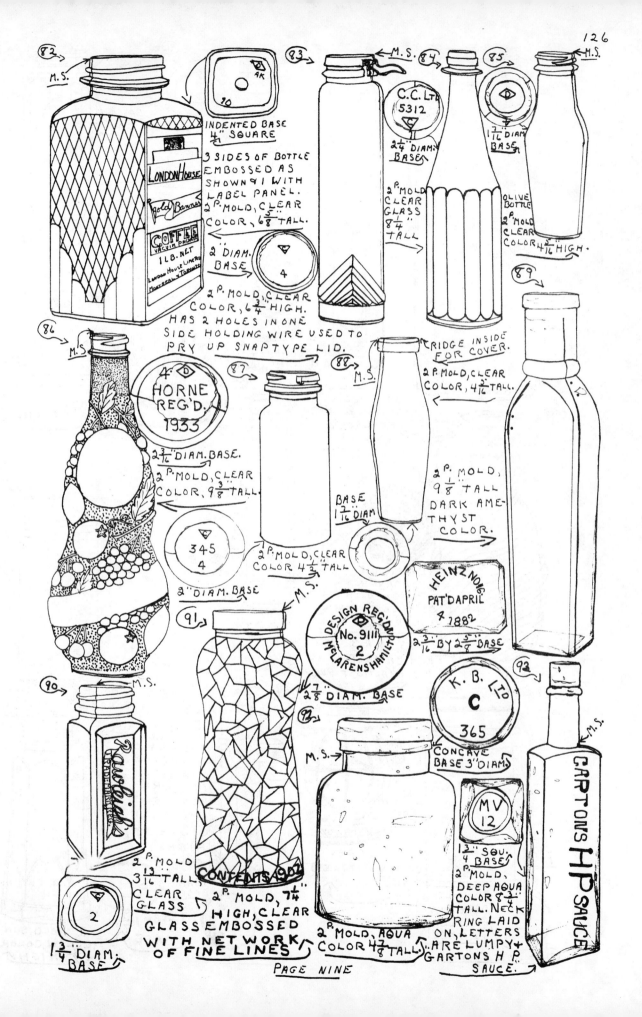

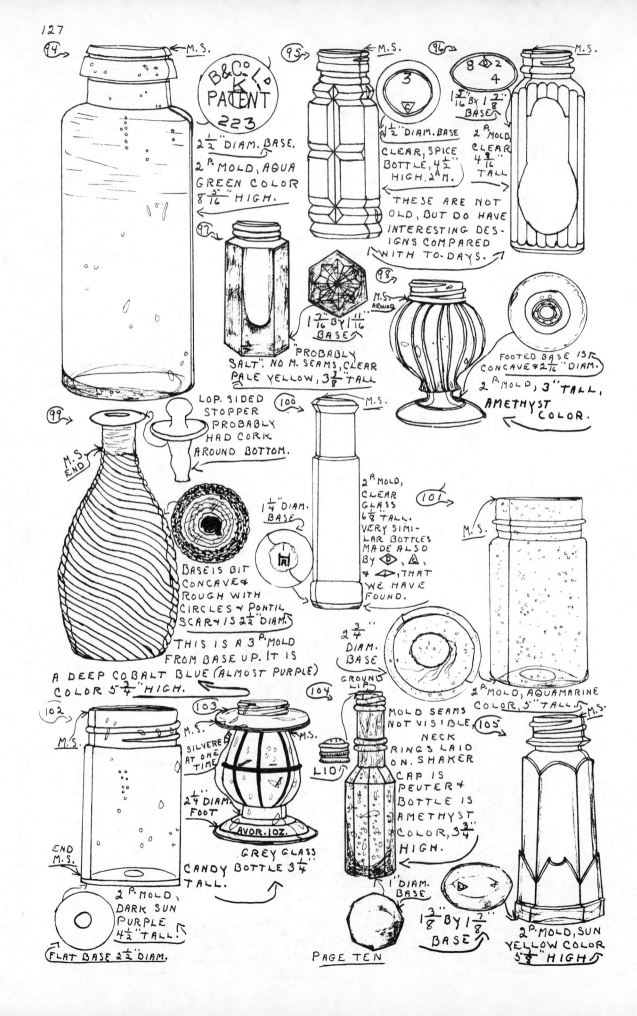

94 → ← M.S.

B&Co. L.D
K
PATENT
223

2½" DIAM. BASE.

2 P. MOLD, AQUA
GREEN COLOR
8 5/16" HIGH.

95 → ← M.S.

96 →

8 ◇ 2
4
1 5/16" BY 1 2/8"
BASE

← M.S.

2 P. MOLD
CLEAR
4 9/16"
TALL

3
◇
√ ½" DIAM. BASE

CLEAR, SPICE
BOTTLE, 4½"
HIGH, 2 A.M.

THESE ARE NOT
OLD, BUT DO HAVE
INTERESTING DES-
IGNS COMPARED
WITH TO-DAYS.

97 →

1 7/16 BY 1 11/16
BASE

"PROBABLY
SALT". NO M. SEAMS, CLEAR
PALE YELLOW, 3 3/8" TALL

98 →

M.S.
AROUND

FOOTED BASE IS
CONCAVE & 2 1/16" DIAM.

2 P. MOLD, 3" TALL,
AMETHYST
COLOR.

99 →

M.S.
END

LOP. SIDED
STOPPER
PROBABLY
HAD CORK
AROUND BOTTOM.

100 → M.S.

1¼" DIAM.
BASE

2 P. MOLD,
CLEAR
GLASS
6 5/8 TALL.
VERY SIMI-
LAR BOTTLES
MADE ALSO
BY ◇, △,
& ◁, THAT
WE HAVE
FOUND.

BASE IS BIT
CONCAVE &
ROUGH WITH
CIRCLES & PONTIL
SCAR & IS 2½" DIAM.

THIS IS A 3 P. MOLD
FROM BASE UP. IT IS
A DEEP COBALT BLUE (ALMOST PURPLE)
COLOR 5 3/4" HIGH.

2 3/4
DIAM.
BASE

GROUND
LIP

101 →

M.S.

2 P. MOLD, AQUAMARINE
COLOR, 5" TALL.

← M.S.

102 →

M.S.

END
M.S.

2 P. MOLD,
DARK SUN
PURPLE
4½" TALL!

FLAT BASE 2½" DIAM.

103 →

SILVERED
AT ONE
TIME

2¼" DIAM
FOOT

← M.S.

AVOR. 1 OZ.

GREY GLASS
CANDY BOTTLE 3¼"
TALL.

104 →

LID

MOLD SEAMS
NOT VISIBLE,
NECK
RINGS LAID
ON. SHAKER
CAP IS
PEUTER &
BOTTLE IS
AMETHYST
COLOR, 3 3/4"
HIGH.

1" DIAM.
BASE

1 3/8" BY 1 7/8"
BASE

105 →

← M.S.

2 P. MOLD, SUN
YELLOW COLOR
5 5/8" HIGH.

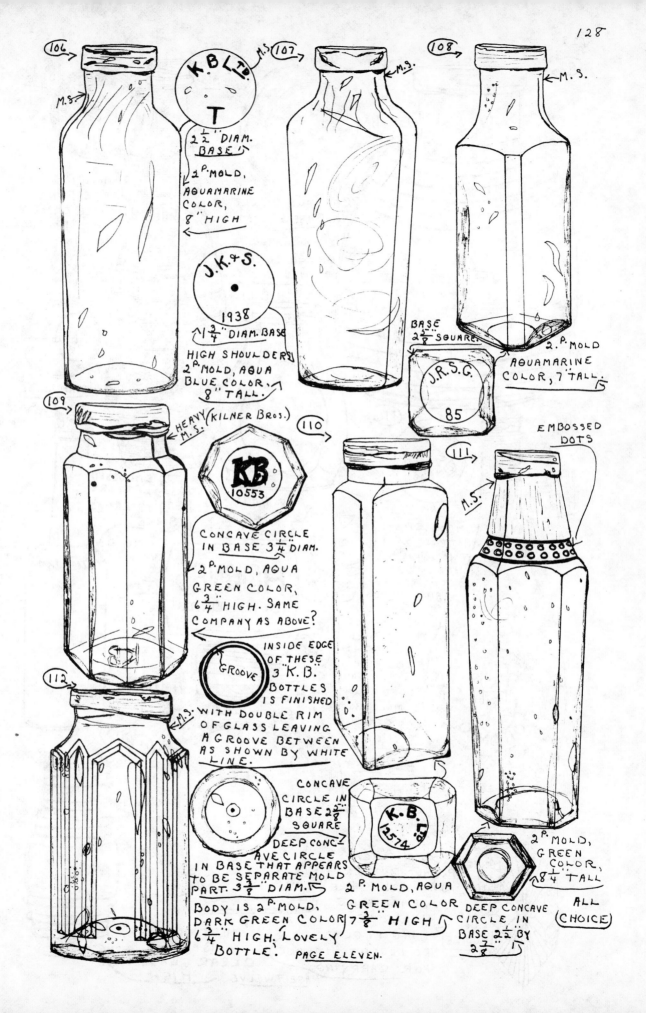

106 →

M.S. →

K.B.LTD.

T

M.S. 107 →

M.S. →

108 →

M.S. →

2 1/2" DIAM.
BASE

2 P. MOLD,
AQUAMARINE
COLOR,
8" HIGH

J.K.&S.

1938

1 3/4" DIAM. BASE

HIGH SHOULDERS
2 P. MOLD, AQUA
BLUE COLOR,
8" TALL.

BASE
2 5/8" SQUARE

J.R.S.G.

85

2 P. MOLD
AQUAMARINE
COLOR, 7" TALL.

109 →

HEAVY (KILNER Bros.)
M.S.

110 →

KB
10553

CONCAVE CIRCLE
IN BASE 3 1/4" DIAM.

2 P. MOLD, AQUA
GREEN COLOR,
6 3/4" HIGH. SAME
COMPANY AS ABOVE?

111 →

EMBOSSED
DOTS

M.S. →

GROOVE

INSIDE EDGE
OF THESE
3 "K.B."
BOTTLES
IS FINISHED
WITH DOUBLE RIM
OF GLASS LEAVING
A GROOVE BETWEEN
AS SHOWN BY WHITE
LINE.

112 →

M.S. →

CONCAVE
CIRCLE IN
BASE 2 3/8"
SQUARE

DEEP CONC-
AVE CIRCLE
IN BASE THAT APPEARS
TO BE SEPARATE MOLD
PART. 3 3/8" DIAM.

BODY IS 2 P. MOLD,
DARK GREEN COLOR,
6 3/4" HIGH. LOVELY
BOTTLE.

K.B.Ltd.
12574

2 P. MOLD, AQUA
GREEN COLOR
7 3/8" HIGH

PAGE ELEVEN.

2 P. MOLD,
GREEN
COLOR,
8 1/4" TALL

DEEP CONCAVE
CIRCLE IN
BASE 2 1/2" BY
2 7/8"

ALL
(CHOICE)

129

113 →

M.S.

CONCAVE CIRCLE
IN BASE 3½ DIAM.

2 P. MOLD, AQUA
GREEN COLOR
7" HIGH

114 →   M.S.

DESIGN REGISTERED
9
D
6
1929
2" DIAM.
BASE

2 P. MOLD "McLARENS
GRAPE PUNCH."
BOTTLE EMBOSSED
WITH 2 PANELS
ON FRONT FOR
LABELS.
CLEAR COLOR
9 7/16 HIGH

McLAREN'S
GRAPE PUNCH
SYRUP

DIRECTIONS — USE 2 TABLE SPOONS
TO A LARGE GLASS
A DRINK FOR EVERY SCALE

6 OZ
8
2" DIAM BASE

M.S.

115 →   M.S.

ALSO
MADE
WITH
SNAP CAP

DESIGN
2
REG'D 1926
1 3/8" DIAM. BASE

EMBOSSED
BOTTLE HAS
TWO LABEL
PANELS ON
OTHER SIDE.
LABEL READS
"HORNES
CONCENTRATED
GRAPE PUNCH
SYRUP, FORTI-
FIED FRUIT
FLAVOR, CONTAINS
ADDED COLOR."
2 P. MOLD BOTTLE
GREY COLOR,
9 3/8" HIGH

2 3/4 BY 3½ BASE

2 P. MOLD,
CLEAR GLASS
6 5/8" HIGH.

HORNE
TORONTO

DESIGN
ON
SIDE'S
OF
GOOD
LUCK
BOTTLE

116 →

M.S.

C
4
2½ DIAM.
BASE

8 PANELS,
2 P. MOLD, CLEAR
GLASS, 4¼ TALL

HORNE'S
REG. APPLIED FOR

118

M.S.

Good Luck

"Good Luck"
PEANUT BUTTER
JAR HAS HOLE
ON EACH SIDE
UNDER NECK
RING IN GLASS
TO INSERT HANDLE
FOR CARRYING.

PAGE TWELVE

117 →   EMBOSSED
LETTERS
READ "PATERSON'S
SAUCE"

2 P. MOLD
SUN YEL-
LOW,
7¼ TALL →

1 7/8" DIAM.
BASE

Paterson's

8 OZ

119   M.S.

M.S.

M.S.

"MUSTARD
BARREL
CLEAR GLASS 4 L
HIGH

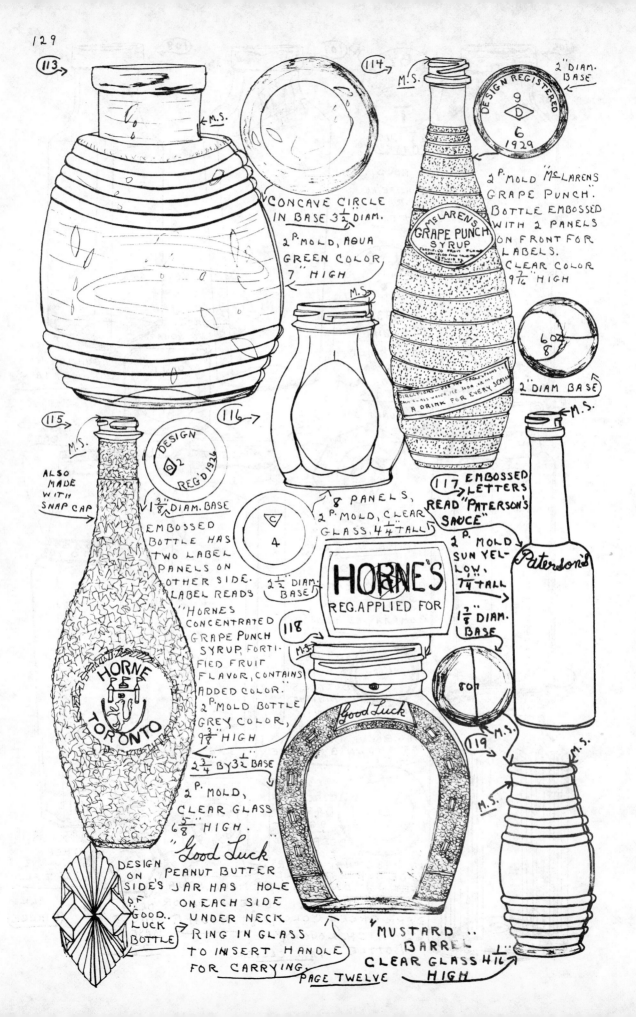

120 — M.S. SLIGHTLY CONCAVE BASE 1 3/4" DIAM. 2 P. MOLD, SUN PURPLE COLOR 4 7/8" HIGH. "MUSTARD BARREL".

121 — M.S. CONCAVE CENTRE IN BASE 3" DIAM. 2 P. MOLD, DARK GREEN COLOR, 5 7/8" HIGH

CONCAVE CIRCLE IN 2 1/2" SQU. BASE 681 C.S.&CO

122 — M.S. M.S. 3 P. MOLD, PEA GREEN COLOR, 5 1/4" HIGH (FOOD BOTTLE)

123 — M.S. BASE 3" DIAM. REG. 1932 5 2 P. MOLD, 5" TALL, CLEAR GLASS

124 — 2 1/2" DIAM. BASE 2 P. MOLD 7 5/16" TALL, PALE AMETHYST COLOR

125 — C.B 3" DIAM. BASE 2 P. MOLD, 7 3/4" TALL, AQUA GREEN COLOR — OPALIZED RAINBOW HUES.

288 1 1/8" BY 1 1/2" BASE

126 — M.S. 2 1/4" DIAM. BASE HORNE DESIGN REG'D 1932 2 P. MOLD, 6 1/2" TALL, CLEAR GLASS "HORNE VANILLA BOTTLE"

127 — HORNE'S 1 5/8" BY 2 3/4" BASE

"CONTENTS 8 FL. OZ. EMBOSSED JUST BELOW HANDLE; BOTH SIDES HAVE SAME EMBOSSING."

128 — MS MS 2 OZ BOVRIL TED 2 P. MOLD, 2 7/8" TALL, CORN SYRUP AMBER COLOR. "2 OZ. BOVRIL EMBOSSED ON ONE SIDE" "2 OZ BOVRIL LIMI-TED" ON OTHER SIDE

129 — M.S. M.S. R911 C BASE DIAM. 1 1/8" IMPERIAL EXTRACT Co. TORONTO 2 P. MOLD, 4 1/2" HIGH, COLOR AMETHYST.

PAGE THIRTEEN

131

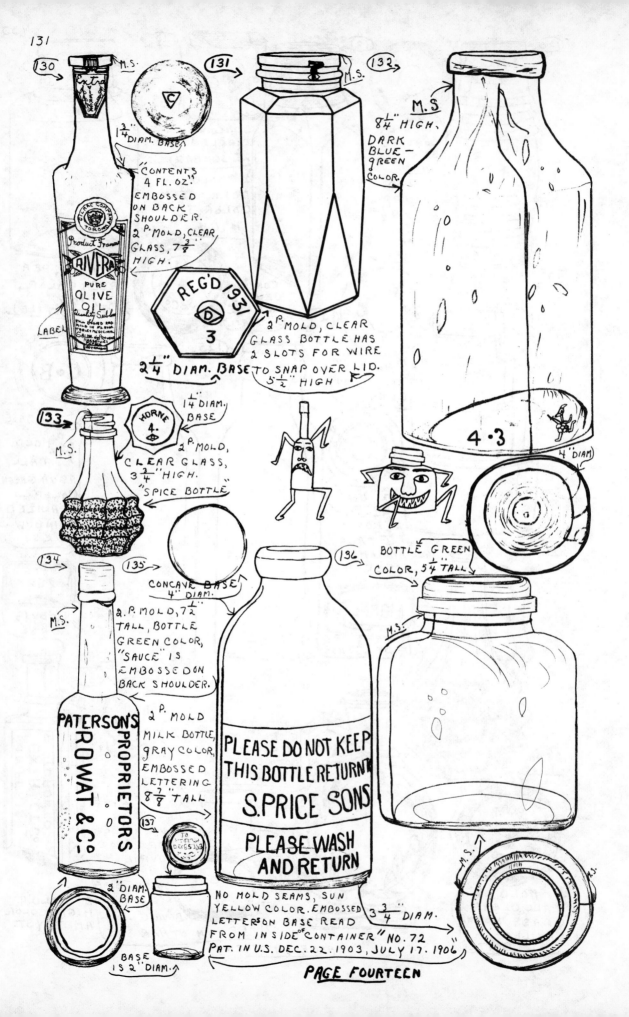

130
M.S.

3/4" DIAM. BASE

131
M.S.

132
M.S.
8 1/4" HIGH.
DARK
BLUE-
GREEN
COLOR.

"CONTENTS 4 FL. OZ." EMBOSSED ON BACK SHOULDER. 2 P. MOLD, CLEAR GLASS, 7 3/8" HIGH.

REG'D 1931
3

CLEAR COMPANY
TORONTO

Product Francais
RIVERA
PURE
OLIVE
OIL

LABEL

2 1/4" DIAM. BASE

2 P. MOLD, CLEAR GLASS BOTTLE HAS 2 SLOTS FOR WIRE TO SNAP OVER LID. 5 1/2" HIGH

4·3

4" DIAM

133
M.S.

HORNE
4.

1 1/4" DIAM. BASE

2 P. MOLD, CLEAR GLASS, 3 3/4" HIGH. "SPICE BOTTLE"

BOTTLE GREEN COLOR, 5 1/4" TALL

134
M.S.

135

CONCAVE BASE 4" DIAM.

136

2 P. MOLD, 7 1/2" TALL, BOTTLE GREEN COLOR, "SAUCE" IS EMBOSSED ON BACK SHOULDER.

2 P. MOLD MILK BOTTLE, GRAY COLOR, EMBOSSED LETTERING 8 7/8" TALL

PATERSON'S
PROPRIETORS
ROWAT & Co.

PLEASE DO NOT KEEP THIS BOTTLE RETURN
S. PRICE SONS
PLEASE WASH AND RETURN

M.S.

137

2" DIAM. BASE

BASE IS 2" DIAM.

NO MOLD SEAMS, SUN YELLOW COLOR. EMBOSSED LETTER ON BASE READ FROM INSIDE OF CONTAINER" NO. 72 PAT. IN U.S. DEC. 22. 1903, JULY 17. 1906"

3 3/4" DIAM.

M.S.

M.S.

PAGE FOURTEEN

138 → NECK IS ROLLED TO FORM MOUTH

BASE 3" DIAM.

139 → GROUND TOP

M.S.

M.S.

M.S.

C.B K

2 P. MOLD, LIGHT GREEN COLOR, 7 HIGH

B & Co LTD K 1740

C. K B

CONCAVE CIRCLE IN BASE 3" DIAM.

CONCAVE BASE 3" SQUARE

2 P. MOLD 7¼" TALL. HAS EMBOSSED DESIGN & LETTERING IS AMETHYST COLOR.

FANCY PICKLES

M.S.

140 →

M.S.

GROOVED MOUTH

141 →

2 P. MOLD, 8 PANELS, AQUA GREEN COLOR, 6 ¾" TALL.

142

M.S.

949C

1 ¾" BY 2 ⁷⁄₁₆" BASE

EMBOSSED LETTERS, AMETHYST COLOR, 2 P. MOLD 7½" TALL.

2½ DIAM. BASE

LEA'S

2½ DIAM. BASE

2 P. MOLD, SUN YELLOW COLOR, EMBOSSED LETTERS & 6¼" TALL. THIS WAS AN UXBRIDGE ONT. DAIRY.

143 →

M.S.

144 →

M.S.

CROXALL

Cousins DAIRY

2¼" DIAM. BASE

2 P. MOLD, CLEAR GLASS 4" TALL. EMBOSSED LETTERING.

MAPLE LEAF EMBOSSED ON 2¼" DIAM. BASE

145

2 P. MOLD, SUN PURPLE COLOR 9 ⅜" HIGH

Canada Dairies LIMITED

SUN YELLOW COLOR, 2 P. MOLD WITH EMBOSSED LETTERS & 4" TALL.

133

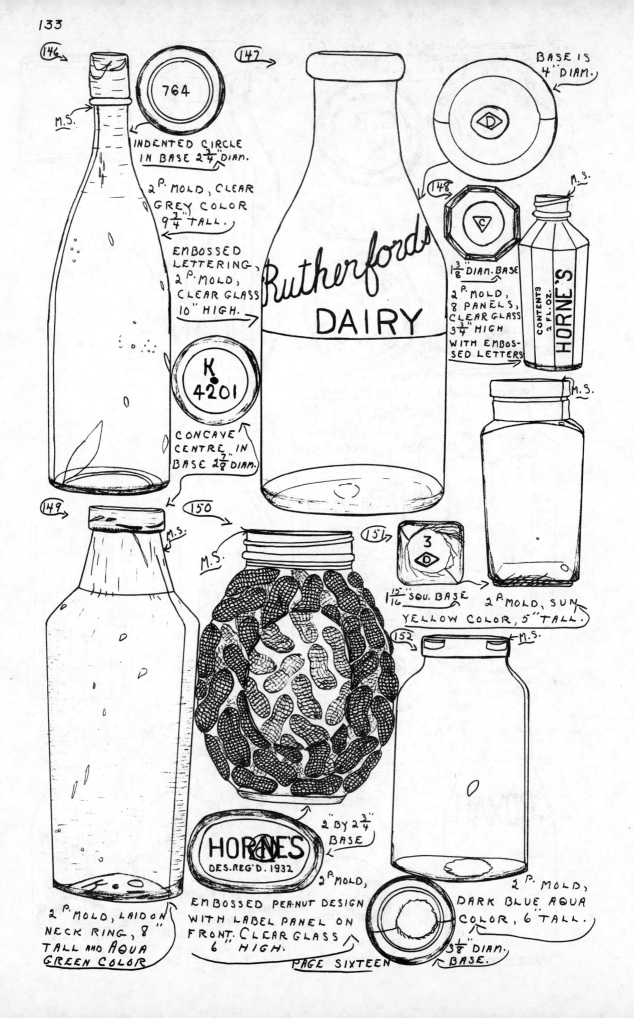

146

M.S.

147

764

INDENTED CIRCLE
IN BASE 2¾" DIAM.

2 P. MOLD, CLEAR
GREY COLOR
9¾" TALL.

EMBOSSED
LETTERING,
2 P. MOLD,
CLEAR GLASS
10" HIGH.

K.
4201

CONCAVE
CENTRE IN
BASE 2⅞" DIAM.

Rutherfords
DAIRY

BASE IS
4" DIAM.

148

M.S.

1⅜" DIAM. BASE

2 P. MOLD,
8 PANELS,
CLEAR GLASS
3¾" HIGH
WITH EMBOS-
SED LETTERS

CONTENTS
2 FL. OZ.
HORNE'S

M.S.

149

M.S.

150

M.S.

151

3

1 15/16" SQU. BASE

2 P. MOLD, SUN
YELLOW COLOR, 5" TALL.

152

M.S.

HORNE'S
DES. REG'D. 1932

2" BY 2¾"
BASE

2 P. MOLD,
EMBOSSED PEA-NUT DESIGN
WITH LABEL PANEL ON
FRONT. CLEAR GLASS
6" HIGH.

2 P. MOLD, LAID ON
NECK RING, 8"
TALL AND AQUA
GREEN COLOR

2 P. MOLD,
DARK BLUE AQUA
COLOR, 6" TALL.

3⅜" DIAM.
BASE.

PAGE SIXTEEN

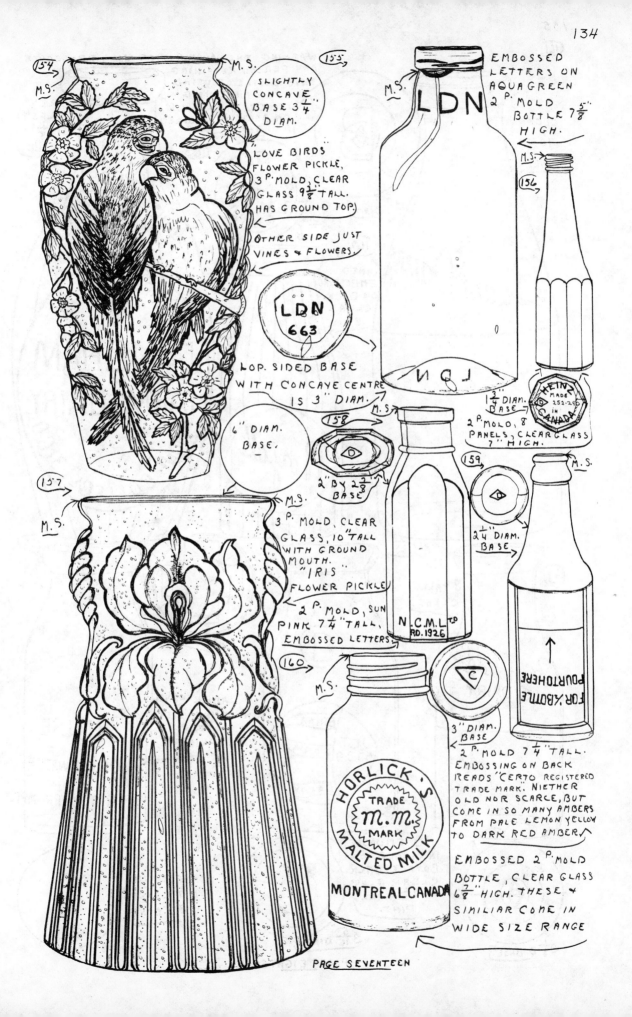

154

M.S.

M.S.

155

SLIGHTLY
CONCAVE
BASE 3¼"
DIAM.

"LOVE BIRDS"
FLOWER PICKLE,
3 P. MOLD, CLEAR
GLASS 9⅜" TALL.
HAS GROUND TOP.

OTHER SIDE JUST
VINES & FLOWERS.

LDN
663

LOP. SIDED BASE
WITH CONCAVE CENTRE
IS 3" DIAM.

6" DIAM.
BASE.

EMBOSSED
LETTERS ON
AQUA GREEN
2 P. MOLD
BOTTLE 7⅝"
HIGH.

M.S.

LDN

M.S.

156

LDN

1¾" DIAM.
BASE

2 P. MOLD, 8
PANELS, CLEAR GLASS
7" HIGH.

HEINZ
MADE
252-250
IN
CANADA

M.S.

158

2" BY 2⅞"
BASE

M.S.

157

M.S.

M.S.

3 P. MOLD, CLEAR
GLASS, 10" TALL
WITH GROUND
MOUTH.
"IRIS"
FLOWER PICKLE

2 P. MOLD, SUN
PINK 7¼" TALL,
EMBOSSED LETTERS.

160

M.S.

N.C.M.L ᵀᴰ
RD. 1926

159

M.S.

2¼" DIAM.
BASE

FOR ½ BOTTLE
POUR TO HERE

3" DIAM.
BASE

HORLICK'S
TRADE
m.m.
MARK
MALTED MILK
MONTREAL CANADA

C

2 P. MOLD 7¼" TALL.
EMBOSSING ON BACK
READS "CERTO REGISTERED
TRADE MARK." NIETHER
OLD NOR SCARCE, BUT
COME IN SO MANY AMBERS
FROM PALE LEMON YELLOW
TO DARK RED AMBER.

EMBOSSED 2 P. MOLD
BOTTLE, CLEAR GLASS
6⅞" HIGH. THESE &
SIMILIAR COME IN
WIDE SIZE RANGE

PAGE SEVENTEEN

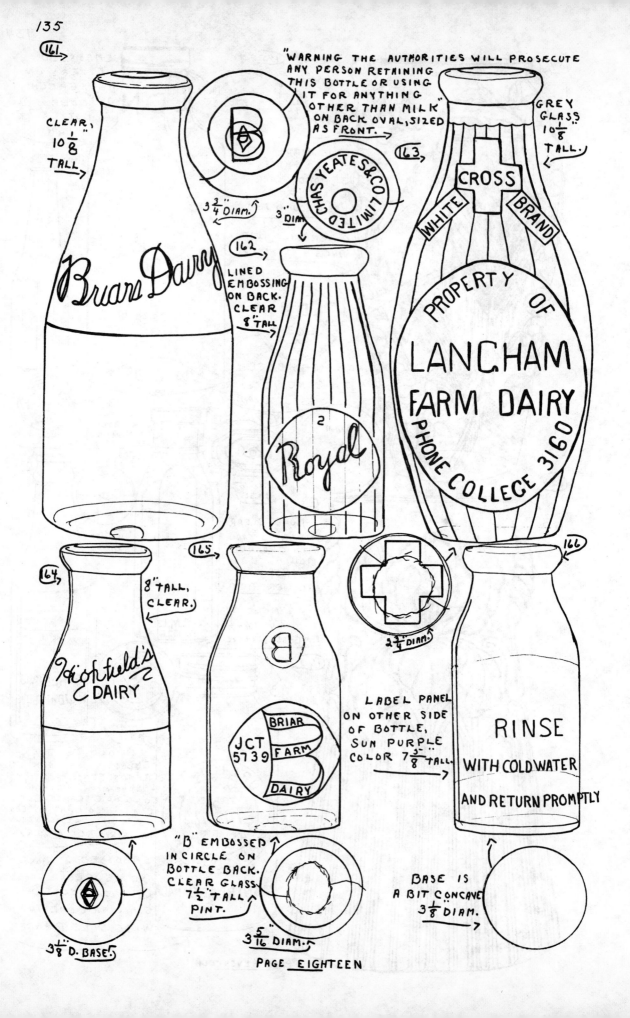

161

CLEAR,
10⅛"
TALL →

"WARNING THE AUTHORITIES WILL PROSECUTE
ANY PERSON RETAINING
THIS BOTTLE OR USING
IT FOR ANYTHING
OTHER THAN MILK"
ON BACK OVAL, SIZED
AS FRONT. →

GREY
GLASS
10⅛"
TALL. →

Briar Dairy

B

3¾" DIAM. →

163 →

CROSS

WHITE   BRAND

CHAS YEATES & CO LIMITED

3" DIAM →

162 →

LINED
EMBOSSING
ON BACK.
CLEAR
8" TALL →

PROPERTY OF

LANCHAM
FARM DAIRY

2
Royal

PHONE COLLEGE 3160

165 →

166 →

164 →

8" TALL,
CLEAR.) →

Highfield's
DAIRY

B

2¼" DIAM. →

RINSE

LABEL PANEL
ON OTHER SIDE
OF BOTTLE,
SUN PURPLE
COLOR 7⅜" TALL →

WITH COLD WATER

AND RETURN PROMPTLY

JCT
5739

BRIAR

FARM

DAIRY

"B" EMBOSSED
IN CIRCLE ON
BOTTLE BACK.
CLEAR GLASS
7½" TALL
PINT.

BASE IS
A BIT CONCAVE
3⅛" DIAM.

3⅛" D. BASE;

3 5/16" DIAM. →

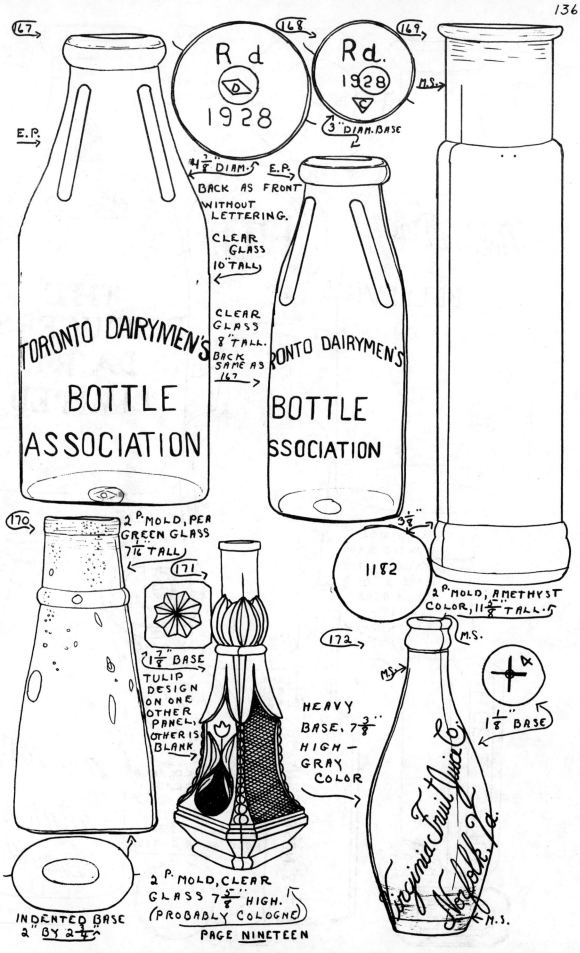

167

168

169

E.P.

Rd
1928

Rd.
1928

M.S.

3" DIAM. BASE

4⅞" DIAM. E.P.

BACK AS FRONT

WITHOUT
LETTERING.

CLEAR
GLASS
10" TALL

CLEAR
GLASS
8" TALL.
BACK
SAME AS
167

TORONTO DAIRYMEN'S
BOTTLE
ASSOCIATION

RONTO DAIRYMEN'S
BOTTLE
ASSOCIATION

3"

1182

⅜"

2 P. MOLD, AMETHYST
COLOR, 11⅝" TALL.

M.S.

170

2 P. MOLD, PEA
GREEN GLASS
7 1/16" TALL

171

172

M.S.

1⅞" BASE
TULIP
DESIGN
ON ONE
OTHER
PANEL,
OTHER IS
BLANK

HEAVY
BASE. 7⅜"
HIGH —
GRAY
COLOR

1⅛" BASE

Virginia Fruit Juice Co.
Norfolk, Va.

M.S.

INDENTED BASE
2" BY 2¼"

2 P. MOLD, CLEAR
GLASS 7⅝" HIGH.
(PROBABLY COLOGNE)

PAGE NINETEEN

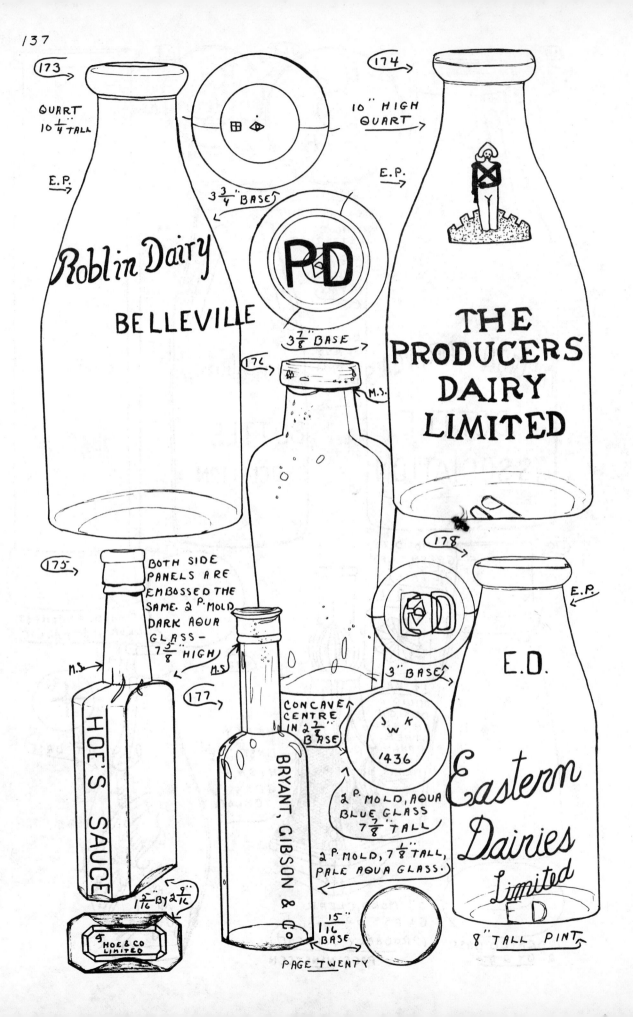

137

173
QUART
10¼" TALL

E.P.

Roblin Dairy
BELLEVILLE

174
10" HIGH
QUART

E.P.

THE
PRODUCERS
DAIRY
LIMITED

3¾" BASE

PD

3⅞ BASE

176

M.S.

178

PD

3" BASE

175

BOTH SIDE
PANELS ARE
EMBOSSED THE
SAME. 2 P. MOLD
DARK AQUA
GLASS -
7⅝" HIGH

M.S.

M.S.

177

CONCAVE
CENTRE
IN 2⅞"
BASE

E.D.

HOE'S SAUCE

BRYANT, GIBSON & Co.

J W K
1436

2 P. MOLD, AQUA
BLUE GLASS
7⅞" TALL

2 P. MOLD, 7⅛" TALL,
PALE AQUA GLASS.

Eastern
Dairies
Limited
E.D.

1 7/16 BY 2 9/16

HOE & CO
LIMITED

1 15/16
BASE

PAGE TWENTY

8" TALL PINT

179
6 ³/₈" TALL

M.S.

5302
C. S & Co LD

3 ¹/₈" BASE

2 P. MOLD, DARK AQUA GREEN GLASS.

180
2 P. MOLD, AMETHYST COLOR QT.

M.S.

EDWARDSBURG
CROWN BRAND
REGISTERED
PURE
CORN SYRUP
PERFECT SEAL JAR

M.S.

3 ³/₈" SQU. BASE

183

2 ¹/₈" DIAM.

184

RD B 1912

M.S.

D 3

1 ½" BY 2 ¼"

2 P. MOLD, CLEAR GLASS, 6 ⁵/₁₆" TALL

D 3842

1 ³/₄" BY 2 ⁵/₁₆"

181

182

M.S.

M.S.

PATERSON'S ESS CAMP COFFEE & CHICORY

Moyer's

186

FRONT & BACK HAVE SAME EMBOSSING. CLEAR GLASS 2 P. MOLD, 6 ¹³/₁₆" TALL.

M.S.

2 P. MOLD, 8" HIGH, PALE AQUA GLASS

185

M.S.

B & Co LD 104

2" SQU. BASE

106

2 ³/₈"

2 P. MOLD, AMETHYST COLOR, 9 ¹/₈" TALL

4050
D
6

2" BY 2 ¼"

3 ⁵/₁₆" HIGH, CLEAR GLASS

N C M

"GLASGOW" EMBOSSED ON LEFT SIDE. 2 P. MOLD, AQUA COLOR, 8 ⁹/₁₆" TALL

139

187

M.S.

C.L.

THIS IS A VERY
DARK GRASS
GREEN COLOR,
AND THE ONLY
ONE I HAVE SEEN.)

3 3/4" BASE

188

Caulfields

CREAM TOP
PATENTED 1923

Silverwoods

10 1/4" HIGH.
CLEAR GLASS.

3 3/4" DIAM.

3 P. MOLD, CLEAR
GLASS, 8 1/2"
TALL

189

190

3" BASE.

GREY COLOR,
8 1/2" TALL.

191

CLEAR GLASS
7 1/2" TALL.

CITY DAIRY CO

Masons OK Sauce

LIMITED

1666
09

1 11/16" BASE

"LOANED-RETURN
WHEN EMPTY" EMBOSSED
ON BACK.

PAGE TWENTY-TWO

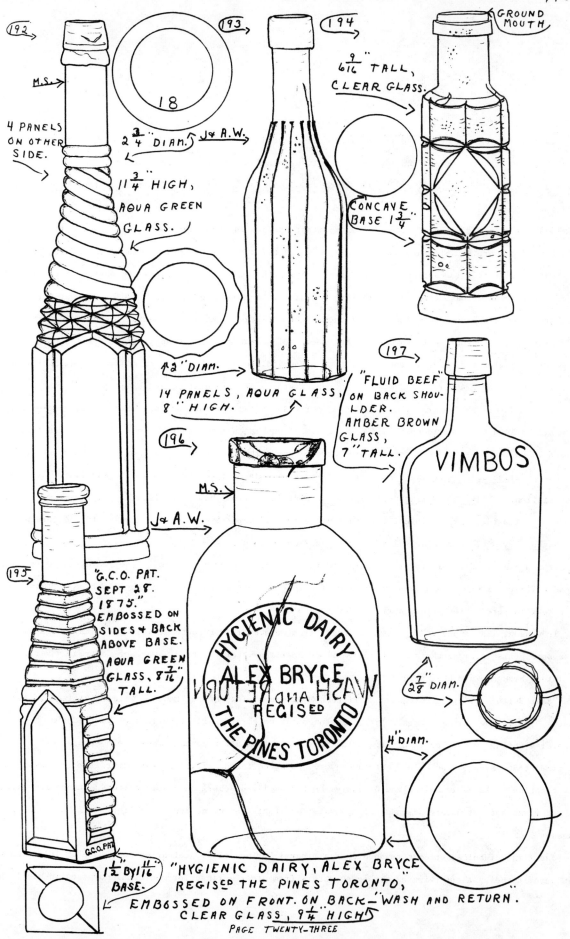

192

M.S.

4 PANELS
ON OTHER
SIDE.

18

$2\frac{3}{4}$" DIAM.

J & A.W.

$11\frac{3}{4}$" HIGH,
AQUA GREEN
GLASS.

193

194

$6\frac{9}{16}$" TALL,
CLEAR GLASS.

GROUND
MOUTH

CONCAVE
BASE $1\frac{3}{4}$"

1.2" DIAM.

14 PANELS, AQUA GLASS,
8" HIGH.

196

M.S.

J & A.W.

197

"FLUID BEEF"
ON BACK SHOU-
LDER.
AMBER BROWN
GLASS,
7" TALL.

VIMBOS

195

"G.C.O. PAT.
SEPT 28.
1875."
EMBOSSED ON
SIDES & BACK
ABOVE BASE.
AQUA GREEN
GLASS, $8\frac{7}{16}$"
TALL.

HYGIENIC DAIRY
ALEX BRYCE
WASH AND RETURN
REGISED
THE PINES TORONTO

$2\frac{7}{8}$" DIAM.

4" DIAM.

G.C.O. PAT

$1\frac{1}{2}$" BY $1\frac{11}{16}$"
BASE.

"HYGIENIC DAIRY, ALEX BRYCE
REGISED THE PINES TORONTO,
EMBOSSED ON FRONT. ON BACK-"WASH AND RETURN."
CLEAR GLASS, $9\frac{1}{4}$" HIGH"

PAGE TWENTY-THREE

XI   MINERAL AND SODA WATERS

A.   Mineral Waters.

Mineral Waters have been used from a very early period as remedial agents. The oldest Greek Physicians had great faith in their curative powers and temples were often erected close to mineral springs. The Greeks considered mineral waters a distinct order of medicaments and a special boon from the Deity, and dedicated them to Hercules, the god of strength.

The Romans also discovered some of the important springs in other parts of Europe over which they had dominion. Roman Physicians praised mineral waters as highly in the fifth century as others did in the nineteenth.

Henry IV, visited the springs of the Pyrenees during his youth and noticing the abuses of their employment, sought to correct them after his accession to the French throne. In 1603, he nominated by letters patent, superintendants over baths, fountains and mineral waters of the kingdom, giving them entire control. Even though they had been in use for centuries, it was not until 1670 that the Academy of Sciences in Paris appointed a commission to fully analyse mineral waters and almost a hundred years later before Bayen discovered the means of separating sulphur from sulphurious waters (1766). In 1774 Bergmann demonstrated the existance of sulphuretted hydrogen gas.

Mineral Waters are generally divided into four classes and some are hot and others cold. Acidulated or Carbonated are characterised by an acrid taste and the release of bubbles as they contain four or five times their volume of carbonic acid gas. The salts they contain are muriates and carbonates of lime and magnesia, carbonate and sulphate of iron etc. Saline Springs consist in general of salts of soda or lime, or of magnesia and lime, with carbonic acid and oxide of iron. Chalybeate Springs (ferruginous - containing iron) have a decided styptic taste. The iron is sometimes in a state of oxide, held in solution by carbonic acid, and sometimes exists as a sulphate and carbonate. The fourth are Sulphur Springs, containing sulphur and recognised by odour.

It had been fashionable for the wealthy to visit Watering Places or Spas as they were called for many years in Europe. Various kinds of amusement were also offered to lure the healthy. For those not so fortunate as to be able to visit them in person, the waters were bottled and sold.

In Canada, listed under "Imports St. Johns, from October 1818 to October 1819" were "Saratoga Water Boxes - 15". These some years later became a heavily advertised American water. Alfred Savage of Montreal advertised them as "being but lately brought into use" around 1840.

"Salt Springs to be let situated at Fifteen Mile Creek, Township of Louth", were advertised in the Upper Canada Gazette, 1797. The Yarmouth Herald 1833, mentioned the celebrated Wilmot Springs of Nova Scotia in telling of a newly discovered spring in the Parish of St. David, four miles from St. Stephen. There were several other springs in use at the time at St. Stephen and Calais but these were not named in the article. The water from the new spring did not sound very tempting - "They are saline and offensive to the smell, discharging a soft white substance resembling curdled milk. The water has not yet undergone chemical analysis; but there can be no doubt that they will be found efficacious in many diseases".

The first organised attempt to develop the Mineral Springs of St. Catharines was made in 1816. Moorman mentions this water as being about twice as strong as waters from other springs for medicinal purposes in his 'Mineral Springs of North America', 1873. He listed the following as being the most important Canadian Springs:

Caledonia Springs	-	midway between Ottawa and Montreal
Tuscarora Acid Spring	-	Tuscarora Township, 21 miles north of Port Dover
Charlotteville Sulphur Spring	-	near Port Dover on Lake Erie
The Mineral Artesian Wells	-	at St. Catharines
Varennes Springs	-	on the St. Lawrence, 17 miles below Montreal
The St. Leon Springs	-	no location given
Plantagenet Springs	-	no location given
Caxton Springs	-	no location given

These last were two in number, one sulphur and the other saline, situated in the Township of Caxton about three miles from Three Rivers. They were brought into active use around 1838.

The Plantagenet Springs were called the Georgian Springs in 1840. They were situated twenty-two miles above the Longue Sault on the Ottawa River in the Township of Plantagenet. By 1848, the Plantagenet Spring Spa and Water were being advertised in many Canadian newspapers.

The St. Leon Springs, situated about four miles from the River du Loup, were advertised by a John Grant, St. Leon, as proprietor in 1846, and mentioned as newly discovered. "Varennes Mineral Water may be had in boxes of one dozen each", 1842, also a recent discovery.

Pure and healthy Spring Water Ice from the Yorkville Fountain-head was advertised by R.B. Richard in 1861; in this he thanked his customers for their past seventeen years of patronage. York Springs Water - natural; York Sparks (charged with purified carbonic gas); York Ginger Ale; York Sarsaparilla; York Soda; York Potash Water; and York Aperients (the perfect laxative) were advertised by The Mineral Springs Ltd., Toronto, in 1906. York Springs were later purchased by O'Keefe's.

A. 11.   CALEDONIA SPRINGS AND THE CALEDONIA GLASS WORKS

The Caledonia Springs first came to the notice of man other than the native Indian around 1806, when the Honourable Mr. Grant and a party of beaver hunters came upon them. There were signs of them being known and resorted to by the Indians. A beaten path led to their source and some of the surrounding trees showed traces of rude figures, and hiero-glyphical emblems. These had been observed to mark several other mineral springs in the Province. The thirsty hunters drank some of the water and the effects produced caused Mr. Grant to later evaporate some of it and find left a variety of salts.

No further interest was taken of these springs until a settler in the area named Kellogg came upon them while deer hunting some years later. The taste and smell of the waters first attracted his attention and by their use he soon became convinced of their medical properties. His informing other inhabitants of the neighbourhood soon led to their shortly being in general use for the purgative effects of the water. "Unlooked for powers gradually developed themselves and diseases over which they were never expected to exert a salutary influence, were found to succumb and fly before their use" - "The cramped and stiffened limb, in that distressing form of rheumatism, the effect of constant exposure to wet and cold, by which settlers and otherwise hardy hunters are so much afflicted, recovered its elasticity and strength, the bent and pain-wracked body became lithe and easy; the waters seemed to instil new vigour into the emaciated frame, to redeem from time and years the feeling of youth and to disarm the power of age, by removing its infirmities".

Kellogg erected a log shanty at the place and began charging a small fee for the use of the waters and they soon became a general resort on Sundays. Their advancement became more rapid and visitors from more distant parts started attending. A house was built for their reception and another log shanty. The Springs, three in number - saline, gas and sulphur - and surrounding property were sold to a Mr. Lemuel Cushing in 1835. The "Caledonia Springs Hotel" was advertised by a Thomas Woodbury in 1836 and the following year a Mr. William Parker advertised the Caledonia Springs .

Due to Parker's efforts, the newspapers of the time soon became interested in the Springs and frequent mentions were made of the cures they were performing and the improvements Mr. Parker was making at the place. An analysis of the different waters had been made by James Chilton, M.D. of New York in 1836 and this was frequently in print afterwards. Mr. Parker built a new hotel at Caledonia Springs in 1837 that was destined to burn down less than a year later. The hotel was not insured so was quite a loss to Mr. Parker, who made do for the balance of the season by adding an extension to the old hotel. He ran notices of a lottery at the end of the year in which 100 lots at Caledonia Springs were the prizes and lost no time in putting the money to use.

The following year, 1840, again needing money, he decided on another lottery or "Tirage au Sort". The first prize to be worth $10,000 - the winner being entitled to an undivided half of the property on which the Springs sat, or the cash - his choice. Second prize was worth $7000, third, $4000, etc. The winner or winners being entitled to an undivided half of the lot and hotel or other buildings already on it.

Lotteries were common in Canada at this time but on a much smaller scale, so Mr. Parker's "Tirage au Sort" received a lot of free publicity from the papers by their urging people to buy tickets at £5 each. Mr. Parker pledged himself to build a church and school among other promised improvements, thus gaining support from a wider section than he might otherwise have done.

This time in his advertisements for carpenters, brick-makers, etc., he stipulated they must also be able to play some kind of musical instrument, so a band could be formed for the amusement of the guests.

During 1841, 'Life in the Woods' were more enjoyable with the addition of another New Hotel, Clean Beds, attentive servants, good foods and wines, billiard table, piano, ball-room and dancing, archery, etc. "The Steamer Caledonia will commence running for passengers to the Springs in the course of this week (June 17th), and will leave Lachine for Port Fortune three times a week and return from the Springs Monday, Wednesday and Friday" - "Caledonia Spring Stages will be in readiness at Port Fortune on the arrival of the Steamer Caledonia to convey passengers to the Spa the same evening".

A small newspaper was started by Mr. Parker that year, with himself as editor, called "Life at the Springs". This paper contained a "Visitors List" and reports on the various events occuring and was available by subscription.

A circular railroad for the amusement of guests was a new addition in 1842. By this time, Caledonia Waters were being sold in England, France and the United States. An ad. from a New York Paper was mentioned in Montreal as saying "the Waters are bottled under the surface of the water in such a manner as to preserve the gas and all the medicinal virtues of the Waters, to be forwarded in wooden casks to Montreal, Quebec, New York and Agents in other places".

Another new larger Hotel was opened in 1843 and still more improvements made, with mention of a swimming bath in contemplation. A fourth spring was discovered about two miles from the others and soon called the Intermittent Spring.

A board walk was laid down to it. A guest at the Springs in later describing them said, "In the immediate vicinity of the Springs is the Bathing House containing hot, cold, shower and vapour Baths, and adjoining this is the Bottling House, where thousands of gallons are bottled annually and sent to all parts of Canada and the United States. Round about the Springs in a circular direction are the various Hotels and Dwelling Houses erected. Mr. Parker's own Hotel is very spacious, with every modern comfort and convenience and the luxuries of life as readily available as in the cities of New York and Montreal..." etc. Further improvements in contemplation by Mr. Parker were told about including plans to make navigable a large creek, (L'Attican) that turned a saw mill in the village and a large observatory about to be erected to give an extended view of the Ottawa and surrounding country.

The Caledonia Springs were by this time a very popular resort, and many prominent names were to be found on the 'Visitors List'. The Caledonia Races held each year with horses coming from all over to participate assured Mr. Parker support from the sporting element.

The following from a Montreal paper was published August 2, 1844. "The Intermittent Spring is destined to cap the climax - to crown the work of Divine Providence and finish the most complete assortment of Mineral Water in the world. The Waters at the Intermittent Springs are at present brought out on men's backs. The Spa is not accessible by other means of conveyance; but a railroad is in contemplation, and the Waters are of such valuable consideration that the Proprietor feels justified in commencing the road forthwith, a good part of which will be run with his pleasur cars, thus affording a treat to the public that cannot be enjoyed elsewhere in Canada. This Spring is in the second concession of Caledonia, about two miles from the main Springs. It has been named the Intermittent Spring on account of the ebbing and flowing of the Water, which appears to run off only when it is thrown out by the gas, which rises in great quantities every four minutes, and on applying a torch, it burns and flashes like powder. The Water is very powerful without being disagreeable, and has been named by some of the visitors the 'Phlegm-cutter'. Its action upon bile is like the effect of calomel, and as an assistant to the Saline and Gas Springs, the Intermittent Spring, to say nothing of the pleasure trip to it, will to the other Springs no doubt, form a most valuable addition".

July 24, 1844 - from the Toronto Star: "(CALEDONIA GLASS WORKS) A glass manufactury', principally for making bottles for the Caledonia Waters, is now being established at the Springs. The immense quantity of bottles required for the transport of the Waters, has induced Mr. Parker to give encouragement to an enterprise of the kind, the first we believe, that has been attempted in Canada. The manufacture will not be confined to bottles alone, but will include a variety of utensils of glass and pottery for domestic purpose".

Thur., Sept. 19, 1844   (Montreal Transcript)
"GLASS WORKS AT THE SPRINGS - The new furnace having been completed, a second and most successful attempt has been made at the Caledonia Springs for the manufacture of Glass Bottles. Samples of which were exhibited on Tuesday last, which are superior to those generally imported, both in quality and shape.
The workmen declare the materials to be the best they have ever used in any country; and all the ingredients for making glass are procured at, and very near to, the Springs. Thus another improvement has been added to the Springs, which promises to be of greater advantage to the Proprietor than anything hitherto attempted.
Mr. Parker will in the course of a few weeks be able to try the experiment of making white glass such as decanters,

dishes and tumblers, the latter of which, as well as bottles, he will require no small quantity for his own use. We

understand the principal ingredients for this kind of ware are to be found within a short distance from the Springs."

"Go on Mr. Parker, and while your friends kindly wish you all sorts of good luck (and at the same time exhibit conside-

rable skepticism in nearly all your projects) you must soon arrive at the height of your laudable ambition -

Communicated. -

(No - not till we see a small iron steam boat along side the factory. - Ed.)"

"In the absence of news we may speak of curiosities, and among the wonders of this place the Glass Works at present

rank the first, being the only thing of the kind in British America. It is not strange that the men, old women, and

young children of the neighbourhood, throng the place, and open their eyes with astonishment at the blaze of this seven-

times heated Furnace, containing two immense pots of solid red hot glass, which is handled with as much familiarity

by the workmen with their iron pipes, as an old woman would stir up her oatmeal porridge with a spoon; whilst children

by dozens, and children of a larger growth, are seen snatching up little curiosities of glass falling from the pipes,

spun out and curled in all manners of shapes, which none but the best of material would hold together to handle; and

owing to the superior quality, a trial has been made to melt and blow bottles without potash, which has succeeded beyond

all expectations."

Sept. 21, 1844   (from Montreal Transcript)

"CALEDONIA INTERMITTENT SPRING - The Powerful Waters from this Spring are coming into vogue through the most respectable

recommendations in this city, which are given from actual experience..." etc., etc. "...warrant the Proprietor in going

to a very considerable expence in making them available to the public..." etc., etc. "Fresh supplies from the four

Caledonia Springs will be forwarded to the Caledonia Water Depot, no. 4, Place d'Armes every week.

Wm. Parker.

Samples of the CALEDONIA GLASS WORKS may be seen at the Depot."

Dec. 14, 1844   (from Montreal Transcript)

"A large and valuable bed of White Sand has just been discovered in opening a winter road from the Caledonia Springs to

the Military Road in Lockie and this valuable material is pronounced by the bottle makers at the Springs to be the best

kind for the manufacture of White Glass of all descriptions. Should this be the case, it will be a discovery of no

small importance to the Glass Works now in operation."

'Life at the Springs' went pretty much as usual during 1845. A Mr. Clifton leased the Canada House (Mr. Parker's

largest hotel, and now so called) and because of hard times reduced prices. 'Hard Times' or not, Mr. Parker had a

weather eye out for business and although Canada was heading into a depression, he had not run out of ideas to attract

visitors to the Springs. In that year, he sponsored a 'Pedestrian Match', with a Mr. Eaton, the baker at the Canada

House, the attraction. In this match, Mr. Eaton was to perform what was known as the 'Barclay Feat'. Captain Barclay

had walked a thousand miles in a thousand successive hours, at the rate of one mile in each and every hour, in October,

537 MILES
JOSIAH EATON Æ 77.

1808. Mr. Eaton was in his seventy-eighth year at the time and his walking to be during the summer heat. The sporting element were busy with their bets for and against Mr. Eaton completing his walk, and the Springs crowded with visitors to watch. "Public opinion both here and in the United States, New York in particular, is decidedly against a man of Mr. Eaton's age being able to accomplish this feat successfully. Every precaution is taken by his backer, Mr. Parker, to have the match thoroughly and correctly formed, according to the strictest meaning of the numerous wagers against the undertaking. We learn that a gentleman of undoubted veracity has been employed by those concerned from the States, to come in and remain at the Springs for the whole match, to look after and testify himself to the due performance of eight hours out of each twenty-four, which is a fourth part of the task, during the time hundreds will be watching daily, besides those sworn in for the express purpose."

Mr. Eaton, despite all thoughts to the contrary, finished his walk to "the cheers of the multitude".

Sept. 1846 - "The question has often been said 'What does Mr. Eaton get by all this?' and Mr. Parker has no objection to satisfying the public on the subject." etc., etc. "...namely Mr. Parker advanced all expenses, giving Mr. Eaton half if he won, and Mr. Parker was to pay all bets and expenses if Mr. Eaton lost."

(Ad. from same paper - 'Life at the Springs') - "BOTTLE BLOWERS WANTED at the Caledonia Springs - Two men acquainted with the manufactury of BLACK BOTTLES, will find employment by calling at the Caledonia Water Depot, no. 4, Place d'Armes, Montreal."

Lord Metcalf was among the visitors at the Springs during 1846, and at the time of his visit, Mr. Parker obtained the then Governor's consent to build a 'retreat for Royalty', and when finished named it "Governer's Cottage". It was in the latter part of this same year that Mr. Parker sold the Springs and property on which they were situated to a Mr. Wilkinson for "over $44,000".

From a letter written by the Editor of the British Whig dated Aug. 7, 1848: "The small village has grown quite into a little town, with post-office, churches, stores, saw-mill, bottle manufactury, race course - with stands, stables, and other conveniences for sportsmen, hotels, boarding houses, and taverns".

Thus, the Bottle Factory was in production at least four years. The Waters from Caledonia Springs continued to be advertised along with the hotels and boarding houses for some years after.

The Caledonia Springs Hotel Property was sold under the Insolvent Act of 1875, at public auction. "Comprising about 175 acres of land, on which has been erected a magnificent New Hotel, Amusement Building, Farm House, etc. The justly celebrated Caledonia Springs, three in number...are also on the property..." etc., etc. From this and another description of Caledonia Springs written in the 1890's, Mr. Parker's town in the forest would seem to have disappeared.

The Caledonia Springs, Grand Hotel, was incorporated in 1876 and sold out in 1906. The Caledonia Springs Hotel was advertised the same year under the management of the C.P.R. Co. - "A charming place for week-end outings, and open for guests all winter".

Duncan Aperient Water, bottled at the Springs was sold by the Caledonia Springs Co. Ltd., with water analysis on the label as made by a Dr. J.T. Donald of Montreal in 1915. A still later bottle is embossed "Property of Red Arrow Caledonia Water Company Limited".

XI   MINERAL AND SODA WATERS - cont'd

B.   Soda Waters.

Seltzer Water derived its name from the village of Lower Selters near Limburg, in the Duchy of Nassau where several springs are united in one basin, yielding a sparkling and effervescing mineral water. Joseph Priestly, an English chemist, is credited with being the first man to produce artificial carbonated water when he invented a method for dissolving carbon dioxide in water, in the latter 1700's.

Carbonic Acid Water, the commonest type, was prepared on a large scale by placing whiting, chalk, or carbonate of lime in a lead vessel with water and sulphuric acid, in an early description. The combination formed stucco or sulphate of lime, and carbonic acid evolved as gas. "The latter is received in a reservoir, and is thereafter forced into water, so that the latter dissolves about five times its own volume of the gas."

The less common aerated waters were - Aerated Soda Water, Potash Water, Selters Water, Carrara Water (obtained by dissolving fine chips of carrara marble in acid charged water), Lime Water (when other forms of lime than carrara marble are used), Magnesia Water and Chalybeate Water (by dissolving a compound of iron in carbonic acid water).

Seltzer Water in baskets of fifty bottles each were for sale and could be tasted at Messrs Dixon and Viney, Galley-Key Custom-house, England, in 1785. Scheppe's Soda and Potash Waters had been constantly in use by the "Royal Palaces in London and Windsor as well as by the principal Nobility and Gentry in the United Kingdom" and manufactured by their powerful machinery for half a century in 1844, according to their advertising.

Richard Sheperd offered his "Chimically termed (Oxygenated Gas Water) far surpassing any yet offered to the public", in Quebec, 1810, and "N.B. one shilling per dozen allowed for return of bottles". It does not seem as if this were a new product to the area but rather an improvement to others already on sale. By 1817, J.T. Turnbull of Montreal was advertising a soda and mineral water establishment as number two. Alfred Savage, a Montreal Druggist and Chemist, had flavoured "Aerated Soda Water" in 1841 and Ginger Nectar, made by themselves. They were shortly offering their "Carrara Water, made the same as Soda Water but substituting Lime for Soda". James Neel, Yarmouth advertised that he had purchased equipment for making soda water in 1841. He had at the same time purchased a recipe for making Dr. Beard's Root Beer together with Bottled Cider and Ginger Beer.

James Crapper, plumber, had Soda Water Apparatus for sale in Toronto in 1859. Four years later Thomas Smith had the same but manufactured by himself. "Likewise wire caps for bottles, much cheaper than they can be imported for and quite as good." These too were made by him.

T. Bickle & Son, Hamilton, had one of the best class London Machines in operation for manufacturing Soda Water at their Medical Hall in 1853. John Green of Chatham manufactured and peddled Soda Water, Lemon Soda, Sarsaparilla Etc., by wagon to Cook's Corners, Bridge, Buckhorn, Trog, Morpeth, Ridgetown, Blenhelm, McKay's Corners, Kinney's Tavern, Wallaceburg, Dresden, Dawn Mills, Thamesville, Kent Bridge, Louisville, and all other places on those routes, three times a week in 1866.

B. ii.   CHARLES WILSON

Charles Wilson's Ginger Ales is listed in a 1871 Directory as having been established in Montreal in 1845. Charles Wilson came to Canada with his parents in 1839 and started working at the bottling table in Montreal when twelve years of age. He later became a partner of the owner, Mrs. Farquhar, and by 1867 was advertising under his own name as Late Farquhar & Wilson.

The Wilson family, originally from Northern Ireland, moved to Toronto and set up business as "Manufacturers of Ginger Ales and Mineral Waters" in 1875. When the plant first started at 519 Sherbourne St., full capacity was three hundred dozen bottles a day. Mr. Wilson soon put in new machinery to increase production to one hundred thousand bottles daily.

Wilson products were awarded a certificate and medal at the International Exhibition at Philadelphia in 1876.

A new Wilson's Plant was officially opened in Don Mills on May 3rd, 1969, on the 94th anniversary of the arrival of the Wilson family in Toronto.

This bottling plant has the capacity to process fifty thousand bottles per hour, from 'wash' to casing. The cases are conveyed to a huge loading bay, there to be stacked on freshly washed Wilson's trucks, a far cry from the two decker horse drawn vans still in use in 1910 and later.

B. iii.   HIRES ROOT BEER

The Hires Division of Consolidated Foods, Chicago, was acquired by Crush International in 1962, bringing to the company an old and respected name in Root Beer.

Charles E. Hires left school at ten to help support his family by working in a drug store. At eighteen he was owner and later attended the College of Pharmacy and Jefferson Medical School, during which time he thought up the idea of a root drink.

Working with a mixture of roots, barks and herbs he came up with a 'herb tea' which his customers had to steep in water - in 1869.

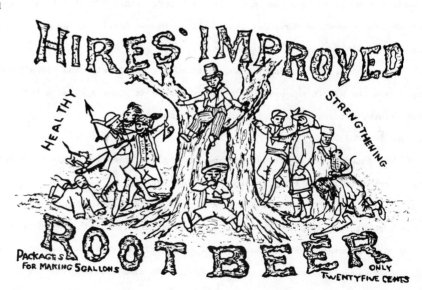

Demand grew for the product which was soon sold in three ounce bottles to which sugar, water and yeast were added for a 'carbonated' drink. This was called "Hires' House-hold Extract". A friend who was also a teetotaler thought the name 'Root Beer' might appeal to the hard drinking miners, and help stop them squandering their pay at the local saloon, so the name was changed to "Hires' Root Beer".

It soon became evident that another change in form was needed so that soda water manufacturers could use it by merely adding sugar and soda water for a finished beverage. The first franchise bottler of Hires' Root Beer was the Crystal Bottling Co. of Philadelphia in 1893. A number of others soon followed.

The company later built a number of plants in areas where there were no franchise plants, including one in Toronto, the first in Canada. This was later transferred to Montreal and became the Canadian Head Office of the Charles E. Hires Co. Ltd.

By 1897, Hires' Root Beer was advertised in Toronto both by package and bottle. "Remember the genuine 'Hires Root Beer Carbonated' is sold only in pint bottles with the name blown in the glass". These bottles were pictured with the ad., but I have yet to see one.

By the 1930's, Hires' Root Beer was the undisputed leader in the Root Beer market. The company remained under the Hires' family control until 1960 when it was sold to Consolidated Foods Corp. Crush International Ltd. purchased the formula and trade mark rights of Hires' Root Beer in 1962 and with this, some 400 franchise bottles throughout the world.

B. iv.   BOTTLE DESIGNS

The dump-shaped bung stoppered seltzer was the first specially designed glass bottle to be used in England for mineral waters. The rounded bottom bottle was patented by an English man, William Hamilton, in 1814, to combat the problem of popping corks caused by aerated water. These Hamilton 'egg' bottles are called various names by collectors as bowlers, bombs and torpedos; they remained in use until the end of the century. A modified form of the egg was patented in 1870, having a flat bottom.

Hiram Codd, another Englishman, invented the bottle with the sides pinched in to hold a marble in 1872. The pressure from the gas in the beverage held the marble in place against a rubber ring. This bottle was used in England for many years, but only a few Canadian beverage manufacturers used it. Special bottling machinery was required in order to use the Codd.

The Internal screw stopper was another English invention; this was patented by Henry Barret in 1872, but seems to have been more in use for beers than soda bottles.

Charles de Quillfeldt of New York city invented the Lightning stopper found on both beer and soda bottles in 1875. This type stopper is still in use in some countries. The most common type of soda bottle next to the crown cork invented by William Painter, an American, in 1891 (and still in use), is the Hutchinson stopper patented in 1875 by Charles Hutchinson, another American. William Painter is also credited for the Baltimore loop seal, invented in 1887 for beer bottles.

Whatever the style, mineral and soda water or 'pop' bottles are a favourite with many Canadian collectors. Sometime, somewhere, I am still hoping to find one from the Caledonia Glass Works.

References

Papers -

Byetown Gazette - 1836 to 45
Chatham Tribune - 1866
The Globe, Toronto and name changes - 1848, 59, 61, 63, 75, 92, 1906
Hamilton Gazette - 1853
Kingston Chronicle & Gazette - 1843-44
La Gazette de Quebec - 1810
Life at the Springs (Caledonia Springs) - 1843-46
London Daily Register (England) - 1785
London Times (England) - 1844
Montreal Herald - 1819
Montreal Pilot - 1840, 41, 42, 43, 44, 45, 46
Montreal Transcript - 1844
Ottawa Citizen - 1851
Three Rivers Gazette - 1817
Toronto Herald - 1846
Toronto Star - 1844-46
Upper Canada Gazette (Newark) - 1797
Yarmouth Herald & Western Advertiser (Nova Scotia) - 1833-41
Western Herald (Sandwhich) - 1839
The Macaully Papers - 1839-41

Books -

Baudoin, Philibert, Notary of Department of Agriculture, Incorporated Bodies, Part I & Part II, Montreal

Grantees Longueuil Township, Prescott, Ontario. 1845-55

Chambers Information for the People, Vol. II, 1842

Chambers Encyclopaedia, 1873, Vol. VIII; 74, Vol. VI; 75, Vol I.

Moorman, J.J., M.D. - Mineral Springs of North America, 1873

Beck, Doreen - The Book of Bottle Collecting, 1973

Munsey, Cecil - The Illustrated Guide to Collecting Bottles, 1970

Company information from -

Mr. Cooper of Charles Wilson's Ltd., Toronto

Mr. W.N. Gilchrist, Vice President Marketing for Crush Beverages Ltd., Toronto

-X-X-X-X-X-X-X-X-X-X-X-X-X-X-X-X-X-X-X-X-X-X-X-X-X-X-X-X-X-X-X-X-X-X-X-X-X-X-X-X-X-X-X

THE SWELLING TIDE OF SOFT DRINKS

Year	Sales in U.S.A. ($ millions)	Total Cases* (millions)	Total Bottles (millions)	Per Capita (bottles)
1869	4.2	8.4	202	6.4
1879	4.7	9.5	227	4.5
1889	14.3	26.1	626	9.9
1899	23.3	38.8	930	12.2
1909	43.5	62.2	1,491	16.2
1919	135.3	169.2	4,060	38.4
1929	214.3	272.4	6,538	53.1
1939	299.8	293.2	7,037	54.9
1949	860.9	1012.9	24,309	162.0
1960	1500.0	1536.0	36,976	205.0

*24 bottles to the case estimated

Summary: Since 1869, per capita comsumption of soft drinks has multiplied
           32 times, production 190 times and sales volume 360 times, to a
           staggering $1.5 billion in 1960.

-X-X-X-X-X-X-X-X-X-X-X-X-X-X-X-X-X-X-X-X-X-X-X-X-X-X-X-X-X-X-X-X-X-X-X-X-X-X-X-X-X-X-

1

M.S.

2 1/8" BASE

1 5/8" DIAM.

"SPRING WATER" ON OTHER SIDE. PALE GREEN COLOR, 9" TALL.

SUN PURPLE, 9 1/8" HIGH.

YORK SPRINGS

2

M.S.

2 1/4" DIAM.

THE COBALT AERATED WATER Co COBALT ONT.

3

M.S.

2 1/4" DIAM.

PETERSONS LIMITED TORONTO

AQUA, 9" TALL

4

M.S.

PERTH BOTTLING WORKS. PERTH ONT.

CLEAR, 9" TALL

5

END OF M.S.

PURITY QUALITY
SUPERIOR BELFAST
GINGER ALE
JAS. T. WALSH
BARRIE AND ONT. STRENGTH
TRADE MARK

8 1/2" TALL, AQUA GREEN COLOR. HAS PAPER LABEL

6

"1114" ON BOTTOM. AQUA GREEN, 9 3/4" HIGH

7

M.S.

THE IMPERIAL SODA WATER WORKS
REGISTERED
TRADE MARK
J. T. WALSH
BARRIE

DEEP AQUA BLUE COLOR, 10 1/2" HIGH

ONE

8

DEEP AQUA BLUE COLOR, 6 7/8" HIGH

9

W.H. DONOVAN

HALIFAX

REG'D D TRADE MARK

1 1/8" DIAM.

AQUA GLASS, 7" HIGH.

3 1/4" DIAM.

10

M.S.

2 3/8" IN DIAM.

1 1/2" BASE

AQUA GREEN, 8 3/4" TALL.

J.B. BAKER HALIFAX

"SOUTH END PLEASANT ST., EMBOSSED ON BACK OF ABOVE BOTTLE

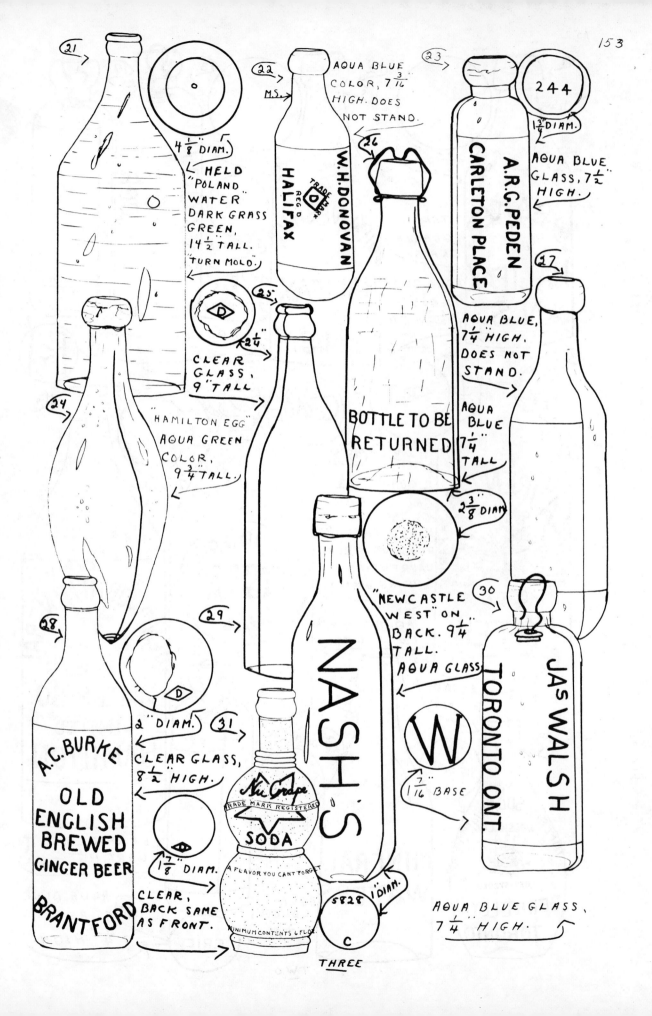

THREE

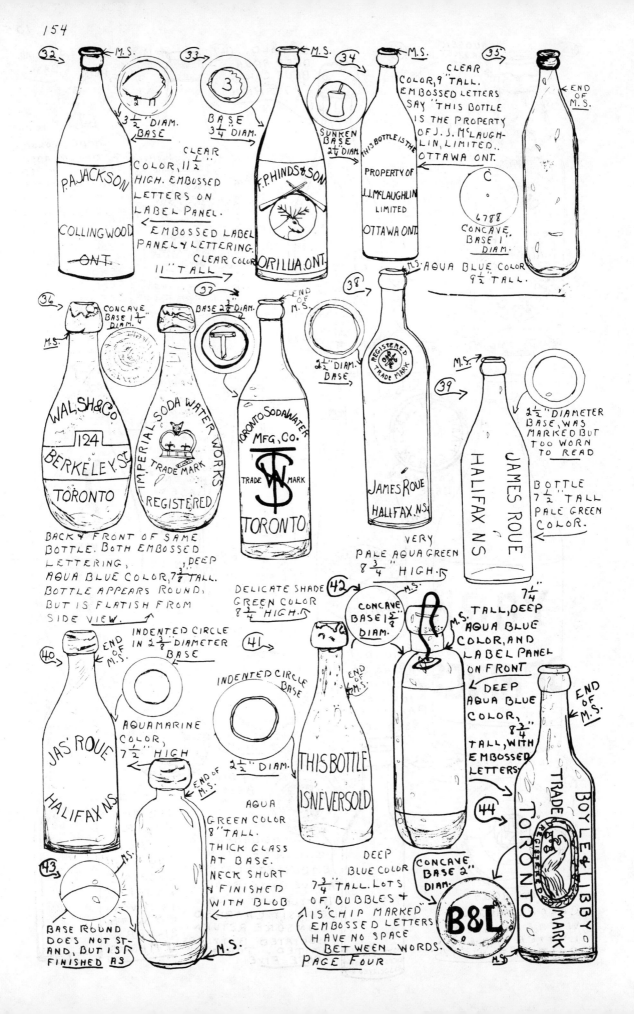

32

3½" DIAM. BASE

33

3

BASE ¾ DIAM.

CLEAR COLOR, 11½" HIGH. EMBOSSED LETTERS ON LABEL PANEL.

← EMBOSSED LABEL PANEL, LETTERING. CLEAR COLOR 11" TALL

P.A.JACKSON COLLINGWOOD ONT.

34

M.S.

SUNKEN BASE 2¼" DIAM.

F.P.HINDS & SON ORILLIA.ONT.

M.S.

CLEAR COLOR, 9" TALL. EMBOSSED LETTERS SAY "THIS BOTTLE IS THE PROPERTY OF J.J. McLAUGHLIN, LIMITED.. OTTAWA ONT.

THIS BOTTLE IS THE PROPERTY OF J.J.McLAUGHLIN LIMITED OTTAWA ONT.

M.S. AQUA BLUE COLOR 9½" TALL.

35

END OF M.S.

C 6788

CONCAVE, BASE 1" DIAM.

36

CONCAVE BASE 1¼ DIAM.

M.S.

WALSH & CO. 124 BERKELEY ST. TORONTO

BACK & FRONT OF SAME BOTTLE. BOTH EMBOSSED LETTERING, DEEP AQUA BLUE COLOR, 7⅞" TALL. BOTTLE APPEARS ROUND, BUT IS FLATISH FROM SIDE VIEW.

BASE 2¼ DIAM.

37

IMPERIAL SODA WATER WORKS TRADE MARK REGISTERED.

END OF M.S.

2¼" DIAM. BASE

TORONTO SODA WATER MFG. CO. TRADE TSW MARK TORONTO

DELICATE SHADE GREEN COLOR 8¾" HIGH.

38

REGISTERED TRADE MARK

JAMES ROUE HALIFAX. N.S.

VERY PALE AQUA GREEN 8¾" HIGH.

39

M.S.

2½" DIAMETER BASE, WAS MARKED BUT TOO WORN TO READ

BOTTLE 7½" TALL PALE GREEN COLOR.

JAMES ROUE HALIFAX N.S.

40

END OF M.S.

INDENTED CIRCLE IN 2¾" DIAMETER BASE

JAS. ROUE HALIFAX.N.S.

41

INDENTED CIRCLE BASE

2¼" DIAM.

AQUAMARINE COLOR, 7½" HIGH

AQUA GREEN COLOR 8" TALL. THICK GLASS AT BASE. NECK SHORT & FINISHED WITH BLOB

END OF M.S.

43

M.S.

BASE ROUND DOES NOT STAND, BUT IS FINISHED AS

THIS BOTTLE IS NEVER SOLD

DEEP BLUE COLOR 7¾" TALL. LOTS OF BUBBLES & IS "CHIP MARKED" EMBOSSED LETTERS HAVE NO SPACE BETWEEN WORDS.

42

CONCAVE BASE 1½" DIAM.

M.S. TALL, DEEP AQUA BLUE COLOR, AND LABEL PANEL ON FRONT

↳ DEEP AQUA BLUE COLOR, 8¾" TALL, WITH EMBOSSED LETTERS

44

CONCAVE BASE 2" DIAM.

B&L

7¼" TALL, DEEP AQUA BLUE

END OF M.S.

BOYLE & LIBBY TORONTO TRADE MARK REGISTERED

M.S.

PAGE FOUR

45 → RUBBER GASKET

M.S. M.S.

419

CONCAVE BASE 1½" DIAM.

2 P. MOLD, AQUA GREEN COLOR, EMBOSSED LETTERING, 8¼" HIGH.

MILTON AERATED'S N. QUEENS CO. WATER WORKS

CONCAVE BASE 2¾" DIAM.

46 →

2 P. MOLD, DEEP AQUA BLUE COLOR. 7¾" HIGH

M.S. M.S.

S. BELCH BELLEVILLE C.W.

47 → ← M.S.

2¾" DIAM. BASE

DES. REGD. 1939.

2 P. MOLD, AMBER COLOR, 7" TALL. LABEL PANEL IS IN RED & WHITE ENAMEL & BRICKS ARE EMBOSSED. BACK HAS LABEL SAME DESIGN AS FRONT BUT ALL IN WHITE. IT READS "A JOLLY GOOD MIXER. ZIP IN EVERY SIP" IN SCRIPT & PRINTED UNDER "AMBER BOTTLE PROTECTS THE FLAVOR."

12 FL. OZ. DOUBLE DRINK WEBB'S Stubby REGISTERED BEVERAGES

48 → M.S.

HAMILTON GLASS WORKS

CONCAVE BASE 2½" DIAM.

YORK SPRINGS

CONCAVE BASE 3½" DIAM.

49 →

← M.S.

D.P →

C.C. NELSON & CO ST. CATHERINES

2 P. MOLD, AQUA-MARINE COLOR, 7¾" HIGH. OVAL LABEL PANEL & EMBOSSED LETTERS.

50 →

M.S. → 2 P. MOLD AQUAMARINE COLOR, 7¾" HIGH

D.P →

SAME AS 49 BUT NO EMBOSSING ON BASE & LABEL PANEL UP-SIDE-DOWN.

ST. CATHERINES C.C. NELSON & CO.

CONCAVE BASE 2½" DIAM

51 →

← M.S.

D.P. →

YORK

2 P. MOLD AQUA COLOR 9¾" TALL. EMBOSSED ON BOTH SIDES. OTHER SIDE SAYS "SPRINGS"

52 →

M.S.

W

2 P. MOLD, AQUA COLORED BOTTLE, WITH EMBOSSED LETTERS ON LABEL PANEL, 10⅞" HIGH!

BOTTLE NOT SOLD DEPOSIT CHARGED ASSOCIATED BOT

2¼" DIAM. BASE

PLB TRADE MARK

1 P. MOLD, AQUAMARINE COLOR 8⅛" HIGH. EMBOSSED LETTERS ABOVE BASE READ "BOTTLE NOT SOLD, DEPOSIT CHARGED TO INSURE RETURN. ASSOCIATED BOTTLERS LIMITED, TORONTO" PAGE FIVE

53 → ← M.S.

2" DIAM. BASE

2 P. MOLD, RED AMBER COLOR, 8" HIGH. FULL OF BUBBLES & SURFACE IS COVERED WITH SILVERY V MARKS.

156

54 →

M.S.

MF

1¼" DIAM. CONCAVE BASE

55 →

P.C. FOY TORONTO

3⅜" DIAM. BASE.

2 P. MOLD, SUN YELLOW COLOR, 10¾" HIGH. BACK EMBOSSING SIMILAR TO FRONT BUT NO LABEL PANEL & READS "DESSIN ENRG." ABOVE BASE.

H.F. WHITHAM BRANTFORD

2 P. MOLD, 7⅞" TALL AQUA COLOR WITH EMBOSSED LETTERING.

56 →

JOHN LYNCH N° 750 SOUTH AVENUE ROCHESTER N.Y.

L

CONCAVE BASE 2⅜" DIAM.

2 P. MOLD, 7¼" TALL, HAS EMBOSSED LETTERING AND IS AQUA GREEN COLOR

MEUNIER FRERE MONTREAL

CONTIENT 28 FL. OZ.

57 →

M.S.

MACK

INDENTED CIRCLE IN BASE 1½" DIAM

AQUAMARINE COLOR, 7¾" TALL, 2 P. MOLD. EMBOSSED LETTERING READS "MACK MINERAL SPRINGS, ST. CATHARINES, ONT."

58 →

INDENTED CIRCLE IN BASE 3½" DIAM.

M.S.

M.S.

C. DARLINGTON

TRADE MARK

UXBRIDGE

MACK MINERAL SPRINGS ST. CATHARINES ONT.

2 P. MOLD WITH EMBOSSED LETTERING 10½" HIGH, PALE AQUA GREEN COLOR

59 →

3⅜" DIAM. BASE

2 P. MOLD. PALE GREEN COLOR, 10⅞" HIGH, WITH EMBOSSED LETTERS.

60 →

NIAGARA FALLS BOTTLING WORKS NIAGARA FALLS ONT.

CONTENTS 30 OZ

2 P. MOLD, AQUA GREEN COLOR, EMBOSSED LETTERS 7⅞" HIGH.

M.S.

TOSSELL

T

CONCAVE BASE 1¼" DIAM.

INDENTED BASE 2¼" DIAM.

S.M.

M.S.

K

TOSSELL & SON NIAGARA FALLS.

61 →

2 P. MOLD, AQUAMARINE COLOR, 7½" TALL WITH EMBOSSED LETTERING.

62 →

2 P. MOLD AQUA GREEN COLOR 7⅞" TALL

M.S. END.

TRADE

EMBOSSED

MARK

BACK READS "CALEY & SON – NORWICH."

PAGE SIX

158

73

M.S.

CONCAVE CIRCLE IN 3¼ DIAM. BASE

2 P. MOLD, DEEP AQUA BLUE COLOR, 10⅜ TALL.

2¼" BASE DIAM.

2 P. MOLD, SUN PURPLE COLOR 7 9/16 TALL. EMBOSSING ABOVE BASE ON BACK SIDE "THIS BOTTLE NOT SOLD."

74

M.S.

Coca-Cola
TRADE MARK REGISTERED
TORONTO ONT.

3 9/16" TALL.

75

M.S.

Coca-Cola
TRADE MARK
RED
DA PROPERTY OF 5

7⅛" DIAM. BASE

Coca-Cola

2 P. MOLD, DARK GREEN COLOR 7¾ HIGH. FRONT & BACK HAVE SAME EMBOSSING "COCA-COLA, TRADE MARK. REGISTERED & ABOVE BASE "PROPERTY OF THE COCA-COLA COMPANY CANADA."

76

M.S.

77

MS

Coca-Cola
TRADE MARK REGISTERED
MIN CONTENTS 6-FL-OZS.

2 P. MOLD, PEA GREEN COLOR 7 11/16 TALL. OTHER SIDE SAME EMBOSSING LESS "MIN CONTENTS 6 FL OZ."

MODERN VERSION MORE STREAM- LINED

2⅜" BASE DIAM.

78

M.S.

CONTENTS 7 OZ
PENETANG BOTTLING
PENETANG ONT.
COY

2 P. MOLD, CLEAR GLASS 7½ TALL WITH EMBOSSED LETTERS.

2⅛" DIAM. BASE

BASE OF NUMBER '79' IS 2¼" DIAMETER.

E F

79

M.S.

ELZEAR FORTIER
QUEBEC

2" DIAM. BASE

"ELZEAR FORTIER & Cⁱᵉ, QUEBEC" EMBOSSED ON ABOVE 2 P. MOLD, DEEP AQUA GREEN BOTTLE 8¾" TALL.

S

2⅛" BASE DIAM.

2 P. MOLD, DARK GREY COLOR, 7⅝ TALL. SAME EMBOSSING ON BOTH SIDES. BASE LINE READS "PROPERTY OF THE COCA COLA COMPANY CANADA.

Coca-Cola
TRADE MARK REGISTERED
COLA COMPANY CANADA

80

O'K
3

O'K

2 P. MOLD, DARK GREEN COLOR, 7 13/16 HIGH. "O.K." EMBOSSED ON BOTH SIDES OF NECK AS WELL AS BASE.

PAGE EIGHT

81 →
2 P. MOLD, AQUA GREEN COLOR WITH EMBOSSED LETTERING & DESIGN.

J.K.

A & W. BURNS
TRADE MARK
TORONTO

82 →
2 P. MOLD, AQUA GREEN COLOR 9½" TALL.

ROUNDED BOTTOM DOES NOT STAND

M.S.

2 P. MOLD, AQUAMARINE COLOR, 13½" HIGH. EMBOSSED DESIGN & LETTERING. "ST LEON MINERAL WATER CO. LTD.

83 →

M.S.
CONCAVE BASE 4¼" DIAM.

ST. LEON MINERAL WATER CO. LTD.
SPRINGS AT ST. LEON QUE.
TRADE MARK REGISTERED
HEAD-OFFICE
TORONTO
CANADA

84 →
M.S.

CONCAVE CIRCLE ON BASE ABOUT 3" DIAM.

D. KNOX.
TRADE & MARK
REGISTERED
PETERBORO_ONT.

LABEL PANEL ON FRONT OF THIS 2 P. MOLD, AQUAMARINE COLORED, 11" TALL BOTTLE. DESIGN & LETTERING ARE EMBOSSED.

85 →
M.S.
M.S.
1417
M.S.

BASE IS ROUNDED BUT DOES HAVE SMALL CONCAVE RING TO STAND ON ⅞" DIAM.

2 P. MOLD, AQUA GREEN COLOR 9½" TALL.

86 →
M.S.

MINERAL WATER

CONCAVE BASE 2¾" DIAM.

EMBOSSED LETTERS, 2 P. MOLD BOTTLE 7½" HIGH, AQUA BLUE COLOR.

87 →
M.S.

2⅜" DIAM. BASE

2 P. MOLD, EMERALD GREEN, 8¾" TALL.

VESS DRY
REGISTERED
RY VESSD
OZS. BOTTLE PA

PAGE NINE

160

88 →

M.S. →

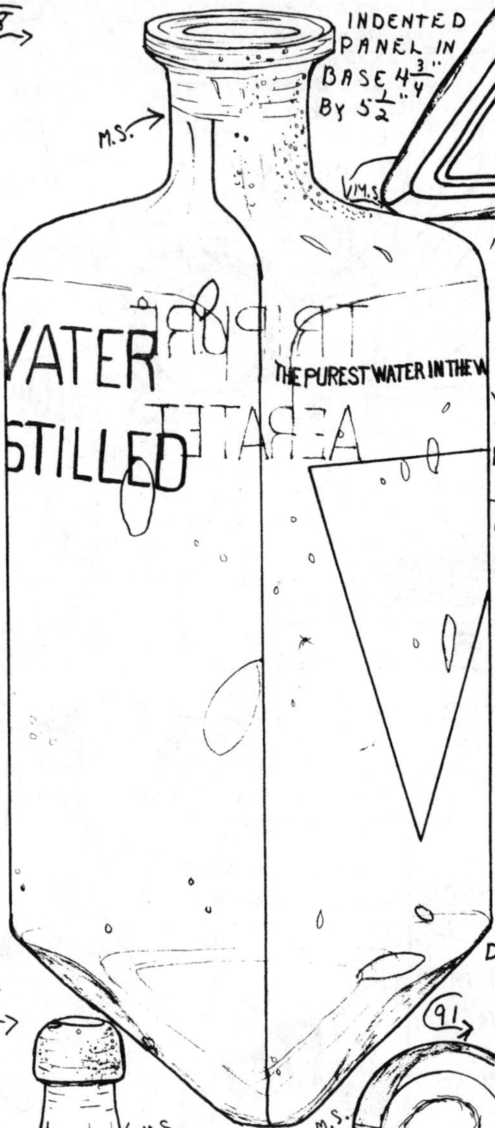

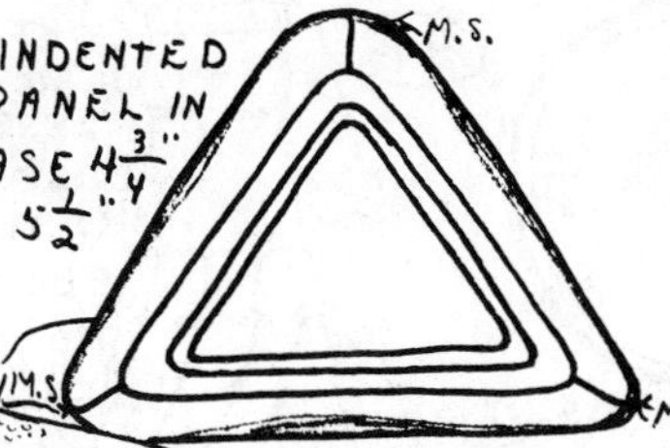

INDENTED
PANEL IN
BASE 4¾"
BY 5½"

M.S.

89 →

M.S. →

WATER
DISTILLED

TRIPURE
THE PUREST WATER IN THE W

AERATE

M.S.

"TRIPURE AERATED"
EMBOSSED ON BACK,
"WATER DISTILLED"
ON LEFT & "THE PURE-
EST WATER IN THE
WORLD" ABOVE A
TRIANGULAR LABEL
PANEL ON RIGHT SIDE.
3 P. MOLD, AQUA GREEN
GLASS, 11¼" TALL.

INDENTED CIRCLE
IN BASE 3⅞" DIAM.

"F. M. PILGRIM
BROCKVILLE." 2 P.
MOLD, DARK GREEN COLOR, 11" TALL.
DESIGN & LETTERING EMBOSSED.

F.M.PILGRIM

BROCKVILLE

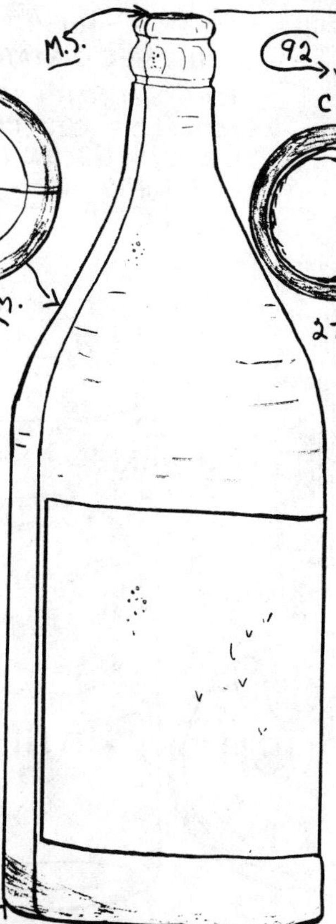

M.S.

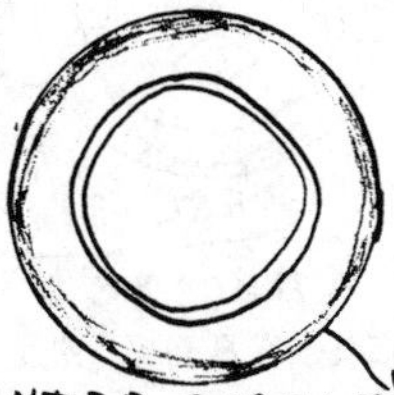

90 →

M.S. →

A.C. →

M.S.

326

91 →

M.S.

3½" DIAM.
BASE.

92 →

"PERTH BOTTLING
WORKS" IN EMBOSSED
CIRCLE. 2 P. MOLD,
PEA GREEN
COLOR, 8" TALL.

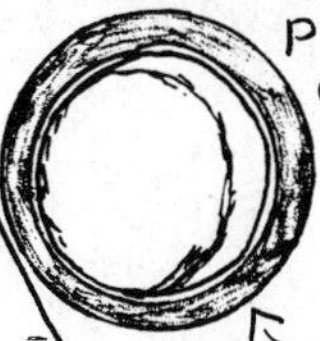

2¼" DIAM.
BASE

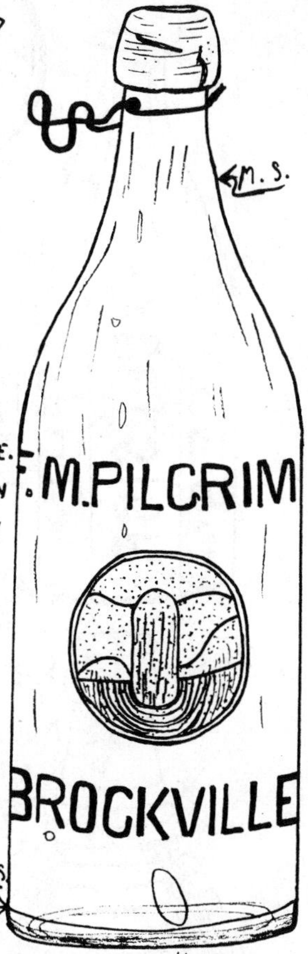

M.S.

INDENTED CIRCLE
IN BASE 3" DIAM.

2 P. MOLD, AMETHYST
COLOR 10½" TALL
WITH EMBOSSED
LETTERING.
"1000 ISLANDS
MINERAL WATER
CO. BROCKVILLE.
F. M. PILGRIM."
2 P. MOLD BOTTLE
HAS LABEL PANEL.
AQUAMARINE
GLASS, 10¾" TALL.

ISLANDS MINERAL WATER CO.

F.M. PILGRIM

BROCKVILLE

PERTH BOTTLING WORKS
K & C
PERTH. ONT.

PAGE TEN.

93 →
M.S.

THE EXCELSIOR WA-T-E-R

2 ¾" DIAM. BASE HAS SCAR

2 P. MOLD, VERY DARK OLIVE GREEN COLOR, 7 1/16" HIGH & HAS 8 PANELS.

4 D

2 1/24" (BASE DIAM.)

94
M.S.

"CONTENTS 6½ OZ. 95 DESIGN REGISTERE 1925. PROPERTY OF BEST & BENNETT LTD. HAMILTON" EMBOSSED ABOVE BASE. 2 P. MOLD, CLEAR GLASS, 7½" TALL.

BASE 2¼" DIAM.

DESIGN REGISTERED 1925
BENNETT LTD. HAMIL

2 P. MOLD, 8 ⅛" TALL, EMBOSSED LETTERS ON LABEL PANEL. AQUA GREEN GLASS.

M.S.

F.P. HINDS & SON

ORILLIA. ONT.

96 →
M.S.

BACK EMBOSSED LETTERS ON PANEL SAME AS FRONT READS "REG'D AUG. 22. 1922 ORANGE CRUSH BOTTLE. 2 P. MOLD, 11 ½" HIGH. STYLE MADE IN CLEAR & AMBER GLASS.

2 P. MOLD, 7 ¼" TALL, EMBOSSED WORDS "TRADE MARK" AT SIDES OF CENTRE DESIGN. GREEN GLASS

Orange Crush
30 FL OZ.

2 P. MOLD AQUA BLUE GLASS, 11" TALL

2 P. MOLD, PEA GREEN COLOR 8 ¾" TALL.

97
M.S.

CONTENTS 10 OZ

THE DAVERN GINGER ALE CO COBOURG

2
D

2 7/16" DIAM. BASE.

98
M.S.

YORK SPRINGS

99 →
M.S.

JAMES WALSH

TORONTO

ORANGE CRUSH BOTTLE

3 ¼" DIAM. BASE.

J.W

2" DIAM. CONCAVE BASE

WS

3 ½" DIAM. BASE

162

100

M.S.

101

2¼" BASE

AQUA BLUE GLASS, 7½" TALL, 2 P. MOLD.

M

M.S.

102

⅝" BASE

"REDFEARN BROS. BOTTLE MAKERS BARNSLEY" EMBOSSED ON BACK OF BOTTLE ABOVE BASE. 2 P. MOLD, AQUA GLASS, 7½" TALL.

R B B

103

JAS MATTHEWS TORONTO

TRADE MARK

2 P. MOLD 7¾" TALL. AMBER GLASS

BASE IS 2½" DIAM. & SAME STYLE AS-100

JAS. MATTHEWS

TRADE MARK

REGISTERED. TORONTO.

SPENCER CONNOR & Cº MANCHESTER

F.S.

M.S.

CLARK BROS TORONTO

2 P. MOLD, PALE GREEN COLOR, 7⅛" HIGH, HAS ROUND BOTTOM.

M.S.

104

105

M.S.

106

1¼" BASE

M.S.

2 P. MOLD, AQUA GLASS, WITH ROUNDED BASE 7" HIGH.

AQUA BLUE GLASS, 11" TALL, 2 P. MOLD

TORONTO JNO VERNER TORONTO

TRADE MARK

F.S.

ST CATHARINES

TRADE

MARK

THOS TUNE & SON

AQUA BLUE GLASS, 6¾" TALL, 2 P. MOLD.

D.J.

CHAS. WILSON LIMITED

TRADE MARK

REGISTERED TORONTO

107

F.S.

M.S.

CHARLES WILSON TORONTO LATE OF MONTREAL

108

M.S.

109

1¾" BASE

F.S.

M.S.

AQUAMARINE COLOR, 7½" TALL, 2 P. MOLD.

2 P. MOLD, 6¾" TALL, AQUA COLOR.

R.A. PILGRIM & CO. HAMILTON, C.W.

L.V. GARNER WELLAND

1⅞" BASE

PAGE TWELVE

C.W.

3¼" DIAM.

2 P. MOLD, AQUA GREEN GLASS, 7½" HIGH. ROUNDED BASE, DOES NOT STAND.

164

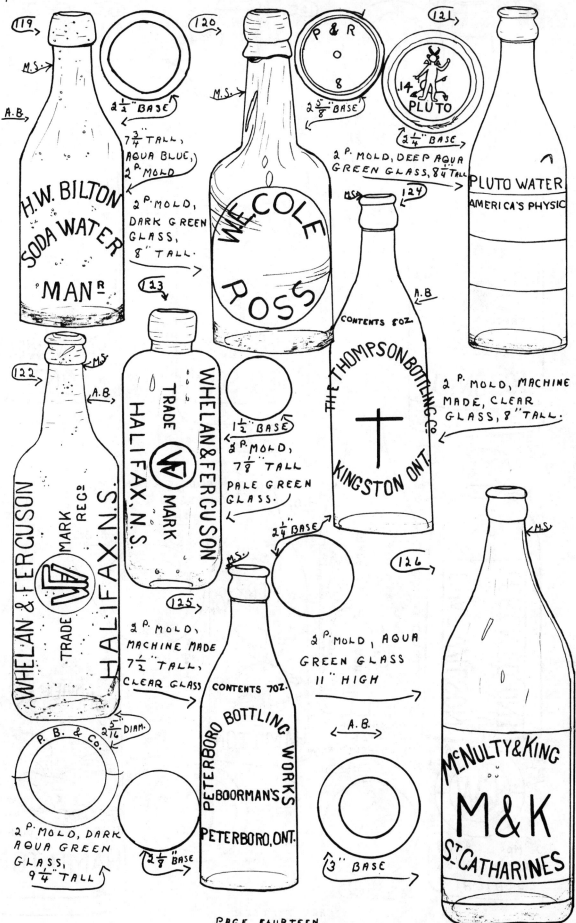

119

M.S.

A.B.

H.W. BILTON
SODA WATER
MAN.R

2½" BASE

7¾" TALL,
AQUA BLUE,
2 P. MOLD

2 P. MOLD,
DARK GREEN
GLASS,
8" TALL.

120

M.S.

P & R

o

8

2⅝" BASE

2 P. MOLD, DEEP AQUA
GREEN GLASS, 8¼" TALL

121

.14
PLUTO

2¼" BASE

PLUTO WATER
AMERICA'S PHYSIC

W.E. COLE
ROSS

113

124

M.S.

CONTENTS 8 OZ.

The THOMPSON BOTTLING Co.

KINGSTON ONT.

A.B.

2 P. MOLD, MACHINE
MADE, CLEAR
GLASS, 8" TALL.

122

M.S.

A.B.

WHELAN & FERGUSON
TRADE MARK REC.D
HALIFAX. N.S.

WHELAN & FERGUSON
TRADE MARK
HALIFAX. N.S.

1½" BASE

2 P. MOLD,
7⅞" TALL
PALE GREEN
GLASS.

125

2¼" BASE

126

M.S.

2 P. MOLD,
MACHINE MADE
7½" TALL,
CLEAR GLASS

M.S.

CONTENTS 7 OZ.

PETERBORO BOTTLING WORKS
P.E. BOORMAN'S
PETERBORO, ONT.

2 P. MOLD, AQUA
GREEN GLASS
11" HIGH

A.B.

McNULTY & KING
M & K
St. CATHARINES

P. B. & Co.

2 5/16" DIAM.

2 P. MOLD, DARK
AQUA GREEN
GLASS,
9¼" TALL

2⅛" BASE

3" BASE

MALE
WM TAYLOR
& SON

OWEN
SOUND
REG'D
1931

127 → M.S.

K

3⅛" BASE

A.B. →

AMETHYST
COLOR, 11¼
TALL, 2 P.
MOLD, MACHINE
MADE.

2 P. MOLD,
AQUA BLUE
GLASS -
11" HIGH →

L.A. KIRKLAND

TRADE   MARK

REGIS TERED

TORONTO

128 → M.S.

A.B. →

2 P. MOLD, PALE
GREEN GLASS -
11" TALL

3¼" BASE

A.B. →

TAYLOR & PRINGLE
Co. LIMITED

TRADE   MARK

REGISTERED

OWEN SOUND

129 → M.S.

NEIL McPHAIL

COLLINGWOOD
ONT.

30 → M.S. A.B. →

CHAS. WILSON
TORONTO, ONT.
CM

BASE
2½"

C.W.

2 P. MOLD, AQUA
GREEN GLASS
6¾" HIGH

131 → M.S.

TRADE
MARK

COLLINGWOOD ON

"CUMMER & SON
HAMILTON
2 P. MOLD PALE GREEN
COLOR, 8" TALL

2¼" BASE

132 → M.S. A.B. →

AQUA GREEN
GLASS 11¼"
HIGH →

3⅛" BASE

AQUA COLOR
7¾" HIGH

CUMMER & SON

TRADE   MARK

HAMILTON

2¼" BASE

C

133 → M.S. A.B. →

CUMMER & SON

TRADE   MARK.

HAMILTON

166

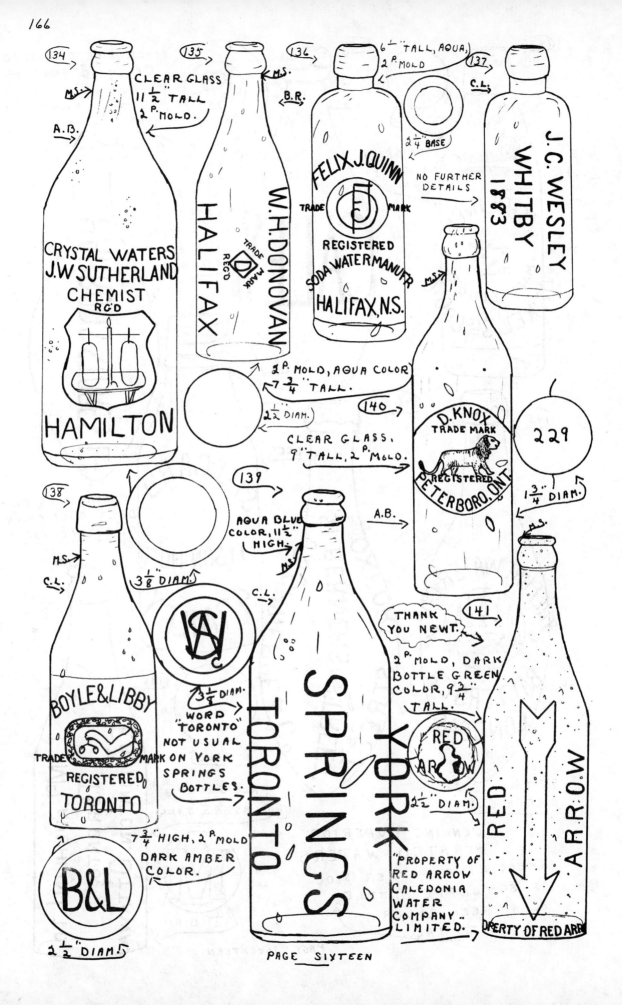

134

135

136

137

138

139

140

141

229

A.B.

M.S.

CLEAR GLASS
11½" TALL
2 P. MOLD.

M.S.

B.R.

6½" TALL, AQUA,
2 P. MOLD

C.L.

CRYSTAL WATERS
J.W.SUTHERLAND
CHEMIST
RG'D

HAMILTON

HALIFAX

W.H.DONOVAN

TRADE
MARK
RG'D

FELIX J.QUINN

TRADE MARK

REGISTERED

SODA WATER MANUF.R

HALIFAX, N.S.

2¼" BASE

NO FURTHER
DETAILS

J.C.WESLEY
WHITBY
1883

M.S.

2 P. MOLD, AQUA COLOR
7¾" TALL.

2½" DIAM.

CLEAR GLASS,
9" TALL, 2 P. MOLD.

D.KNOX
TRADE MARK

REGISTERED

PETERBORO.ONT.

229

1¾" DIAM.

AQUA BLUE
COLOR, 11½"
HIGH.

A.B.

M.S.

THANK
YOU NEWT.

2 P. MOLD, DARK
BOTTLE GREEN
COLOR, 9¾"
TALL.

M.S.

C.L.

3⅛" DIAM.

M.S.

C.L.

BOYLE&LIBBY

TRADE

REGISTERED

TORONTO

WA C

3¼" DIAM.

"WORD
"TORONTO"
NOT USUAL
MARK ON YORK
SPRINGS
BOTTLES.

TORONTO

SPRINGS

YORK

RED
ARROW

2½" DIAM.

RED

ARROW

"PROPERTY OF
RED ARROW
CALEDONIA
WATER
COMPANY..
LIMITED.

B&L

7¾" HIGH, 2 P. MOLD
DARK AMBER
COLOR.

2½" DIAM.

PROPERTY OF RED ARROW

PAGE SIXTEEN

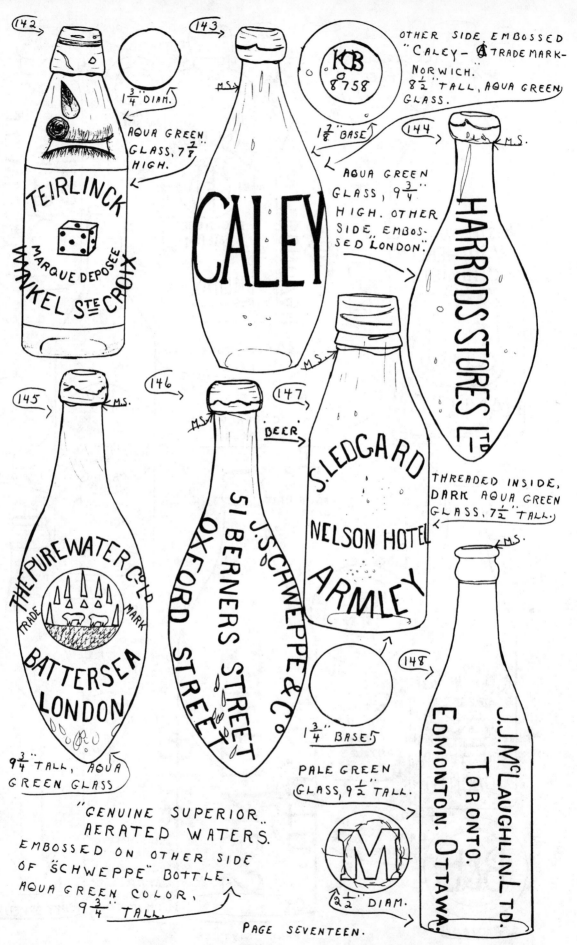

142 →

1 3/4" DIAM.

AQUA GREEN GLASS, 7 7/8" HIGH.

TEIRLINCK
MARQUE DÉPOSÉE
WINKEL Ste CROIX

143 →

MS.

KCB 8758

1 7/8" BASE

OTHER SIDE EMBOSSED "CALEY - TRADE MARK - NORWICH. 8 1/2" TALL, AQUA GREEN GLASS.

CALEY

AQUA GREEN GLASS, 9 3/4" HIGH. OTHER SIDE, EMBOSSED "LONDON".

144 →   DIA.   MS.

HARRODS STORES LTD

145 →   MS.

146 →   MS.

BEER

147 →   MS.

S. LEDGARD
NELSON HOTEL
ARMLEY

THREADED INSIDE, DARK AQUA GREEN GLASS, 7 1/2" TALL.

THE PURE WATER Co LD
TRADE   MARK
BATTERSEA
LONDON

9 3/4" TALL, AQUA GREEN GLASS

51 BERNERS STREET
J. SCHWEPPE & Co.

1 3/4" BASES

PALE GREEN GLASS, 9 1/2" TALL.

M

2 1/2" DIAM.

148 →   MS.

J.J. McLAUGHLIN.LTD.
TORONTO.
EDMONTON. OTTAWA.

"GENUINE SUPERIOR" AERATED WATERS. EMBOSSED ON OTHER SIDE OF "SCHWEPPE" BOTTLE. AQUA GREEN COLOR, 9 3/4" TALL.

PAGE SEVENTEEN.

168

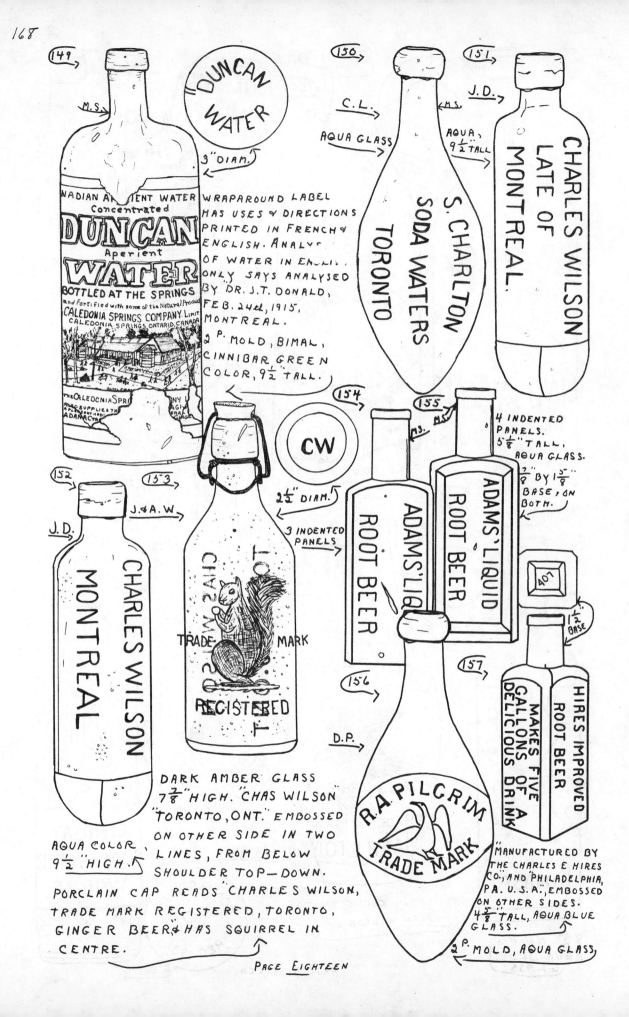

149
M.S.

"DUNCAN WATER"

3" DIAM.

WRAPAROUND LABEL HAS USES & DIRECTIONS PRINTED IN FRENCH & ENGLISH. ANALYSIS OF WATER IN ENGLISH ONLY SAYS ANALYSED BY DR. J.T. DONALD, FEB. 24th, 1915, MONTREAL.

2 P. MOLD, BIMAL, CINNIBAR GREEN COLOR, 9½ TALL.

150
C.L.
AQUA GLASS

S. CHARLTON SODA WATERS TORONTO

AQUA, 9½ TALL

M.S.

151
J.D.

CHARLES WILSON LATE OF MONTREAL.

154
CW
2½" DIAM.

155
M.S. M.S.

4 INDENTED PANELS. 5⅝" TALL. AQUA GLASS.
⅞ BY 1⅝ BASE, ON BOTH.

152
J.D.

CHARLES WILSON MONTREAL

153
J.&A.W

3 INDENTED PANELS

TRADE MARK
REGISTERED

ADAMS' LIQUID ROOT BEER

ADAMS' LIQUID ROOT BEER

407

½ BASE

AQUA COLOR 9½" HIGH.

DARK AMBER GLASS 7⅞" HIGH. "CHAS WILSON" "TORONTO, ONT." EMBOSSED ON OTHER SIDE IN TWO LINES, FROM BELOW SHOULDER TOP—DOWN. PORCLAIN CAP READS "CHARLES WILSON, TRADE MARK REGISTERED, TORONTO, GINGER BEER" & HAS SQUIRREL IN CENTRE.

156
D.P.

R.A. PILGRIM TRADE MARK

157
HIRES IMPROVED ROOT BEER
MAKES FIVE GALLONS OF A DELICIOUS DRINK

"MANUFACTURED BY THE CHARLES E HIRES CO., AND PHILADELPHIA, PA. U.S.A.", EMBOSSED ON OTHER SIDES. 4⅝" TALL, AQUA BLUE GLASS.

2 P. MOLD, AQUA GLASS.

158

M.S.

159

160

M.S.

161

M.S. 169

$3\frac{1}{4}''$ DIAM.

J.B. BEGG

LINDSAY ONT.

BEGG BROS

LINDSAY

THE IMPE

SODA WATER

MARK

HORSFIELD
RRIE

FROM AQUA BLUE
QUART.

$2\frac{1}{4}''$ DIAM.

B

J.B. BEGG

LINDSAY

$8\frac{1}{8}''$ TALL, AMETHYST
COLORED GLASS.

PALE AQUA GLASS

11" TALL, AQUA GLASS

162

163

164

M.S.

M.S.

M.S.

$2''$ DIAM.
BASE

$8\frac{1}{2}''$ TALL, NICE
DARK AMETHYST
COLOR.

$2\frac{1}{4}''$ DIAM.

$8\frac{5}{8}''$ TALL,
AQUA BLUE.

165

M.S.

J.B. BEGG

CUMMER & SON

TRADE   MARK
HAMILTON

McLAUGHLIN'S
TRADE MARK
HYGEIA
WATERS
REGISTERED
TORONTO

LINDSAY
SODA WATER
WORKS

LINDSAY

CLEAR GLASS, $7\frac{5}{8}''$ TALL.

CON G. CO. LTD
C
REG 1931

ALL FROM COLLECTION OF
JOAN & ALAN WILSON.

$8\frac{1}{2}''$ HIGH,
AQUA BLUE
GLASS

PAGE NINETEEN

$2''$ DIAM.

Ink Powder was imported from England for sale in Canada for many years. Around 1820, it began to be offered in bottles but was still in powder form for some years. The druggists were among the first to sell it in liquid - probabl simply mixing the powder with water and selling it under their own name. Mr. Lamb was an established Ink and Blacking manufacturer on New Street, Toronto, by 1841 and sold out to Thomas Anderson in 1843. By 1870 Dredge & Co., also of Toronto, were advertising inks of all colours of their own manufacture. Dalley and Kennedy of Hamilton both made ink along with their other goods but James Kennedy advertised his as "Kennedy's Liquid Bluing" - for writing ink or washing purposes.

Sullivan and Stotesbury reduced the price on Japan Blacking of their own manufacture in York, 1822. C.H. Sabine, druggist, Toronto, stated that after "infinite labour" he had produced a composition that if regularly used imparted to leather boots the properties of India Rubber. This was in liquid form. Charles Shrimpton, Montreal Blacking Manufactu offered to buy or exchange for his product, blacking bottles in 1837. Lack of both ink and blacking bottles seems to have been a problem of these earlier manufacturers - they were often advertising for these. By the amount of stone ink bottles around there must have been many of these in use, but inks were listed under glassware by Budden and Vennor, Montreal, in 1839 as imported from England.

The only blacking bottles of any interest to the collector that are generally available are those where the maker is identified by the lettered plate. Mucilage bottles are similar to inks and often included in the same collection. Ink bottles were made in a variety of styles and aside from the larger 'master inks' do not occupy much space - should this be a consideration. Some interesting designs were used here, and these, while not plentiful, do turn up from time to time to the seeker with patience. Amber appears to be a fairly scarce colour. Cobalt blue while relatively scarce in the pre-machine ink bottle is common in the later.

Figurals are favoured by some collectors; these were and are made to resemble anything other than a bottle. Anoth bottle of some interest is the feeding or baby bottle. Breast glasses were advertised in Quebec in 1764, and various other equipment of a like nature, including bottles, were among the druggists wares, with no indication as to whether o not they were glass until 1845 when Robert Love, Toronto, listed glass feeding bottles along with breast pipes, breast glasses and nipple shells.

Nursing bottles with tubes adjusted were for sale by Garrison and Everett of Yarmouth in 1848. These bottles had a tube reaching to the bottom of the bottle through which the baby could draw out the milk or whatever. Unsanitary as they must have been they remained in use for some number of years in various styled bottles.

The Coghill and Walsh Fire Grenade was advertised simply as I have pictured it and "The Canadian Grenade Fire Extinguisher". Fire Grenade bottles were made to be thrown into fires when they would burst by the impact to release the contents and help put out the fire, These bottles were made in varied designs but for obvious reasons not too many hav survived.

(References re 'Miscellaneous' , page 101)

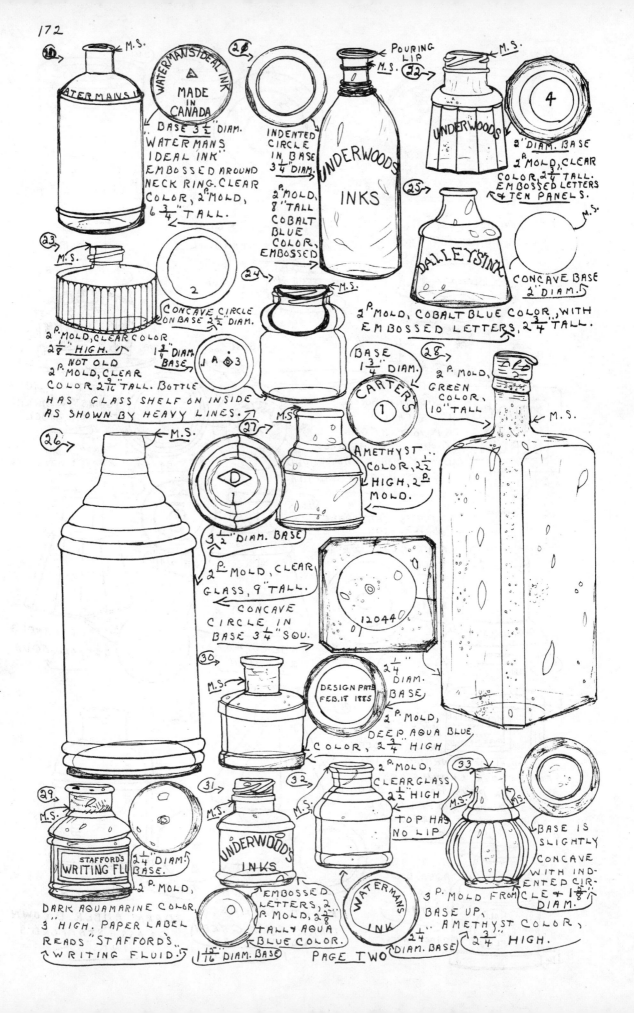

10 → M.S.

WATERMANS IDEAL INK
⚠
MADE IN CANADA

BASE 3¼" DIAM. "WATERMANS IDEAL INK" EMBOSSED AROUND NECK RING. CLEAR COLOR, 2 P. MOLD, 6¾" TALL.

2 P.

INDENTED CIRCLE IN BASE 3¾" DIAM.

2 P. MOLD, 8" TALL COBALT BLUE COLOR. EMBOSSED

POURING LIP
32

M.S.

UNDERWOODS INKS

UNDERWOODS

4

2" DIAM. BASE
2 P. MOLD, CLEAR COLOR, 2¾" TALL. EMBOSSED LETTERS & TEN PANELS.

25 →

DALLEYS INK

M.S.

CONCAVE BASE 2" DIAM.

2 P. MOLD, COBALT BLUE COLOR, WITH EMBOSSED LETTERS, 2¾" TALL.

23 →
M.S.

2

CONCAVE CIRCLE ON BASE 2½" DIAM.

2 P. MOLD, CLEAR COLOR 2⅛" HIGH.

NOT OLD
2 P. MOLD, CLEAR COLOR 2⁹⁄₁₆" TALL. BOTTLE HAS GLASS SHELF ON INSIDE AS SHOWN BY HEAVY LINES.

24 →
M.S.

J A ◇ 3

1½" DIAM. BASE

BASE 1¾" DIAM.

CARTERS
1

AMETHYST COLOR, 2½" HIGH, 2 P. MOLD.

28 →
2 P. MOLD, GREEN COLOR, 10" TALL

M.S.

26 →
M.S.

27 →

D

3½" DIAM. BASE

2 P. MOLD, CLEAR GLASS, 9" TALL.

CONCAVE CIRCLE IN BASE 3¼" SQU.

12044

DESIGN PAT. FEB. 17 1885

2¼" DIAM. BASE

2 P. MOLD, DEEP AQUA BLUE COLOR, 2¾" HIGH

30 →
M.S.

2 P. MOLD, CLEAR GLASS 2½" HIGH

TOP HAS NO LIP

33 →
M.S.

M.S.

BASE IS SLIGHTLY CONCAVE WITH INDENTED CIRCLE & 1⅞" DIAM.

29 →
M.S.

STAFFORD'S WRITING FLU

2¼" DIAM. BASE.

2 P. MOLD, DARK AQUAMARINE COLOR, 3" HIGH. PAPER LABEL READS "STAFFORD'S WRITING FLUID."

31 →
M.S.

UNDERWOOD'S INKS

EMBOSSED LETTERS, 2 P. MOLD, 2⅛" TALL & AQUA BLUE COLOR.

1⁵⁄₁₆" DIAM. BASE

32 →
M.S.

WATERMANS INK

2¼" DIAM. BASE

3 P. MOLD FROM BASE UP, AMETHYST COLOR, 2¾" HIGH.

PAGE TWO

34 M.S.

PAT.

E.P.

"PAT. NOVEMBER 25, 1879"
CLEAR GLASS IN METAL STAND.
2 P. MOLD BOTTLE.

35 M.S. GROUND M.S. **36**

ABOUT 2½" DIAM.
2 P. MOLD, CLEAR GLASS.
MADE FOR STAND. **39**

2" BASE. AQUA BLUE
GLASS 2¼" TALL.

37 M.S.

M.S.

A.B.

38 M.S.
2 P. MOLD, AQUA
GLASS.
2½" HIGH.

BASE 2½"
DIAM.

CARTER'S
79

2 1/16" BASE

BLUE BLACK
PREMIUM
XXX
WRITING INK
MANUFACTURED TORONTO MUCILAGE MAN. CO. TORONTO

2¾" TALL, AQUA
GLASS, 2 P. MOLD.
PAPER LABEL.

"TORONTO MUCILAGE
MAN. CO., TORONTO."

MOODY'S
INKS
BERLIN

DEEP AQUA
BLUE INK BOTTLE
IS 1½" TALL
WITHOUT NECK.
(HAVE SEEN LABELLED
BOTTLE, "MOODY'S HOUSEHOLD
LIQUID, BERLIN CANADA".)

2⅛" BY 2 7/16"

40
C.L.

EDWARDS CATCHPOL

"EDWARDS CATCHPOLE
& Co., TORONTO."
AQUA GLASS, 1½"
TALL.

1⅞" BASE

41 **42**
162
2¼" DIAM.

AMBER GLASS,
2⅞" HIGH.

2¼"
2⅝" TALL, AQUA.
10 PANELS

43 M.S.
M.S.

HALL'S BLUE B
ONCE USED, ALWAY
TAKES PRESID
OVER ALL OTHER

PAPER LABEL

"HALL'S MODERN
WRITING FLUID.
FOR LEDGER, COPYING OR
FOUNTAIN PENS. PATRONIZED BY
KING'S PRINTER AND PRINCIPAL
CORPORATIONS. PEA GREEN
GLASS, 2¼" HIGH."

2¼" DIAM.

44

5/16" DIAM.

2¾" HIGH,
EIGHT PANELS,
DARK AQUA GREEN
COLORED GLASS

45

STAFFORD'S
INK

2¼" DIAM.

3⅛" HIGH,
DARK AMBER BROWN
GLASS. "STAFFORD'S
INK."

46 M.S.
M.S.

BLACK
S USED
DENCE
OTHERS

HALLS
MODERN
WRITING
FLUID

FOR LE
FOUN
PATRO
KINGS
PRINC

AQUA BLUE
COLOR,
2¾" TALL.)

PAPER LABEL.

15/16"

PAGE THREE

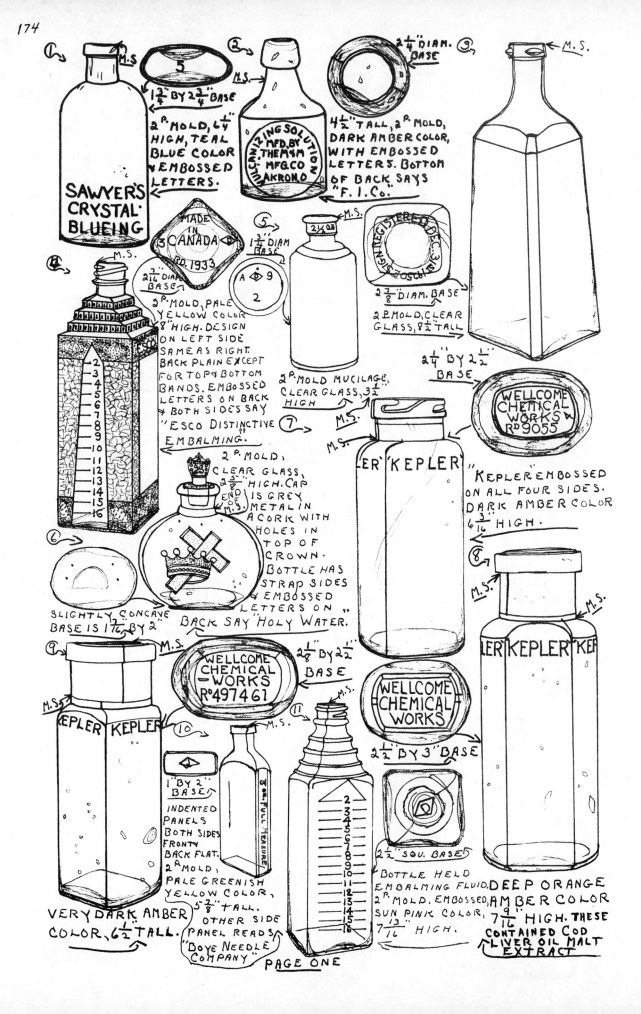

1 → M.S.

5

$1\frac{3}{4}$ BY $2\frac{3}{4}$ BASE

2 P. MOLD, $6\frac{1}{4}$ HIGH, TEAL BLUE COLOR ¢ EMBOSSED LETTERS.

SAWYER'S CRYSTAL BLUEING

2 → M.S.

..CANIZING SOLUTION MFD. BY THE M ¢ M MFG. CO AKRON O.

$2\frac{1}{4}$ DIAM. BASE

3

$4\frac{1}{2}$ TALL, 2 P. MOLD, DARK AMBER COLOR, WITH EMBOSSED LETTERS. BOTTOM OF BACK SAYS "F. I. Co.

M.S.

MADE IN CANADA RD. 1933

3

$2\frac{1}{4}$ DIAM BASE

2 P. MOLD, PALE YELLOW COLOR 8" HIGH. DESIGN ON LEFT SIDE SAME AS RIGHT. BACK PLAIN EXCEPT FOR TOP ¢ BOTTOM BANDS. EMBOSSED LETTERS ON BACK ¢ BOTH SIDES SAY "ESCO DISTINCTIVE EMBALMING.

4 → M.S.

ESCO

2 3 4 5 6 7 8 9 10 11 12 13 14 15 16

5

$1\frac{3}{4}$ DIAM BASE

$2\frac{1}{2}$ oz

M.S.

A ◈ 9 2

2 P. MOLD MUCILAGE, CLEAR GLASS, $3\frac{1}{4}$ HIGH

7 →

M.S.

...IGN REGISTERED DEC. 3 ...O 5C...

$2\frac{3}{8}$ DIAM. BASE

2 P. MOLD, CLEAR GLASS, $8\frac{1}{2}$ TALL

$2\frac{1}{4}$ BY $2\frac{1}{2}$ BASE

WELLCOME CHEMICAL WORKS RD 9055

M.S.

2 P. MOLD, CLEAR GLASS, $2\frac{5}{8}$ HIGH. CAP IS GREY METAL IN A CORK WITH HOLES IN TOP OF CROWN. BOTTLE HAS STRAP SIDES ¢ EMBOSSED LETTERS ON BACK SAY "HOLY WATER.

END OF M.S.

6

SLIGHTLY CONCAVE BASE IS $1\frac{7}{16}$ BY 2"

...LER "KEPLER"

M.S.

M.S.

"KEPLER" EMBOSSED ON ALL FOUR SIDES. DARK AMBER COLOR $6\frac{3}{16}$ HIGH.

8

M.S.

...LER "KEPLER" KEP...

M.S.

9 → M.S.

KEPLER KEPLER

M.S.

WELLCOME CHEMICAL WORKS RD 497461

$2\frac{1}{8}$ BY $2\frac{1}{2}$ BASE

M.S.

10

11

M.S.

1" BY 2" BASE

INDENTED PANELS BOTH SIDES FRONT ¢ BACK FLAT. 2 P. MOLD, PALE GREENISH YELLOW COLOR, $5\frac{7}{8}$ TALL. OTHER SIDE PANEL READS "DOYE NEEDLE COMPANY"

VERY DARK AMBER COLOR, $6\frac{1}{2}$ TALL.

3 OZ. FULL MEASURE

2 3 4 5 6 7 8 9 10 11 12 13 14 15 16

WELLCOME CHEMICAL WORKS

$2\frac{1}{2}$ BY 3 BASE

$2\frac{1}{4}$ SQU. BASE

BOTTLE HELD EMBALMING FLUID. 2 P. MOLD, EMBOSSED SUN PINK COLOR, $7\frac{7}{16}$ HIGH.

DEEP ORANGE AMBER COLOR $7\frac{9}{16}$ HIGH. THESE CONTAINED COD LIVER OIL MALT EXTRACT

PAGE ONE

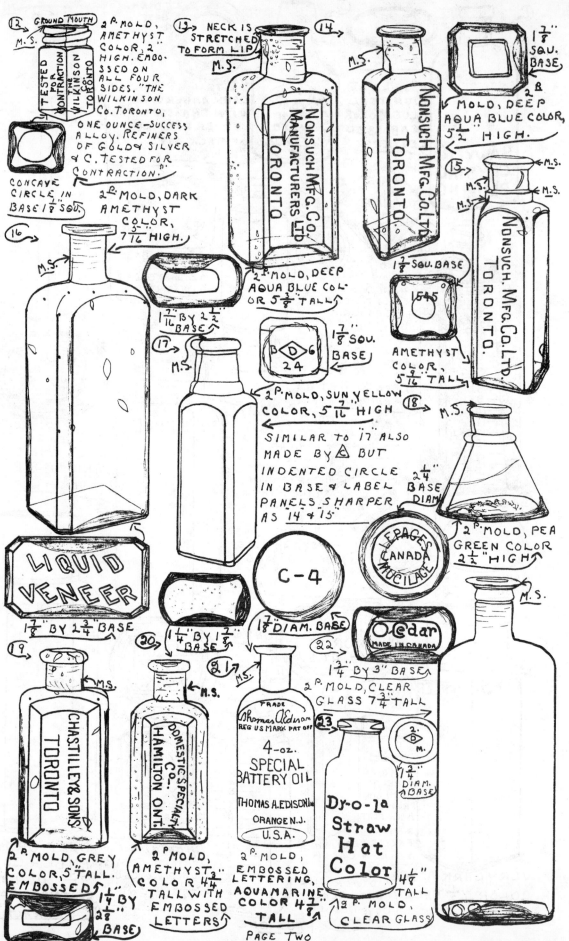

12 GROUND MOUTH — M.S. 2 P. MOLD, AMETHYST COLOR, 2" HIGH. EMBOSSED ON ALL FOUR SIDES. "THE WILKINSON Co. TORONTO, ONE OUNCE—SUCCESS ALLOY. REFINERS OF GOLD & SILVER & C. TESTED FOR CONTRACTION.

TESTED FOR CONTRACTION / THE WILKINSON Co. TORONTO

CONCAVE CIRCLE IN BASE 1⅛" SQU.

2 P. MOLD, DARK AMETHYST COLOR, 7 5/16 HIGH.

13 NECK IS STRETCHED TO FORM LIP. M.S.

NONSUCH MFG. CO. MANUFACTURERS LTD. TORONTO

2 P. MOLD, DEEP AQUA BLUE COLOR 5 ⅜ TALL

14 M.S. NONSUCH MFG. CO. LTD. TORONTO

1⅞" SQU. BASE

MOLD, DEEP AQUA BLUE COLOR, 5½ HIGH.

1⅛" SQU. BASE — 1545

15 M.S. M.S. M.S. NONSUCH MFG. CO. LTD. TORONTO.

AMETHYST COLOR, 5 9/16 TALL

16 M.S. LIQUID VENEER

1⅞" BY 2¾" BASE

1 7/16" BY 2½" BASE

17 M.S.

D 6 24 B — 1⅞" SQU. BASE

2 P. MOLD, SUN YELLOW COLOR, 5 7/16 HIGH

SIMILAR TO 17 ALSO MADE BY △ BUT INDENTED CIRCLE IN BASE & LABEL PANELS SHARPER AS 14 & 15.

18 M.S. 2 P. MOLD, PEA GREEN COLOR 2½"HIGH 2¼" BASE DIAM.

LEPAGES CANADA MUCILAGE

C-4

1⅞" DIAM. BASE

1¼" BY 1⅞" BASE

O Cedar MADE IN CANADA — 1¼" BY 3" BASE

2 P. MOLD, CLEAR GLASS 7¾" TALL

19 M.S. CHAS. TILLEY & SONS TORONTO

2 P. MOLD, GREY COLOR, 5" TALL. EMBOSSED — 1¼" BY 2⅛" BASE

20 M.S. DOMESTIC SPECIALTY Co. HAMILTON ONT.

2 P. MOLD, AMETHYST COLOR 4¾" TALL WITH EMBOSSED LETTERS

21 M.S. TRADE Thomas A. Edison REG US MARK PAT OFF 4-oz. SPECIAL BATTERY OIL THOMAS A. EDISON INC ORANGE N.J. U.S.A.

2 P. MOLD, EMBOSSED LETTERING, AQUAMARINE COLOR 4⅞" TALL

22 **23** Dy-o-la Straw Hat Color

2 M. — 1¾" DIAM. BASE

4⅛" TALL — 2 P. MOLD, CLEAR GLASS

M.S.

PAGE TWO

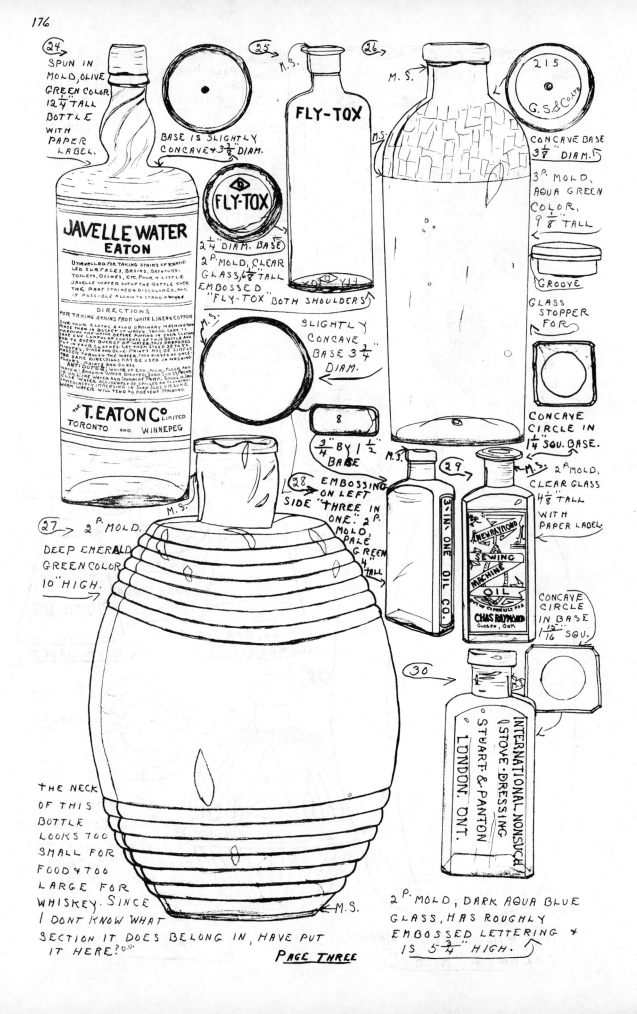

176

24 SPUN IN MOLD, OLIVE GREEN COLOR 12¼" TALL BOTTLE WITH PAPER LABEL.

BASE IS SLIGHTLY CONCAVE + 3⅜" DIAM.

25 M.S.

26 M.S.

FLY-TOX

215 G.S.&Co.Ltd.

CONCAVE BASE 3⅛" DIAM.

3P. MOLD, AQUA GREEN COLOR, 9⅛" TALL

JAVELLE WATER
EATON

Unexcelled for taking stains of enamelled surfaces, basins, bathtubs, toilets, dishes, etc. Pour a little Javelle water out of the bottle over the part stained & discolored, and if possible allow to stand a while.

DIRECTIONS

For taking stains from white linen & cotton. Give your cloths a good ordinary washing then rinse them in bucket of water, taking care to prepare the water before putting in your cloths. Add one cupful of contents of this bottle and put in every bucket of water thus prepared. Put in your clothes. Let them steep 35 to 50 minutes, rinse and dry. Paints may be simply passed through the water, then rinsed at once. The same directions may be used in washing flannels, prints and glass.

ANTIDOTES: White of egg, milk, flour and water. Ammonia water diluted, soap suds, paches lime water and stomach pump. Should Javelle water accidently be spilled on clothing, immediately immersing in soap suds or lime water will tend to prevent staining.

THE T. EATON Co. LIMITED
TORONTO AND WINNIPEG

FLY-TOX

2¼" DIAM. BASE

2P. MOLD, CLEAR GLASS, 6⅞" TALL EMBOSSED "FLY-TOX" BOTH SHOULDERS

M.S.

SLIGHTLY CONCAVE BASE 3¾" DIAM.

M.S.

8
¾" BY 1½" BASE

28 EMBOSSING ON LEFT SIDE "THREE IN ONE." 2P. MOLD, PALE GREEN 4" TALL

27 2P. MOLD, DEEP EMERALD GREEN COLOR 10" HIGH.

M.S.

3-IN-ONE OIL CO.

29

NEW RAYMOND SEWING MACHINE OIL
CHAS RAYMOND GUELPH, ONT.

GROOVE

GLASS STOPPER FOR

CONCAVE CIRCLE IN 1¼" SQU. BASE.

M.S. 2P. MOLD, CLEAR GLASS 4⅛" TALL WITH PAPER LABEL.

CONCAVE CIRCLE IN BASE 1 15/16 SQU.

30

INTERNATIONAL NONSUCH STOVE DRESSING
STUART & PANTON LONDON. ONT.

THE NECK OF THIS BOTTLE LOOKS TOO SMALL FOR FOOD & TOO LARGE FOR WHISKEY. SINCE I DON'T KNOW WHAT SECTION IT DOES BELONG IN, HAVE PUT IT HERE? D.U.

M.S.

PAGE THREE

2P. MOLD, DARK AQUA BLUE GLASS, HAS ROUGHLY EMBOSSED LETTERING & IS 5¾" HIGH.

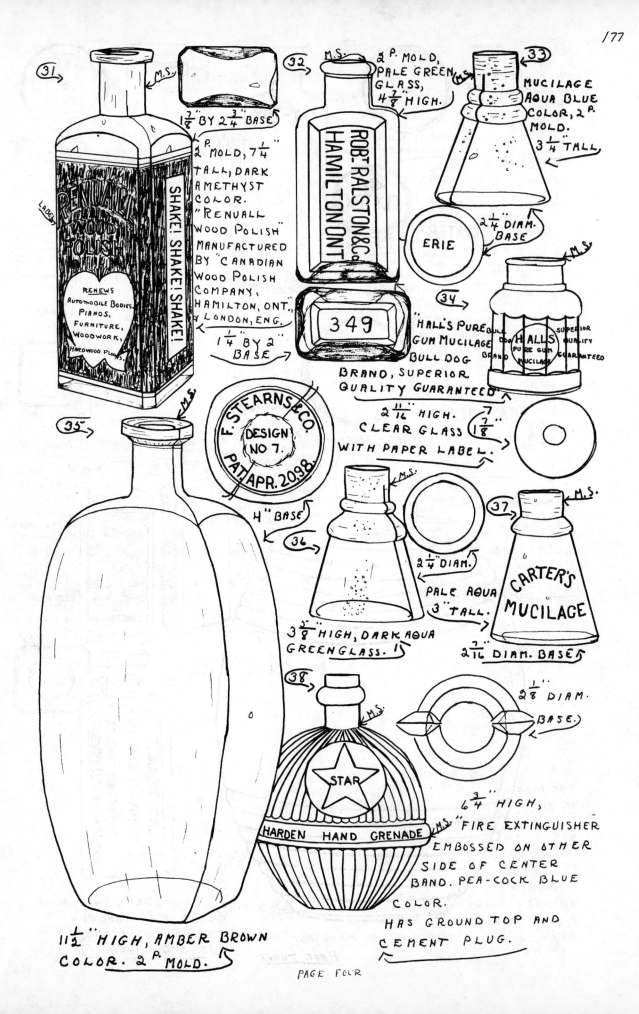

31 → M.S.

1⅞" BY 2¾" BASE

2 P. MOLD, 7¼" TALL, DARK AMETHYST COLOR. "RENUALL" WOOD POLISH MANUFACTURED BY "CANADIAN WOOD POLISH COMPANY, HAMILTON, ONT.", & LONDON, ENG.

RENUALL WOOD POLISH

RENEWS AUTOMOBILE BODIES, PIANOS, FURNITURE, WOODWORK, HARDWOOD FLOORS.

SHAKE! SHAKE! SHAKE!

LABEL

1¼" BY 2" BASE

32 → M.S.

ROBᵗ. RALSTON & Coᵒ. HAMILTON ONT.

349

2 P. MOLD, PALE GREEN GLASS, 4⅞" HIGH.

33 →

MUCILAGE AQUA BLUE COLOR, 2 P. MOLD. 3¼" TALL

2¼" DIAM. BASE

ERIE

34 →

"HALL'S PURE GUM MUCILAGE BULL DOG BRAND, SUPERIOR QUALITY GUARANTEED"

HALL'S PURE GUM MUCILAGE   BULL DOG BRAND   SUPERIOR QUALITY GUARANTEED

2¹¹⁄₁₆" HIGH. CLEAR GLASS WITH PAPER LABEL.

1⅞"

35 → M.S.

F. STEARNS & CO. DESIGN NO 7. PATᵈ APR. 20.98.

4" BASE

36 →

2¼" DIAM.

PALE AQUA

3" TALL.

3⅜" HIGH, DARK AQUA GREEN GLASS.

37 → M.S.

CARTER'S MUCILAGE

2¹¹⁄₁₆" DIAM. BASE

2⅛" DIAM. BASE.

38 →

M.S.

STAR

HARDEN HAND GRENADE   M.S.

6¾" HIGH, "FIRE EXTINGUISHER" EMBOSSED ON OTHER SIDE OF CENTER BAND. PEA-COCK BLUE COLOR. HAS GROUND TOP AND CEMENT PLUG.

11½" HIGH, AMBER BROWN COLOR. 2 P. MOLD.

PAGE FOUR

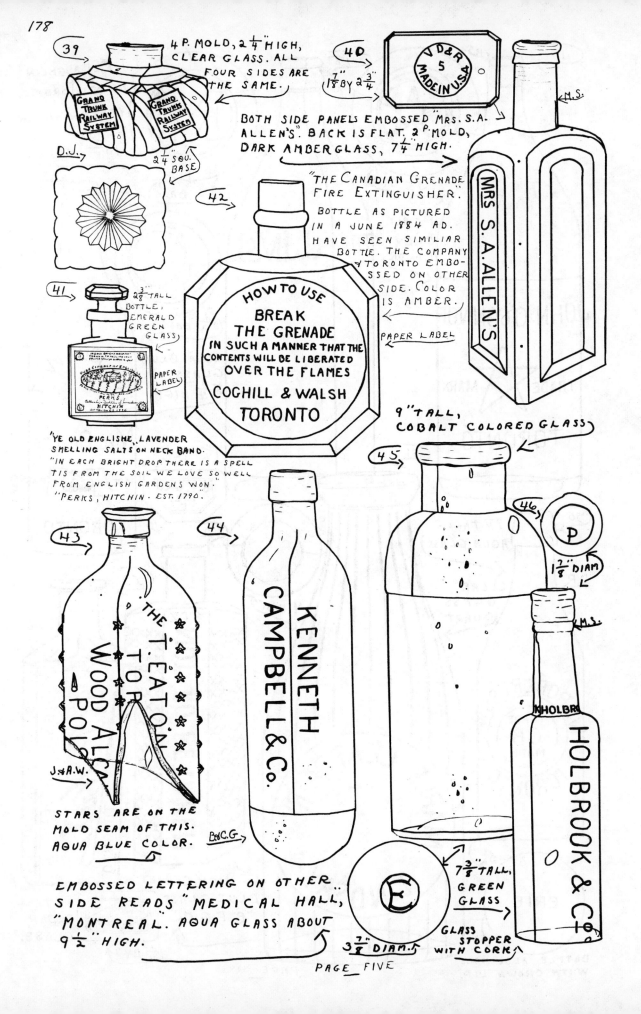

39 → 4 P. MOLD, 2 1/4 HIGH, CLEAR GLASS. ALL FOUR SIDES ARE THE SAME.

GRAND TRUNK RAILWAY System
GRAND TRUNK RAILWAY System

D.J. →

2 1/4" SQU. BASE

40 → V D & R 5 MADE IN U.S.A.

7" 1 8/8 BY 2 3/4

M.S. →

BOTH SIDE PANELS EMBOSSED "MRS. S.A. ALLEN'S". BACK IS FLAT. 2 P. MOLD, DARK AMBER GLASS, 7 1/4 HIGH.

42 →

"THE CANADIAN GRENADE FIRE EXTINGUISHER". BOTTLE AS PICTURED IN A JUNE 1884 AD. HAVE SEEN SIMILIAR BOTTLE. THE COMPANY TORONTO EMBOSSED ON OTHER SIDE. COLOR IS AMBER.

PAPER LABEL

MRS. S.A. ALLEN'S

41 →

2 3/8" TALL BOTTLE, EMERALD GREEN GLASS

PAPER LABEL →

PERKS HITCHIN

HOW TO USE
BREAK
THE GRENADE
IN SUCH A MANNER THAT THE CONTENTS WILL BE LIBERATED OVER THE FLAMES
COGHILL & WALSH
TORONTO

9" TALL, COBALT COLORED GLASS

45 →

46 →

P

1 7/8" DIAM

"YE OLD ENGLISHE" LAVENDER SMELLING SALTS ON NECK BAND. "IN EACH BRIGHT DROP THERE IS A SPELL TIS FROM THE SOIL WE LOVE SO WELL FROM ENGLISH GARDENS WON." "PERKS, HITCHIN. EST. 1790.

43 →

THE T. EATON CO TORONTO WOOD ALCOHOL POLISH

J & A.W. →

M.S. →

KENNETH CAMPBELL & Co.

KHOLBRO

HOLBROOK & Co.

STARS ARE ON THE MOLD SEAM OF THIS. AQUA BLUE COLOR.

B & C.G.

EMBOSSED LETTERING ON OTHER SIDE READS "MEDICAL HALL, "MONTREAL. AQUA GLASS ABOUT 9 1/2" HIGH.

E

3 7/8" DIAM.

7 3/8" TALL, GREEN GLASS

GLASS STOPPER WITH CORK

PAGE FIVE

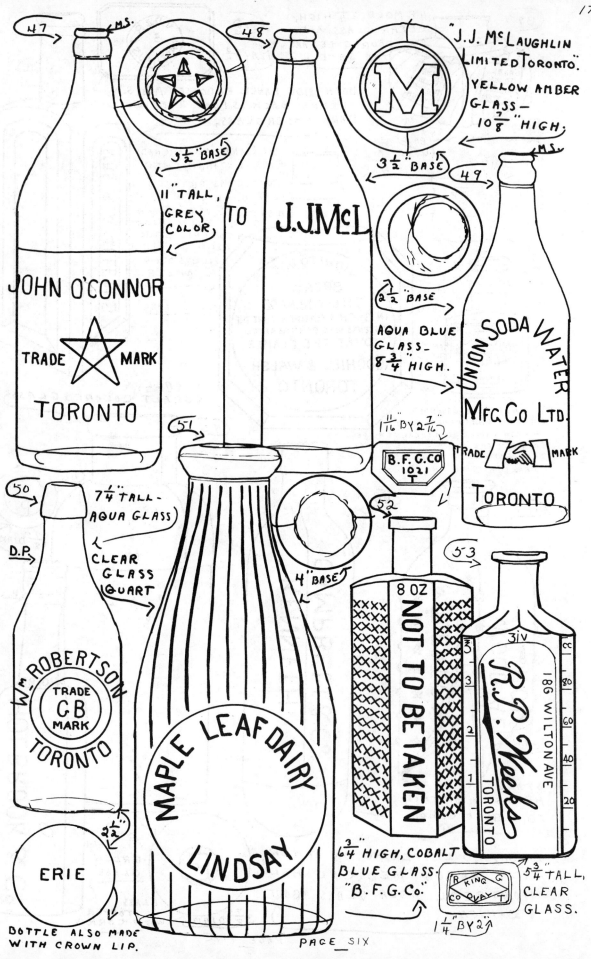

179

PAGE SIX

180

54 →

TURN MOLD, 11¼" TALL
AMBER GLASS,
3⅛" BASE,
PAPER LABEL.

55 →

56 →

T. A. LYTLE & CO. TORONTO

2¾" BY 3¼" BASE.

11½" TALL, 3¾" BASE,
PAPER LABEL,
TURN MOLD.
AMBER GLASS.

MATURED as WHISKEY
SHOULD BE

"T. A. LYTLE & CO. TORONTO".
PALE GREEN GLASS
11⅝" HIGH. GLASS
LID "PAT⁰ JAN.Y. 11TH
'86 81".

N⁰905

Imperial
Whisky.
Distilled and Bottled by
Hiram Walker & Sons
Limited
Walkerville Ontario Canada

MATURED in CASK, in WAREHOUSES VARIED DURING THE COLD SEASON
AND BOTTLED BY THE DISTILLERS IN BOND UNDER CUSTOMS SUPER
OFFICIAL STAMP OVER THE CAPSULE OF EVERY BOTTLE
Our Cork & Capsules bear our name
This Brand Trade mark & Label are registered

ESTABLISHED
FOR OVER HALF A CENTURY
Corbys
Canadian Whisky
Distilled & Bottled in Bond by
H. Corby Distillery Co Limited
Corbyville, Ont.

THE AGE & CONTENTS OF EACH BOTTLE IS GUARANTEED BY THE CANADIAN GOVT
WITH THE AGE CERTIFIED OVER EACH CAPSULE DATE OF MANUFACTURE

58 →

59 →

57 →

ESTABLISHED 1832
GOODERHAM and WORTS, LIMITED
CANADIAN ✳ RYE WHISKY
AGE STRENGTH & QUANITY
GUARANTEED
By GOVERNMENT
See Label ✳
1878   ✳ ON CORK   1885
GOLD MEDAL AWARDED PARIS   GOLD MEDAL AWARDED ANTWERP
TORONTO, CANADA

LABEL ON BOTTLE SAME AS ABOVE NO— 54

J. D. BROWN
TRADE MARK
REGISTERED
GRAVENHURST

MACDONALD
& CO.
COBALT

60 →

C. ROBERTSON

"C. ROBERTSON & C⁰ L⁰
LONDON", INK—
3 P. MOLD, 3" TALL,
AQUA GREEN GLASS.
1⅞" DIAM. BASE.

"J.D.B." ON 2¼" BASE.
"SPRING WATER" ON
BACK OF THIS 8⅜"
HIGH, AQUA
BLUE BOTTLE.

11" HIGH, AQUA BLUE
GLASS. 3⅝" BASE

PAGE SEVEN

ALBERTA

Brewers and Distillers

Blairmore Brewing & Malting Co.		1909	Directory
Calgary Brewing & Malting Co. Ltd.	inc. 1882	1909	D.
Calgary - Golden West Brewing Co. Ltd.		1909	D.
Edmonton Breweries Ltd.		1909	D.
Edmonton Brewing & Malting Co.		1909	D.
Lethbridge Brewing & Malting Co. Ltd.		1909	D.
Strathcona Brewing & Malting Co. Ltd.		1909	D.

Mineral Springs and Soda Water Manufacturers

Calgary - Berg, Paul	s.w.	1909	Directory
Calgary - Langston, Fred	s.w.	1909	D.
Edmonton - Neher Bros.	general	1909	D.
Edmonton - McLaughlin, J.J. Ltd.		1909	D.

BRITISH COLUMBIA

Brewers and Distillers

Anaconda - Hartman, Oscar	brewer	1909	Directory
Atlin - Northern Brewing Co. Ltd.		1909	D.
Cranbrook - Kerrigan, Jas. & Co.	brewers	1909	D.
Cumberland - Comox Brewing Co.		1899	D.
Fernie - Fort Steele Brewing Co. Ltd.		1909	D.
Grand Forks - Columbia Brewing Co.		1909	D.
Grand Forks - Cox, Eli	brewer	1899	D.
Grand Forks - Houbeck, Jno.	brewer	1909	D.
Greenwood - Columbia Bottling Works		1899	D.
Greenwood - Elkhorn Brewing Co.		1909	D.
Hedley - Dillier & Sherbauer	brewers	1909	D.
Hedley Brewing Co.		1909	D.
Kamloops - Imperial Brewing Co. Ltd.		1896-1909	D.
Kamloops - Jamieson, C.M.	brewer	1896-7	D.
Ladysmith - Union Brewing Co. Ltd.		1909	D.
Michel - Elk Valley Brewery		1909	D.
Moyie - Inderweis, Chas.	brewer	1909	D.
Nanaimo Brewing Co.		1892-3	D.
Nanaimo - Hasenfratz, August & Co.	brewers	1896-7	D.
Nanaimo - Maher, John	brewer	1890-3	D.
Nanaimo - Marwick & Hoelfe	brewer	1890	D.
Nanaimo - Union Brewing Co.		1892-1909	D.
Nanaimo - Weigle & Anderson	brewers	1892-3	D.
Nanaimo - Weigle, Peter	brewer	1909	D.
Nelson Brewing Co. Ltd.		1909	D.
Nelson - Reisterer, Robt.	brewer	1896-7	D.
Nelson - Righton, Thos.	brewer	1896-7	D.
New Westminster - Andrezjeuski, John	brewer	1890-7	D.
New Westminster - Jameson, Ralph	brewer	1890	D.
New Westminster - Nelson, Nels	brewer	1909	D.
New Westminster - Westminster Brewery		1909	D.
New Westminster - Wright & Jamieson	brewers	1890-3	D.
Phoenix - Biner & Sons	brewers	1909	D.
Phoenix Brewing Co.		1899-1909	D.
Powel - Columbia Brewery, Kappler & Co.		1896-7	D.
Powel - Doering & Marstrand	brewers	1896-7	D.
Powel - Farrall, H. jun.	brewers	1896-7	D.
Princeton - Nelson Brewing Co. Ltd.		1909	D.
Revelstoke - Allan, O.H.	brewer	1896-7	D.
Revelstoke Brewing & Bottling Works		1899	D.

British Columbia - cont'd

Revelstoke - Enterprise Brewing Co.		1909	Directory
Revelstoke - Long, Jas.A.	brewer	1909	D.
Rossland - Le Roi Brewing Co.		1909	D.
Rossland Spring Brewery		1896-7	D.
Rossland - Union Brewing Co.Ltd.		1897-8	D.
Rossland - Victoria, Phoenix Brewing Co. Ltd.		1896-7	D.
Rossland - Weigel, Peter	brewer	1896-7	D.
Sandon - New York Brewery		1909	D.
Sandon - Towgood & Bruder	brewers	1909	D.
Sapperton - Nelson, N.	brewer	1909	D.
South Vancouver - Royal Brewing Co. Ltd.		1909	D.
South Vancouver - Thorson, Chas.	brewer	1909	D.
Trail - Flahrer	brewer	1909	D.
Trail - Kootenay Brewing, Malting & Distilling		1899	D.
Trail - Yuengling Brewing Co. Ltd.		1899	D.
Vancouver - Baker & Williams	brewers	1896-7	D.
Vancouver Bottling Works, Gore Ave.		1899	D.
Vancouver Breweries Ltd.		1909	D.
Vancouver City Brewery		1890	D.
Vancouver - Denckert, Wm.	brewer	1891	D.
Vancouver - Doering, Chas.	brewer	1890	D.
Vancouver - Doering, Chas. & Co.	brewers	1896-7	D.
Vancouver - Doering & Marstrand Brewing Co., The		1899	D.
Vancouver - Kappler & Co.	brewers	1891-1909	D.
Vancouver - Knickerbocker Bottling Co.		1890-1	D.
Vancouver - Mitchell & Squier	brewer	1890	D.
Vancouver - Reisterer, Robt.	brewer	1890	D.
Vancouver - Royal Brewing Co. Ltd.		1909	D.
Vancouver - Stanley Park Brewery		1909	D.
Vancouver - Thorson, Chas.	brewer	1909	D.
Vancouver - Williams, John	brewer	1891-2	D.
Vernon - Klausman, N.	brewer	1891-1909	D.
Victoria Brewing Co.		1891-2	D.
Victoria - Carter & Ferris	brewers	1890	D.
Victoria - Excelcior Brewing Co.		1896-7	D.
Victoria - Fairall, H.S. & Co.	brewers	1890	D.
Victoria - Fairall Bros.	brewers	1909	D.
Victoria - Gowen, G.&N.	brewers	1890	D.
Victoria - Hasenfrotz & Lowson	brewers	1890	D.
Victoria - Leahy, John	brewer	1890-7	D.
Victoria - Loewen & Erb	brewer	1891-2	D.
Victoria - Milwaukee Brewing Co. Ltd.		1899	D.
Victoria - Silver Spring Brewing Co. Ltd.		1909	D.
Victoria - Stichnoth & Hermann	brewers	1891-2	D.
Victoria, Phoenix Brewing Co. Ltd.		1909	D.
Wellington - Ferrerro, Catharine	brewer	1899	D.

Chemists, Druggists and Manufacturers

Ainsworth - Henry & Adams	retail druggists	1892-3	Directory
Clinton - Foster, F.W.	retail druggists	1892-3	D.
Kamloops - Clarke & Co.	retail druggists	1892-3	D.
Kamloops - Harding, A.W.	retail druggists	1892-3	D.
Nanaimo - McCartney & Planta	retail druggists	1892-3	D.
Nanaimo - Prinbury, E. & Co.	retail druggists	1892-3	D.
Nelson - Henry & Adams	retail druggists	1892-3	D.
Nelson - Teetzel, W.F. & Co.	retail druggists	1892-3	D.
New Westminster - Burnett, G.T.	retail druggists	1892-3	D.
New Westminster - Curtis, D.S. & Co.	retail druggists	1892-3	D.
New Westminster - Herring, A.M.	retail druggists	1892-3	D.
New Westminster - Macpherson & Thompson	retail druggists	1892-3	D.
New Westminster - Muir, T.A. & Co.	retail druggists	1892-3	D.
New Westminster - Yuen Wo.	retail druggists	1892-3	D.
Revelstoke - Teetzel, W.F.	retail druggists	1892-3	D.
Vancouver - Atkins & Atkins	retail druggists	1892-3	D.
Vancouver - Clark, Mrs. Jos.	retail druggists	1892-3	D.
Vancouver - Fung King	retail druggists	1892-3	D.
Vancouver - Hip Tuck Lung & Co.	retail druggists	1892-3	D.
Vancouver - Horrocks & Co.	retail druggists	1892-3	D.

British Columbia - cont'd

Vancouver – Kong Man Lung Co.	retail druggists	1892-3	Directory
Vancouver – McAlpin, D.L.	retail druggists	1892-3	D.
Vancouver – McDowel, H. & Co.	retail druggists	1892-3	D.
Vancouver – Morrow, John W.	retail druggists	1892-3	D.
Vancouver – Nelson, Chas.	retail druggists	1892-3	D.
Vancouver – Reed, John	retail druggists	1892-3	D.
Vancouver – Rosenbaum & Co. whlsl.	retail druggists	1892-3	D.
Vancouver – Vancouver Drug Co.	retail druggists	1892-3	D.
Vancouver – Zemmir, Louis (herbs)	retail druggists	1892-3	D.
Van Winkle – Choy Chong	retail druggists	1892-3	D.
Vernon – Chipp, John	retail druggists	1892-3	D.
Victoria – Bowes, C.H. & Co.	retail druggists	1892-3	D.
Victoria – Campbell, D.E.	retail druggists	1892-3	D.
Victoria – Chu Chung & Co.	retail druggists	1892-3	D.
Victoria – Cochrane & Munn	retail druggists	1892-3	D.
Victoria – Dean & Cryderman	retail druggists	1892-3	D.
Victoria – Fish, Thos.	retail druggists	1892-3	D.
Victoria – Fook, Yuen & Co.	retail druggists	1892-3	D.
Victoria – Hanson, Samuel	retail druggists	1892-3	D.
Victoria – Hip Lung Co.	retail druggists	1892-3	D.
Victoria – Jackson, Wm. jun. & Co.	retail druggists	1892-3	D.
Victoria – Jones, C.E.	retail druggists	1892-3	D.
Victoria – King Tye Co.	retail druggists	1892-3	D.
Victoria – Kwong, On, Lung & Co.	retail druggists	1892-3	D.
Victoria – Langley & Co.	retail druggists	1892-3	D.
Victoria – Lee Chung	retail druggists	1892-3	D.
Victoria – Moore & Co.	retail druggists	1892-3	D.
Victoria – Morison, George	retail druggists	1892-3	D.
Victoria – Shotbolt, Thomas	retail druggists	1892-3	D.
Victoria – Sing Wo Tong	retail druggists	1892-3	D.
Victoria – Tai Yune & Co.	retail druggists	1892-3	D.
Victoria – Tong Yik Dan	retail druggists	1892-3	D.

Mineral Springs and Soda Water Manufacturers

Courtenay – Eureka Soda Water Works		1899	Directory
Cranbrook – East Kootenay Bottling Co.		1909	D.
Cumberland – Picket, J.H.	s.w.	1909	D.
Grand Forks – Lion Bottling Works		1909	D.
Hedley – Gillan, J.	s.w.	1909	D.
Kamloops – Duprat & Son	s.w.	1890-1	D.
Kaslo – Kapps, C.J.		1899	D.
Ladysmith – Rumming, W.E.		1909	D.
Nanaimo – Adams & Lawrence		1890-1	D.
Nanaimo – Lawrence, Louis		1896-9	D.
Nanaimo – Mitchell, John		1890-1	D.
Nanaimo – Rumming, W.E.		1899, 1909	D.
'77 Nelson – Thorpe & Co.		1899, 1909	D.
New Westminster – Henley, Jos.		1899, 1909	D.
Princeton – Gillan, J.	s.w.	1909	D.
Revelstoke – O'Brien, M.J.		1899	D.
Rossland – Columbia Bottling Works		1909	D.
Rossland – Harper, Jas.		1909	D.
Sandon – Day, M.W.		1899	D.
Sandon – Fitzgerald, Paul		1899	D.
Sandown – Bigney, C.A.		1909	D.
Vancouver – British Canadian Man. Co.		1909	D.
Vancouver – Cally & Co. Ltd.		1896-7	D.
Vancouver – Cross & Co.		1899, 1909	D.
Vancouver – Deckinsale, D.R.		1890-1	D.
Vancouver – McPhee, D.	s.w.	1909	D.
Vancouver – Meikle Bros.		1899	D.
Vancouver – Meikle Bros. Ltd.		1909	D.
Vancouver – Murchison, C.		1890-1	D.
Vancouver – Pacific Bottling Works Ltd.		1909	D.
Vancouver – Suckling, A.E. & Co.		1909	D.
? 77 Vancouver – Thorpe & Co.		1890, 1909	D.

British Columbia - cont'd

Vernon - O'Brien, M.J.		1899	Directory
Victoria - Fairall, H.S.		1896-9	D.
Victoria - Morley, Christopher		1890-9	D.
Victoria - Phillips Bros.		1896-7	D.
Victoria - Thorpe & Co. Ltd.		1896-7	D.

MANITOBA

Brewers and Distillers

Brandon Brewing Co.		1909	Directory
Brandon - Drewry, E.L.	brewer	1909	D.
Brandon - Empire Brewing Co. Ltd.		1909	D.
Minnesdosa - Davies, C.L.	brewer	1890-1	D.
Portage La Prairie - Bell, James	brewer	1890-1	D.
Portage La Prairie - Cairns, Thos.	brewer	1890-1	D.
Winnepeg - Blackwood Bros.	brewers	1890-1	D.
Winnepeg - Crown Brewing Co.		1909	D.
Winnepeg - Drewry, E.L. Redwood Brewery, Main N.		1890-1909	D.
Winnepeg - Edelweiss Brewery		1909	D.
Winnepeg - Empire Brewing & Malting Co.	inc. 1885	1890-1	D.
Winnepeg - English Brewing		1909	D.
Winnepeg - Manitoba Brewing Co.	inc. 1871	1909	D.
Winnepeg - Manitoba Milling & Brewing Co.	inc. 1885	1909	D.
Winnepeg - McDonagh & Shea	brewers	1890, 1909	D.
Winnepeg - Noel, J.H.	brewer	1890-1	D.
Winnepeg - Riedle, A.W.	brewer	1909	D.
Winnepeg - Versene, John	brewer	1890-1	D.

Chemists, Druggists and Manufacturers

Ash Creek - Brown, Thos.	retail druggists	1892-3	Directory
Birtle - Latimer, Victor	retail druggists	1892-3	D.
Boissevain - Wright, J.A.	retail druggists	1892-3	D.
Brandon - Fleming & Sons	retail druggists	1892-3	D.
Brandon - Halpin, N.J.	retail druggists	1892-3	D.
Brandon - Rose & Co.	retail druggists	1892-3	D.
Carberry - Boyd, W.M.	retail druggists	1892-3	D.
Carberry - Munson, A.E.	retail druggists	1892-3	D.
Cypress River - Butchart, G.N. & J.C.	retail druggists	1892-3	D.
Deloraine - Cowan, W.E.	retail druggists	1892-3	D.
Elkhorn - Rolston, P.M.	retail druggists	1892-3	D.
Emerson - Casselman, Ezra	retail druggists	1892-3	D.
Glenbore - Morrison & Gordon	retail druggists	1892-3	D.
Grenta - Donovan, P.C.	retail druggists	1892-3	D.
Hamiota - Lawson, Alexander	retail druggists	1892-3	D.
Hartney - Woodhull, F.W.	retail druggists	1892-3	D.
Killarney - Oliver, R.W.	retail druggists	1892-3	D.
Manitou - Scarlett, Edward	retail druggists	1892-3	D.
Melita - A.N.	retail druggists	1892-3	D.
Minnedosa - Patton, J.K.	retail druggists	1892-3	D.
Morden - Duncalfe, W.P.	retail druggists	1892-3	D.
Morden - McLaren, G.W.	retail druggists	1892-3	D.
Napinka - Snider, S.H., M.D.	retail druggists	1892-3	D.
Neepawa - Harrison & Co.	retail druggists	1892-3	D.
Neepawa - Herrel, C.W.	retail druggists	1892-3	D.
Oak Lake - Wright, Henry	retail druggists	1892-3	D.
Pilot Mound - Hobbs, J.A.	retail druggists	1892-3	D.
Portage La Prairie - Cannif, B.M.	retail druggists	1892-3	D.
Portage La Prairie - Stork, J.	retail druggists	1892-3	D.
Portage La Prairie - Taylor, Jos.	retail druggists	1892-3	D.

Manitoba - cont'd

Rapid City - Campbell, R.J.	retail druggists	1892-3	Directory
Rapid City - Crookshank, R.P. & Co.	retail druggists	1892-3	D.
St. Boniface - Lampert, J.H.A.	retail druggists	1892-3	D.
Selkirk - Gilhuly, R.H.	retail druggists	1892-3	D.
Souris - Sherrin, N.A.	retail druggists	1892-3	D.
Souris - Stoyte, J.C.	retail druggists	1892-3	D.
Stonewall - Leonard, A.R.	retail druggists	1892-3	D.
Treherne - Taylor, S.L.	retail druggists	1892-3	D.
Virden - Higginbotham, J.N	retail druggists	1892-3	D.
Virden - Steel, Robt.	retail druggists	1892-3	D.
Wawanesa - Jump, Jos.	retail druggists	1892-3	D.
Winnepeg - Blakely, E.A.	retail druggists	1892-3	D.
Winnepeg - Bole, Wynne & Co.	retail druggists	1892-3	D.
Winnepeg - Eddington, C.M.	retail druggists	1892-3	D.
Winnepeg - Flexon & Co.	retail druggists	1892-3	D.
Winnepeg - Gordon, J.C.	retail druggists	1892-3	D.
Winnepeg - Howard, J.P. & Co.	retail druggists	1892-3	D.
Winnepeg - Inman & Monckton	retail druggists	1892-3	D.
Winnepeg - Jackson & Co.	retail druggists	1892-3	D.
Winnepeg - Martin, Rooser & Co.	retail druggists	1892-3	D.
Winnepeg - Mitchell, W.J.	retail druggists	1892-3	D.
Winnepeg - Neelands & Co.	retail druggists	1892-3	D.
Winnepeg - Parkinson, Jos.	retail druggists	1892-3	D.
Winnepeg - Pulford, Walter	retail druggists	1892-3	D.
Winnepeg - Rose, J.H.	retail druggists	1892-3	D.
Winnepeg - Sugden Pill & Drug Co. inc. 1894	retail druggists	1892-3	D.
Winnepeg - Stewart, James	retail druggists	1892-3	D.

Mineral Springs and Soda Water Manufacturers

Boissevain - Allan, E.D.		1890-9	Directory
Brandon - Cleverly & Ferguson		1890-9	D.
Brandon - West, Ephraim	s.w.	1890-1	D.
Portage La Prairie Soda Water Works		1909	D.
Portage La Prairie - Meyer, F.A.	s.w.	1890-1	D.
Selkirk Aerated Water & Bottling Works		1909	D.
Souris - Grant, F.W.		1899	D.
West Lynne - Pilgrim, T.M.		1890-1	D.
Winnepeg - American Soda Water Co.		1909	D.
Winnepeg - Blackwood Bros.	est. 1882, article	1899	D.
Winnepeg - Blackwood's Ltd.		1909	D.
Winnepeg - Drewry, E.L. (prop. Golden Key Aerated Water Factories)		1909	D.
Winnepeg - Hygiene Kola Co.		1909	D.
Winnepeg - Kelly Bros., 184 James		1899	D.
Winnepeg - McLaughlin, J.J. Ltd.		1909	D.
Winnepeg - North West Aerated Water Co.		1891	D.
Winnepeg - Pelisser & Son	s.w.	1909	D.
Winnepeg - Stanley Mineral Springs Ltd.		1909	D.
Winnepeg - West, S.E. & Co.	soda & mineral water	1891	D.

NEW BRUNSWICK

Brewers and Distillers

✱ SEE ST. JOHN UNDER N.S.			
Edmonton - Thibault, A.E.	brewer	1899	Directory
Frederickton - Lee, Newton	brewer	1899	D.
Frederickton - Thomalson, Wm.	brewer	1899	D.
St. John - Carling Brewing & Malting Co. Ltd.		1899	D.
St. John - Dolan Bros. Haymarket Sq.	brewers	1899	D.
St. John - Jones, Simeon, 2 Carmarthen	brewers	1899	D.
St. Stephen - Barter, E.H.	brewer	1891-9	D.
St. Stephen - Tyrrel, F.H.	brewer	1899	D.
Woodstock - Garden Bros.	brewers	1899	D.
Woodstock - Groves, Daniel	brewers	1891	D.

New Brunswick - cont'd

Mineral Springs and Soda Water Manufacturers

Bathurst - Ellis, Mrs. John		1899	Directory
Butternut Ridge - Havelock Mineral Spring Co.		1899	D.
Chatham - Ready, James		1899	D.
Edmundson - Thibault, A.E.		1909	D.
Fairville - Hooley, Tim	s.w.	1909	D.
Moncton - Givans, Wm. Sons		1896, 1909	D.
Moncton - Legere, P.P.		1899	D.
Moncton - Legere, O.S., 50 Main		1899, 1909	D.
Peticodiac - Havelock Mineral Spring Co.		1896-7	D.
St. John - Dolan Bros.		1909	D.
St. John - Jones, Simeon Ltd.		1909	D.
St. John - Nash, Thomas, 51 Douglas Ave.		1899	D.
St. John - Ready, Jas.		1909	D.
St. John - Terris, J.J., 51 City Rd.		1899, 1909	D.
St. Mary's - Emack Bros.		1909	D.
St. Stephen - Tyrell, F.H.		1909	D.
Sussex Mineral Spring Co. Ltd.		1899, 1909	D.
Upham - Mahpu Mineral Spring Co. Ltd.		1909	D.
Woodstock - Baird Co. Ltd.	s.w.	1899	D.
Woodstock - Denton, A.E.	s.w.	1909	D.
Woodstock - Garden Bros.		1899	D.

NEWFOUNDLAND

Brewers and Distillers

St. Johns - Gaden, G.H.	brewer		1891	Directory
St. Johns - Miller & Co.	brewer		1891	D.
St. Johns - Newfoundland Brewery Ltd.			1899-1909	D.
St. Johns - Lindberg, John	brewer		1891-1909	D.

Mineral Springs and Soda Water Manufacturers

Duckworth - Bennet, John R.		1891, 1909	Directory
Signal Hill - Lindberg, John Sr.		1899	D.
St. Johns - Gaden, George H.		1899	D.
St. Johns - Gaden Aerated Water Works		1909	D.
St. Johns - Klavanagh & Co.		1899	D.
St. Johns - Lindberg, John	s.w.	1891	D.
St. Johns - Wood, F.B.C. Ltd.	s.w.	1909	D.

NORTHWEST TERRITORIES

Brewers and Distillers

Battleford - Graff, J.J.	brewer	1890-1	Directory
Battleford - Williams, W.	brewer	1890-1	D.
Calgary Brewing & Malting Co.		1899	D.
Calgary Wine & Spirit Co.		1899	D.
Lethbridge - Alberta Brewing Co.		1890-1	D.
Lethbridge - McKenzie, M.	brewer	1890-1	D.
Lethbridge - Noel, J.H.	brewer	1890-1	D.
Pine Creek - Crea, W.	brewer	1890-1	D.

Northwest Territories - cont'd

Strassburg - Heck, A.	distiller	1890-1	Directory
Stobart - Dugal, Julias	brewer	1890-1	D.

Chemists, Druggists and Manufacturers

Anthracite - Brett, R.G.	retail druggists	1892-3	Directory
Banff - Ross, Peter	retail druggists	1892-3	D.
Battleford - J.B.	retail druggists	1892-3	D.
Calgary - Feild, John	retail druggists	1892-3	D.
Calgary - MacLean, Wendell	retail druggists	1892-3	D.
Calgary - Newson, Alfred C.	retail druggists	1892-3	D.
Calgary - Thornton, Wm.	retail druggists	1892-3	D.
Edmonton - McDonald, D.W.	retail druggists	1892-3	D.
Edmonton - Bleasdell, A.W. & Co.	retail druggists	1892-3	D.
Fort McLeod - Barnes, R.B.	retail druggists	1892-3	D.
Fort McLeod - Thompson, Geo.	retail druggists	1892-3	D.
Grenfell - Sweete, H.	retail druggists	1892-3	D.
Indian Head - Orchard, A.G.	retail druggists	1892-3	D.
Lethbridge - Higginbotham, J.D. & Co.	retail druggists	1892-3	D.
Lethbridge - Little & Cleveland	retail druggists	1892-3	D.
Medicine Hat - Hughes, Albert	retail druggists	1892-3	D.
Medicine Hat - Walton, E.J.R.	retail druggists	1892-3	D.
Moose Jaw - Bole, W.W.	retail druggists	1892-3	D.
Moosomin - Carman, F.T. (estate)	retail druggists	1892-3	D.
Moosomin - Scott, E.H.	retail druggists	1892-3	D.
Saltcoats - Patrick, T.A.	retail druggists	1892-3	D.
Swift Current - Knight, W.J.	retail druggists	1892-3	D.
Pincher Creek - Bleasdell, A.W. & Co.	retail druggists	1892-3	D.
Prince Albert - Neely, J.M.R. & Co.	retail druggists	1892-3	D.
Prince Albert - White, G.J. & Co.	retail druggists	1892-3	D.
Qu'Appelle - Hall, Wm.	retail druggists	1892-3	D.
Qu'Appelle Station - Brydon, Wm.	retail druggists	1892-3	D.
Qu'Appelle Station - Carthew, C.E.	retail druggists	1892-3	D.
Regina - Hill, G.S. & Co.	retail druggists	1892-3	D.
Regina - Martin, Robt.	retail druggists	1892-3	D.
Regina - Pettingell, W.G.	retail druggists	1892-3	D.
Regina - Waldon, A.E.	retail druggists	1892-3	D.
Whitewood - McDonald, J.A.	retail druggists	1892-3	D.
Whitewood - Sweet, T.C.	retail druggists	1892-3	D.
Yorkton - Watson, F.	retail druggists	1892-3	D.

Mineral Springs and Soda Water Manufacturers

Grenfell Mineral Water Co.		1896-7	Directory
Grenfell Mineral Water Factory		1899	D.

NOVA SCOTIA

Brewers and Distillers

Bathurst - Ellis, John	brewer	1891	Directory
Butternut Ridge - Keith, Wm.	brewer	1891	D.
Campbellton - Hodge & Charette	brewer	1891	D.
Canterbury Station - Donovan, Patrick	brewer	1891	D.
Dartmouth - Maritime Brewing & Malting Co.		1896-7	D.
Fairville - Ready, Jas.	brewer	1909	D.
Frederickton - McKee, S.H. & Son	brewers	1891-1909	D.
Halifax Brewery Ltd.		1909	D.
Halifax - Dawes & Co., 209 Barrington	brewers	1896-7	D.
Halifax - Foyle Brewery		1891	D.

Nova Scotia - cont'd

Halifax - Highland Spring Brewery			1909	Directory
Halifax - Keith & Son, 88 Lower Water	brewers		1896-7	D.
Halifax - Lager Beer Brewery			1896-7	D.
Halifax - Nova Scotia Bottling Co., Hayward & Co. props.			1909	D.
Halifax - Ol & J.C. Brewers, 41 Bedford Row			1896-7	D.
Moncton - Givan, Wm.	brewer		1891	D.
Moncton - Leger, O.S.	brewer		1891	D.
North Sydney - Excelsior Bottling Co.			1899	D.
Nova Scotia Brewery			1909	D.
St. John - Carling's Brewing & Malting (agency)			1909	D.
St. John - Labatt Jno. (agency)	brewing		1909	D.
St. John - Ready, James	brewer		1890-1909	D.
St. John - Simeon, Jones Ltd.	brewer		1891	D.
St. John - Wallis, J.A. & Son	brewer		1891	D.
St. Stephen - Barter, E.H.	brewer		1891	D.
St. Stephen - Tyrell, Frank	brewer		1891	D.
Sydney - Barker, J.H.	brewer		1909	D.
Truro - Bigelow, J.E. & Co.	brewer		1891	D.
Yoho - Petty, J.F.	brewer		1891	D.

Chemists, Druggists and Manufacturers

Bridgetown - Piper, A.B.	druggist		1854	Ad.
Bridgetown - Hoyt, C.	druggist		1854	Ad.
Digby - Oakes ,E.M.	druggist		1854	Ad.
Halifax - Atlantic Manufacturing Co. (Cod Liver Oil)			1870	Ad.
Halifax - Brown & Webb (man. Puttner's Emulsion)			1882	Ad.
Halifax - Cogswell & Forsythe (cosmetic mans.)			1842	Ad.
Halifax - Humphrey, T. & Co. Medical Hall			1841	Ad.
Halifax - Morton, G.E.	druggist		1842, 54	Ads.
Halifax - Rogers & Co. (Rogers Medicines)			1866	Ad.
New Glasgow - K.D.C. Co. Ltd. (dyspepsia Med.) started in 1892, opened a branch office in Boston the following year.				Ads.
Truro - Malto Peptonized Porter	started 1891			Ad.
Wolfville - Scoda Discovery Co.			1893	Ad.
Yarmouth - Bingay, John	druggist		1856	Ads.
Yarmouth - Burrel, Wm.	druggist		1852	Ads.
Yarmouth - Burton, D. & Co.	druggist		1854	Ads.
Yarmouth - Bush ,Alfred	druggist		1865	Ads.
Yarmouth - Davis, J.D., Dr. Remedies Co. Ltd.	inc. 1892			
Yarmouth - Garrison & Evert, Apothecary Hall			1848	Ad.
Yarmouth - Garrison, G.	druggist		1852	Ad.
Yarmouth - Guest, R.	druggist		1848	Ad.
Yarmouth - Hood Bros.	druggist		1865	Ad.
Yarmouth - Jackson, Mary (prop. Mrs. Jackson's Gold Liniment)			1867	Ad.
Yarmouth - Parr & Co's Pain Eradicator			1865	Ad.
Yarmouth - Parr, H.A.	druggist		1865	Ad.
Yarmouth - Redding, F.	druggist		1858	Ad.
Yarmouth - Tupper, E.A.	druggist		1865	Ad.
Yarmouth - Stoneman, Jos. jun.	druggist		1855	Ad.
St. John - Fellows Co., extracts			1848	Ad.
St. John - Fellows, James I. Chemist & Manufacturer			1867	Ad.
St. John - Fellows Medical Manufacturing Co. inc. 1876				
St. John - Garrison, G.	druggist		1852	Ad.
St. John - Pendleton, Mw. (man. Botanic Medicines)			1865	Ad.
St. John - Rudman, Allen, chemist & druggist (Scott's Cure)			1890	Ad.

Mineral Springs and Soda Water Manufacturers

Amherst - Canadian Beverage Co. Ltd.			1909	Directory
Amherst - Barker, J.H.	s.w.		1891	D.
Amherst - Taylor & Tennant	s.w.		1899-1909	D.
Bridgewater Aerated Water Co.			1909	D.
Butternut Ridge - Havelock Mineral Springs Co.			1909	D.
Campbellton - Ray & Damboise	s.w.		1909	D.
Dartmouth - Atlantic Mineral Water Co.			1899	D.
Dartmouth - Glendinning, J.R.	s.w.		1891	D.
Dartmouth Mineral Water Co. Ltd.			1899	D.
Glace Bay - McKinley & Oglivie	s.w.		1909	D.

Nova Scotia - cont'd

Halifax - Bent, J.K.	s.w.	1891	Directory
Halifax - Booth, Thos.	s.w.	1891-9	D.
Halifax - Crosskill, J. & Son		1891-9	D.
Halifax - Donovan, W.H., 43 Grenville		1891-1909	D.
Halifax - Nova Scotia Bottling Co.		1909	D.
Halifax - Quinn, F.J., 371 Barrington		1891-1909	D.
Halifax - Ramey, G.R. & Son		1909	D.
Halifax - Roue, Jas. Woods Wharf		1891-1909	D.
Halifax - Strachan, John		1909	D.
Halifax - Walke, E.J.		1899	D.
Halifax - Walke, J.T.		1899	D.
Halifax - Walker, E.		1896-7	D.
Halifax - Wheelan & Ferguson		1891-1909	D.
Inverness - Quigley, John		1909	D.
Milton Aerated Water Co.		1891	D.
Milton - Kempton Bros. & Co.		1899-1909	D.
Milton - Harlan & Kempton		1891	D.
New Glasgow - Drake, Francis		1899-1909	D.
North Sydney - Gannon, P.&J.	s.w.	1899	D.
North Sydney - Home Bottling Co.		1909	D.
North Sydney - Maple Leaf Bottling Co.		1909	D.
North Sydney - McCallum, W.H.		1909	D.
North Sydney Mineral Water Works		1891	D.
North Sydney - Smith, S.B.		1909	D.
North Sydney - Walker, J.	s.w.	1891	D.
Parrsboro Bottling Co.		1909	D.
Port Hood Bottling Co.		1909	D.
Red Mines - McKinley & Oglivie		1909	D.
Sydney - Barker, G.H.	s.w.	1899	D.
Sydney - Crown Bottling Co. Ltd.		1909	D.
Sydney - Doherty, Patrick	s.w.	1909	D.
Sydney - Havelock Bottling Co. Ltd.		1909	D.
Sydney - Mayflower Bottling Co. Ltd.		1909	D.
Sydney - Nash & McAllister	s.w.	1909	D.
Springhill - Cumberland Beverages Co.		1909	D.
Springhill Mineral Water Co.		1909	D.
Springhill - O'Connel, Thos.		1909	D.
Truro - Bigelow, J.E. & Co.		1891	D.
Truro - Bigelow & Hood		1899-1909	D.
Yarmouth - Garrison, G. Apoth. & Drug., Pure Soda Water Man.		1852	Ad.
Yarmouth - Neel, Jas., Soda Water, Root Beer & Ginger Ale Man.		1841	Ad.
Yarmouth - Nickerson, Grant & Co.		1909	D.
Yarmouth - Standard Soda Water Co.		1899, 1909	D.
Yarmouth Mineral Bottling Co.		1899	D.

ONTARIO

Brewers and Distillers

Amherstburg - Turk & Bullock	brewers	1841	Ad.
Amherstburg - Turk, John	brewer	1851	Directory
Amherstburg - Douglas & Williams	brewers	1851	D.
Ashburnham - Calcutt, Henry	brewer	1882	D.
Ashburnham - Calcutt Brewing & Malting	inc. 1898		
Ashburnham - Caleuth Brewing & Malting	inc. 1898		
Aurora - Mort, Wm.	brewer	1862	Ad.
Ayr Brewery, Cunningham, Peter, prop.		1855	Ad.
Ayr - Glenlivet Distillery, Colcleugh, G., prop.		1861	Ad.
Ayr - Hall, John	dist.	1851	D.
Baden - Ernst Bros.	brewers	1871	D.
Baden - Dantzer, brewer & maltster		1892-3	D.
Baden - Lierch, Henry	brewer	1861	D.
Bamberg - Heiss, Lorentz	brewer	1882	D.
Bamberg - Korwan, M.	brewers	1892-3	D.
Barrie - Anderson Bros.	brewers	1882	D.
Barrie - Anderson, James	brewers	1892-3	D.

Ontario - cont'd

Barrie - Anderson, Wm.	brewers	1862	Directory
Barrie - Anderton & Co. brewers & maltsters		1909	D.
Barton - Matheral, James brewery & tavern		1842	Ad.
Bayfield - Heath, A.H.	dist.	1851	D.
Beamsville - Dewitt, J.	dist.	1851	D.
Beaverton - Calcutt, Henry	brewer	1876-89	D.
Beaverton - Calder, D.	dist.	1851	D.
Beaverton - Proctor, Geo.	dist.	1860	D.
Beaverton - Stuart, A.	dist.	1851	D.
Belleville - Blacklock, Jas. (bottled goods)		1860	Ad.
Belleville - Corby, Henry	dist.	1862, 92-3	D.
Belleville - Corby, H. Distillery Co. Ltd.		1909	D.
Belleville - Clifford, C.	brewer	1862	D.
Belleville - Hall, Jos.	brewer	1851-61	D.
Belleville - McCarty, William	brewer	1832	Ad.
Belleville - Nash, Abner	brewer	1831	Ad.
Belleville - Read, Robt.	dist.	1863	Ad.
Belleville - Roy, J.A.	brewer	1882, 1909	D.
Belleville - Samson, J.H.	brewer	1833	Ad.
Belleville - Severns, Wm.	brewer	1896-7	D.
Belleville - Smith, D.	brewer	1862	D.
Belleville - Thompson, Wm.	brewer	1860	Ad.
Belleville - Thorpe, Louis	dist.	1831	Ad.
Belleville - Turnbull, John	brewer	1831	Ad.
Berlin - Huether, C.N.	brewer	1909	D.
Berlin - Kuntz, L.	brewer	1890-7	D.
Berlin - Pipscher, Peter	brewer	1860	D.
Berlin - Seipe, George & Co.	brewer	1862	D.
Berlin - Reinhardt, E.N.	brewer	1890	D.
Berlin - Spencer & Sons	brewer	1861-2	D.
Berlin - Spencer, Thos.	brewer	1871	D.
Berlin - Stein, Wm., brewer & malster		1892-3	D.
Boulton - Goodfellow & Warbrick	dist.	1850	Ad.
Bowmanville Distillery, Raynor, F.		1863	Ad.
Brantford - Bampfylde, J.P.	brewer	1890	D.
Brantford - Bixel Brewing & Malting Co.		1892, 1909	D.
Brantford - Brant Brewing & Malting Co.		1882	D.
Brantford Brewing Co.	inc.1906	1909	D.
Brantford - Pelee Island Wines, J.S. Hamilton & Co.		1884, 1905	Ads.
Brantford - Spencer & Sons	brewers	1861	D.
Brantford - Spencer, Thos.	brewers	1871	D.
Brantford - Strobridge & Botham	dist.	1860	Ad.
Brantford - West Brantford Brewery		1861-62	D.
Brideport - Luft, Henry, brewer & malster		1892-3	D.
Brockville - Bowie & Bate	brewers	1882	D.
Brockville - Bowie & Co's Brewery	inc. 1905	1909	D.
Brockville - Best Brewing Co.	inc. 1898	changed to next	
Brockville - Consumers Brewing Co.		1903	D.
Brockville - Highbury Brewery, Sabine, J. & Son. est. 1838			Ad.
Brockville - McNaughton, John brewer & distiller		1862	D.
Brockville - Sanderson, George	dist.	1839	Ad.
Byetown - Barriele & Aumond (dealers, wood & bottle)		1836	Ad.
Byetown - Black, James (dealer and tavern)		1845	Ad.
Camden Distillery, Johnson, J. prop.		1862	Ad.
Carlsruhe - Schwann, David	brewer	1882, 1909	D.
Chatham - Allenor, John	brewer	1882	D.
Chatham - Aldis, S.& A.	dist.	1851-2	D.
Chatham Brewery, Slagg, J.& H. est. around 1841			Ads.
Chatham - Bennet, Thos.	dist.	1861-2	D.
Chatham - Coupland, W.G. & Co.	brewers	1882	D.
Chatham - Garner, John	brewers	1861-2	D.
Chatham - Halpin, Martin	brewers	1861-2	D.
Chatham - Howard & Northwood	brewers	1882	D.
Chatham - Wood, M.D.	brewers	1861-2	D.
Chepstowe - Graf, Peter	brewers	1882	D.
Chepstowe - Schwann, Wm.	brewers	1883-93	D.
Chesley - Schumacher Bros.	brewers	1896-7	D.
Chippawa Brewery, Macklem, Thos. & Co.		1855	Ad.
Chippawa Brewery, Thomas, J. (for sale)		1868	Ad.
Chippawa - Tench, W.E.	brewer	1882	D.
Clinton - Robinson, Wm.	brewer	1890	D.
Cobourg - Calcutt, Kingsley	brewer	1871	D.

Ontario - cont'd

Cobourg Distillery (whiskey)		1837	Ad.
Cobourg Distillery & Brewery, Calcutt prop.		1849	Ad.
Cobourg - Jones, George F.	dist.	1864	Ad.
Cobourg - MacKechne, Henry	brewer	1882	Directory
Cobourg - Macpherson, Gordon & Co.	brewers	1892-9	D.
Cobourg - Ontario Distillery, 1847 ad. for sale by auction		1869	Ad.
Cobourg - Wallace, P.	dist.	1843, 1850	Ads.
Cobourg - Wallace, John	dist.	1862	D.
Cornwall Distillery, Bell, John prop.		1852	Ad.
Cornwall - Nutter, Seth C. Brewery Ltd.		1909	D.
Delaware - Tuplone, C.	brewer	1882	D.
Demorestville - Munro, Samuel	dist.	1831	Ad.
Doncaster - Davies, Robt.	brewer	1896-7	D.
Dover - Howse, brewery - notice of fire at...		1847	
Drummondville - Fisher, Fred	brewer	1882	D.
Duart Brewery, Russel, John prop.		1887	Ad.
Duart - Ramsrein, Jos.	brewer	1882	D.
Dundas - Bennet, George W.	brewer	1882	D.
Dundas Brewery		1861-2	D.
Dundas Distillery, property of late Richard Hatt, for rent 1821, again 1830			
Dundas Distillery (distiller wanted)		1857	Ad.
Dundas - Leslie, John	brewer	1861-2	D.
Dundas - Patterson, John (brewery for sale)		1844	Ad.
Dundas - Racy, A.	brewer	1861-2	D.
Dundas - Robertson & Wardle	brewers	1868	Ad.
Dundas - Holt & Cray	malsters	1863	Ad.
Dundas - Wilson, Steele Malting Co.		1909	D.
Dundas - Wright, M.	brewer	1882	D.
Dunneville - Dominion Brewery	inc. 1901		
Egmondville - Brant, A.	brewer	1892-9	D.
Egmondville - Colbert, Henry	brewer	1882-92-93	D.
Egmondville Brewery Co.		1909	D.
Elora - Carter & Co.	brewers	1882	D.
Elora - North Wellington Distillery		1857	Ad.
Exeter Brewery, est. 1862, for sale ...		1882	Ad.
Fergus Brewing Co.	inc. 1883		
Fergus - Holland & Co.	brewers	1882	D.
Formosa - Fehrenback, John	brewer	1882	D.
Formosa - Heisy, Lawrence	brewer	1909	D.
Formosa - Messner, Francis X.	brewer	1892-3	D.
Formosa - Schwartz, Jno. S.	brewer	1896-7	D.
Fort William - Kakabeca Falls Brewery,	inc. 1906	1909	D.
Galt Brewery, Whitney, E. prop.		1861-2	D.
Galt - Brogden, James	brewer	1882	D.
Galt - Cranston, Adam	brewer	1882	D.
Galt Distillery		1860	Ad.
Galt - Lutz, W.H.	brewer	1909	D.
Galt - Peck, Thos.	malster	1863-Ad. 1882-D.	
Galt - Todd, Thos.	brewer	1882	D.
Galt - Whitney, E.	brewer	1861-2	D.
Georgetown Brewery, Brinkerhoff, B.H.		1870-Ad. 1892-3-D.	
Goderich - Blake Bros.	brewers	1892-3	D.
Grafton - Archer, James	brewer	1847	Ad.
Grafton - Campbell & Pim	dist.	1862	D.
Grafton - Halimand Distillery, 1847 Ad., for sale...		1874	Ad.
Grafton - Roddick, John	dist.	1845	Ad.
Grafton - Spaulding, Thos.	brewer	1862	D.
Greensville - Steel, James	brewer	1892-3	D.
Guelph - Allen, David	dist.	1863	Ad.
Guelph - Fred, George & Co.	dist.	1856	Ad.
Guelph - Hamilton Spring Brewery (agency)		1862	D.
Guelph - Hogbert, James	brewer	1854	Ad.
Guelph - Holliday, Thos., Waterloo Ave.	brewer	1862-97	D.
Guelph - Holliday Bros.	brewers	1909	D.
Guelph - Lleunau Brewing & Malting	inc. 1900		
Guelph - Sleeman, George (Silver Creek Brewery)		est. 1850	Ad.
Guelph - Sleeman's Brewing & Malting	inc. 1901	1909	D.
Guelph - Sleeman & Sons	brewers	1909	D.
Guelph - Williams, W.	brewer	1862	D.
Hamilton - Cahusac, Wm. & Arnold, John, brewers, dissolved partnership-1834			Ad.
Hamilton Brewery, Cahusac, Wm. prop.		1835	Ad.

Ontario - cont'd

Hamilton - Baner, H.	brewer	1862	Directory
Hamilton - Bell, John	brewer	1861-2	D.
Hamilton Brewing Association	inc. 1903	1909	D.
Hamilton - Carling Brewing & Malting Co. Ltd.		1909	D.
Hamilton - Charlton's Vinegar Works		1862	D.
Hamilton - Dalley, E. (wines, liquors etc.)		1857	D.
Hamilton Distillery, Hon. Adam Perrie prop.		1860	Ad.
Hamilton Distilling Co. Ltd.	inc. 1884		
Hamilton Distillery	inc. 1901		
Hamilton - Dominion Brewery, Kuntz, H., prop., 19 Bay		1892-3	D.
Hamilton - Eydt, John	brewer	1882	D.
Hamilton - Grant, P.& Co.	brewers	1857	D.
Hamilton - Grant, Middlewood & Townsend	brewers	1861-2	D.
Hamilton - Grant, P. & Sons	brewers	1871-D., 1876-Ad.	
Hamilton - Grant, Lottridge Brewing Co.	inc. 1892	name changed - next	
Hamilton - Grant's Spring Brewery	inc. 1899		
Hamilton - Grant Spring Brewery Co. Ltd.		1909	D.
Hamilton - Snowdon, Grant & Co., Spring's Brewery		1851	D.
Hamilton - Hyatt's Spring Brewery (barrel or bottle)		1841	Ad.
Hamilton - General Distillery	inc. 1898		
Hamilton - Gompf, John, Ontario Brewery		1882, 96-7	D.
Hamilton - Hunt & Co. Peel St.	brewers	1851	D.
Hamilton - Independent Brewing Co. Ltd.		1909	D.
Hamilton - Kendall Brewery, 1861-2 - Directory. Destroyed by fire, 1880...			Article
Hamilton - Kuntz, David	brewer	1882	D.
Hamilton - Kuntz, Henry, 19 Bay N. 1892 - Directory. Inc. 1902. Sold out...			1906
Hamilton - Labatt, R.H., 18 Hughson St.		1892-3	D.
Hamilton - Linfoot, John H.	brewer	1892	D.
Hamilton - Palmerston Brewery		1882	D.
Hamilton - Regal Brewing Co. Ltd.	Est. 1875		Ad.
Hamilton - Royal Distillery		1905	Ads.
Hamilton - Saunders, W.	brewer	1882	D.
Hamilton - Silver Creek Brewery Agency		1892-3	D.
Hamilton - Thomas, W.H.	dist.	1861-2	D.
Hillier - Nash, Abner	brewer	1830	Ad.
Holland Landing - Tait, Wm.	brewer	1892-3	D.
Hollowell - Boone, George	brewer	1833	Ad.
Hollowell - Chapman, R.J.	dist.	1830	Ad.
Hollowell - Gardner, R. Hollowell Brewery		1830	Ad.
Hollowell - Munroe, Allen distillery & tavern		1830	Ad.
Hornby - Bain Bros.	brewers	1882, 92-3	D.
Hornby - Kemp, D.C.	brewers	1909	D.
Ingersol - Bixel, Matthew	brewer	1882	D.
Kemptville - Becket, Thos.	brewer	1862	D.
Kincardine Brewery for sale, owner retiring		1862	Ad.
Kingston - Bajus, John	brewer	1862	D.
Kingston - Bajus, Phillip jun.		1882	D.
Kingston - Bajus, Mrs. Grace		1909	D.
Kingston - Boiton, August	dist.	1810	Ad.
Kingston Brewery, Dalton, Thos. prop.		1819	Ad.
Kingston Brewery		1892-3	D.
Kingston - Burgess, J. brewer & dist. Wellingston St.		1851	D.
Kingston - Burn's Brewery		1820	Ad.
Kingston - Cameron & Livingston, Ontario St.	brewers	1851	D.
Kingston - Cameron, L.	brewer	1862	D.
Kingston - City Brewery Co., Mason, Micah prop. est. 1840			Ad.
Kingston - Cornell Brewing & Malting Co. Ltd.		1909	D.
Kingston - Creighton, G.W.	brewer	1862-71	D.
Kingston - Frontenac Brewery		1862	D.
Kingston - Garret, Wm.	dist.	1816	Ad.
Kingston - Gillespie & Burley	brewers	1816	Ad.
Kingston - Hayward & Downing	brewers	1862	D.
Kingston - Hawley, S.	dist.	1818	Ad.
Kingston - Jackson & Co.	brewers	1890	D.
Kingston - MacKay, R.& A.	brewers	1817	Ad.
Kingston - McDonnel, A.	brewers	1817	Ad.
Kingston - Molson, Thos.	bottled beer	1824	Ad.
Kingston - Morton, James, brewer & dist. 1844 Ad., died 1870, for sale...			1874
Kingston - Nickle, Wm.	brewer	1862	D.
Kingston - Nichalls, John	brewer	1890	D.
Kingston - Norton & Sons	brewer	1890	D.

Ontario - cont'd

Kingston - Patterson, J. Portsmouth Brewery		1851	Directory
Kingston - Pipe, Wm.	brewer	1890	D.
Kingston - Robinson, James	brewer	1815	Ad.
Kingston - Roderick, MacKay & Co.	brewers	1816	Ad.
Kingston - Rogers, Job beer in pts. & quts.		1843	Ad.
Kingston - Thompson Bottling Co. 292 Princess, beer		1899	D.
Kingston - Westlake, G. Portsmouth Rd. brewer & dist.		1851	D.
Laudewick - Essex Distilling Co.	inc. 1887	defunct 1906	
Lindsay Brewery		1896-7	D.
Lindsay - Hallam, W.H.	brewer	1893	D.
Lindsay - Lloyd, Cyril H.	brewer	1882	D.
Lindsay - Victoria Brewery		1871	Ad.
Listowell - Roth Bros.	brewer	1882	D.
Listowell - Roth, Robt.	brewer	1892-3	D.
Listowell - Watson, John	brewer	1909	D.
London - Arkell, Robt.	brewer	1882	D.
London Brewery, Labatt, John K. brewer & maltster		1861-2	D.
London - Carling, W.& J. est. 1840	brewers	1851	D.
London City Brewery, Carling, W.& J.		1861	D.
London - Carling Brewing & Malting Co.	inc. 1882	1909	D.
London - Cosgrave Brewing Co. of London	inc. 1894		
London - Dundas Brewery		1861-2	D.
London - Ferguson, C.M. 145 Queens Ave.	brewer	1892-3	D.
London - Forest City Malt House		1869	Ad.
London - Gage, T.	dist.	1861-2	D.
London - Gore Mills & Distillery	for sale...	1863	Ad.
London - Hamilton, John	brewer	1862-82	D.
London - Hamilton, Joseph	brewer	1896-1909	D.
London - Humpridge, Wm.	brewer	1862	D.
London - Kent Brewery, 197 Ann		1892-3	D.
London - Kompass, Fred	brewer	1861-2	D.
London - Labatt & Eccles	brewers	1851	D.
London - Labatt & Co.	brewers	1871	D.
London - Labatt, John K., Simcoe St.		1862, 1909	D.
London - Moore, W.	dist.	1861-2	D.
London - Slater, James	brewer	1882	D.
Maitlandville - Long, Wm.	brewer	1882	D.
Maitlandville - Potts, Wm.	brewer	1882	D.
Maitlandville - Wells, Henry	brewer	1882	D.
Maitlandville - Wells, James	brewer	1882	D.
March - Berry, W.H.	brewer	1892-3	D.
Marmion - Tedford, Ed.	dist.	1892-3	D.
Napanee - Bradford, E.B. & Co.	dist.	1862	D.
Napanee Distillery		1862	D.
Napanee - Fisher, Jos.	brewer	1870	Ad.
Napanee - Empey, Thos.	brewer	1892-3	D.
Napanee - Taylor, R.	brewer	1862	D.
Napanee - Wilkinson, Wm. H. new distillery		1862	Ad.
Newboro - Garshore, J.	brewer	1856	Ad.
New Hamburg Brewery		1882	D.
New Hamburg - Rare, S.& J.	brewers	1862	D.
New Hamburg - Rare, Mrs. John	brewers	1892-3	D.
New Hamburg - Rau, (?) Mrs. Mary	brewers	1909	D.
New Market - Gamble, N.A. brewery business for sale		1863	Ad.
New Market - Sykes, Sam	brewer	1882	D.
Neustadt - Berther, Henry	brewer	1871	D.
Neustadt - Huether, David	brewer	1882	D.
Neustadt - Huether, Henry	brewer	1871, 96-7	D.
Neustadt - Huether, William	brewer	1909	D.
New Edinburgh - Ardagh, A.W. & Co.	brewers	1862	D.
Niagara Falls - Cataract Wine & Spririts	inc. 1903		
Niagara Falls - Wine & Spirit Co.	inc. 1903		
Niagara Falls - Brewing & Malting	inc. 1905	operated 1 year	
North Bay - New Ontario Brewing	inc. 1904	1909	D.
Norval Distillery, Scott, A.F. prop.	sale or let	1859	Ad.
Oakville - Brown, Jas.	brewer	1860	Ad.
Oakville - Hogben, H. Victoria Brewery, 1861-D. Died 1865 & brewery sold,			Ad.
Ontario - Ontario Whiskey Exporting Co.	inc. 1896		
Ontario - Quebec City Malting Co. of Ontario	inc. 1882		
Orillia - Clarke & Graham	brewers	1892-3	D.
Orillia - Wright, A.J.	brewer	1909	D.

Ontario - cont'd

Oshawa - Spaulding, David	brewer		1857	Directory
Oshawa Brewery, occupied by late David Spaulding, for sale...			1864	Ad.
Osnawa - Wallace, George	dist.		1862	D.
Ottawa - Anderson, A., 726 Wellington S.	brewer		1871-97	D.
Ottawa - Brading, H.F., 457 Wellington S.	brewer, est. 1863		1896-7	D.
Ottawa - Brading Brewing Co. Ltd.			1909	D.
Ottawa - Burke, G.R.	brewer		1857	D.
Ottawa - Canadian Brewers Ltd.			1909	D.
Ottawa - Capital Brewing Co.	inc. 1899		1909	D.
Ottawa - Carling & Co.	brewers		1871-82	D.
Ottawa - Carling Bros. 144 Albert			1892-93	D.
Ottawa - Carling Brewing & Malting Co. Ltd.			1899-1909	D.
Ottawa - Christin, Jos. & Co.	brewers		1871-82	D.
Ottawa - Dawes & Co. (branch)	brewers		1882-93	D.
Ottawa - Dennison, John	brewers		1857	D.
Ottawa - Dorney, J.F.	brewers		1862	D.
Ottawa - Doyle, John	brewers		1862	D.
Ottawa - Gilmour, A.L., 435 Sussex	brewer		1892-3	D.
Ottawa - Gilmour, R.P., 431 Sussex	brewer		1899	D.
Ottawa - Kerr, J.	brewer		1862	D.
Ottawa - Labatt, John, 275 Kent	brewer		1899-1909	D.
Ottawa - McCarthy, J. & Sons Co., 474 Sussex	brewers		1899-1909	D.
Ottawa - Moran, John A., 181 Queen	brewer		1892-99	D.
Ottawa - Murphy Bros., Canal & Queen	brewer		1892-3	D.
Ottawa - O'Keefe Brewing Co. Ltd. 427 Nepean			1899	D.
Ottawa Brewing Co.	inc. 1893			
Ottawa Brewing & Malting Co., 851 Wellington			1899	D.
Ottawa - Pocklington, Jas.	brewer		1882	D.
Ottawa - Quinn, Michael	brewer		1882	D.
Ottawa - Ranger, D.V., 3 Clarence	brewer		1892-3	D.
Ottawa - Rochester, J. jun.	brewer		1862	D.
Ottawa - Rown, Jos. & Co.	brewer		1892-3	D.
Ottawa - Sampson, J.B., 450 Sussex	brewer		1899	D.
Ottawa - Sleeman & Kuntz, 349 Sparks	brewers		1899	D.
Ottawa - Stirling, George	brewers		1857	D.
Ottawa - Union Brewery, 461 Wellington			1882, 92-3	D.
Ottawa - Victoria Brewery			1862	D.
Ottawa - Weir, Wm., 58 Walker	brewer		1892-3	D.
Ottawa - Williamson, W.G.	brewer		1871	D.
Otterville - Williams, J.G.	dist.		1857	D.
Owen Sound - Eaton Bros. Brewery	inc. 1895		1903	Ads.
Owen Sound - Malone, Henry	brewer		1882	D.
Owen Sound - Riddle's Brewery	to let		1878	Ad.
Owen Sound - Schwan Bros.	brewers		1892-7	D.
Owen Sound - Sleeman's Brewery Agency			1896-7	D.
Owen Sound - Wilkinson, G.R.	brewer		1892-3	D.
Palmer - Clarke, L.H.	brewer		1892	D.
Palmer - Clark, Wm.	brewer		1892	D.
Palmerston Brewery	inc. 1889		defunct 1900	
Palmerston - Canada Malting Co.			1909	D.
Palmerston - Clarke, L.H.	brewer		1909	D.
Pelee Island Wine & Vineyards	inc. 1901			
Pembroke - Mattman, Frank	brewer		1892-3	D.
Penetangore C.W. - Browne, G.	brewer		1857	D.
Penville Distillery, St. Clair A. prop. for sale			1855	Ad.
Perth - Canwith, Wm.	brewer		1857	D.
Perth - Crystal Spring Brewery			1896-7	D.
Perth - Gemmel, R.	dist.		1862	D.
Perth - McLaren, J.A.	dist.		1862	D.
Perth - Scott & Campbell	brewers		1857	D.
Perth - Spaulding, James	brewers		1862	D.
Perth - Spaulding, James jr.	brewers		1882, 92-3	D.
Perth - Spaulding & Stuart	dist		1892-3	D.
Perth - Wordie, Wm.	brewer		1862	D.
Peterboro' - Boswell, W.W.	brewer		1862	D.
Peterboro' - Ritchie, Jas.	brewer		1862	D.
Peterborough Malting Co.	inc. 1881			
Picton - Despard, Wm.	brewer		1882	D.
Picton - MacCuaig, Paul	brewer		1871	D.
Picton - Niles, N.	dist.		1857	D.
Picton - Pickering, C.	brewer		1857	D.

Ontario - cont'd

Plantagenet - Ledue, P.	brewer	1899	Directory
Plantagenet - Winning, Hill & Ware	dist.	1870, 1900	Ads.
Port Arthur - Gehl, Conrad	brewer	1892-3	D.
Port Arthur - Guerard, A. & Son	brewers	1909	D.
Port Arthur - Superior Brewing & Malting	inc. 1900	1909	D.
Port Colborne - Cronmiller & White	brewers	1896-7	D.
Port Colborne - Cronmiller & White Brewing & Malting Co. Ltd.		1909	D.
Port Colborne - Lake Erie Brewery		1882	D.
Port Colborne - North, Jacob	brewer	1871	D.
Port Grandby - Elliott, G.	dist.	1862	D.
Port Hope - Ambrose & Winslow	brewers	1882	D.
Port Hope - Ambrose, W., brewer & maltster	inc. 1897	defunct 1907	
Port Hope Brewery, Dr. H. Bradley, Rochester N.Y. prop. for sale	1847	Ad.	
Port Hope Brewing & Malting Co. Ltd.		1909	D.
Port Hope - Bourne, Jas.	brewer	1857	D.
Port Hope - Calcutt, Jas.	brewer	1862-82	D.
Port Hope - Fothergill, Chas.	brewer	1819	Ad.
Port Hope - Lambert, Chas.	brewer	1857	D.
Port Hope - Lynne & White	dist.	1857	D.
Port Hope - McPhadden, C.	dist.	1857	D.
Port Hope - Protestant Hill Brewery		1862	D.
Port Hope - Spaulding, J.B.	brewer	1857	D.
Port Hope - Spaulding, M. brewery for sale or let	1865	Ad.	
Port Hope - Winslow & Allen	brewers	1871	D.
Port Nelson - O'Niel, J.	dist.	1857	D.
Port Rowan - Laymond, W.E.	brewer	1857	D.
Portsmouth - Fisher, James	brewer	1851-71	D.
Portsmouth - Fisher Bros.	brewer	1896-1909	D.
Portsmouth - Morton, James	brewer	1857	D.
Prescott - Averell, James G. & Co.	dist.	1857	D.
Prescott Brewing & Malting	inc. 1875	sold out 1905	
Prescott - Conway, D.B.	dist	1857	D.
Prescott - Crane, S. & Co.	dist.	1857	D.
Prescott - Crichton, J.B.	dist.	1857	D.
Prescott - Daniels, John	brewer	1892-3	D.
Prescott - Ellis, Wm.	brewer	1862	D.
Prescott - Egert, C.P. & Co.	dist.	1862	D.
Prescott - Grenville Brewery		1882	D.
Prescott - McCarthy, John & Sons	brewers	1882-99	D.
Prescott - McCarthy, John & Sons Co. Ltd.	brewers	1909	D.
Prescott - Smith, J.C.	brewer	1862	D.
Prescott - Wiser, J.P. & Sons	dist.	inc. 1893	
Preston - Bernhardt, Henry	brewer	1861-2	D.
Preston - Bernhardt, Henry & Son	brewers	1882	D.
Preston - Bernhardt, Peter	brewers	1892-7	D.
Preston - Bernhardt, Peter & Sons	brewers	1909	D.
Preston - Hitsch, Andrew	brewer	1882	D.
Preston - Hummel, David	brewer	1892-7	D.
Preston Lager		1861-2	D.
Preston Lager Bier		1861-2	D.
Preston - Martin, J. & Co.	brewers	1857	D.
Preston - Roos, George	brewer	1857	D.
Prince Arthur's Landing - Gehl, C.	brewer	1882	D.
Prince Arthur's Landing - Hale, John P.	brewer	1882	D.
Rat Portage - Lake of the Woods Brewery	inc. 1898	defunct 1904	
Richmond - Lyon, Thos.	dist.	1857	D.
Salem - Andrick, E.C. & Bros.	brewers	1909	D.
Salem Brewery		1882	D.
Salem - Doerbecker, Conrad	brewer	1882-93	D.
Salem - Doerbecker, Michael	brewer	1882	D.
Salem - Reuter, George	brewer	1892-3	D.
Saltford - Blake Bros.	brewer	1892-3	D.
Saltford - Wells, Henry	brewer	1882	D.
Sandwhich - Essex Distillery Co.	inc. 1903		
Sangster - Donnell, Patrick	dist.	1892-3	D.
Sarnia - Barry, James	brewer	1882	D.
Sarnia - Farr, Charles	brewer	1890	D.
Sarnia - Heusor, Henry & Co.	brewers	1890-7	D.
Sarnia - Russel, George	brewers	1871	D.
Sarnia - Russel, John	brewers	1882	D.
Sarnia - Union Brewery	inc. 1903	1909	D.
Saulte Ste. Marie - St. David's Wine Growers	inc. 1901	defunct 1902	

Ontario - cont'd

Saulte Ste. Marie - Superior Brewing	inc. 1901 as Algoma Brewery		
Saulte Ste. Marie - Soo-Falls Brewing Co.		1909	Directory
Simcoe - Finlay, H.D. & Co.	brewers	1882	D.
Simcoe - Kent, Edwin P.	brewers	1871	D.
Sincoe Steam Brewery		1882	D.
Smith's Falls - Burke, Thos.	dist.	1862	D.
South March - Barry, W.H.	brewer	1882-93	D.
St. Catharines - Hope, Robt. A.	brewer	1882	D.
St. Catharines - O'Keefe & Co.	brewer	1892-3	D.
St. Catharines - Taylor & Bates est. 1834	brewers	1861-1909	D.
St. David's - Henry, William	brewer	1882	D.
St. George - Bixel Brewing & Malting	inc. 1900	defunct 1906	
St. Jacobs - Jackson, Henry	distillery for sale - 1857		Ad.
St. James - Assineboine Brewing & Distillery	inc. 1876		
St. Lawrence Distillery Co.	inc. 1900		
St. Mary's - Guest, James R.	brewer	1862	D.
St. Thomas - Anson, brewer & distiller		1832	Ad.
St. Thomas - Bixel, M. & Son	brewers	1882	D.
St. Thomas - Blackwood, Jas. distillery erected 1849, burned out 1851			
St. Thomas - Gilbert & Co.	brewers	1882	D.
St. Thomas - Luke, Rich.	brewers	1861-2	D.
St. Thomas - Reiser, Wm. & Sons	brewers	1882	D.
St. Thomas - Rudolph & Begg	brewers	1892-7	D.
St. Thomas - Rudolph & Begg Brewing Co. Ltd.		1909	D.
Stratford - Beck, George	brewer	1892-3	D.
Stratford - Devlin & Steele	brewer	1896-7	D.
Stratford - Devlin, F.	brewer	1909	D.
Stratford - Empire Brewery		1896-7	D.
Stratford - Hamilton Spring Brewery		1862	D.
Stratford - Hargott Bros.	brewers	1892-3	D.
Stratford - Jones, W.C.	brewer	1872	Ad.
Stratford - Kuntz, L. (estate of)		1909	D.
Stratford - Russel, Wm.	brewer	1882	D.
Stratford - Sheard, Henry	brewer	1890	D.
Strathroy - Bixel Brewing & Malting Co. Strathroy		inc. 1890	
Strathroy Brewing & Malting Co.	inc. 1872	1909	D.
Strathroy - Snell, Thos.	brewer	1882	D.
Sudbury Brewing & Malting Co. Ltd.		1909	D.
Tilsonberg - St. Malo Vineyards (wines)		1880's	Ads.
Tilsonberg - Luke, J. & Sons	brewers	1892-7	D.
Toronto - Aldwell's Brewery, William St. 1857-D., chancery sale 1874			Ad.
Toronto - Alexander, Jas., wine man. est. 1855, sold out to J. Leask - 1860			
Toronto - Alexander, Hugh & Co.	brewers	1861-2	D.
Toronto - Allen, Thos. & Son, East End Brewery		1878-Ad. 1882-D.	
Toronto - Bailey & Bunting, 61-63 Front St. (vaults)		1869	Ad.
Toronto - Barclay & Perkins Porter, King St.		1856	Ad.
Toronto - Batland's Concertina Depot (wines)		1863	Ad.
Toronto - Beech St. Brewery, Defries, Robt. prop.		1861	article on.
Toronto - Bloor Brewery, Rosedale Ravine	- 1820		
Toronto - Bole, A., Colborne St.	brewer	1884	Ad.
Toronto - Brazil, F.P. & Co. 166 King St.	wines	1890	Ad.
Toronto - Borst, Halliday & Co.	dist.	1861-2	D.
Toronto - British American Brewing Co., Toronto, inc. 1903, defunct 1907			
Toronto - Brunskill, Thos.	dist.	1849	Ad.
Toronto - Burrel, Christopher	dist.	1857	Ad.
Toronto - Canada Malting Co.	inc. 1900	1909	D.
Toronto - Canadian Wine & Spirits	inc. 1905	defunct 1907	
Toronto - Carling Brewing & Malting Co. 13 Front W.		1892-9	D.
Toronto - Carling Brewing & Malting Co. Ltd., 45 Simcoe		1909	D.
Toronto - Clark, Jos., 64 Richmond St.	brewer	1851	D.
Toronto - Commercial Steam Mills Distillery		1855	Ad.
Toronto - Cook & Hamburger, wine man.		1856	Ad.
Toronto - Copeland, W., 220 King St.	brewer	1851	D.
Toronto - Copeland, W. jun., 220 King St.	brewer	1871	D.
Toronto - Copland, Wm. J.	brewer	1862-82	D.
Toronto - Copland Brewing Co., The, 55-65 Parliament		1892-99	D.
Toronto - Copland Brewing Co. Ltd., 337 King E.		1909	D.
Toronto - Corby, H. Distillery	inc. 1905		
Toronto - Cornell, John	brewer	1882	D.
Toronto - Cosgrave & Co.	brewers	1868	Ad.
Toronto - Cosgrave & Sons, 297 Niagara	brewers	1876	Ad.
Toronto - Cosgrave Brewing & Malting Co. of Toronto		inc. 1882	

Ontario - cont'd

Toronto - Cosgrave Brewing Co., inc. 1894, - 99D., Ltd.			1909	Directory
Toronto - Crabb, Sam., (wines, spirits & vinegar works) dist.			1860	Ad.
Toronto - Crocker, W., Palace St.		dist.	1851	D.
Toronto - Day, John		dist.	1861-2	D.
Toronto - Davies, Thomas & Nathaniel, Yonge St.		brewers	1846	(see Yonge)
Toronto - Davies, Thomas, Don Bridge Brewery			1849	Ad.
Toronto - Davies Brewing & Malting, Queen & King E. inc. 1883			defunct 1901	
Toronto - Davies Brewing Co., 580 Queen E.			1909	D.
Toronto - Dawson, John		brewer	1850's-Ads. 1862-D.	
Toronto - Denison, R.L. dist. Third Mile Stone, Dundas St.			1845	Ad.
Toronto - Don Brewery, Helliwell, Thos. & Jos.			1831	Ad.
Toronto - Dominion Brewery, Davies, Robt. prop. est. 1878				Article
Toronto - Dominion Brewery Co. Ltd., 496 Queen E.			1890-1909	D.
Toronto - Dominion of Canada Malting		inc. 1905	defunct 1907	
Toronto - Dominion Wine & Spirits, inc. 1906, changed name to C. Edwards & Co. same year.				
Toronto - Eaton Bros., 4 Louisa		brewers	1896-99	D.
Toronto - Essex Wines		inc. 1902		
Toronto - Farr, John, Queen W.		brewer	1851	D.
Toronto - Foster, Dawson		wine man.	1870	Ad.
Toronto - Foy, George J. (dealer)		inc. 1905		
Toronto - Fulton, Jobis & Co. (vaults)			1857	Ad.
Toronto - Fulton, Michie & Co. (vaults)			1864	Ad.
Toronto - George, T.H., 699 Yonge		brewer	1899	D.
Toronto - Gilpin, Robt.		dist.	1855	Ad.
Toronto - Girardot, E. Wines		inc. 1902	defunct 1906	
Toronto - Glassford, H.A.		wines etc.	1856	Ad.
Toronto - Globe Wine Vaults (under Globe paper)			1857	Ads.
Toronto - Gooderham & Worts, 216 Trinity,		dist.	1851 - D. Inc. - 1892	
Toronto - Greey, Samuel		brewer	1860's	Ads
Toronto - Hannath & Hart, Victoria Brewery, Gold & Victoria			1848	Ads.
Toronto - Harding, Jas.		brewer	1861-2	D.
Toronto - Harris, Jas.		brewer	1861-2	D.
Toronto - Harris, J.A., Louisa St.		wine man.	1890	Ad.
Toronto - Henderson, Wm. & Co., King St.		dist.	1849	Ad.
Toronto - Hogben, H., brewer, King W., (The Vine, Bottled Ale & Porter Vaults) 1859-65 Ads.				
Toronto - Jardine & Co., 143 Kinsington Ave.		brewers	1892-3	D.
Toronto - Jennings, W.J.		wine & spirit man.	1858	Ad.
Toronto - Korman's Brewery, 105 Duchess			1899 - D. Inc. - 1903	
Toronto - Korman's Brewery Ltd.			1909	D.
Toronto - Knapp, Lyman		dist.	1855	Ad.
Toronto - Labatt, John, 49 Elm			1899-1909	D.
Toronto - Leask, James, Man. ginger wine etc.			1860's	Ads.
Toronto - London Dock Vaults, Grand Bros. 1850's Ads. Sold 1857 and name changed-Globe Wine Vaults.				
Toronto - Mace, J.A.		brewer	1890	D.
Toronto - McCormack Bros.		brewers	1871-82	D.
Toronto - McKay, Adam, Eliza St.		brewer(wood & bottle) 1842		Ad.
Toronto - McKay, Adam, Spadina Ave.		brewer	1851	D.
Toronto - Medcalf, F.H.		brewer	1861-2	D.
Toronto - Moffat, Murray & Co. (beer & liquors in pts. & qts.)			1856	Ad.
Toronto - Moor, J.C., 433 Yonge St.		brewer	1899	D.
Toronto - Morrison, M. brewer (bottled Ale & Porter Vaults)			1868-Ad. 1871-D.	
Toronto - Nash, Cayley & Co., Ontario Brewery, Front St. 1851 D. for sale, 1856 Ad.				
Toronto - Nicholls, H.E.		dist.	1841	Ad.
Toronto - O'Keefe & Co. improve premises known as the Victoria Brewery-1864, Article.				
Toronto - O'Keefe & Co., Gould, corner Victoria, brewers			1882	D.
Toronto - O'Keefe Brewing Co. of Toronto Ltd.			1892-99	D.
Toronto - O'Keefe Brewery Co. Ltd., 11 Gould			1909	D.
Toronto - Ontario Brewing & Malting Co., 311 King E. 1853 Ad. inc. 1883. 1899 D.				
Toronto - Ontario Liquor Co.		inc. 1883	defunct 1901	
Toronto - Platt, Samuel, Front St.		brewer	1851	D.
Toronto - Queen City Brewery			1861-2	D.
Toronto - Queen City Malting		inc. 1882		
Toronto - Rae Distillery on the River Don		for sale...	1856	Ad.
Toronto - Reinhardt & Co., 22 Mark,			1892-3 - D. 1910 - Ads.	
Toronto - Rioroan, D.& J.S., (foot of Bay)		dist.	1857	Ad.
Toronto - Risdan, Julian & Dennis, Front St.		dist.	1859	Ad.
Toronto - Rogers & Frink		brewers	1862	D.
Toronto - Rowell, George, Agnes St.		brewers	1851	D.
Toronto - Rowell, W.J.		brewers	1862	D.
Toronto - Saunders, W.C.		brewer	1890	D.
Toronto - Severn's Brewery, bottled ale, 1848 Ad. Sheriff's sale of brewery & equipment - 1885, Ad.				

Ontario - cont'd

Toronto - Shaw, Duncan, brewer, bottled ale etc.	1870	Ad.
Toronto - Silver Creek Brewery Agency, 23 Church	1896-7	Directory
Toronto - Southley, E.R., brewer, Kingston Rd., sold out	1858	Ad.
Toronto - Sovereign, John, Yonge St. brewer	1851	D.
Toronto - Spadina Brewery, (late McKay's) for auction	1855	Ad.
Toronto - Spadina Brewery beer & ale	1865	Ad.
Toronto - St. Malo Vineyard inc. 1884		
Toronto - Thompson, Isaac brewer	1857-63	D.
Toronto - Todd Wine Co. of Toronto Ltd. inc. 1888		
Toronto Brewing & Malting co., 272 Simcoe, inc. 1874	1899	D.
Toronto Brewing & Malting Co. Ltd., The, 284 Simcoe	1909	D.
Toronto - Turner, Enoc, Palace & Parliament (brewery for sale)	1853	Ad.
Toronto - Turner Brewing Co. inc. 1905		
Toronto - Victoria Brewery, orders taken at	1852	Ad.
Toronto - Walkerville Brewing Co. Ltd., 11 Colborne St.	1892-3	D.
Toronto - Walker, Hiram & Sons inc. 1890		
Toronto - Wallis & Moss brewers	1861-2	D.
Toronto - Warner & Waltz brewers	1857	D.
Toronto - Warner's Lager Beer, 92 Yonge	1862	Ad.
Toronto - Waltz, John brewer	1862-82	D.
Toronto - West Toronto Brewery, Barnes & Thompson (keg or bottle)	1857 - Ad.	1882 - D.
Toronto - Wendigo Wines of Ontario inc. 1900	defunct 1902	
Toronto - William Street Brewery	1861-2	D.

Toronto - Yonge St. Brewery operated by Thomas & Nathaniel Davies. In 1848 they dissolved
partnership and Thomas took over the Don Bridge Brewery same year.

Toronto - Yonge St. Brewery to let by Thos. Davies, Don Brewery	1865	Ad.
Trent Distillery, property of late Dennis Weaver, for sale...	1868	Ad.
Trenton - Flindall, John F. brewer	1882	D.
Uxbridge - Bowman, W.J. dealer	1876	Ad.
Vittoria - Norfolk Distillery for rent, Mrs. Woolnough prop.	1869	Ad.
Walkerton - Farquharson & Grainger brewers	1892-1909	D.
Walkerville Brewing Co. Ltd. inco. 1890	1909	D.
Walkerville - Walker, Hiram & Sons Ltd. dist.	1892-3	D.
Waterdown - Dyke - brewer	1861	D.
Waterloo - Hespeler & Randall dist.	1862	D.
Waterloo - Huether, Chris. brewer	1862	D.
Waterloo - Huether, Chris. & Son brewers	1892-3	D.
Waterloo - Kuntz, David est. 1840 brewer	1862	D.
Waterloo - Kuntz, Louis brewer	1882-93	D.
Waterloo - Kuntz, Louis (estate of) brewers	1909	D.
Waterloo - Seagram, J.E. dist.	1892-3	D.
Waterloo Malting Co.	1909	D.
West Flamboro Distillery, Crook, Jas. prop.	1859	Ad.
Weston Brewery, Thompson, G. (bottled ale & porter)	1861	Ad.
Whitby Brewery for sale or lease	1855	Ad.
Whitby Brewery, Clark & Woodward	1862	D.
Windsor - Baby & Hanrahan brewers	1890	D.
Windsor - Beniteau, Pat. dist.	1892-3	D.
Windsor - British American Brewing Co. Ltd. est. 1882	1909	D.
Windsor - Connel Brewing & Malting inc. 1904		
Windsor - Consumers Brewing inc. 1899	defunct 1906	
Windsor - Copland Brewing inc. 1903		
Windsor - Cronk, Albert brewer	1882	D.
Windsor - Girardot Wine Co. inc. 1906		
Windsor - Griesinger, Louis brewer	1892-3	D.
Woodstock - Berhardt, Louis, Norwich Ave. brewer	1882	D.
Woodstock - Collens, S. & James brewers	1882	D.
Woodstock - Otterbein, C. brewer	1909	D.
York Distillery & Potashery on the River Don, Wood & Anderson	1831	Ad.
Yorkville Brewery - Severn, G.& H.	1862-82	D.
Yorkville - Morgan & Rose, brewery & distillery	1856	Ad.
Yorkville - Wharfinger & Reed, distillery & malthouse for sale	1855	Ad.

Ontario Cider Mills

Albury - Dempsey, W.R.	1892-3	Directory
Almira - Hisey, A.	1892-3	D.
Ameliasburg - Roblin, R.	1892-3	D.
Ancaster - Lyons, E.	1892-3	D.

Ontario - cont'd

Aylmer Canning & Evaporating Co.	1882	Directory
Aylmer - Lewis, W.C.	1892-3	D.
Ayton - Dieterich, G.	1892-3	D.
Baden - Meisel Bros.	1892-3	D.
Bamberg - Kieswater, L.	1882	D.
Bayfield - Gemenhardt, J.	1892-3	D.
Belleville - Graham, R.J.	1892-3	D.
Belleville - Leavers & Corby	1882	D.
Bethesda - Leary, J. & Co.	1892-3	D.
Blyth - McCreight, A.	1892-3	D.
Bowmanville - Souch, S.	1892-3	D.
Bright - Evans, Jas. E.	1892-3	D.
Brooksdale - Young, Edwd.	1892-3	D.
Brougham - Cowie, Wm.	1892-3	D.
Burnaby - Schooley, D.B. & Sons	1892-3	D.
Carlsruhe - Lobsinger, L.	1882	D.
Carlsruhe - Lobsinger, Mrs. C.	1892-3	D.
Cashmere - Moyer, Abraham	1892-3	D.
Cedar Grove - Lapp, Peter	1882	D.
Cedar Grove - Lapp & Son	1892-3	D.
Cherry Valley - Hughes & Palmeter	1892-3	D.
Clinton - Andrews, Jerome	1892-3	D.
Cranbrook - Cameron, J.	1882, 92-3	D.
Deemerton - Ruland Bros.	1892-3	D.
Delaware - Hammond & Weld	1892-3	D.
Doon - Cluthie, C.	1892-3	D.
Dunkeld Cider Man. Co.	1892-3	D.
Dunkheld - Tschirhart, J.B.	1892-3	D.
Eden - Gray, A.N.	1892-3	D.
Egmondville - Jackson, G.& H.	1882, 92-3	D.
Fairview - Helpin, Jas.	1882	D.
Forks Road - Smith, John	1892-3	D.
Frankford - Sweetman, Jas.	1892-3	D.
Fullerton - Getlar, John	1882	D.
Hamilton - Toronto Cider & Fruit Vinegar Co.	1892-3	D.
Harley - Bennet, Wm.	1892-3	D.
Harrington - White, E.	1892-3	D.
Hensall - Thomson, B.	1892-3	D.
Hespeler - Groh, Issac	1892-3	D.
Hillier - Cripper, John	1892-3	D.
Hills Green - Coleman, Thos.	1892-3	D.
Hills Green - Troyer, John	1882	D.
Ingersoll - McKenzie, Ed.	1882	D.
Innerskip - Hotson, George	1892-3	D.
Jordon - Moyer, Jos. B.	1882, 92-3	D.
Kurtsville - Kurtz, John	1892-3	D.
Langstaff - Langstaff, John	1882	D.
Luton - Doolittle, Ephraim	1882, 92-3	D.
Marden - Hook, David	1882	D.
Milverton - Noll, Fred	1892-3	D.
Millbrook - Derbyshire, Wm.	1882	D.
Moltke - Weigel Bros.	1892-3	D.
Mount Vernon - Griffin, J.P.	1892-3	D.
Musselburg - Yost, John R.	1892-3	D.
New Hamburg - Asmus, W.	1882	D.
New Hamburg - Ritz, Daniel	1892-3	D.
Nobleton - Elviss, Jos.	1892-3	D.
Norwich - Allen, Soloman	1892-3	D.
Norwich - Donald, D.M.	1882	D.
Norwich - Palmer Bros.	1882	D.
Oakville - Hilton, Henry	1892-3	D.
Otterville - Lossing, S.B.	1892-3	D.
Petersburg - Holman, J.S.	1882	D.
Petersburg - Minor, H.Z.	1882	D.
Plattsville - Whitmore, D.	1882, 92-3	D.
Port Dover - Silverthorn, W.	1882	D.
Port Perry - Davy & Atkinson	1892-3	D.
Princeton - Henderson, Jas. S.	1882	D.
Rednersville - Dempsey, Wm. R.	1892-3	D.
Ridgetown - Patterson, Archibald	1892-3	D.
Ringwood - Reamer, John	1892-3	D.

Ontario - cont'd

Rockwood - Bragg, W.S.	1892-3	Directory
Rodney - McCallum, F.A.	1892-3	D.
Roseville - Detwieler, Enoc W.	1882, 92-3	D.
St. Clement - Weher, J.& M.	1892-3	D.
Salem - Wissler, Ezra	1892-3	D.
Sebringville - Barthel, George	1892-3	D.
Sebringville - Pfrimmer, George	1882	D.
Simcoe - Nickerson, Wilson & Co.	1882	D.
Smithfield - Drewery Bros.	1892-3	D.
St. Clements - Weber, J.M.	1882	D.
Stirling - Bradley, T.H.	1892-3	D.
Tavistock - Krauntz, Henry	1892-3	D.
Tavistock - Schmidt, Christian	1892-3	D.
Tavistock - Wettlaufer, Eckhardt	1892-3	D.
Thamesville - Weitzel, Oscar	1892-3	D.
Toronto - Crawford, John	1892-3	D.
Toronto - Kemp, Jones & Peck	1892-3	D.
Toronto - Patterson, S.	1892-3	D.
Toronto Cider & Fruit Vinegar Co.	1892-3	D.
Union - Doolittle, George	1892-3	D.
Wellesley - Meyer, Caspar	1882	D.
Wellesley - Weismiller, John	1892-3	D.
Willowdale - Morgan, John	1892-3	D.
Wolverton - Chesney, Henry	1892-3	D.
Woodstock - Passage, Ike	1892-3	D.
Woodstock - Watkins, Fred	1882	D.

Chemists, Druggists and Manufacturers

Acton - McGarvin, James E.	druggist	1882	Directory
Acton - Kannawin, J.V.	druggist	1892-3	D.
Acton - Morrow, R., M.D.	druggist	1882	D.
Ailsa Craig - Hey, T.	druggist	1882	D.
Ailsa Craig - Stewart, D.A.	druggist	1892-3	D.
Ainleyville - Grant, John R.	druggist	1871	D.
Albion - Snell, Samuel J.	druggist	1892-3	D.
Alexandria - McDonald, A.L.	druggist	1892-3	D.
Alexandria - Ostram Bros.	druggist	1892-3	D.
Allanburg - Mussen, Henry	druggist	1892-3	D.
Allandale - Sanders, F.J.	druggist	1892-3	D.
Allenford - Taylor, A.B.	druggist	1882, 92-3	D.
Alliston - McMahon, Isaiah	druggist	1882, 92-3	D.
Alliston - Pine Malt Medicine	inc. 1895		
Alliston - Stewart, John	druggist	1892-3	D.
Almonte - Dowdall, P.C.	druggist	1882, 92-3	D.
Almonte - MacFarlane, M.R.	druggist	1892-3	D.
Almonte - Patterson, M.	druggist	1892-3	D.
Alton - Kibblewhite, E.J.	druggist	1892-3	D.
Alton - Holden, John F.	druggist	1882	D.
Alvinston - Mackinnon, D.	druggist	1882	D.
Alvinston - McDiarmid, D.	druggist	1882, 92-3	D.
Alvinston - Pine Malt Medicine Co. of Ont.	inc. 1895		
Ameliasburg - File, A.J.	druggist	1892-3	D.
Amherstburg - Johnston, Wm.	druggist	1882	D.
Amherstburg - Kane, John A.	druggist	1871	D.
Amherstburg - Kane, Mrs. M.A.	druggist	1892-3	D.
Amherstburg - Lushington, J.S.	druggist	1882, 92-3	D.
Amherstburg - Thomas, C.M.S.	druggist	1882, 92-3	D.
Amsterdam - Young, J.H. (prop. Rowan's Tonic)		1834	Ad.
Ancastor - Donnelly, B.W.	druggist	1882, 92-3	D.
Angus - Nesbitt, W.T.	druggist	1892-3	D.
Annon - Sloane, A.C.	druggist	1892-3	D.
Arkona - Everest, J.M.	druggist	1892-3	D.
Arnprior - Menzies, A.	druggist	1892-3	D.
Arnprior - Shaw, Wm.	druggist	1882	D.
Arnprior - Wait, J.T.	druggist	1882, 92-3	D.
Arthur - Kilgour, D.F.	druggist	1882, 92-3	D.
Arthur - Henderson, W., M.D.	druggist	1871	D.
Arthur - Robertson, Wm. J.	druggist	1892-3	D.

Ontario – cont'd

Athens – Lamb, J.P.	druggist	1892-3	Directory
Atwood – Public D ngs,	inc. 1904		
Aurora – Ashton, S.H.	druggist	1882	D.
Aurora – Hartman, H.J.	druggist	1882	D.
Aurora – Patterson, G.	druggist	1892-3	D.
Aurora – Rutherford, J.R.	druggist	1892-3	D.
Aurora – York, F.E.	druggist	1892-3	D.
Aylmer – Comport, Thos.	druggist	1892-3	D.
Aylmer – Lyon, Warner	druggist	1871	D.
Aylmer – Mann, T.T.	druggist	1892-3	D.
Aylmer – Richards, J.E.	druggist	1892-3	D.
Ayr – McGeorge	apothecary	1851	
Ayr – McGeorge, Charles chemist &	druggist	1882, 92-3	D.
Ayr – Wylie, John	druggist	1871	D.
Ayton – McLean, P.	druggist	1882, 92-3	D.
Bancroft – Rose, D.E.	druggist	1892-3	D.
Barrie – Georgen, Wm. T.	druggist	1882	D.
Barrie – Kidd, Jas. P.	druggist	1892-3	D.
Barrie – McLean, Wm. C.	druggist	1892-3	D.
Barrie – Monkman, J.G.	druggist	1882	D.
Barrie – Woods, John	druggist	1882, 92-3	D.
Barrie – Workman, G.	druggist	1892-3	D.
Bath – Price, R., M.D.	druggist	1871	D.
Bayfield – Hewston, J.H.	druggist	1882, 92-3	D.
Beachburg – Forbes, G.	druggist	1882, 92-3	D.
Beamsville – Riggins, C.E.	druggist	1882, 92-3	D.
Beaverton – McKinnon, J.	druggist	1882	D.
Beaverton – Thompson, S.	druggist	1892-3	D.
Beeton – Ashton, W.	druggist	1892-3	D.
Beeton – Borland, E.B.	druggist	1882	D.
Beeton – Howland, W.H.	druggist	1882	D.
Belleville – Bennet, Badgely & Co.	druggist	1882	D.
Belleville – Carmichael, W.R.	druggist	1882, 92-3	D.
Belleville – Chandler, E.	druggist	1851, 71	D.
Belleville – Clarke, J. & Co.	druggist	1882	D.
Belleville – Clarke, F.C.	druggist	1892-3	D.
Belleville – Green, A.L.	druggist	1882, 92-3	D.
Belleville – Holden & Sawyer	druggist	1846	Ad.
Belleville – Holden, Jas. C. chemist &	druggist	1871	D.
Belleville – Levesconte, C.G. & Co.	druggist	1851	D.
Belleville – Mundy, Mark	druggist	1882	D.
Belleville – Scott & Bowne (Scott's Emulsion man.)		1876	Ad.
Belleville – Templeton, Robt.	druggist	1882, 92-3	D.
Belleville – Waters, D.M.	druggist	1892-3	D.
Belleville – Yeoman, L.W. & Co.	druggist	1882, 92-3	D.
Belwood – Smith, N. L.	druggist	1892-3	D.
Berlin Chemical Co. (Vandaline Hair Tonic)	1892 Ad., inc. 1902, def. 1905		
Berlin – Bowman, W.H.	druggist	1882, 92-3	D.
Berlin – Forster, M., M.D.	druggist	1882	D.
Berlin – Hoffman, J.S.	druggist	1882	D.
Berlin – Hoffman, C.E.	druggist	1892-3	D.
Berlin – Landreth, J.H. & Co.	druggist	1892-3	D.
Berlin – Neville, J.E.	druggist	1892-3	D.
Bethany – Brereton, T.G., M.D.	druggist	1892-3	D.
Bethany – Earkwell, H.	druggist	1882	D.
Bethany – Leach, Alf.	druggist	1882	D.
Bethany – Ryley, Thos. G.	druggist	1882	D.
Bewdley – Sidey, John, M.D.	druggist	1882	D.
Blenheim – Arkell & Son	druggist	1892-3	D.
Blenheim – Crookshank Bros.	druggist	1892-3	D.
Blyth – Hamilton, J.M.	druggist	1892-3	D.
Bobcaygeon – McCamus, W., M.D.	druggist	1882	D.
Bobcaygeon – McCamus, Thos.	druggist	1892-3	D.
Bobcaygeon – Sloane, Wm., M.D.	druggist	1882	D.
Bobcaygeon – Ventress, R.	druggist	1871, 82	D.
Bolton – Snell, S.J.	druggist	1882	D.
Bolton – Stork, James, Dr.	druggist	1871, 82	D.
Bowmanville – Higginbotham, J.	druggist	1882	D.
Bowmanville – Higginbotham & Son	druggist	1892-3	D.
Bowmanville – Neads, Martin E.	druggist	1892-3	D.
Bowmanville – Stott & Jury	man.	1882, 92-3	D.

Ontario - cont'd

Location - Name	Type	Date	Source
Bothwell - Pope, F.H., M.D.	druggist	1882	Directory
Bracebridge - Bridgeland, S.	druggist	1882, 92-3	D.
Bracebridge - Thomson, J.	druggist	1892-3	D.
Bradford - Williams, J.F.	druggist	1882	D.
Bradford - Edmanson, Thos.	druggist	1882, 92-3	D.
Brampton - Bannister, E.	druggist	1882, 92-3	D.
Brampton - Hodgson, R.H.	druggist	1882, 92-3	D.
Brampton - Magurn & Bannister	druggist	1871	D.
Brampton - Stork, C. & Son	druggist	1882, 92-3	D.
Brantford - Bachelor, Ben	druggist	1892-3	D.
Brantford - Blackeder & Mills	druggist	1882	D.
Brantford - Brantford Chemical Man. Co. Ltd.	inc. 1899		
Brantford - Golding, G.I.	druggist	1892-3	D.
Brantford - Higinbotham, Wm.	druggist	1892-3	D.
Brantford - Mason, C.S. & Co.	druggist	1871	D.
Brantford - McGregor & Parke	druggist	1892-3	D.
Brantford - Phillips, Kincard & Co.	druggist	1882	D.
Brantford - Pilkey, Albert E.	druggist	1882	D.
Brantford - Popplewell, A.A.	druggist	1882	D.
Brantford - Sager, D.S.	druggist	1892-3	D.
Brantford - Stratford, Jos.	druggist	1882	D.
Brantford - Tappscott, S. & Co.	druggist	1882, 92-3	D.
Brantford - Turner, Robt. (man. Turner's Tonic Bitters)		1883	Ad.
Brantford - Wallace, J.A.	druggist	1882, 92-3	D.
Bright - Bromley, E., M.D.	druggist	1882, 92-3	D.
Brighton - Barker, Robt.	druggist	1882	D.
Brighton - Haines, A.	druggist	1892-3	D.
Brighton - Rolls, J.F., M.D.	druggist	1882	D.
Brighton - Rowan, J.E.	druggist	1892-3	D.
Brockville Chemical & Superphosphate Co.		1871	D.
Brockville - Comstock, W.H. man. etc.,	est. 1834	1892	Article
Brockville - Cribb & Co.	druggists	1846	Agency for cal. spr's.
Brockville - Donnelly, B.	druggist & man.	1851	Ad.
Brockville - Dunham, Dr. Medical Hall		1843	Ad.
Brockville - Fulford & Co.	man.	1871, 92-3	D.
Brockville - Fullerton Drugs		1897	Ad.
Brockville - Hawkes, Jas.	druggist	1871	D.
Brockville - Harding, T.J.B.	man.	1876-Ad. 1882, 92-3-D.	
Brockville - Hays Soloman (prop. Hay's Liniment)		1840	Ad. (Comstock agent)
Brockville - LaLonde, F.C.	druggist	1892-3	D.
Brockville - Libby, Dr. (Dr. Libby's Bitters)		1840	Ad.
Brockville - Libby, Dr.	man. & agent	1842	Ad.
Brockville - McDonald, A.N. & Co.	man. chem.	1866	Ad.
Brockville - McMillan, P.	druggist	1892-3	D.
Brockville - Turner, Allan & Co.	druggist	1871, 92-3	D.
Brockville - Williams, J.	druggist	1882, 92-3	D.
Brockville - Wilson & Co.	druggist	1882	D.
Brockville - Wilson, Robt. A.	druggist	1882	D.
Brougham - Soule, Dr. E.L. & Co. (man. Sovereign Balm)		1848	Ad.
Brougham - Woodruff, Benley & Co. (Dr. M. Caldwell's Dyspepsia Remedy) 1869			Ad.
Brussels - Deadman, G.A.	druggist	1882, 92-3	D.
Brussels - Pepper, J.T.	druggist	1892-3	D.
Burford - Chrysler, Wm. H., M.D.	druggist	1882, 92-3	D.
Burford - Harbottle, R.	druggist	1882, 92-3	D.
Burks Falls - Caughell, C.	druggist	1892-3	D.
Burlington - Wells, Richardson & Co.	man.	1882	Ad.
Burlington - Halson, Robt.	druggist	1882	D.
Burlington - LePatourel	druggist	1892-3	D.
Bytown - Bishoprick, H. druggist & ginger beer man.		1836	Ad.
Bytown - Kneeshaw, R. (late with Lyman & Co. Mont.)		1843	Ad.
Bytown - Graham, R.	drugs, etc.	1839	Ad.
Bytown - Summer, Chas.	druggist	1846	Agency for cal. spr's.
Caledonia - Buck, Alexis C. druggist & man. est. 1846 Ads.		1871	D.
Caledonia - Roper, John (man. Duncan's Indian Liniment)		1866-Ad. 1892-3-D.	
Caledonia - Thynne, R.	chemist & druggist	1867	Ad.
Caledon East - Lawrence, R. & Co.	druggist	1882	D.
Cambray - Lytle, H.J.	druggist	1892-3	D.
Campbellford - Loucks, W.F.	druggist	1892-3	D.
Campbellford - Wood, F.W.	druggist	1892-3	D.
Cannington - Elwell, Wm., M.D.	druggist	1871	D.
Cannington - Fead Bros.	druggist	1892-3	D.
Cannington - Wyatt, A.	druggist	1892-3	D.

Ontario - cont'd

Cardinal - Birks, John	druggist	1882, 92-3	Directory
Cardinal - Dowsley	druggist	1892-3	D.
Carleton Place - Hughes, W.J.	druggist	1897-8	D.
Carleton Place - McEwen, F., M.D.	druggist	1882	D.
Carleton Place - McEwen, H.	druggist	1892-3	D.
Carleton Place - McIntosh, D.M., M.D.	druggist	1882	D.
Carleton Place - Preston, R.F.	druggist	1882	D.
Carleton Place - Robertson, W.S.	druggist	1882	D.
Carleton Place - Switzer & Bros.	druggist	1882	D.
Cayuga - Thompson, D.	druggist	1892-3	D.
Chatham - Bray, W.T. (prop. Hill's Bucha Extract)		1878	Ad.
Chatham - Bright, J.C.	druggist	1892-3	D.
Chatham - Burt, R.C.	druggist	1882, 92-3	D.
Chatham - Conklin, W.P.	druggist	1875	Ad.
Chatham - Hall, H.C. (prop. Sparkhall's Specific, Qt. bottle)		1884	Ad.
Chatham - McLaren, J.W.	druggist	1892-3	D.
Chatham - Pilkey, A.E. & Co.	druggist	1892-3	D.
Chatham - Powell, G.A.	druggist	1882	D.
Chatham - Powell & Davis	druggist	1892-3	D.
Chatham - Priddy, R.	druggist	1892-3	D.
Chatham - Radley & Patton	druggist	1882	D.
Chatham - Radley, S.D. (Radley's Cough Syrup)	druggist	1886-Ad. 1892-3-D.	
Chatham - Robertson, A.R.	druggist	1842	Ad.
Chatham - Rolls, A.M.	druggist	1882	D.
Chatsworth - Hopkins, Thos.	druggist	1882, 92-3	D.
Chatsworth - Elliot, J.W.	druggist	1882	D.
Chesley - Goodine, A.S.	druggist	1892-3	D.
Chesley - Goulding, G.H.	druggist	1882	D.
Chesley - Stinson, J.O.	druggist	1892-3	D.
Chesterville - Bolster, W.G.	druggist	1892-3	D.
Chesterville - Casselman, Chas.	druggist	1882	D.
Chippawa - Campbell, Jos., M.D.	druggist	1882	D.
Claremont - Eastwood, W.F., M.D.	druggist	1892-3	D.
Claremont - Milne, Wm., M.D.	druggist	1882	D.
Clarksburg - Sine, C. & Co.	druggist	1892-3	D.
Clifford - Rowntree, R.	druggist	1892-3	D.
Clinton - Combe, J.H.	druggist	1882, 92-3	D.
Clinton - Mackid, J.M.	druggist	1882	D.
Clinton - Watts & Co.	druggist	1871, 92-3	D.
Clinton - Worthingham, A., M.D.	druggist	1892-3	D.
Cobourg - Boyer, G. Dr.	druggist	1848	Ad.
Cobourg - Gowans, F.M. & Co.	druggist	1892-3	D.
Cobourg - Gravelly & Jackson	druggist	1846	Ad.
Cobourg - Kennedy, John E.	druggist	1882	D.
Cobourg - McNichol, E.C., M.D.	druggist	1882	D.
Cobourg - Osgood, Dr. (man. Osgood's Indian Cholagogue)		1848	Ad.
Cobourg - Templeton, J.	druggist	1892-3	D.
Cobourg - Wilson, R.	druggist	1882, 92-3	D.
Coe Hill Mines - Bothby, H.N.	druggist	1892-3	D.
Colborne - Griffis, W.G.	druggist	1892-3	D.
Coldwater - Millard, C.G.	druggist	1892-3	D.
Collingwood - Carpenter, E.H.	druggist	1882, 92-3	D.
Collingwood - Douglas, Wm.	druggist	1892-3	D.
Collingwood - Greaves, Jos.	druggist	1882	D.
Collingwood - Johnston, A.H.	druggist	1892-3	D.
Collingwood - Oliphant, D.	druggist	1882, 92-3	D.
Comber - Abbot, R.H.	druggist	1892-3	D.
Conestogo - Passmore, Wm., M.D.	druggist	1882	D.
Cookstown - Green, Sam. G.	druggist	1882	D.
Cookstown - Green, Mrs. S.G.	druggist	1892-3	D.
Cookstown - Harper, H.	druggist	1871	D.
Cookstown - Meecham, J.B. & Co.	druggist	1892-3	D.
Cooksville - Green, Josiah	druggist	1882, 92-3	D.
Cornwall - Brown, E.H.	druggist	1892-3	D.
Cornwall - Machaffie & Elvidge	druggist	1892-3	D.
Cornwall - Medical Hall Co.	druggists, etc.,	1892-3	D.
Cornwall - Pringle, George, M.D.	druggist	1882	D.
Cornwall - Thompson, W.E.	druggist	1882	D.
Courtright - Dale, George	druggist	1892-3	D.
Creemore - Colver, Orlando	druggist	1892-3	D.
Creemore - Corbett, W.J.	druggist	1892-3	D.

Ontario - cont'd

Cromarty - King, James	druggist	1882	Directory
Delta - Whaley, R.J.	druggist	1892-3	D.
Desboro - Dickinson, J.G.	druggist	1892-3	D.
Desoronto - Egar, W.C.	druggist	1892-3	D.
Desoronto - Malley, W.J.	druggist	1892-3	D.
Dickinsons Landing - Weagand, A.	druggist	1892-3	D.
Dorchester Station - Graham, A.	druggist	1892-3	D.
Drayton - Babcock, G.N.	druggist	1892-3	D.
Drayton - Fitsgerald, W.	druggist	1882	D.
Dresden - Clarke, Sibree	druggist	1871	D.
Dresden - Miller, E.& Co.	druggist	1892-3	D.
Dresden - McInnes, Thos., M.D.	druggist	1871	D.
Dresden - Switzer, W.H.	druggist	1892-3	D.
Drumbo Chemical Light Co. Ltd.		1892-3	D.
Drumbo - McKenzie, James	druggist	1871	D.
Drumbo - Pentland, W.R.	druggist	1892-3	D.
Duart - Elfred, Chas.	druggist	1882, 92-3	D.
Dundalk - Deans, E.A.	druggist	1882, 92-3	D.
Dundalk - Parsons, George	druggist	1882, 92-3	D.
Dundalk - Phillips, R.	druggist	1882	D.
Dundas - Canister Medicine	inc. 1897		
Dundas - Lyman & Son	druggist	1841	Ad.
Dundas - Niblitt, W.C.	druggist	1882, 92-3	D.
Dundas - Ralph, H.W.	druggist	1892-3	D.
Dundee - Butchart, James (Butchart's Family Medicines)		1844	Ad.
Dungannon - McKay, James	druggist	1892-3	D.
Dunneville - Harrison, R.A.	druggist	1882, 92-3	D.
Dunneville - Michener, J.H.	druggist	1882, 92-3	D.
Dunneville - Smith, J.	druggist	1892-3	D.
Durham - MacFarlane & Co.	druggist	1882, 92-3	D.
Durham - Parker, Henry	druggist	1882, 92-3	D.
Dutton - Kirkland, J.A.	druggist	1892-3	D.
East Toronto - Walters. Wm. R.	druggist	1892-3	D.
Eganville - Channonhouse, J.	druggist	1882, 92-3	D.
Elginton - Watson, David A.	druggist	1892-3	D.
Egmondville - Jackson, G.	druggist	1882, 92-3	D.
Elmira - Wamsley, D.L.	druggist	1882, 92-3	D.
Elmira - Werner, A.	druggist	1892-3	D.
Elmvale - Nettleton, C.A.	druggist	1892-3	D.
Elmvale - Shelley, E.G.	druggist	1892-3	D.
Elmwood - Bonnar, H.A., M.D.	druggist	1882	D.
Elmwood - Evans, J., M.D.	druggist	1892-3	D.
Elora - Hele & Co.	druggist	1871	D.
Elora - McDonald, A.J.	druggist	1882	D.
Elora - Morrow, J.H.	druggist	1882, 92-3	D.
Elora - Smith, T.P.	druggist	1882, 92-3	D.
Embro - Adams, H., M.D.	druggist	1871	D.
Embro - Duncan, R.A.	druggist	1892-3	D.
Enterprise - Carscallen, A.B., M.D.	druggist	1882, 92-3	D.
Erin - Wood, Robt. & John	druggist	1882	D.
Erin - Wood, Robt.	druggist	1892-3	D.
Essex Centre - St. Marie, N.G.	druggist	1882	D.
Essex - Brien & Co.	druggist	1892-3	D.
Essex - Thorn, J.	druggist	1892-3	D.
Everett - Keanton, A.J., M.D.	druggist	1892-3	D.
Exeter - Browning, J.W.	druggist	1882, 92-3	D.
Exeter - Cowan, Young, M.D.	druggist	1882	D.
Exeter - Lutz, Calvin	druggist	1882, 92-3	D.
Farmersville - Lamb, J.P.	druggist	1882	D.
Fenelon Falls - Barber & Ellis	druggist	1882	D.
Fenelon Falls - Everest, W.E.	druggist	1871	D.
Fenelon Falls - Madill, W.R.	druggist	1892-3	D.
Fenelon Falls - Phillips, R.	druggist	1892-3	D.
Flesherton - Christoe, Wm.	druggist	1892-3	D.
Flesherton - Richardson, Wm.	druggist	1882, 92-3	D.
Florence - Charteris, C.R.	druggist	1892-3	D.
Fordwich - Bell, John	druggist	1892-3	D.
Fordwich - Spence, A., M.D.	druggist	1892-3	D.
Forest - Bartram, W.H.	druggist	1892-3	D.
Forest - Everest, G.M.	druggist	1882	D.
Forest - Scott, R.E.	druggist	1892-3	D.

Ontario - cont'd

Fort Erie - Ferrol Medicine Co.		inc. 1897	
Fort Erie - Fort Erie Drug Co. Ltd.		inc. 1895	
Fort William - Hamilton, W.H.	druggist	1892-3	Directory
Fort William - Smeller, T.S.T.	druggist	1892-3	D.
Frankford - Cranhyatekha, M.D.	druggist	1871	D.
Frankford - Ostram, B.R.	druggist	1892-3	D.
Fredericksburg - Blake, W.H., M.D.	druggist	1871	D.
Fredericksburg - Garvey, J.M.	druggist	1882	D.
Fuller - McEvoy, Pat.	druggist	1892-3	D.
Galt - Bond, F.C.	druggist	1892-3	D.
Galt - Ferrah, Robt.	druggist	1892-3	D.
Galt - Gibbard Bros.	druggist	1882	D.
Galt - Graham, J.Y.	druggist	1882	D.
Galt - Howell, H.B.	druggist	1892-3	D.
Galt - Lutz, W.H.	druggist	1882, 92-3	D.
Galt - McLellan, T.E.	druggist	1892-3	D.
Galt - Strong, R.S. & Co.	druggist	1882, 92-3	D.
Gananoque - Brown, R.	druggist	1882	D.
Gananoque - Fullerton's	druggist	1882	D.
Gananoque - Gamsby, G.A.	druggist	1892-3	D.
Georgetown - Morrow, G.E.	druggist	1882, 92-3	D.
Georgetown - Rushton, Thos.	druggist	1882, 92-3	D.
Glencoe - Barclay, M.F.	druggist	1882	D.
Glencoe - McFarlane & Co.	druggist	1892-3	D.
Glencoe - Meek, F.W.	druggist	1892-3	D.
Goderich - Bond, J.R.	druggist	1882	D.
Goderich - Fear, G.A.	druggist	1892-3	D.
Goderich - Jordan, F.	druggist	1882, 92-3	D.
Goderich - Rhynas, Geo.	druggist	1882	D.
Goderich - Wilson, J.	druggist	1882, 92-3	D.
Gore Bay - Johnston, Jos.	druggist	1892-3	D.
Gore Bay - McGregor, J.R.	druggist	1892-3	D.
Grafton - Hildreth, Truman M.D.	druggist	1882	D.
Grafton - Lang, H.	druggist	1892-3	D.
Gravenhurst - Cornell, A.P.	druggist	1892-3	D.
Grimsby - Fitch, J.D.	druggist	1861	D.
Grimsby - Fitch, M.	druggist	1892-3	D.
Grimsby - Whittaker, S.A.	druggist	1892-3	D.
Guelph - Herod & Co.	druggist	1882, 92-3	D.
Guelph - Petrie, A.B.	druggist	1882, 92-3	D.
Guelph - Rolls, Wm.	druggist	1882	D.
Guelph - Shaw, C.E.	druggist	1892-3	D.
Guelph - Smith, W.G.	druggist	1892-3	D.
Guelph - Spurrin & Weeks	druggist	1871	D.
Guelph - Stewart, A.	druggist	1892-3	D.
Hagersville - Howard, S.W.	druggist	1892-3	D.
Hagersville - Jones, Peter, M.D.	druggist	1871	D.
Hagersville - Seater, John	druggist	1892-3	D.
Haliburton - Giles, Wm., M.D.	druggist	1892-3	D.
Hallowell - Chapman, R.J.	druggist	1831	Ad.
Hamilton - Cartwright, G.E. chemist & Apothecary		1851	D.
Hamilton - Barr, John A. & Co.	druggist	1882, 92-3	D.
Hamilton - Bickle, T. & Son	est. 1835 Ad.	1871	D.
Hamilton - Blaicher & Reche	druggist	1892-3	D.
Hamilton - Bleasdale & Harrison	druggist	1882	D.
Hamilton - Bond, F.C.	druggist	1882	D.
Hamilton - Boulter, Thos.	druggist	1892-3	D.
Hamilton - Boyle, Arthur	druggist	1882, 92-3	D.
Hamilton - Brierley, R. & Co. (late with T. Bickle & Son)		1866	Ad.
Hamilton - Brierley, Richard	druggist	1892-3	D.
Hamilton - Bridge, G.& S.	druggist	1866	Ad.
Hamilton - Briggs, G.C. & Co.	pat. meds.	1861, 92-3	D.
Hamilton - Calder & Co.	druggist	1882	D.
Hamilton - Case, H.S.	druggist	1892-3	D.
Hamilton - Chapman, Sam.	druggist	1882, 92-3	D.
Hamilton - Clark, J.A.	druggist	1882, 92-3	D.
Hamilton - Cochenour, W.E.	druggist	1892-3	D.
Hamilton - Copland, Thos.	druggist	1882	D.
Hamilton - Cosley, John (Cosley's Shrub, hair tonic)		1866	Ad.
Hamilton - Dalley, F.F. & Co.	man., etc.	1844-Ads. 1861,92-3-D.	
Hamilton - Davidson, G.W.W.	druggist	1892-3	D.
Hamilton - Doherty, Arthur	druggist	1892-3	D.

Ontario - cont'd

Hamilton - Dominion Drugs,	inc. 1900		
Hamilton - Garland & Rutherford	druggist	1882	Directory
Hamilton - Gerrie, J.W.	druggist	1882, 92-3	D.
Hamilton - Gilmore & Diemert	druggist	1882	D.
Hamilton - Graham & Rutherford	druggist	1892-3	D.
Hamilton - Hamilton & Kneeshaw	chemists	1851	D.
Hamilton - Hamilton, Muir & Co.	druggists	1861	D.
Hamilton - Hamilton, A. & Co.	druggists	1866-Ad.	1892-3-D.
Hamilton - Harrison Bros.	druggists	1892-3	D.
Hamilton - Hitchcock & Bastock	chemists	1851	D.
Hamilton - Hollbrook & Stark	chemists & druggists	1866-Ad.	1871-D.
Hamilton - Howell, W.A.	druggist	1882, 92-3	D.
Hamilton - Kennedy, James meds. 1861, bluing for inks or wash		1869	Ads.
Hamilton - Kelly, D.	med.	1861	Ad.
Hamilton - Lawrence, Thos.	druggist	1882	D.
Hamilton - Lincoln Medicine Co.	inc. 1900		
Hamilton - Mackay Bros. & Co.	chemists & druggists	1851	Ad.
Hamilton - McDonald & Co.	chemists	1861	D.
Hamilton - McGregor & Park	druggist	1882	D.
Hamilton - Meldrum, Henry	druggist	1861	D.
Hamilton - Mills, F.W.	druggist	1892-3	D.
Hamilton - Mundy, Mark	druggist	1871, 92-3	D.
Hamilton - Rock, Thos.	druggist	1861, 82	D.
Hamilton - Sloan Medicine	inc. 1894		
Hamilton - Smith, W.B.	druggist	1882, 92-3	D.
Hamilton - Spackman, J.W. & Co.	druggist	1892-3	D.
Hamilton - Stark, Robt. & Co.	druggist	1892-3	D.
Hamilton - Sutherland, J.W.	druggist	1892-3	D.
Hamilton - Taylor, R.N. & Co.	druggist	1882	D.
Hamilton - Thompson, Alfred	druggist	1882	D.
Hamilton - Vincent, A. & Co.	druggist	1882, 92-3	D.
Hamilton - Wild, M.C.	druggist	1892-3	D.
Hamilton - Wilson, Ardale & Co.	druggist	1882, 92-3	D.
Hamilton - Winer, J. (Red Drop & Canadian Vermifuge, Winer's)		1842	Ad.
Hamilton - Winer & Sims, est. 1830 chemists & druggists		1851	D.
Hamilton - Winer, J. & Co.	inc. 1903		
Hamilton - Woodworth, B.H.	chemists & druggists	1851	D.
Hamilton - Woolverton, Mrs. F.E.	druggist	1892-3	D.
Hamilton - Yapp, F.H.	druggist	1892-3	D.
Hamilton - Zimmerman, J.A.	druggist	1892-3	D.
Hanover - Ball, John	druggist	1892-3	D.
Hanover - Goodene, W.H.	druggist	1892-3	D.
Harriston - Fitsgerald, Wm.	druggist	1892-3	D.
Harriston - Smith, W.B.	druggist	1882	D.
Harriston - Taylor, Wm.	druggist	1882, 92-3	D.
Harriston - Walden, F., M.D.	druggist	1882	D.
Harrow - Campeau, W.J., M.D.	druggist	1892-3	D.
Hastings - Coughlin, Rich.	druggist	1892-3	D.
Hastings - Sinclair, J.A., M.D.	druggist	1892-3	D.
Havelock - Jeffs, W.H.	druggist	1892-3	D.
Hawkesville - Ahrens, August	druggist	1892-3	D.
Hawkesville - Hilborne, J.G.	druggist	1882	D.
Hensall - McDiarmid, J., M.D.	druggist	1892-3	D.
Hepworth - Campbell, L.E.	druggist	1892-3	D.
Hespeler - Kirkland, W.M.	druggist	1892-3	D.
Hillsburgh - Hamilton, J.H.	druggist	1892-3	D.
Hillsburgh - Sowerby, John	druggist	1892-3	D.
Holstien - Brown, A.L.	druggist	1892-3	D.
Honeywood - Lawrence, Robt., M.D.	druggist	1892-3	D.
Huntsville - Sieveright, Arch.	druggist	1892-3	D.
Huntsville - Watson, C.A.	druggist	1892-3	D.
Ingersoll - Browett, J.W.	druggist	1892-3	D.
Ingersoll - Gayler, John	druggist	1882, 92-3	D.
Ingersoll - Hutchinson, D.	druggist	1892-3	D.
Ingersoll - Kneeshaw, R. & Co.	druggist	1882, 92-3	D.
Ingersoll - Revell, R.H.	druggist	1882	D.
Ingersoll - Secord, Dan.	druggist	1882	D.
International Bridge - Hazen Morse	man.	1890	Ad.
Iroquois - Ault, Ed.	druggist	1882	D.
Iroquois - Serviss, Gordon	druggist	1871, 92-3	D.

Ontario - cont'd

Jarvis - Mills Bros.	druggist	1892-3	Directory
Keewatin - Coate, W.D.	druggist	1892-3	D.
Kemptville - Bascomb, O.	druggist	1882, 92-3	D.
Kemptville - Buchannon, A.	druggist	1882, 92-3	D.
Kemptville - Holmes, Hiram	druggist	1871	D.
Kincardine - Cooke, J.C.	druggist	1882, 92-3	D.
Kincardine - MacKendrick, G.M.	druggist	1882, 92-3	D.
Kincardine - Martyn De Witt, H.	druggist	1882, 92-3	D.
Kincardine - Wright, J.P.	druggist	1882	D.
Kingston - Abbot & Bascom	druggist	1810	Ads.
Kingston - Barker, Robt. Atheneum Dispensary		1847	Ad.
Kingston - Bethel, Wm.	druggist	1882	D.
Kingston - Binley, Wm.	meds. & drug.	1828	Ads.
Kingston - Brent, J.W.	druggist	1846	Ad.
Kingston - Brent, Charles druggist & apothecary		1851	D.
Kingston - Catarrhozone Co., The		1915	Ad.
Kingston - Chown, A.P.	druggist	1899	Ad.
Kingston - Heath, C. chemist & druggist		1851	D.
Kingston - Heath & Gunn	druggist	1871, 82	D.
Kingston - Hobert, G.S.	druggist	1882, 92-3	D.
Kingston - King, J.C.	druggist	1882, 92-3	D.
Kingston - McCammon, James	druggist	1882	D.
Kingston - Mitchell, E.C.	druggist	1892-3	D.
Kingston - Palmer, E.W. apothecary & chemist		1851	D.
Kingston - Parker, E.H.	druggist	1851	Ad.
Kingston - Polson, N.C. & Co.	man.	1882-D. 1895-Ads.	
Kingston - Scott, Joseph Surgeon	pat. meds.	1817	Ads.
Kingston - Scott & McGee, surgeons & druggists		1818	Ads.
Kingston - Skinner, H. & Co.	druggist	1882, 92-3	D.
Kingston - Stringer & Haskin Medicine Co.		1899	Ad.
Kingston - Wade, Henry	druggist	1882, 92-3	D.
Kingston - Wilson, W.J.	druggist	1892-3	D.
Kingsville - Doan, James	druggist	1892-3	D.
Kingsville - Miller, C.S.	druggist	1892-3	D.
Kintore - Eldon, Robt.	druggist	1892-3	D.
Kleinburg - Joelinskie, Jockiel	druggist	1871	D.
Kleinburg - Joelinskie, Jacob	druggist	1892-3	D.
Lakefield - Bird, T.J.	druggist	1892-3	D.
Lakefield - Burgess, J.A.	druggist	1892-3	D.
Lambton Mills - Green, Josiah	druggist	1892-3	D.
Lanark - Cameron, A. & Co.	druggist	1892-3	D.
Lancaster - Bolster, Thos.	druggist	1892-3	D.
Leamington - Chamberlain, Chas., M.D.	druggist	1882	D.
Leamington - Smith, W.J.	druggist	1892-3	D.
Leamington - Sutherland, J.T.	druggist	1892-3	D.
Lindsay - Britton, Chas.	druggist	1892-3	D.
Lindsay - Gregory, Edmond	druggist	1882, 92-3	D.
Lindsay - Higginbotham, A.	druggist	1882, 92-3	D.
Lindsay Medicine & Dispensay Co. Ltd.	inc. 1899		
Lindsay - Morgan, Phillip	druggist	1892-3	D.
Lindsay - Perrin, Samuel	druggist	1882, 92-3	D.
Lindsay - Michener, J.H., M.D.	druggist	1882	D.
Linwood - Veitch, George	druggist	1892-3	D.
Lion's Head - Freeborn Bros.	druggist	1892-3	D.
Listowel - Hacking, J.A.	druggist	1882, 92-3	D.
Listowel - Livingston, John jr.	druggist	1882, 92-3	D.
Listowel - Michener, J.H., M.D.	druggist	1882	D.
Little Current - Currie, H.	druggist	1892-3	D.
London - Anderson & Nells	druggist	1892-3	D.
London - Barkwell, W.S.B.	druggist	1892-3	D.
London - Barkwell Chemical Co. of London Ltd.	inc. 1892		
London - Barret, M. & Co.	druggist	1871	D.
London - Burkholder, J.F.	druggist	1892-3	D.
London - Cairncross, L.	druggist	1892-3	D.
London - Callard, John	druggist	1892-3	D.
London - Campbell, A.	druggist	1882	D.
London - Canada Chemical Man. Ltd.	inc. 1891		
London - Canadian Drug Syndicate	inc. 1902		
London - Harkness & Co.	druggist	1882	D.
London - Holman, F.	druggist	1892-3	D.
London - Jepson, J.J.	druggist	1892-3	D.

Ontario - cont'd

London - Kennedy, J.A. & Co.	druggist	1892-3	Directory
London - London Drug Co.		1892-3	D.
London - McCallum, C.	druggist	1882, 92-3	D.
London - Mitchell, B.A.	druggist	1851, 92-3	D.
London - Mitchell & Platt	druggist	1871	D.
London - Rippin, George (Rippin's Remedy, pts. & ½ pts.)		1880	Ads.
London - Robinson, Wm. H.	druggist	1882	D.
London - Salter, John (est. 1829, bus. for sale, 1855 - Ad.)			
London - Saunders, Wm. (herbal medicines & extracts)		1862	Ad.
London - Saunders, Wm.	chemist & druggist	1882	D.
London - Saunders, D.E. & Co.	chemist & druggist	1892-3	D.
London - Shuff, G.J.	druggist	1892-3	D.
London - Smallman, T.H. & Co.	druggist	1882	D.
London - Strong, W.T.	druggist	1882, 92-3	D.
London - Smith, Walter J.	druggist	1882	D.
London - Wildern, Isaac	druggist	1892-3	D.
London - Wismer, C.A.	druggist	1892-3	D.
Loydtown - Eastwood, Alf.	druggist	1871	D.
Lucan - Farrel, John	druggist	1882, 92-3	D.
Lucknow - Congram, A.B.	druggist	1892-3	D.
Lucknow - Days, Henry	druggist	1892-3	D.
Lucknow - Sheppard, C.A.	druggist	1882	D.
Lucknow - Tennant, J., M.D.	druggist	1882	D.
Lyn - Taylor, C.M.	druggist	1892-3	D.
Lyn - West, Frank	druggist	1882	D.
Lyndhurst - McKay, Wm.	druggist	1892-3	D.
Madoc - Deans, John G.	druggist	1882	D.
Madoc - Dunlop, A.H.	druggist	1892-3	D.
Madoc - Wilson, C.G.	druggist	1871, 92-3	D.
Magnetawan - McMillan, D.	druggist	1892-3	D.
Manilla - Ellis, Wm.	druggist	1882	D.
Manilla - Okedon, J. Kent	druggist	1882	D.
Manitowaning - Tucker, W.J.	druggist	1882, 92-3	D.
Manotick - Rickey, Jos. A.	druggist	1892-3	D.
Markdale - Stephen, Rich. L.	druggist	1892-3	D.
Markdale - Turner, W.	druggist	1892-3	D.
Markham - Byer Remedy C. Ltd.	inc. 1900		
Markham - Holden, Sinclair	druggist	1871, 82	D.
Markham - Mason, R.A.	druggist	1892-3	D.
Markham - Millar, Wm. & Co.	druggist	1882	D.
Markham - Turner, Walter	druggist	1892-3	D.
Marlbank - Allan, W.J.	druggist	1892-3	D.
Marmosa - Pomeroy & Bly	druggist	1892-3	D.
Marmosa - Jones, Henry M.	druggist	1892-3	D.
Marsh Hill - De Geers, Jas. prop. (Dr. Carson's Bitters & Medicines) 1874			Ad.
Matawa - Gray, R.B.	druggist	1892-3	D.
Meaford - Carr, Thos.	druggist	1871	D.
Meaford - Manley, Henry	druggist	1882	D.
Meaford - McCarrol, Thos.	druggist	1892-3	D.
Meaford - Stephens & McCarrol	druggist	1882	D.
Meaford - Stephens, W.W. & Co.	druggist	1892-3	D.
Meaford - Stephens Bros.	druggist	1892-3	D.
Merlin - Bell, J.C.	druggist	1892-3	D.
Merrickville - Church, M.K.	druggist	1892-3	D.
Merrickville - Jacques, H.W.	druggist	1882, 92-3	D.
Merrickville - Merrick, P. Young	druggist	1882	D.
Merritton - Greenwood, W.W.	druggist	1882	D.
Merritton - Vanderburgh, J.F.	druggist	1882, 92-3	D.
Midland - Canadian Drug & Chemical, inc. as Nation Drug & Chemical 1906			
Midland - Hudson, Frs.	druggist	1882	D.
Midland - Macartney, H.E.	druggist	1892-3	D.
Midland - Nettleton, C.A.	druggist	1892-3	D.
Mildmay - Clapp, R.E.	druggist	1892-3	D.
Millbank - Harren, Wm.	druggist	1882	D.
Millbank - Neads, M.E.	druggist	1892-3	D.
Millbrook - Elliott, A.T.	druggist	1892-3	D.
Millbrook - Leach, Alfred	druggist	1882, 92-3	D.
Millbrook - Turner, Wm.	druggist	1871	D.
Millbrook - Turner, F.G.	druggist	1892-3	D.
Millbrook - Smith, John B.	druggist	1882	D.

Ontario - cont'd

Milton - McCollom, Jos.	druggist	1892-3	Directory
Milton - Watson, Henry	druggist	1871, 92-3	D.
Milton - Willmot, J.B.	druggist	1871	D.
Milverton - Egbert	druggist	1892-3	D.
Milverton - Torrance, J.	druggist	1892-3	D.
Mimico - Mingay, G.W.	druggist	1892-3	D.
Minden - Curry, F.R.	druggist	1882, 92-3	D.
Mitchell - Coates, John	druggist	1892-3	D.
Mitchell - Cull, Jos. W.	druggist	1882	D.
Mitchell - Hodge, S.A.	druggist	1882, 92-3	D.
Mitchell - Thomson, H.W.	druggist	1892-3	D.
Moore - Gamble, A. Walter, M.D.	druggist	1871	D.
Moorefield - Crawford, George	druggist	1892-3	D.
Morpeth - Pickering, C.	druggist	1892-3	D.
Morrisburg - Bruce, Jos.	druggist	1892-3	D.
Morrisburg - Carman, F.B.	druggist	1882, 92-3	D.
Morrisburg - Chamberlin, T.F., M.D.	druggist	1871	D.
Morrisburg - Selleck, L.F.	druggist	1882, 92-3	D.
Mount Albert - Hammil, W.E., M.D.	druggist	1882	D.
Mount Albert - Loyd, W.T.	druggist	1892-3	D.
Mount Bridges - Meek, F.W. & Co.	druggist	1882	D.
Mount Forest - Colcleugh, James	druggist	1871	D.
Mount Forest - Colcleugh, Wm.	druggist	1882, 92-3	D.
Mount Forest - Jamieson, Alex	druggist	1892-3	D.
Mount Forest - Yeomans, L.H.	druggist	1882, 92-3	D.
Napanee - Detlor & Fullerton	druggist	1892-3	D.
Napanee - Grange, A.W. & Bros.	druggist	1892-3	D.
Napanee - Huffman, T.A.	druggist	1892-3	D.
Napanee - Perry, J.J.	druggist	1882, 92-3	D.
Neustadt - Brown, Wm. McE.	druggist	1892-3	D.
Newboro - Hart, E.J.	druggist	1892-3	D.
Newboro - Killburn, Horace	druggist	1892-3	D.
Newburgh - Caton, Allen	druggist	1882	D.
Newburgh - Duff & Dunwoody	druggist	1892-3	D.
Newburgh - Grange, Wm.	druggist	1882	D.
Newcastle - Farncomb Bros.	druggist	1892-3	D.
Newcastle - Northrop & Lyman	druggist	1866	Ad.
Newcastle - Tuttle, Moses & Northrop	est. 1854		
New Hamburg - Boullee, W.H.	druggist	1892-3	D.
New Hamburg - McCallom, F.H.	druggist	1871, 82	D.
New Hamburg - McCallom, Miss Isabella	druggist	1892-3	D.
Newmarket - Bentley, Wm., M.D.	druggist	1882	D.
Newmarket - Campbell, Duncan	druggist	1892-3	D.
Newmarket - Kelman, James	druggist	1882, 92-3	D.
Newmarket - Scott, Stewart	druggist	1892-3	D.
Newmarket - Simpson, Chas. H.	druggist	1871, 82	D.
Newmarket - Simpson, Mrs. C.H.	druggist	1892-3	D.
Niagara City - Nitzsche	druggist	1861	D.
Niagara - Pafford, Henry	chemist & druggist	1871, 92-3	D.
Niagara Chemical Co.	inc. 1906		
Niagara Falls - Hobson & Co.	druggist	1892-3	D.
Niagara Falls - Macartney, J.L.	druggist	1882, 92-3	D.
Niagara Falls - Means, E.C.	druggist	1892-3	D.
Niagara Falls - Rundfield, Theo.	druggist	1861	D.
Niagara Falls - Russel & Griffith	druggist	1861	D.
Niagara Falls - Skinner, R.P.	druggist	1882	D.
Niagara Falls South - Book, Mrs. E.E.	druggist	1892-3	D.
Niagara Falls South - Land, Abel	druggist	1892-3	D.
North Bay - Cormack, J.G.	druggist	1892-3	D.
Norwich - Bannon, J.J.	druggist	1892-3	D.
Norwich - Dager, H.J.	druggist	1892-3	D.
Norwich - Kirk, D.A.	druggist	1882	D.
Norwich - Lount, G., M.D.	druggist	1882	D.
Norwich - McCay, S.B.	druggist	1892-3	D.
Norwich - Moffat, J.C.	druggist	1892-3	D.
Norwich - Tidey, John A.	druggist	1871, 82	D.
Norwood - Rutherford, Wm.	druggist	1892-3	D.
Oakville - Balmer, R.C.	druggist	1882, 92-3	D.
Oakville - James, F.W.	druggist	1892-3	D.
Oakville - Pearce, Chas.	druggist	1882	D.
Oakville - Urquhart, John	druggist	1861, 92-3	D.

Ontario - cont'd

Odessa - Booth, D.B., M.D.	druggist	1882	Directory
Odessa - Booth, Donald B.	druggist	1892-3	D.
Oil City - Adamson & Hunter	druggist	1882	D.
Oil Springs - Hanks, A.R.	druggist	1892-3	D.
Omemee - Higginbotham, Wm., M.D.	druggist	1882	D.
Omemee - Mulligan, R.J.	druggist	1892-3	D.
Omemee - Norris, George A., M.D.	druggist	1882	D.
Orangeville - Dodds, J.R.	druggist	1882, 92-3	D.
Orangeville - Heal, H.H.	druggist	1882	D.
Orangeville - Holden, James	druggist	1871	D.
Orangeville - Stevenson, Thos. Medical Hall		1882, 92-3	D.
Orangeville - Turner, Adam	druggist	1892-3	D.
Orford Chemical Co.	inc. 1894		
Orillia - Cooke, H. & Co.	druggist	1882, 92-3	D.
Orillia - Elwell, George	druggist	1871	D.
Orillia - Robinson, T.H.	druggist	1882, 92-3	D.
Orillia - Slaven, John W.	druggist	1871, 92-3	D.
Orono - Gamsby, L.A.	druggist	1892-3	D.
Orono - Gilfillan, L.	druggist	1871	D.
Oshawa - Atkinson, Wm.T.	druggist	1882	D.
Oshawa - Higginbotham, J. & Son	druggist	1882	D.
Oshawa - Maxwell, L.J.	druggist	1892-3	D.
Oshawa - Ryley, T.J.	druggist	1892-3	D.
Oshawa - Symonds, Chas.	druggist	1892-3	D.
Oshawa - Woon, Wm.	druggist	1882	D.
Osnabruck Township - Ontario Chemical Co.	inc. 1897		
Ottawa - Abbot & Wooten	druggist	1892-3	D.
Ottawa - Ahearn, E.M.	druggist	1892-3	D.
Ottawa - Allen & Cochrane	druggist	1899	Ad.
Ottawa - Beattie & Argue	druggist	1900	Ad.
Ottawa - Belanger & Co.	druggist	1892-3	D.
Ottawa - Brethor Pharmacy Hall	druggist	1892-3	D.
Ottawa - Brownlee, A.J.	druggist	1892-3	D.
Ottawa - Brownlee, T.A.	druggist	1897	D.
Ottawa - Cambell, N.W.	druggist	1897	D.
Ottawa - Culbert, C.G.	druggist	1897	D.
Ottawa - Christie, A. & Co.	druggist	1871, 82	D.
Ottawa - Dacier, C.O.	druggist	1882	D.
Ottawa - Day, F.W.	druggist	1892-3	D.
Ottawa - Davidson & Daniel	druggist	1871	D.
Ottawa - Durocher, E.J.	druggist	1892-3	D.
Ottawa - Elwell, G.T.	druggist	1882	D.
Ottawa - Frazer, H.J.	druggist	1892-3	D.
Ottawa - Graham, K.D.	druggist	1882	D.
Ottawa - Graham, Dr. K.D.	druggist	1892-3	D.
Ottawa - Graham & Elliot	druggist	1899	Ad.
Ottawa - Jamieson, W.A.	druggist	1882, 92-3	D.
Ottawa - Kirby Bros.	druggist	1892-3	D.
Ottawa - Langford & Co.	druggist	1882	D.
Ottawa - Lloyd, W.A.	druggist	1882, 92-3	D.
Ottawa - MacCarthy, H.F.	druggist	1871, 92-3	D.
Ottawa - MacCormack, R.A.	druggist	1892-3	D.
Ottawa - Martin, E.D.	druggist	1882	D.
Ottawa - Mill, R.J.	druggist	1882	D.
Ottawa - Mortimer, George	druggist	1882	D.
Ottawa - Musgrove, J.A.	druggist	1892-3	D.
Ottawa - Payment, T.	druggist	1897-8	D.
Ottawa - Roberts, John	druggist	1882, 92-3	D.
Ottawa - Savard, Dr. & Co.	druggist	1892-3	D.
Ottawa - Shillington & Co.	druggist	1892-3	D.
Ottawa - Skinner, J. & Co.	druggist	1882, 92-3	D.
Ottawa - Stalker, D.J.	druggist	inc. 1897	
Ottawa - Stevenson, S.J.	druggist	1897-8	D.
Ottawa - Story, E.D.	druggist	1897-8	D.
Ottawa - Valade & Co.	druggist	1892-3	D.
Ottawa - Voligny, L.L., M.D.	druggist	1882	D.
Ottawa - Waters, Henry	druggist	1892-3	D.
Otterville - Colver, Addison	druggist	1892-3	D.
Otterville - McKibbon, J.H.	druggist	1882	D.
Owen Sound - Cameron, D.A. & Co.	druggist	1882, 92-3	D.
Owen Sound - Lang Bros.	druggist	1871, 82	D.

Ontario - cont'd

Owen Sound - Manley, Arthur W.	druggist	1892-3	Directory
Owen Sound - McCallum, John F.	druggist	1892-3	D.
Owen Sound - Parker & Co.	druggist	1882, 92-3	D.
Owen Sound - Oakland Chemical Co.	inc. 1901		
Owen Sound - Ontario Chemical Co.	inc. 1896		
Owen Sound - Taylor, Wm. H.	druggist	1892-3	D.
Owen Sound - Wightman, Robt.	druggist	1892-3	D.
Paisley - Bain, D.J.	druggist	1882, 92-3	D.
Paisley - Hargreaves, W.A.	druggist	1882	D.
Paisley - Hargreaves Bros.	druggist	1892-3	D.
Paisley - Hildreth, A.R.	druggist	1871	D.
Pakenham - Baird, James G.	druggist	1882	D.
Palmerston - Brown, G.H.	druggist	1882	D.
Palmerston - Forster, Moffat	druggist	1892-3	D.
Palmerston - Standish, J.M.	druggist	1882, 92-3	D.
Paris - Allworth, E.C.	druggist	1882	D.
Paris - Chase, John A.	druggist	1882	D.
Paris - Roberts, C.H.	druggist	1882, 92-3	D.
Paris - Scott, G.L.	druggist	1871	D.
Paris - Scott, J.L.	druggist	1892-3	D.
Parkdale - Devlin, Geo. A.	druggist	1882	D.
Park Hill - Owens, Thos	druggist	1892-3	D.
Park Hill - Roberts, J.F.	druggist	1892-3	D.
Parry Sound - Appele, James	druggist	1892-3	D.
Parry Sound - Foot, W.R.	druggist	1892-3	D.
Pembroke - Dickson, W.W.	druggist	1882, 92-3	D.
Pembroke - Findlay, Jas.	druggist	1892-3	D.
Pembroke - Gray, R.B.	druggist	1882, 92-3	D.
Pembroke - Gray, W.L., M.D.	druggist	1882	D.
Pembroke - Lafferty, A.M. & Co.	druggist	1882	D.
Penetanguishine - Darling, J.S.	druggist	1882	D.
Penetanguishine - Macartney, A.E.	druggist	1892-3	D.
Penetanguishine - Nettleton, C.A.	druggist	1892-3	D.
Perth - Bower, Jos. & Co.	druggist	1882	D.
Perth - Bower, Jos. & Son	druggist	1892-3	D.
Perth - Coombs, John S.	druggist	1871, 82	D.
Perth - Grant, Wm., M.D.	druggist	1871	D.
Perth - Hanna, A.E. & F.	druggist	1892-3	D.
Perth - Kellock, J.D., M.D.	druggist	1871	D.
Perth - Kellock, J.F.	druggist	1882, 92-3	D.
Perth - Lane, Freeman	druggist	1871	D.
Perth - Rug, Henry C. & Co.	druggist	1882	D.
Perth - Wampole, Henry K. Co. 1898 Ad. Wampole, inc. 1906.			
Peterboro' - Lynch, J.	druggist	1864	Ad.
Peterboro' - McPhail, A.	druggist	1846	Ad.
Peterboro' - Poole, Thos., M.D. (Botonical Medicines)		1862	Ads.
Peterborough - Bell, Wm., M.D.	druggist	1871	D.
Peterborough - Greatrex, W.R.	druggist	1892-3	D.
Peterborough - Kempt, A.W.	druggist	1871	D.
Peterborough - Kincaid & Co.	druggist	1871	D.
Peterborough - Macdonald, H.S.	druggist	1892-3	D.
Peterborough - Maddill, Wm.	druggist	1892-3	D.
Peterborough - McKee, John	druggist	1882, 92-3	D.
Peterborough - Membray Medicine Co. Ltd.	inc. 1893		
Peterborough - Newbray Medicine Co. Ltd.	inc. 1896		
Peterborough - Norval, Dr. medicine	inc. 1906		
Peterborough - Nugent, John	druggist	1892-3	D.
Peterborough - Ormand & Walsh	druggist	1871, 92-3	D.
Peterborough - Peterborough Medicine Co.	inc. 1892		
Peterborough - Rushton, Thos.	druggist	1882	D.
Peterborough - Schofield, G.A.	druggist	1892-3	D.
Peterborough - Taylor, Wm. H., M.D.	druggist	1871	D.
Peterborough - Taylor & Macdonald	druggist	1882	D.
Peterborough - Tully, J.D.	druggist	1882, 92-3	D.
Petrolia - Bray, Wm.	druggist	1882	D.
Petrolia - Cuthbertson & Co.	druggist	1892-3	D.
Petrolia - Dale, W.H.	druggist	1882, 92-3	D.
Petrolia - Denham, George	druggist	1882, 92-3	D.
Petrolia - Dudfield, John	druggist	1892-3	D.
Pickering - Bateman, R.M.	druggist	1892-3	D.
Picton - Allison, C.B. & Co.	druggist	1882, 92-3	D.

212

Ontario - cont'd

Picton - Branscombe, H.W.	druggist	1882, 92-3	Directory
Picton - Caniff, B.M.	druggist	1882	D.
Picton - Morden, J.B., M.D.	druggist	1882	D.
Pinkerton - Morrison, W.C.	druggist	1892-3	D.
Plantagenet - Pattee, Richard	druggist	1892-3	D.
Plattsburgh - Platt, K.M. & Co. man. Mothers Relief		1846	Ad.
Platsville - Veitch, W.M.	druggist	1892-3	D.
Point Edward - Geary, Rich.	druggist	1882	D.
Point Edward - Ingersoll, G.G.	druggist	1892-3	D.
Pontypool - Phillips, J.A.	druggist	1892-3	D.
Port Arthur - Clarke, W.J.	druggist	1892-3	D.
Port Burwell - McConnell, G.B.	druggist	1882	D.
Port Burwell - McCollom, Wm. A.	druggist	1871	D.
Port Colborne - Brown, F.K.	druggist	1892-3	D.
Port Colborne - Lugsdin, Chas.	druggist	1882	D.
Port Colborne - Noble, F.D.	druggist	1892-3	D.
Port Colborne - Thuresome, F.D.	druggist	1882	D.
Port Dalhousie - Considine, J.W., M.D.	druggist	1882, 92-3	D.
Port Dover - Ansley & Tibbetts	druggist	1882	D.
Port Dover - Ansley, H.W.	druggist	1892-3	D.
Port Dover - McBride, J.	druggist	1882, 92-3	D.
Port Elgin - Eby, Martin F.	druggist	1871	D.
Port Elgin - Eby, M.A.	druggist	1892-3	D.
Port Elgin - Muir, R.S.	druggist	1892-3	D.
Port Hope - Brent, Chas.	druggist	1871	D.
Port Hope - Deyell, Robt.	druggist	1892-3	D.
Port Hope - Hughs, C.	druggist	1846	Ad.
Port Hope - Michell, G.& W.	druggist	1871	D.
Port Hope - Watson, T.J.	druggist	1892-3	D.
Port Hope - Wilson, Richard	druggist	1892-3	D.
Port Hope - Woolhouse & Deyell	druggist	1871	D.
Port Perry - Allison, S.E.	druggist	1882	D.
Port Perry - Davis, A.J.	druggist	1882, 92-3	D.
Port Perry - McClinton, N., M.D.	druggist	1882	D.
Port Perry - McGlashon, C.C.	druggist	1882	D.
Port Perry - Nichols, T.C.	druggist	1892-3	D.
Port Robinson - Park, H., M.D.	druggist	1882	D.
Port Rowan - Pearsall, F.H.	druggist	1892-3	D.
Port Rowan - Stewart, G. & Co.	druggist	1892-3	D.
Port Stanley - Price, J.	druggist	1892-3	D.
Prescott - Harding, A.O.	druggist	1871, 92-3	D.
Prescott - Melville, T.R.	druggist	1871, 92-3	D.
Prescott - Peck, C.H.	druggist	1843	Ad.
Prescott - Raney, W.H.	druggist	1892-3	D.
Preston - Duck, E.J.	druggist	1892-3	D.
Preston - Nispel, C.	druggist	1882, 92-3	D.
Princeton - Gissing, A.W.	druggist	1892-3	D.
Rat Portage - Cannif & Johnson	druggist	1892-3	D.
Rat Portage - Coate, W.D.	druggist	1892-3	D.
Renfrew - Clark, James	druggist	1892-3	D.
Renfrew - Davey & Clark	druggist	1882	D.
Renfrew - Walford, S.& J.H.	druggist	1871, 92-3	D.
Riceville - Switzer, Dr.	druggist	1892-3	D.
Richmond Hill - Sanderson, H. & Sons	druggist	1871	D.
Richmond Hill - Sanderson Bros.	druggist	1892-3	D.
Ridgetown - Bawden, Peter	druggist	1892-3	D.
Ridgetown - Clark, R.A. (Pride of the Valley Medicines)		1888	Ad.
Ridgetown - Clark, R.A.	druggist	1892-3	D.
Ridgetown - Graham, W.B.	druggist	1892-3	D.
Ridgetown - Kyle, Thos. H.	druggist	1882	D.
Ridgetown - Meads, M.E.	medicines	1880	Ad.
Ridgetown - Smith, J., M.D.	druggist	1871	D.
Ridgeway - Brewster & Allan	druggist	1882	D.
Ridgeway - Brewster, Nathaniel	druggist	1892-3	D.
Ripley - Amith, D.F.	druggist	1882, 92-3	D.
Rodney - Harvey, E.C.	druggist	1892-3	D.
Rodney - Madconald, D., M.D.	druggist	1882	D.
Rodney - Munger, J.S.	druggist	1892-3	D.
Rosemount - Corbett, Richard	druggist	1871	D.
Roseneath - Noden, Wm., M.D.	druggist	1882	D.
Rowena - Freemont, A.	druggist	1892-3	D.

Ontario - cont'd

Ruthven - Wigle, T.H. & Co.	druggist	1892-3	Directory
Sarnia - Clement & Co.	druggist	1882	D.
Sarnia - Clement, J.J.	druggist	1892-3	D.
Sarnia - Geary, R.T.	druggist	1882, 92-3	D.
Sarnia - Gemmil, F.H.	druggist	1871	D.
Sarnia - Johnston, S.	druggist	1882, 92-3	D.
Sarnia - McLean, J.S.	druggist	1882	D.
Sarnia - Scott, R.D.	druggist	1892-3	D.
Sault Ste. Marie - Adams, W.A.	druggist	1892-3	D.
Sault Ste. Marie - Bishoprick & Co.	druggist	inc. 1900	
Sault Ste. Marie - Hunter, G.A.	druggist	1892-3	D.
Seaforth - Fear, I.V.	druggist	1892-3	D.
Seaforth - Lumsden, Robt.	druggist	1871	D.
Seaforth - Lumsden & Wilson	druggist	1882, 92-3	D.
Seaforth - Roberts, J.S.	druggist	1882, 92-3	D.
Sebringville - Eby, A.	druggist	1892-3	D.
Sebringville - Johns, E.J.	druggist	1882	D.
Seeley's Bay - Bowen, G., M.D.		1882, 92-3	D.
Selby - Beeman, T.W.	druggist	1882	D.
Selkirk - Derby & Derby	druggist	1892-3	D.
Selkirk - Phillips, E.E.	druggist	1892-3	D.
Shelburne - Brown, F.	druggist	1892-3	D.
Shelburne - Gamon, C.A. & Co.	druggist	1892-3	D.
Simcoe - Austin, J. & Co.	druggist	1882, 92-3	D.
Simcoe - Hayes & Livingston	druggist	1871	D.
Simcoe - Hayes & Co.	druggist	1892-3	D.
Simcoe - Wilson, J., M.D.		1882	D.
Smith's Falls - Brodi, J.R.	druggist	1892-3	D.
Smith's Falls - Lavell Drug Co.		1892-3	D.
Smith's Falls - McCallum, J., M.D.		1882	D.
Smithville - Eastman, D.W.	druggist	1892-3	D.
Southhampton - Douglas, J.G.	druggist	1892-3	D.
Southhampton - Holden, W.J.	druggist	1882	D.
South Mountain - Cleland, M.J.	druggist	1892-3	D.
Sparta - Eakins, J.M.	druggist	1892-3	D.
Sparta - Hewitt, C.	druggist	1892-3	D.
Spring Brook - Stewart, Robt.	druggist	1892-3	D.
Springfield - Chandler, E.	druggist	1892-3	D.
Springfield - Tufford, A.F.	druggist	1892-3	D.
Stayner - Coleman & Perdue	druggist	1871, 82	D.
Stayner - Sanders, Wm. B.	druggist	1882, 92-3	D.
Stayner - Stewart, F.J.	druggist	1892-3	D.
St. Catharines - Beeton & Co.	druggist	1882	D.
St. Catharines - Boyle, Arthur	druggist	1871	D.
St. Catharines - Greenwood, A.J.	druggist	1882, 92-3	D.
St. Catharines - Greenwood, Wm., W.	druggist	1871, 92-3	D.
St. Catharines - Jukes, A. & Co.	druggist	1882, 92-3	D.
St. Catharines - Lispinard Co. (face creams, etc.)		1882	Ads.
St. Catharines - Lawson, Dr's (Botanic Medicines)		1849	Ads.
St. Catharines - Parker, George	druggist	1892-3	D.
St. Catharines - Rhumatine Manufacturing Co.	inc. 1897		
St. Catharines - Seymour, J.R.	druggist	1882, 92-3	D.
St. Catharines - Southcott, H.	druggist	1892-3	D.
St. Catharines - Welland Drugs	inc. 1906		
St. George - Fleming, S.H.	druggist	1892-3	D.
St. George - Richardson, J. & Co.	druggist	1892-3	D.
St. Jacobs - Wideman, J.	druggist	1882, 92-3	D.
St. Louis - Jaspar, Dr. (man. Dr. Josephus Shoshawnees Remedy)		1866	Ad.
St. Louis - Lambert Pharmacy	inc. 1901		
St. Mary's - Fraleigh, S.	druggist	1882, 92-3	D.
St. Mary's - McCallum, C.	druggist	1871	D.
St. Mary's - MacLean, J.	druggist	1882, 92-3	D.
St. Mary's - Sanderson, F.G.	druggist	1892-3	D.
St. Thomas - Corlis, Josiah, M.D.		1882	D.
St. Thomas - Duncombe, T.H.	druggist	1892-3	D.
St. Thomas - Foster, W.C. & Co.	druggist	1892-3	D.
St. Thomas - Harrison, A.W.	druggist	1892-3	D.
St. Thomas - Hugill, G.A.	druggist	1882	D.
St. Thomas - Jukes Medicine	inc. 1900		
St. Thomas - Kidd, J.P.	druggist	1892-3	D.
St. Thomas - Leitch, D.C., M.D.		1882	D.

Ontario - cont'd

St. Thomas - McColl, G.R.	druggist	1892-3	Directory
St. Thomas - McCullough, G.B.	druggist	1882	D.
St. Thomas - Mitchell, C.	druggist	1882	D.
St. Thomas - Old, R.J.	druggist	1882, 92-3	D.
St. Thomas - Reynolds, F.P.	druggist	1882, 92-3	D.
St. Williams - McKinnon, Lauchlin	druggist	1892-3	D.
Stirling - Boulter, G.H.	druggist	1882, 92-3	D.
Stirling - Parker & Butler	druggist	1882	D.
Stouffville - Fead, Wm. & Bros.	druggist	1871	D.
Stouffville - Rowan & Co.	druggist	1892-3	D.
Stouffville - Sangster & Co.	druggist	1892-3	D.
Stratford - Bosworth, N.A.	druggist	1882, 92-3	D.
Stratford - Dutton, John	druggist	1882, 92-3	D.
Stratford - Johns, E.J.	druggist	1892-3	D.
Stratford - Nasmyth, Chas. E.	druggist	1882	D.
Stratford - Nasmyth, C.E. & Co.	druggist	1892-3	D.
Stratford - Nasmyth, James H.	druggist	1882	D.
Stratford - Nasmyth, J.H. & Co.	druggist	1892-3	D.
Stratford - Waugh, G.J.	druggist	1882, 92-3	D.
Strathroy - Dyas, W.J.	druggist	1882, 92-3	D.
Strathroy - Meek, F.W.	druggist	1892-3	D.
Strathroy - Springer, M.	druggist	1882	D.
Strathroy - Stepler, W.H.	druggist	1892-3	D.
Streetsville - McClung, R.H.	druggist	1892-3	D.
Streetsville - Thom, J.C., M.D.		1882	D.
Sudbury - Howey, W.R.	druggist	1892-3	D.
Sudbury - Mulligan, W.H.	druggist	1892-3	D.
Sunderland - Baldwin, H.	druggist	1892-3	D.
Sunderland - McDermott, J., M.D.	druggist	1882	D.
Sunderland - Ray, John C., M.D.		1882	D.
Sutton - Tremayne, F.G.	druggist	1882, 92-3	D.
Tamworth - Jones, C.R.	druggist	1892-3	D.
Tamworth - Rose, Dan E.	druggist	1892-3	D.
Tara - Bruce, R.C.	druggist	1892-3	D.
Tara - Hillbourn, W.R.	druggist	1892-3	D.
Tavistock - Niemeir, O.G.	druggist	1892-3	D.
Tavistock - Steele, M.	druggist	1892-3	D.
Teeswater - O'Connor, H.B.	druggist	1892-3	D.
Teeswater - Thurtell, R.N.	druggist	1892-3	D.
Thamesford - McWilliams, J.	druggist	1882, 92-3	D.
Thamesville - Eddington, Chas. & Ed.	druggist	1882	D.
Thamesville - Stewart, Sam.	druggist	1892-3	D.
Thamesville - Tye, Sam. A.	druggist	1882	D.
Thedford - McEdwards, D.	druggist	1892-3	D.
Thornbury - Howe, S.L. & W.A.	druggist	1892-3	D.
Thornbury - McKenny, Thos.	druggist	1871	D.
Thornhill - Lindsay, F. & Co.	druggist	1892-3	D.
Thorold - Brown, John E.	druggist	1861, 71	D.
Thorold - Grant, John	druggist	1861	D.
Thorold - Johnston, J.K.	druggist	1882, 92-3	D.
Thorold - Macartney, W.J.	druggist	1882, 92-3	D.
Tilbury Centre - Johnson, H.	druggist	1892-3	D.
Tilsonburg - McCollom, W.A. (Man. Rheumatic Repellant, 1869 Ad.)		1892-3	D.
Tilsonburg - McDonald, Wm. jr.	druggist	1882	D.
Tilsonburg - McDonald, Wm.	druggist	1892-3	D.
Tilsonburg - McKenny & Co.	druggist	1882	D.
Tilsonburg - Thomson, Chas.	druggist	1892-3	D.
Tiverton - Patterson, J.R., M.D.	druggist	1882	D.
Tiverton - Walker, J.B.	druggist	1892-3	D.
Toledo - Kilborn, R.K., M.D.		1892-3	D.
Toronto - Abbot, Mrs. J.	druggist	1892-3	D.
Toronto - Adam, Dr. Edward (Liver & Bowel remedies)		1893	Ad.
Toronto - Adams, Dr. J. Homoepathic Physician		1864	Ads.
Toronto - Agnew, Dr. (Dr. Agnew's Heart Cure)		1895	Ads.
Toronto - Allan & Co.	druggist sundries	1892-3	D.
Toronto - Anderson, Chas.	chemist & druggist	1861	D.
Toronto - Anderson, Thos. chemist. (blacking & inks man.)		1843	Ads.
Toronto - Arcade Pharmacy		1884	Ad.
Toronto - Armstrong, Wm.	druggist	1892-3	D.
Toronto - Atkinson, W.T. & Co. chemists. (Parision Tooth-paste)		1856	Ad.
Toronto - Augusta, T., Central Medical Hall		1855	Ad.

Ontario - cont'd

Toronto - Austin Bros.	druggist	1892-3	Directory
Toronto - Balm Medicine Co. of Toronto	inc. 1896		
Toronto - Balue Medicine Co. of Toronto	inc. 1896		
Toronto - Bates, Edmanson Co.		1884	Ads.
Toronto - Bauld, E.H.	druggist	1892-3	D.
Toronto - Beasley, Thos.S.	druggist	inc. 1898	
Toronto - Becket, Jos. & Co.	druggist	1846-Ad. 1851-D.	
Toronto - Belfrey, I.F.	druggist	1892-3	D.
Toronto - Belfry's Eastern Pharmacy		1890	Ad.
Toronto - Bentley, John	chemist & druggist	1851	D.
Toronto - Bentley, Frank	chemist & druggist	1882	D.
Toronto - Bentley, Lafayette	chemist & druggist	1892-3	D.
Toronto - Berlin Chemical Co. of Toronto	inc. 1902	defunct 1905	
Toronto - Besant, Mrs. Martha (Indian Medicines)		1890	Ads.
Toronto - Bettridge & Bentley,	chemist & druggist	1848	Ads.
Toronto - Bettridge, J.C.	chemist & druggist	1851	D.
Toronto - Bingham, J.A.	druggist	1892-3-D.	1900-Ad.
Toronto - Bond, J.R.	druggist	1892-3	D.
Toronto - Botham & Hall	druggist	1892-3	D.
Toronto - Botsford, O.F.	druggist	1892-3	D.
Toronto - Bowden, H.K.	druggist	1892-3	D.
Toronto - Boyce, Albert	druggist	1882	D.
Toronto - Boyle, R.W.	druggist	1882	D.
Toronto - Bremer, A.R. & Co. (Coke Dandruff Cure)		1902	Ad.
Toronto - Bright & Wells	druggist	1899	Ad.
Toronto - Brodie, James A.	druggist	1882	D.
Toronto - Bruce, S.E.	druggist	1892-3	D.
Toronto - Brumell, H.L. (man. Lubin Perfumes, etc.)		1961	Ad.
Toronto - Brydon, Wm.	druggist	1882	D.
Toronto - Burgess, F.T.	druggist	1892-3	D.
Toronto - Burgess, H.W.	druggist	1892-3	D.
Toronto - Cameron, Jas.	druggist	1844	Ad.
Toronto - Campbell, Dr. Homoepathic Medicines		1864	Ad.
Toronto - Campbell, R.W.	druggist	1892-3	D.
Toronto - Carter, Henry	druggist	1882	D.
Toronto - Case, John	druggist	1882	D.
Toronto - Chamberlain's Medicine Co. Des Moines & Toronto		1902	Ad.
Toronto - Cleland, Dr. G.S.		1888	Ad.
Toronto - Corker, Edward (man. Stomachic Bitters)		1862	Article
Toronto - Coombe, John Medica Hall		1861-Ad. 1882-D.	
Toronto - Cook,W.V.	druggist	1892-3	D.
Toronto - Colling, J.H.	druggist	1892-3	D.
Toronto - Coutts & Sons (Acetocura)		1885	Ad.
Toronto - Cowen, C.H.	druggist	1892-3	D.
Toronto - Cox, W.H.	druggist	1892-3	D.
Toronto - Cranfield, E.S.	druggist	1892-3	D.
Toronto - Cummings, Dr. (Nerve Anodyne, 1856 - Vegetine)		1880	Ads.
Toronto - Curry, Isaac	druggist	1892-3	D.
Toronto - Daniel, C.D. & Co. (prop. Woofords Sanitary Lotion)		1892	Ad.
Toronto - Davids, Jos.	druggist	1871	D.
Toronto - Davids, Jos. & Co.	druggist	1882	D.
Toronto - Davidson, W.J.	druggist	1892-3	D.
Toronto - Delaporte, A.V.	druggist	1882	D.
Toronto - Devlin, G.A.	druggist	1882	D.
Toronto - Dewar, I.D. & R.	chemist	1892-3	D.
Toronto - Dilworth, Jos.	druggist	1882, 92-3	D.
Toronto - Dingham & Co. (man. Dipsiboicum Indian Tonic)		1883	Ad.
Toronto - Doan's Kidney Pill Co.		1895	Ad.
Toronto - Dodd Medicine Co.	inc. 1893		
Toronto - Dominion Dyes & Chemicals		1892-3	D.
Toronto - Dow, A.M.	druggist	1892-3	D.
Toronto - Doel, Wilt (late E. Lorie)	druggist	1850	Ad.
Toronto - Dr. Gordon Medicine,	inc. 1902	defunct 1906	
Toronto - Dr. Shoop Medicine, Racine Wis., Toronto		inc. 1902	
Toronto - Dr. Slocum, T.A.	inc. 1903		
Toronto - Dr. Unger, Medicine	inc. 1903		
Toronto - Dr. Williams, Medicine	inc. 1906		
Toronto - Dredge & Co. (Inks, mucilage, blacking, etc. man.)		1870	Ad.
Toronto - Drug Trading Co.	inc. 1900		
Toronto - Druggists Corporation of Canada	inc. 1903		
Toronto - Dwyer, H.	druggist	1882	D.

Ontario - cont'd

Toronto - East End Pharmacy		1892-3	Directory
Toronto - Easton, T. Drug Co.		1900	Ad.
Toronto - Edwards, W.H. (man. perfumes, hair tonic, creams etc.)		1841-59	Ads.
Toronto - Elborne, H.	druggist	1892-3	D.
Toronto - Electra Medicine Co.	inc. 1899		
Toronto - Elliot & Co., Front St.	chemists	1882, 92-3	D.
Toronto - Elliot & Chambers, Victoria St.	chemists	1892-3	D.
Toronto - Ellis, Wm.	druggist	1892-3	D.
Toronto - Evans, Sons & Mason (Evan's Steel Meat & Wine)		1885	Ad.
Toronto - Evans & Sons		1892-3	D.
Toronto - Evans, H., Sugden & Do.		1882	D.
Toronto - Fahnestock, B.A. (man. B.A. Fahnestock's Vermifuge)		1848	Ad.
Toronto - Farquar, Alexander	druggist	1848	Ad.
Toronto - Fawcett, A.E.	druggist	1892-3	D.
Toronto - Fenwick, James M.	druggist	1861	D.
Toronto - Ferguson, D.C.	druggist	1892-3	D.
Toronto - Ferrol Co. Ltd. 124 King W. Toronto		1903	Ad.
Toronto - Field, W.H.	druggist	1892-3	D.
Toronto - Fisher, Dr. (meds. for lungs etc.)		1882-D.	1893-Ads.
Toronto - Flett, F.W.	druggist	1892-3	D.
Toronto - Fowler, Dr.		1849	Ads.
Toronto - Fowler & Russel (Canadian Medicines for Canadian People)		1850	Ads.
Toronto - Fraliegh, W.S.	druggist	1892-3	D.
Toronto - Fuller, T.J.	druggist	1848	Ad.
Toronto - Fulton, Michie & Co. (Hydrozon Brain Tonic)		1885	Ad.
Toronto - Galley, W.E.	druggist	1892-3	D.
Toronto - Gamsby, A.T.	druggist	1892-3	D.
Toronto - Gaynor, Walter	druggist	1892-3	D.
Toronto - Gervaise, Mrs. Graham's Face Bleach at Graham Institute		1894	Ad.
Toronto - Gibbard, G.E.	druggist	1892-3	D.
Toronto - Gibbons, J.A. & Co.	druggist	1892-3	D.
Toronto - Gilpin, W.H.	druggist	1892-3	D.
Toronto - Goodman, E.A.	druggist	1892-3	D.
Toronto - Gray, J.C. & Co.	druggist	1892-3	D.
Toronto - Gray Medicine Co. (Gray's Specific Meds.)		1879	Ad.
Toronto - Grant, John	druggist	1882	D.
Toronto - Grant, A.L.	chemist	1892-3	D.
Toronto - Green, C.B. (sucessor to R. Tuton)	chemist	1851	Ad.
Toronto - Green, Josiah	druggist	1882	D.
Toronto - Green, Joseph	druggist	1892-3	D.
Toronto - Green, S.M.	druggist	1892-3	D.
Toronto - Greenwood Drugs	inc. 1896		
Toronto - Hagard, T. (Hagard's Yellow Oil)		1880	Ad.
Toronto - Hall, John B. Homoepathic meds.		1889	Ad.
Toronto - Hallamore Pharmacy	inc. 1902	defunct 1906	
Toronto - Haldenby, Wm. D.	druggist	1892-3	D.
Toronto - Hanna, G.H. & Co.	druggist	1892-3	D.
Toronto - Hamilton & Chettle	druggist	1844	Ad.
Toronto - Hampton, H.M.	druggist	1882	D.
Toronto - Hartwell's Liquid Blue	druggist	1861	Ad.
Toronto - Hartz, J.F.	chem. man.	inc. 1903	
Toronto - Harvard, Albert	druggist	1882	D.
Toronto - Hanford & Son (man. perfumes, creams etc.)		1852	Ads.
Toronto - Hanford & Co. (man. perfumes, creams etc.)		1856	Ads.
Toronto - Hargreaves Bros.	druggist	1892-3	D.
Toronto - Harvey, J.C.	chemist & druggist	1892-3	D.
Toronto - Hastings, C.J. & Co.	druggist	1892-3	D.
Toronto - Hazen, Morse, man. (Maltopepsyn)		1890	Ad.
Toronto - Hazelton, J.E.	druggist	1892-3	D.
Toronto - Hearn, Wm.	druggist	1882	D.
Toronto - Henry, Hollick & Co. (Meds. by mail)		1864	Ad.
Toronto - Hewlett, John (Bitters, Tonics, etc. man.)		1848	Ad.
Toronto - Heys, Thos.	chemist	1892-3	D.
Toronto - Higginbotham, John	druggist	1861	D.
Toronto - Hoar, W.R.	druggist	1892-3	D.
Toronto - Hodgetts, Geo.	druggist	1861, 82	D.
Toronto - Hooper, E. & Co.	druggist	1861, 92-3	D.
Toronto - Horton, H.J.	druggist	1892-3	D.
Toronto - Houston, J.W.	druggist	1892-3	D.
Toronto - Howarth, John	druggist	1851, 61	D.
Toronto - Howarth, Chas. W.	druggist	1882	D.

Ontario - cont'd

Toronto - Howson, Jos.	druggist	1861	Directory
Toronto - Hutty, J.H.	druggist	1882, 92-3	D.
Toronto - Inglis & Co.	druggist	1892-3	D.
Toronto - Jackes, Baldwin	druggist	1882, 92-3	D.
Toronto - Jaffrey, Andrew	druggist	1892-3	D.
Toronto - Jackson, E.E.	druggist	1892-3	D.
Toronto - Jenkins, J.W. York St.	drug store	1870	Ad.
Toronto - Johnson, Thos.	druggist	1892-3	D.
Toronto - Johnson, J.C.	druggist	1892-3	D.
Toronto - Johnston & Johnston Co., The		1892-3	D.
Toronto - Kennedy, A.E.	druggist	1892-3	D.
Toronto - Kerry, Grathern & Co.		1863, 69	Ads.
Toronto - Kipp, H.M.	druggist	1892-3	D.
Toronto - Knowles, H.A.	druggist	1882, 92-3	D.
Toronto - Lamb, P.R. chem. man. (inks & blacking)		1841	Ad.
Toronto - Lambert Pharmacy	inc. 1900		
Toronto - Lander, J.C.	druggist	1882, 92-3	D.
Toronto - Larkin, G.A.	druggist	1892-3	D.
Toronto - Lawrence Williams & Co.,	inc. 1900	1878	Ads.
Toronto - Leader Pharmacy	inc. 1900		
Toronto - Leau Medical Co.	inc. 1895		
Toronto - Lee, J.R.	druggist	1892-3	D.
Toronto - Lemaitre, E.G.	druggist	1882, 92-3	D.
Toronto - Leslie Bros.	druggist	1841	Ad.
Toronto - Lion Medicine Co. of Toronto	inc. 1896		
Toronto - Liquizone Toronto	inc. 1905		
Toronto - Little, G.J.	druggist	1892-3	D.
Toronto - Little, J.L.	druggist	1892-3	D.
Toronto, Lorie, E.	druggist	1847	Ad.
Toronto - Love, Robert (many years with Leslie Bros.)		1844	Ad.
Toronto - Love, Neil	pharmacist	1851, 71	D.
Toronto - Love, Neil C. & Co. dispencing chemists		1886-Ad. 1892-3-D.	
Toronto - Lowden & Co.	druggist	1882	D.
Toronto - Lubon, M.V. (cure for drunkenness)		1868	Ad.
Toronto - Lumbers, Wm. (Lumbers' Botanical Remedies)		1882	Ad.
Toronto - Lyman, Farr & Co.	druggist	1844	Ad.
Toronto - Lyman, Kneeshaw & Co.	druggist	1846	Ad.
Toronto - Lyman, Bros. & Co.	druggist	1851	Ad.
Toronto - Lyman, Elliot & Co. wholesale druggists and manufacturers 1860			Ad.
Toronto - Lyman, Bros., Toronto	inc. 1900		
Toronto, - Lynes & Brown	druggist	1844	Ad.
Toronto - Madill & Hoar, dispensing chemists (Dermaline man.)		1886	Ad.
Toronto - Malta Vita Pure co.	inc. 1905		
Toronto - Marsh Medicine, inc. 1901 - changed name to Marsh Manufacturing Co. 1902 - defunct 1904			
Toronto - Marshal, G.	druggist	1892-3	D.
Toronto - Margach, J.L. & Co.	druggist	1871	D.
Toronto - Manley, W.G.J.	druggist	1892-3	D.
Toronto - Matheson, Angus	druggist	1871, 92-3	D.
Toronto - Matheson, George	druggist	1892-3	D.
Toronto - Matheson, J.D.	druggist	1892-3	D.
Toronto - May & Co.	druggist	1882	D.
Toronto - May Dew Agency (face lotions etc.)		1884	Ad.
Toronto - May, J.P.	druggist	1892-3	D.
Toronto - McArthur, J.A.	druggist	1892-3	D.
Toronto - McBride, Chas. A.	druggist	1882	D.
Toronto - McCann, G.A.	druggist	1892-3	D.
Toronto - McConnell, W.H.	druggist	1892-3	D.
Toronto - McGarvin, J.E.	druggist	1892-3	D.
Toronto - McClean, George	man.	1850's	Ads.
Toronto - McLean, A.	druggist	1892-3	D.
Toronto - McKenzie, Dr. A.F.		1889	Ad.
Toronto - McKenzie, J.A.	druggist	1892-3	D.
Toronto - Meacham & Co.	druggist	1892-3	D.
Toronto - Meldrum, Henry	druggist	1882	D.
77 - Toronto - Milburn, T. & Co. (Burdock Bitters) inc. 1899		1882 & on	Ads.
Toronto - Miller, Hugh, Medical Hall		1844	Ad.
Toronto - Miller, Hugh & Co.		1871, 92-3	D.
Toronto - Mitchell & McLean	druggist	1892-3	D.
Toronto - Mittleburger, G.B.	druggist	1892-3	D.
Toronto - Mnoran, A., King St. (man. Nepenthe Bitters)		1876	Ad.
Toronto - Montgomery, W.B.	druggist	1892-3	D.
Toronto - Moore, W. (Bitters man.)		1862	Ad.

Ontario - cont'd

Toronto - Munyon's Offices (Munyon's Medicines)		1896	Ads.
Toronto - Murchison, Wm.	druggist	1892-3	Directory
Toronto - Neville, J.E.	druggist	1882	D.
Toronto - New Art Medicine	inc. 1899	defunct 1902	
Toronto - Newman, C.H.	druggist	1882, 92-3	D.
Toronto - Northrop & Lyman		1882	D.
Toronto - Noxan, Allan	druggist	1892-3	D.
Toronto - Oakley, Francis	druggist	1892-3	D.
Toronto - O'Connor, Wm.	druggist	1892-3	D.
Toronto - Ogden, Jehu, M.D.		1882, 92-3	D.
Toronto - Ogden, J.J.	pharmacist	1892-3	D.
Toronto - Oliver & Co.	druggist	1851	D.
Toronto - Ontario Remedies, Toronto	inc. 1897		
Toronto - Ozone Co. of Toronto Ltd.	inc. 1898		
Toronto - Petrie, G.M.	chemist	inc. 1897	
Toronto - Phrenoline Medicine Co. Ltd.	inc. 1896		
Toronto - Pugsley Drug Manufacturing Co.	inc. 1900		
Toronto - Pursey, F.J.	druggist	1892-3	D.
Toronto - Rea, Harry J.	druggist	1900	Ad.
Toronto - Rexford & Co. (Camomile Cordial, "R. & Co." on bottle)		1852	Ad.
Toronto - Richardson, C.G.	manufacturers	1892-3	D.
Toronto - Reynolds, A. (prop. Reynolds' Indian Colagogue) est.1835		1848	Ad.
Toronto - Richardson, Francis	druggist	1851	D.
Toronto - Robertson, Robt.	druggist	1892-3	D.
Toronto - Robinson, W.S.	druggist	1871, 92-3	D.
Toronto - Rockhill, C.P.	druggist	1882	D.
Toronto - Roscoe Medicine, Toronto	inc. 1902	defunct 1905	
Toronto - Rose Toilet Co.		1890	Ad.
Toronto - Rose, H.G.	druggist	1882	D.
Toronto - Rosebrugh & Co.	druggist	1892-3	D.
Toronto - Ross, W.C.	druggist	1844	Ad.
Toronto - Sabine, C.H. man. chemist (inks & blacking)		1844	Ad.
Toronto - Sabine & Huggins, New Drug Store		1848	Ads.
Toronto - Salter, H.L.	druggist	1892-3	D.
Toronto - Sampson, T.N.	druggist	1892-3	D.
Toronto - Schofield, Henry	druggist	1882, 92-3	D.
Toronto - Scott, T.W.	druggist	1882, 92-3	D.
Toronto - Scott, Wm.	druggist	1892-3	D.
Toronto - Sanitol Chemical Lab. Co.		1910	Ad.
Toronto - Seagram, Chemist & Druggist		1856	Ad.
Toronto - Scripture, W.H.	druggist	1882, 92-3	D.
Toronto - Sherries, Harry	druggist	1882	D.
Toronto - Shapters Apothecary Hall (prop. Chapters Medicines & Perfumes) 1864			Ad.
Toronto - Shapter & Jeffrey		1882	D.
Toronto - Shaw, Hayes & Comstock (perfumes & medicines)		1847	Ad.
Toronto - Shaw, Jos.	druggist	1882	D.
Toronto - Sheppard, Chris	druggist	1882	D.
Toronto - Shuttleworth, E.B.	druggist	1882	D.
Toronto - Slocum, T.A., M.D., 186 Adelaide St.		1884	Ad.
Toronto - Slocum, T.A., Medicine Co.		1897	Ad.
Toronto - Slocum, T.A., Chemical Co., 179 King W.		inc. 1895	
Toronto - Slocum, T.A. Dr. Ltd.	inc. 1903		
Toronto - Smith, W.H.	druggist	1851	D.
Toronto - Smith, Edwin A.	druggist	1882	D.
Toronto - Smith, G.B. & Co.	druggist	1882	D.
Toronto - Smith & McGlashan	druggist	1882	D.
Toronto - Smith, R.J.	druggist	1892-3	D.
Toronto - Sneath, C.R.	druggist	1892-3	D.
Toronto - Snider, R.O.	druggist	1892-3	D.
Toronto - Stevenson, Hugh	druggist	1892-3	D.
Toronto - Stevenson, S.B.	druggist	1892-3	D.
Toronto - Steward, W.R.	druggist	1892-3	D.
Toronto - Stewart, John	druggist	1892-3	D.
Toronto - Swain, J. & Co., 65 Yonge St. (man. Bitters, Vermifuge, Rhumatine, Pomades, Perfumes etc.) 1847-Ad.			
Toronto - Swain & Co., King St. E.		1851	D.
Toronto - Tallmadge, E.H. & Co.	druggist	1882	D.
Toronto - Taylor, John A.	chemist & druggist	1855	Ads.
Toronto - Taylor, John & Co. (man. soaps, perfumes etc.)		1895	Ad.
Toronto - Todd Remedy Co. Toronto Ltd.	inc. 1899		
Toronto - Thompson, D.L. Homoepathic Medicines		1882, 96	Ads.
Toronto - Thompson, Sam. R.	druggist	1882	D.
Toronto - Thomson, Dr. Botanic medicines		1836	Ad.

Ontario - cont'd

Toronto - Tonicine Co. Ltd.		inc. 1900	defunct 1905
Toronto - Toronto Chemical Co.			1892-3	Directory
Toronto - Toronto Chemical Works			1892-3	D.
Toronto - Toronto Drug Co.		inc. as Holgate	no date
Toronto - Toronto Liquid Carbonate		inc. 1901
Toronto - Toronto Pharmaceutical		inc. 1896	defunct 1902
Toronto - Truss, A.J.	druggist	1892-3	D.
Toronto - Turner, Henry	druggist	1882	D.
Toronto - Tumblety's Vegetable Compound at Dr. T's Office		1858	Ad.
Toronto - Tuthill, Rich.	druggist	1892-3	D.
Toronto - Tuthill, Robt.	druggist	1892-3	D.
Toronto - Tuthill Pharmacy		inc. 1901
Toronto - Urquhart, S.F. Thomsonian Medicines		1847-Ads. 1851-D.
Toronto - Usit Manufacturing Co. Ltd. (Wrinkle Chaser)		1915	Ad.
Toronto - Walterhouse, D.C.	druggist	1892-3	D.
Toronto - Walton, A.E.	druggist	1892-3	D.
Toronto - Ware, P.T. & Co. (man. New England Hair Restorer)		1863	Ad.
Toronto - Warner, H.H. & Co., Tor., Roch., & London. (Safe Cure)		1882, 1900	Ads.
Toronto - West, John C. & Co. (Nerve & Brain med.)		1882	Ad.
Toronto - Wilkins, H.P.	druggist	1892-3	D.
Toronto - Williams Pharmacy		inc. 1905	liqui. 1908
Toronto - Woods, J.O. (man. Adipso, 1880, Dr. King's Blood Purifier) 1892			Ads.
Toronto - Wood, Robt. A.	druggist	1871, 82	D.
Toronto - Wood, W. Loyd	druggist	1892-3	D.
Toronto - Worden, W.H.	druggist	1892-3	D.
Toronto - Woodward Medicine Co.		inc. 1898	succeeded by...
Toronto - Woodward Chemical Co.		in 1900.
Toronto - Wright, J. & Co.	druggist	1871, 82	D.
Toronto - Wright, A.M.	druggist	1892-3	D.
Toronto - Zopesa Chemical Co.		inc. 1901
Toronto Junction - Barland, C.B.	druggist	1892-3	D.
Toronto Junction - Boothe, Wallace	druggist	1892-3	D.
Toronto Junction - Gillespie, W.	druggist	1892-3	D.
Toronto Junction - Holden, John	druggist	1892-3	D.
Toronto Junction - Wright & Co.	druggist	1892-3	D.
Tottenham - Brown & Co.	druggist	1892-3	D.
Tottenham - Hughes, G.P.	druggist	1892-3	D.
Tottenham - Sandford, Wm.H.	druggist	1892-3	D.
Trenton - Barker, Wm. T.	druggist	1882	D.
Trenton - Booth, W.T.	druggist	1897-8	D.
Trenton - Deans & Munn	druggist	1882	D.
Trenton - Dickey, J.H.	druggist	1892-3	D.
Trenton - Hawley, A.W.	druggist	1882, 92-3	D.
Trenton - Meade, Henry	druggist	1882	D.
Trenton - Spaulsbury, J.F.	druggist	1892-3	D.
Tweed - Newton, P.K.	druggist	1892-3	D.
Tweed - Pomroy, T.E., M.D.		1882	D.
Tweed - Tuttle, Lewis, M.D.		1882	D.
Tweed - Tuttle, Leslie	druggist	1892-3	D.
Uxbridge - Bolster Medical Hall		1878	Ad.
Uxbridge - Bolster, Thos. jun.	druggist	1882	D.
Uxbridge - Hardy, A.S. & Co. (prop. Hardy's Oriental Compound)		1877	Ad.
Uxbridge - McGillivray, D.	druggist	1892-3	D.
Uxbridge - Stickney, Lewis P.	druggist	1882	D.
Uxbridge - Weeks, A.D.	druggist	1871, 92-3	D.
Uxbridge - Willis, R.F.	druggist	1892-3	D.
Vankleek Hill - Astron Bros. & Co.	druggist	1892-3	D.
Vankleek Hill - McIntosh, Mrs. S.J.	druggist	1892-3	D.
Vienna - Wilder, Isaac	druggist	1882	D.
Vittoria - Hewitt, Wm. (Hewitt's Anodyne Cordial)		1848	Ad.
Vittoria - Hewitt, Wm. jr.		1862	Ads.
Vittoria - Hewitt, Miss S.M.	druggist	1892-3	D.
Walkerton - Brunskill, Thos.	druggist	1892-3	D.
Walkerton - Cryderman, C.W.	druggist	1892-3	D.
Walkerton - Davidson, H.	druggist	1871	D.
Walkerton - Deans, Henry C.	druggist	1871	D.
Walkerville - Bott, John (Bott's Malt Tonic)		1892	Ad.
Walkerville - Parke, Davis & Co.		1892-3	D.
Walkerville - Parsons, E.E.	druggist	1892-3	D.
Wallaceburg - Brander, A.D.	druggist	1892-3	D.
Wallaceburg - Judson, C.J.	druggist	1882, 92-3	D.

Ontario - cont'd

Wallaceburg - McCann, Geo.	druggist	1882	Directory
Wallaceburg - Mitchell, G., M.D.		1882	D.
Waterdown - Crooker, W.H.	druggist	1892-3	D.
Waterdown - McGregor, J.O.	druggist	1892-3	D.
Waterford - Aitkin, J.F.	druggist	1892-3	D.
Waterford - Kestell, J.R. & Co.	druggist	1882	D.
Waterford - York, T.E.	druggist	1882	D.
Waterford - York, T.E. & Co.	druggist	1892-3	D.
Waterloo - Devitt, E.M.	druggist	1892-3	D.
Waterloo - Snyder, Simon	druggist	1882, 92-3	D.
Waterloo - Zoellner, H.A.	druggist	1892-3	D.
Watford - Brett, R.G.	druggist	1871	D.
Watford - McLaren, W.P.	druggist	1871, 82	D.
Watford - Taylor, T.B.	druggist	1892-3	D.
Webbwood - Ball, S.	druggist	1892-3	D.
Welland - Burger, J.H.	druggist	1882, 92-3	D.
Welland - Cumins, Thos.	druggist	1882, 92-3	D.
Welland - Douglas, A.E.	druggist	1892-3	D.
Welland - Hobson, H.W.	druggist	1882	D.
Wellandport - Horton, C.E.	druggist	1892-3	D.
Wellandport - McKeague, Wm.	druggist	1892-3	D.
Wellesley - Morton, Wm.	druggist	1882, 92-3	D.
Wellington - Yourex, J. McG.	druggist	1892-3	D.
Westport - McGuire & Co. (man. Harper's Arabian Balm)		1902	Ad.
West Winchester - Bow, Wm.	druggist	1882	D.
Weston - Banks, J.H.	druggist	1882, 92-3	D.
Weston - Irwin & Co.	druggist	1892-3	D.
Weston - Roberts, A.J.	druggist	1892-3	D.
Whitby - Gerrie, Jas. H.	druggist	1871	D.
Whitby - Howse, W.R.	druggist	1882, 92-3	D.
Whitby - Willis, J.E.	druggist	1892-3	D.
Whitby - Whitfield, Thos.	druggist	1882	D.
Wiarton - Fisher, R.M.	druggist	1892-3	D.
Wiarton - Manley, J.W.	druggist	1892-3	D.
Wiarton - Patterson, Jas.	druggist	1892-3	D.
Wiarton - Wigle, H.	druggist	1892-3	D.
Winchester - Bow, Wm.	druggist	1892-3	D.
Windsor - D'Avignon, J.E.	druggist	1892-3	D.
Windsor - Eaton, T.H. & Co.	chemists	1892-3	D.
Windsor - Gray, Wm. & Co. (Specific Medicines)		1875	Ad.
Windsor - La Belle, J.S.	druggist	1892-3	D.
Windsor - Laing & Fleming	druggist	1892-3	D.
Windsor - Mack's Magnetic Medicine Co.		1890	Ad.
Windsor - Priddy, Robt. S.	druggist	1871, 82	D.
Windsor - Wood Co., The (Wood's Phosphodine)		1903	Ad.
Wingham - Bray, W.T.	druggist	1871	D.
Wingham - Chisholm, J.H.	druggist	1892-3	D.
Wingham - Hamilton, A.L.	druggist	1892-3	D.
Wingham - Jackson, Thos.	druggist	1871	D.
Wingham - Williams, C.E.	druggist	1882, 92-3	D.
Wolfe Island - Spankle, Wm.	druggist	1892-3	D.
Woodstock - Bradley, B.L.	druggist	1892-3	D.
Woodstock - Comport & Co.	druggist	1882	D.
Woodstock - Dunlop Cure Co. Ltd.	inc. 1892		
Woodstock - Gunn, C.H.	druggist	1892-3	D.
Woodstock - Hall, J.J. & Co.	druggist	1882, 92-3	D.
Woodstock - Karn, J.G.	druggist	1892-3	D.
Woodstock - Karn, W.A.	druggist	1892-3	D.
Woodstock - Phillips, D.B.	druggist	1892-3	D.
Woodstock - Scott & White	druggist	1871	D.
Woodstock - Scott & Son	druggist	1882, 92-3	D.
Woodstock - White, Jas.	druggist	1882	D.
Woodstock - White & White	druggist	1892-3	D.
Woodville - Gunn, A.	druggist	1882	D.
Woodville - Fead, S. & Co.	druggist	1892-3	D.
Wroxeter - Fox, Jas.	druggist	1892-3	D.
Wroxeter - Robinson, W.M.	druggist	1882	D.
Wyoming - Dale, J.B.	druggist	1871, 92-3	D.
York - Moore, Wm. (meds. etc.)		1826	Ad.
York - Oates, R.H.	chemist & druggist	1831	Ad.
York - Sullivan & Stotesbury (Inks & Blacking)		1822	Ad.

Ontario - cont'd

Yorkville - Bauld, Ebonezer	druggist	1882	Directory
Yorkville - Cox, Wm. H.	druggist	1882	D.
Yorkville - Lauder, J.C.	druggist	1882	D.
Yorkville - Leslie, C.H. & Co. (man. Arnica Liniment)		1869	Ad.
Yorkville - Robinson, W.S.	druggist	1871, 82	D.
Zurich - Buchanan, G., M.D.		1882, 92-3	D.

Mineral Springs and Soda Water Manufacturers

Acton - Matthews, L.G.	general	1882	Directory
Alexandria - Stimson, E.H.		1909	D.
Alliston - Aitkin, A.	min. & soda	1890-1	D.
Alliston - Williams, John		1892-3	D.
Almonte - Forgie, Wm.	s.w.	1882	D.
Arnprior - Bell, A.H.	general	1899	D.
Arnprior - Diamond Park Mineral Water Co.	inc. 1897		
Arnprior - Kearns, H.S.	s.w.	1909	D.
Arnprior - Sanitarius Ltd.	s.w.	1909	D.
Aylmer - Winder, J.N.	s.w.	1899	D.
Barrie - Walsh, J.T.		1899	D.
Barrie - Walsh & Horsefield		1909	D.
Belleville - Belch, S.	s.w.	1857	D.
Belleville - Fay Bros.	min. & sod.	1890-1	D.
Belleville - Foy & Irwin		1890, 1909	D.
Belleville - Knox, David		1882	D.
Berlin Soda Water Co.		1909	D.
Bothwell - Adkin, J.F.	s.w.	1899	D.
Brampton - Brown, A.W.		1892, 1909	D.
Brampton - Matthews, F.	min. & sod.	1890-3	D.
Brantford - Blacker, John & Co., 2 Alfred		1890-3	D.
Brantford - Dunlop, R.S. & Co., 30 Market		1899	D.
Brantford - Pilgrim, T.A., 26 West		1899	D.
Brantford - Whitman, Henry F.		1882	D.
Brockville - Bourke & Mooney		1890	D.
Brockville - Bourke, Miles		1892-9	D.
Brockville - Chauvin, Frs. X.		1882	D.
Brockville - Pilgrim, F.M.		1890-9	D.
Brockville - Steeper, Chas & Son		1909	D.
Brockville - Thousand Island Mineral Water Co.	inc. 1901	1909	D.
Brook, The - Denault, F.	s.w.	1909	D.
Byetown - Bishoprick's superior ginger beer at his store		1836	Ad.
Caledonia - Buck, A.C.	soda water man.	1864	Ad.
Caledonia - Clark, W.J.	min. water	1890-3	D.
Caledonia Springs		1836 & on	
Caledonia Springs Co. Ltd.		1909	D.
Campbellford - Horsman, C.L.	s.w.	1909	D.
Carlton Place - Peden, A.R.G.		1899	D.
Chatham - Green, John	general	1866	Ad.
Chatham - Hoon, J.A.		1899	D.
Chatham - Horton & McGregor		1896-7	D.
Chatham - Lambert & Turner		1896, 1909	D.
Chatham Mineral Water Co.	inc. 1900		
Clinton - Liddle & Ryder		1882	D.
Cobalt Aerated Water Co.	inc. 1898	1909	D.
Cobalt - Macdonald & Co.		1890, 1909	D.
Cobalt - Stanley Mineral Water Co.	inc. 1906		
Cobourg - McWilliams, J.A.		1899	D.
Cobourg - Meehan, F.F.	s.w.	1890, 1909	D.
Cobourg - Smith, J.		1909	D.
Colborne - Merriman,	mineral water	1857	Ad.
Collingwood - McPhail, Neil		1899	D.
Cornwall - Eamer & Cameron		1909	D.
Cornwall - Foster, John		1892-3	D.
Cornwall - McLennan & Co.		1890	D.
Cornwall - Stinson & Emar		1899	D.
Essex - Vance, Mrs. Tillie		1899	D.
Fergus - Matthews, Alex		1890	D.
Ft. William Bottling Works		1909	D.
Ft. William - Woeker, E.		1909	D.

Ontario - cont'd

Galt - Hamilton, Thos. & Bros.		1899	Directory
Galt - Hamilton Bros.		1909	D.
Goderich Mineral Water Co.		1909	D.
Goderick - Phillips, Wm.		1890-3	D.
Goderich - Phillips & Co.		1899	D.
Goderich - Walton, P.L.		1909	D.
Gravenhurst - Brown & Co.		1882	D.
Gravenhurst - Brown, J.D.		1891, 1909	D.
Guelph - Atkinson, Oscar		1899	D.
Guelph - Kickley, Geo.		1909	D.
Guelph - Matthews, Alexander		1899	D.
Guelph - Reed, Bros.		1909	D.
Guelph - Royal City Bottling Works		1909	D.
Hamilton - Bickle, T. & Son, flavored soda waters		1853	Ad.
Hamilton - Bilton, George	s.w.	1882	D.
Hamilton - Cummer & Son		1909	D.
Hamilton - Imperial Mineral Water Co.	inc. 1884	1893	D.
Hamilton Mineral Water Co.		)	D.
Hamilton - Pilgrim Bros. & Co., 12 Jarvis		1890-9	D.
Hamilton - Sutherland, J.W., 16 Chancery La.		1899	D.
Hamilton - Sutherland's Ltd.		1909	D.
Hamilton - Tyler's Soda Water Machines for sale		1856	Ad.
Hamilton - Wentworth Mineral Water Co.	inc. 1906	1909	D.
Hawthorn - Borthwick, Thos.		1890-9	D.
Huntsville - Williams, H.A.		1896-7	D.
Ingersol - McKim, W.	s.w.	1892-3	D.
Kemptville - Seeley, C.H.		1896-7	D.
Kemptville - Seeley & Banks		1899	D.
Kincardine - Johnson, D.	s.w.	1890-9	D.
Kingston - Bone, Jas. Kingston Mineral Springs prop.		1843	Ad.
Kingston - Hinds Bros., Market Sq.		1890-3	D.
Kingston - Hinds, J.R., 10 Market Sq.		1899	D.
Kingston - Kronthal Lithia Water	inc. 1904	defunct 1906	
Kingston - Kronthal Lithia Water Co. Ltd.		1909	D.
Kingston - Perry, O.R.		1909	D.
Kingston - Pipe, Wm.	general	1890-9	D.
Kingston - Piper, Wm.	general	1890-1	D.
Kingston - Skinner, S. (Soda Water business for sale)		1880	Ad.
Kingston - Thompson Bottling Co. (estab. of Wm. Pipe)		1899	D.
Kingston - Young, John spruce beer man.		1816	Ad.
Kingston - Whitemarsh & Hay		1890	D.
Kleinburg - Brown, John		1890, 1909	D.
Lindsay - Begg, Jas.	s.w.	1890, 1909	D.
Lindsay - Crimmons, Jack	(Lindsay Post,	1973-4	Article)
Lindsay - Martin, Bob	(Lindsay Post,	1974	Article)
Lindsay - Nichols, Wilbert	(Lindsay Post,	1974	Article)
Lindsay - Taylor, Chas.	(Lindsay Post,	1974	Article)
Lindsay Soda Water Factory		1882	D.
Listowel - Norton, C.H.		1899	D.
Listowel - Welch, Wm.	s.w.	1890-3	D.
London - Bilton, Jos., 263 Dundas		1882, 99	D.
London - Cordery, Jas.		1890-3	D.
London - Ferguson, D., 336 Ridout		1899, 1909	D.
London - Howe, John		1909	D.
London - Hynd, W.M.		1892-3	D.
London - Murray, John, 188 Hamilton Rd.		1899, 1909	D.
London Sulphur Spring		1869	Ad.
London - Tune, Jas. & Son, 145 York	est. 1880	1890, 1909	D.
London - White Sulphur Springs		1870	Ad.
Markham - Reids, George	s.w.	1896-7	D.
Matheson - Peterson, W.H.		1909	D.
Midland - Hinds, M.C.		1909	D.
Midlan - Rooney, Nicholas		1890-3	D.
Morrisburg - Seeley & Dillebaugh		1890	D.
Morrisburg - Seeley, C.H.		1892-3	D.
Mount Forest - Robertson, Alexander		1899, 1909	D.
Napanee - Sexsmith, A.J. (Soda bus. for sale - machine, bottles, wagons and plant) 1876 - Ad.			
New Liskeard - Taylor & Pringle Co. Ltd.		1909	D.
Newmarket - Burk, James		1909	D.
Niagara Falls - Breakey Bros.		1899	D.
Niagara Falls - Tossel, W. & Son		1882	D.
Niagara Falls - Tossel, Charles		1899	D.

223

Ontario - cont'd

Niagara Falls Centre - Doty, Lilian		1909	Directory
Niagara Falls Centre - Glasgow, Mrs. L.E.		1892-3	D.
Niagara Falls Centre - Smyth, S.J.		1890	D.
North Bay - Blanchet & Fitzpatrick		1909	D.
Oakville - Matthews, F.		1899	D.
Oakville - Sproule, Bert		1909	D.
Orangeville - Aiken & Walker		1909	D.
Orangeville - Connor, B.F.		1882, 93	D.
Orangeville - Crozier, Jas.	s.w.	1892-3	D.
Orangeville - Hill & Robertson		1899	D.
Orillia - Fralick, Adam	general	1882	D.
Orillia - Hinds, F.P.		1899, 1909	D.
Orillia - Tune, J.E.	s.w.	1891	D.
Oshawa - Holmes, Daniel		1909	D.
Ottawa - Borthwick, Wm., 87 Besserer		1892-9	D.
Ottawa - Butler & Conway		1909	D.
Ottawa - Canada Mineral Waters Ltd.		1909	D.
Ottawa - Crown Mineral Water Co.		1909	D.
Ottawa - Christie, C.A.		1892-3	D.
Ottawa - Christin, C.A.		1890	D.
Ottawa - Cussans, Henry, 115 George		1892-9	D.
Ottawa - Davis, L.		1909	D.
Ottawa - Drolet, Jos.		1882	D.
Ottawa - Drolet, Melchoir, 424 Sussex		1890	D.
Ottawa - Drolet & Wells		1892-3	D.
Ottawa - Dunn, R.& J.		1909	D.
Ottawa - Forest, Felix		1882	D.
Ottawa - Grand Hotel Co. (Caledonia Springs)		1896-7	D.
Ottawa - Hoggard, George		1896, 1909	D.
Ottawa - Huckels, A. & Co., 326 Queen		1899, 1909	D.
Ottawa - Irvine, R. Ltd.		1909	D.
Ottawa - Miriault, E., 381 Wellington		1899, 1909	D.
Ottawa - Obico Mineral Water	inc. 1893		
Ottawa - Radnor Water Co., 53 Sparks		1899	D.
Ottawa - Ranger & Allard		1892-3	D.
Ottawa - Russel Bottling Works of Ottawa	inc. 1905		
Ottawa - Sarault, N.		1909	D.
Ottawa - Shaw, J.R.		1909	D.
Ottawa - Whitemarsh & Haig		1890	D.
Owen Sound - Malone, Henry		1882	D.
Owen Sound - Smart, John		1882	D.
Owen Sound - Taylor & Pringle		1899	D.
Owen Sound - Taylor & Pringle Co. Ltd.		1909	D.
Parkhill - Haney, R.		1909	D.
Parry Sound - Laughington, H.		1896, 1909	D.
Parry Sound - Mosley, J.F.		1899	D.
Pembroke - Behan, E.& J.		1890	D.
Pembroke - Behan, Edward		1892, 1909	D.
Penetanguishene - Ricalton, A.W.		1890	D.
Penville - Stuart & Bruce		1882	D.
Perth - Johnston, Archibald		1890, 1909	D.
Peterborough - Belch, Edward		1909	D.
Peterborough - Croft, Wm.		1909	D.
Peterborough - Foy & Campbell		1882	D.
Peterborough - Foy & Starr		1888	D.
Peterborough - James, Chas.		1895, 1909	D.
Peterborough - Knox Bros.		1890	D.
Peterborough - Knox, David		1892-9	D.
Peterborough - Knox, Mrs. D.		1909	D.
Peterborough Mineral Water Co.		1895-7	D.
Petrolia - Peninsula Soda Co.	inc. 1895		
Picton - Beech, E. & Co.		1896-7	D.
Picton - Belch, Edward		1890-3	D.
Picton - Hughes & Palmatier		1899	D.
Plantagenet - Bridge & Carre, Georgian Springs prop.		1840	Ad.
Plantagenet - Carratraca Springs Water		1869	Ad.
Plantagenet - La Roque, prop. Plantagenet Springs		1848-61	Ads.
Plantagenet - Irish, John T. prop. Plantagenet Springs		1862	Ads.
Plantagenet - Rodden, R.J. & Boyd, R.W. props. above		1869	Ads.
Plantagenet Springs Hotel & Land inc. as Plantagent Springs Co.		1893	
Port Arthur - Elliot & Co.		1890, 1909	D.
Port Arthur - McKibbon, H.A.		1909	D.

Ontario - cont'd

Port Arthur - Robb, S.J. & Co.	1909	Directory
Port Arthur - Turin & Fauer	1909	D.
Port Colborne - Cronmiller, J.H.	1899	D.
Port Colborne - Cronmiller, J. Henry jr.	1909	D.
Port Colborne - Lake Erie Bottling Co.	1909	D.
Port Hope - Garbutt, George	1899	D.
Port Hope - Garfat, Wm.	1890-3	D.
Port Hope - Walter, J.	1909	D.
Port Perry - Bolton, Ephraham	1892-3	D.
Port Perry - Cook, Thos.	1892, 1909	D.
Prescott - Daniels, John	1882-99	D.
Prescott - Daniels, Mrs. John	1909	D.
Preston Mineral Spring Water	1876	Ad.
Rat Portage - Blackwood Bros.	1899	D.
Renfrew - Deroche, Cleophas	1890	D.
Renfrew - Patterson & Co.	1899	D.
Sarnia - Farr & Sharpe	1899	D.
Sarnia - Jackson, Farr & Co.	1890	D.
Sarnia - Sharpe & Kirkpatrick	1909	D.
Sault Ste. Marie - Dunseath & McKendrie	1890	D.
Sault Ste. Marie - Taylor & Pringle Ltd.	1909	D.
Seaforth - Dodge, John	1890-3	D.
Seaforth - Dodds, John	1899, 1909	D.
Simcoe - Colonial Bottling Works	1909	D.
Simcoe - Pursel, H.W.	1899	D.
Smith's Falls - Irvine, Robt.	1899, 1909	D.
Smith's Falls - Ward, Richard	1909	D.
Southhampton Mineral Water Co. inc. 1886	defunct 1906	
Southhampton - Saugeen Mineral Water Co.	1895	Ad.
Southhampton - Saugeen Magnetic Mineral Water Co., Carey & Creighton props. 1909 D.		
Stratford - Dow, James	1899	D.
Stratford Soda Water Works	1890-9	D.
Stratford - Taylor, Richard	1899	D.
Stratford - Totem of Health Co.	1890	D.
Stratford - Tune & Robertson	1890	D.
Stratford - Tune, G.E.	1892-7	D.
Stratford - Tune Bottling Co.	1909	D.
Stratford - Wilkinson, H.	1899, 1909	D.
Strathroy - Hockin, John	1890	D.
Strathroy - Redmond & Gale	1909	D.
Strathroy - Taylor, Richard	1896-9	D.
St. Catharines - Bain, A.J.	1899	D.
St. Catharines - Hynes, Burton	1890	D.
St. Catharines - Mac Mineral Spring inc. 1901		
St. Catharines - McNulty & King	1909	D.
St. Catharines Mineral Springs & Spa, 1840's through 1890's		Ads.
St. Catharines - Nadell, R.	1909	D.
St. Catharines - Nelson, Chas. C.	1882	D.
St. Catharines - Springbank Mineral Springs inc. 1902	defunct 1906	
St. Catharines - Tyson, W.H.	1909	D.
St. Joseph - Huron Mineral Water Co.	1909	D.
St. Thomas - Gilbert, Daniel	1890	D.
St. Thomas - Hutchinson, T.H., 206 Talbot	1899	D.
St. Thomas - Hutchinson, Thos. B.	1909	D.
St. Thomas - Tune, G.E.	1892-3	D.
Sudbury - Jodouin, L.J.	1899	D.
Sudbury - New Ontario Bottling Works	1909	D.
Sudbury - Taylor & Pringle Ltd.	1909	D.
Thorold - Tuckahoe Lithia Water inc. 1900	defunct 1905	
Thornhill - Hawthorn Mineral Springs Co.	1896-7	D.
Thornhill - Langstaff, John	1896-7	D.
Tillsonburg - Wilcox, Robt. H. & Co.	1909	D.
Toronto - Alexander, Jas. Aerated Waters etc.	1856	Ad.
Toronto - Boyle & Libby, 349 Dundas	1892-9	D.
Toronto - Boyle & Libby, 240 Gladstone Ave.	1909	D.
Toronto - Burns, Alex	1882	D.
Toronto - Butters, Edmond, soda water man. 1846 Ad., sold out... 1855		Ad.
Toronto - Canesda Mineral Water Co. Toronto inc. 1897		
Toronto - Carter, S., soda water & ginger nectar	1857	Ad.
Toronto - Clark Bros., 30 William St.	1882-99	D.
Toronto - Coca Cola Toronto, 65 Bellwoods Ave. inc. 1906		

Ontario - cont'd

Toronto - Cook, Wm., soda water man.		1854	Ad.
Toronto - Eudo Mineral Water Co., 9 Francis		1899	Directory
Toronto - Eves, J.	soda water	1861-2	D.
Toronto - Fauman Bros., 11 Caer-Howell		1909	D.
Toronto - Fletcher Man. Co.		1896-7	D.
Toronto - Forrest, Lorenzo		1892-7	D.
Toronto - Guggishberg & Co.		1896-7	D.
Toronto - Halpern Bros., 80 Louisa		1909	D.
Toronto - Humphries, James (successor to Wm. Cook)		1858	Ad.
Toronto - Hygiena Kola Co., 84 Church		1909	D.
Toronto - Kirkland, L.A., 38 Dundas		1909	D.
Toronto - Langmoore, C.E., 101½ King W.		1890-1	D.
Toronto - Lyman's Soda Water (the props. have purchased machine & bus. of Mr. E. Butters) 1855 Ad.			
Toronto - Matthews, Jas., 29 Ossington Ave.		1890, 1909	D.
Toronto - McLaughlin, J.J., 24 Queen E.		1892-7	D.
Toronto - McLaughlin, J.J., 153 Sherbourne		1899, 1909	D.
Toronto - McVean, F.A., 270 Gerrard E.		1909	D.
Toronto - Non-Alcoholic Beverage Co., 1264 Queen W.		1909	D.
Toronto - O'Connor, Thos., George St.		1896-7	D.
Toronto - O'Connor Bros., 125 George St.		1909	D.
Toronto - Parsons, Johnson & Co., King St.	soda waters	1855	Ad.
Toronto - Queen City Soda Water Co.	inc. 1899		
Toronto - Radnor Water Co., 26 Colborne		1899	D.
Toronto - Riddle, Francis		1871	D.
Toronto - Robertson, Wm., 106 Nassau St.		1890-7	D.
Toronto - Robertson, Wm., 875 Queen W.		1899	D.
Toronto - Ross's Dry Ginger Ale		1906	Ad.
Toronto - Russel Lithia Water bottled at the Spring by Coca Cola Co., Bellwoods Ave. 1910 Ad.			
Toronto - Slatter, James		1861-2	D.
Toronto - Smith, Thos., man. Smith's Soda Water Machines & Wire Caps, good as and cheaper than imported. 1862 Ad.			
Toronto Soda Water Works		1909	D.
Toronto - St. Leon Mineral Water Co., 1909 King St. inc. 1901		1890	Ads.
Toronto - St. Leon Waters Ltd., 101 Adelaide W.		1909	D.
Toronto Mineral Springs	inc. 1905		
Toronto - Tuckahoe Lithia Water Co., 51 King W.		1899	D.
Toronto - Turner's soda water, ginger beer etc.		1855	Ad.
Toronto - Verner, Samuel, 104 Berkeley St.		1899	D.
Toronto - Verner, Mrs. E.J., 120 Richmond W.		1899	D.
Toronto - Verner, John, 132 Berkeley		1890-1	D.
Toronto - Vernor, John, 100 Berkeley		1896-7	D.
Toronto - Vernor, Wm. A., 16 Spruce St.		1896-7	D.
Toronto - Walsh & Co., 124 Berkeley		1882	D.
Toronto - Walsh, James, 132 Berkeley		1896-9	D.
Toronto - Wilson, Charles, inc. 1901		1873	D.
Uxbridge - Colcock, Thos.	soda water	1878	Ad.
Uxbridge - Darlington, Wm.		1871, 1891	D.
Uxbridge - Darlington, Chas.	sold out 1903	1892-9	D.
Walkerton - Barton, Albert		1896-7	D.
Walkerton - Hill, Robt.		1899	D.
Walkerton - McCulloch, J.S.		1882	D.
Waterloo Salt Well & Mineral Co.	inc. 1871		
Wendover - Belenger, D.		1896-7	D.
Whitby - McCrohan, E.O.		1899	D.
Wiarton - Sirley, Walter		1882	D.
Windsor - Baby & Hanrahan		1882	D.
Windsor - Horton, John, 53 Sandwich W.		1899	D.
Windsor - Meisner, George		1899, 1909	D.
Wingham - Hill Bros.		1882	D.
Wingham - Hill, Robt.		1882	D.
Wingham - Orr, John W.		1909	D.
Wingham - Pringle, David		1890-3	D.
Woodstock - Corrigan, Chas.		1909	D.
Woodstock - Young, F.J.		1899	D.

PRINCE EDWARD ISLAND

Brewers and Distillers

Charlottown - Morris, J.& T.B.	brewers	1896-7	Directory
Cherry Valley - Dodd, J.A.	brewer	1899	D.

Mineral Springs and Soda Water Manufacturers

Charlottetown - Ferris & Fredrickson		1891	Directory
Charlottetown - Large, Albert	s.w.	1891-9	D.
Charlottetown - Simmons, G.H.	s.w.	1899, 1909	D.

QUEBEC

Brewers and Distillers

Barnston - Cleveland, S.	dist.	1851	Directory
Barnston - Davis, Edmond	dist.	1851	D.
Beauceville - Turgeon, N.T. & Co.	brewers	1909	D.
Beauharnois - Bedard, J.U.	brewer	1899	D.
Beauharnois - Duncan, George	brewer	1851	D.
Bedford - Bailey, Wm. & Co.	dist.	1851	D.
Bienville - Thibault, Pierre	brewer	1890-9	D.
Buckingham - St. Jacques, Jos.	brewer	1899	D.
Cabano - Levesque, J.	brewer	1909	D.
Chateau Richer - Cauchon, Edward	brewer	1899	D.
Chambly Basin - Petit, E.	brewer	1909	D.
Chicoutimi - Claveau, E.	brewer	1909	D.
Chicoutimi - Morin, C.	brewer	1909	D.
Coaticook - Bouchard, J.A.	brewer	1909	D.
Coaticook - Paradis, Vital & Co.	brewer	1899	D.
Coaticook - Silver Spring Brewery		1909	D.
Courcelles - Blais, H.	brewer	1909	D.
D'Israeli - Bigin, Olivier & Co.	brewer	1899	D.
Drummondville - Piche, E.A.	brewer	1899	D.
Drummondville - Turcotte, J.N.	brewer	1899	D.
Drummondville - Vignault, G.	brewer	1909	D.
Etchemin - Labrecque, Louis	brewer	1899	D.
Farnham Brewing Co.	inc. 1900		
Farnham - Croteau, E.R.	brewer	1899-1909	D.
Farnham - Fontaine, Jos.	brewer	1909	D.
Granby - Choiniere, Antoine	brewer	1909	D.
Granby - Desrochers, P.H. & Co.	brewer	1909	D.
Granby - Tremblay, R.	brewer	1909	D.
Grand Mere - Morrisette, F.	brewer	1909	D.
Grand Mere - Paquet, W.	brewer	1909	D.
Hull - Bureau, Pierre	brewer	1899	D.
Hull - Carriere, Anthime	brewer	1899	D.
Hull - Delisle, Adolphe	brewer	1899	D.
Hull - Durocher, P.H. Co.	brewer	1909	D.
Joliette - Brasseri de Joliette		1896-7	D.
Joliette - Mireault, Abonidius	brewer	1909	D.
Lachine - Dawes & Co., 521 St. James	brewers	1896-7	D.
La Beauce - Lecoeur, P.	brewer	1899	D.
La Beauce - Savard, Gaudiose	brewer	1899	D.
Lake Megantic - Becigneuil, L.	brewer	1899	D.
Lake Megantic - Fortier & Tardiff	brewer	1899	D.
Lambton - Blais, Hilais	brewer	1899	D.
Levis - Beauport Brewing Co.		1909	D.
Levis - Begin, Cleophas	brewer	1899	D.
Levis - Bouchart, A.	brewer	1909	D.
Levis - Caron, Phileas	brewer	1899	D.
Levis - Edmond, C.	brewer	1909	D.

Quebec - cont'd

Levis - Labranche, E.	brewer	1890, 1909	Directory
Levis - Montreuil, P.J.	brewer	1890	D.
Macnider - Fournier, T. & Co.	brewer	1899	D.
Marieville - Arpin, F. & Co.	brewer	1899	D.
Montmagny - Dube, Jos.	brewer	1899	D.
Montmagny - Teter, Cyrille	brewer	1899	D.
Montmorency - Fortier, Adelbert	brewer	1909	D.
Montreal - Beauport Brewing Co., 345 Notre Dame E.		1909	D.
Montreal - Bishop Bottling Co., 1001 Dorchester E.		1909	D.
Montreal - Blackwood & LaRoque (bottled goods)		1817	Ad.
Montreal - Boivin, Wilson & Co.	dist.	1898	Ad.
Montreal - Bourne & Co., La Prairie Brewery		1840	Ad.
Montreal - Bourne, George	brewer	1857	D.
Montreal Brewing Co., 133 3/4 Notre Dame		1890, 96-7	D.
Montreal Brewing Co. Ltd., 490 Notre Dame E.		1909	D.
Montreal - Brown, A.H. & Co. Ltd., 19 Aylmer		1909	D.
Montreal - Buchanan, Harris & Co.	dealers	1857	Ad.
Montreal - Buttery's Brewery		1837	Ad.
Montreal - Canadian Brewing Co.		1896-7	D.
Montreal - Canadian Brewers Ltd.		1909	D.
Montreal - Canada Malting Co. Ltd.		1909	D.
Montreal - Chapman's Brewery, Lemoine St.		1843	Ad.
Montreal - Chaput, Remie	brewer	1909	D.
Montreal - Cook, James, 87 Jane St. (prop. Wilson's Invalid P. Wine)		1905	Ad.
Montreal - Cuvillier & Sons (L.C. whisky)		1838	Ad.
Montreal - Dawes & Co., 215 St. James		1855, 1909	D.
Montreal - Denis, S., 585 St. Dominique	brewer	1899	D.
Montreal Distillery for sale by public auction		1794	Ad.
Montreal - Domphousse, J.	brewer	1890	D.
Montreal - Dow & Co., St. Joseph St.		1851	D.
Montreal - Dow, Wm. & Co., 36 Chaboillez Sq.		1862, 1909	D.
Montreal - Ekers Brewery, (Ald. H.A. prop.) 393 St. Lawrence		est. 1840	Ad.
Montreal - Ekers, Thos., A., 409 St. Lawrence		1882, 96-7	D.
Montreal - Ekers, H.A., 641 St. Lawrence Boul.		1909	D.
Montreal - Gorrie's Brewery (bottles in qts. and pts.)		1842	Ad.
Montreal - Heaven, Thos., Notre Dame (spirits in wood & bottle)		1829	Ad.
Montreal - Howard, Mrs. T.J.	brewer	1890	D.
Montreal - Howard Bottling Co., 181 Dorchester,beer		1899, 1909	D.
Montreal - Kinsella Bottling Works, 237 St. Antoine, beer		1909	D.
Montreal - Labatt, John, 127 Delorimier Ave.		1896, 1909	D.
Montreal - Lachapelle, A., 117 Ste. Mary St.	brewer	1851	D.
Montreal - Laprairie Brewery (bottles in qts. and pts.)		1842	Ad.
Montreal - Mace, T.F.	brewer	1890	D.
Montreal - Maitland, R.F. & Co. (bottled wines)		1838	Ad.
Montreal - McCharles, S.	brewer & dist.	1863	Ad.
Montreal - McCrory, John	brewer	1890	D.
Montreal - Meaghers, Orange Quinine Wine		1892	Ad.
Montreal - Molson, John & Sons, est. 1782, (wood or bottle)		1817	Ad.
Montreal - Molson, T.& W., St. Mary St.	brewers & dist.	1851	D.
Montreal - Molson, John H.R. & Bros.	brewers & dist.	1862	D.
Montreal - Molson, John H.R. & Bros., 1006 Notre Dame		1896-9	D.
Montreal - Molson, John H.R. & Bros., 906 Notre Dame E.		1909	D.
Montreal - Morley, Jas. (agent O'Keefe's) 20 St. Phillip		1909	D.
Montreal - National Brewery, 142 Inspector		1899	D.
Montreal - Pabst Brewing Co., 606 St. Paul		1899	D.
Montreal - Payne, M.& Co.	dist.	1862	D.
Montreal - Perron, P.R., 460 Champlain	brewer	1909	D.
Montreal - Phillips, H.& Co., 170 St. Lawrence	brewers	1851	D.
Montreal - Phillips & Taylor	brewers	1857	D.
Montreal - Pigeon, Sauvageau & Co.	brewers	1857	D.
Montreal - Prentice, E., St. Bernard	brewer	1851	D.
Montreal - Rafferty, Wm.J., 35 Valler	brewer	1909	D.
Montreal - Reinhardt, G.& Sons, 341 German		1882	D.
Montreal - Reinhardt, G.& Sons, 529 Ave del Hotel de Ville		1896-9	D.
Montreal - Reinhardt, G.& Sons, 529 City Hall Ave.		1909	D.
Montreal - Reinhardt & Co. (agency) 617 St. Paul		1909	D.
Montreal - Silver Creek Brewing Co. of Guelph, 8 Lemoine		1896	D.
Montreal - Silver Creek Brewing Co. of Guelph, 58 McGill		1899	D.
Montreal - Sorgius, George, 35 Rivard	brewer	1909	D.
Montreal - Strangman, Chas., 566 St. Mary	brewer	1882	D.
Montreal - Stewart Bottling Co. Ltd.	beer	1909	D.

Quebec - cont'd

Montreal - St. Dennis Distillery (sample bottles to be had)		1837	Ad.
Montreal - St. Pierre Distillery, James, Thos., 1838 Ad. for sale		1851	Ad.
Montreal - St. Roc Brewery, Meiklejohn, Wm. (wood or bottle)		1805	Ad.
Montreal - Stuart, C.D., 49 Notre Dame	dist.	1851	D.
Montreal - Taylor's Brewery, est. 1839 - for sale or rent,		1880	Ad.
Montreal - Taylor & Co., 338 St. Lawrence	brewers	1882	Directory
Montreal - Taylor, R.F., 253 Upper St. Urbain	brewer	1882	D.
Montreal - Union Brewery, inc. 1898, was Atkin heretofor		1909	D.
Montreal - Union Bottling Co., 297 William	beer	1909	D.
Montreal - Vezina, J.B., 1191 Notre Dame	beer	1899	D.
Montreal - Victoria Brewing Co.		1890	D.
Montreal - Virtue, J.& Co.	brewers	1862	D.
Montreal - Vinet, J.G.	brewers	1909	D.
Montreal - Whelan & Rafferty, 30 Vallee	brewers	1899	D.
Montreal - Williams, Miles ju., College St.	brewer	1851	D.
Montreal - Williams, Miles & Co.	brewers	1882, 91-7	D.
Montreal - Wilson, Lawrence A. & Co. (agents)		1900	Ad.
Montreal - Workman, Wm., St. Paul St.	dist.	1845	Ad.
Murray Bay - Gagnon, Jos.	brewer	1899	D.
Nicolet - Desrochers, Jos.	brewer	1909	D.
Nicolet - Duval, J.A.	brewer	1899	D.
Nicolet - Houde, J.H.L.	brewer	1909	D.
Nicolet - Senneville, J.A. & Co.	brewers	1899	D.
Notre Dame de Quebec - Racine, Frank	brewer	1899	D.
Papineauville - Chabot, Chas. ju.	brewer	1890	D.
Plessiville - Rinfret, Oscar	brewer	1899, 1909	D.
Pointe Gatineau - Smith, G.W. & Co.	brewer	1899	D.
Port Rouge - Bedard, D.	brewer	1909	D.
Quebec - Amyot & Gauvin	brewers	1909	D.
Quebec Brewery & Distillery, Young & Ainsley props., 1792 Ads. for sale		1804	Ad.
Quebec Brewing Co.	inc. 1876		
Quebec Bottled Ale Vaults, Rose, James & Co., Market Place, L.T.		1810	Ad.
Quebec - Boutin, Pierre	brewer	1857	D.
Quebec - Beauport Brewing Co., 277 St. Paul		1899, 1909	D.
Quebec - Boswell's Ale from the Racey Brewery		1844	Ad.
Quebec - Boswell, Jos., St. Peter St. L.T.	brewer	1851	D.
Quebec - Boswell & Bros., 96 St. Valier	brewers	1890, 1909	D. (see next)
Quebec Brewery, 1780's Ads. became next			
Quebec - Cape Diamond Brewery, Goddard, Jas. prop. (bottled beer)		1791	Ad.
Quebec - Cape Diamond Brewery, Mr. Brehaut, prop.		1816	Ad.
Quebec - Cape Diamond Brewery, Mrs. Brehaut, prop. 1817 Ad. in partnership with John & Benjamin Racey			
Quebec - Cape Diamond Brewery, Racey, John & Benjamin, props., 1820 and shortly known as the Racey Brewery, Ads.			
Quebec - Cauchon, Chateau Richer	brewer	1896-7	D.
Quebec - Clouthier, Damase	brewer	1896-7	D.
Quebec - Cote, Jos., 39 St. Gabriel	brewer	1899	D.
Quebec - Crawford, A.& Co., 64 St. John		1890-9	D.
Quebec - Doyer, David	dist.	1857	D.
Quebec - Fluet, F.A.	brewer	1909	D.
Quebec - Fortier, D. & Co., 220 St. Valier		1899, 1909	D.
Quebec - Gauvin, Michel	brewer	1890	D.
Quebec - Gorries Brewery off St. Mary St.		1843	Ad.
Quebec - Jenkins & Allsops Red Port Wine neat as imported, Furs or Peltries, Wheat or other products of the country in exchange, L.T.		1765	Ad.
Quebec - Labatt, John, 3 St. Pierre		1899	D.
Quebec - Kennedy, M., 2 Bath		1899	D.
Quebec - Lepper, Paul, St. Paul St. L.T.	brewer	1851	D.
Quebec - Lloyd, Thos.,	brewer	1862	D.
Quebec Liquor Co.	inc. 1896	dissolved 1900	
Quebec - Maquay & Hawkins Liquor Vaults (cask or bottle)		1816	Ad.
Quebec - McCallum, Daniel	brewer	1862	D.
Quebec - Montreuil, N.Y.	brewer	1890	D.
Quebec - Montreuil, P.J., 277 St. Paul		1899	D.
Quebec - O'Donnell, John, 26 St. Angele,	brewer	1890-9	D.
Quebec - O'Regan, C.J., 3 Arsenal	brewer	1890-9	D.
Quebec - Proteau & Carignon, 363 St. Paul		1890, 1909	D.
Quebec - Rock Spring Brewery		1896-7	D.
Quebec - Rousseau, Jos.	brewer	1890	D.
Quebec - Timmons, M. & Son	brewer	1909	D.
Richmond - Janette, J.E.	brewer	1909	D.
Rimouski - Talbot, Jos.	brewer	1890	D.
Robertval - Lalancette, A.	brewer	1909	D.

Quebec - cont'd

Riviere du Loup - Boulanger, Ed.	brewer	1899	Directory
Riviere du Loup - Darisse & Frere	brewer	1899	D.
Riviere du Loup - Martel, Jules	brewer	1899	D.
Riviere du Loup - Montreuil, J.A.	brewer	1890-9	D.
Riviere du Loup - Thibault, J.O.	brewer	1890	D.
Rock Island - Gilmore, C.E.	brewer	1899	D.
Sherbrooke - Archambault, J.O.	brewer	1890	D.
Sherbrooke - Bryant, J.H.	brewer	1899, 1909	D.
Sherbrooke - Burton Brewing Co.	inc. 1886		
Sherbrooke - Odell, C.J.	brewer	1896	D.
Sherbrooke - Wigget, Wm. H.	brewer	1890, 1909	D.
Sorrel - Francoeur, A. & Co.	brewer	1899	D.
Ste. Anne de la Perade - Blouin, A.	brewer	1899	D.
St. Barthelemi - Ringuette, L.	brewer	1899	D.
St. Charles, River Boyer - Doyer, E.	brewer	1899	D.
St. Francois, Beauce - Turgeon, N.T.	brewer	1899	D.
St. Francois, North East - Lambert, A.	brewer	1899	D.
St. Francois, North East - Turgeon, N.T. & Co.	brewers	1899	D.
St. Hyacinth - Bourgeois, J.T.	brewer	1909	D.
St. Hyacinth - Brodeur, Olivier	brewer	1890-9	D.
St. Hyacinth - Lariviere, A.	brewer	1899	D.
St. Hyacinth - Orsali, Chas.	brewer	1899	D.
St. Hyacinth - Orsali & Co.	brewer	1909	D.
St. Hyacinth - Pagnuelo & Frere	brewer	1890-9	D.
St. Hyacinth - St. Pierre, J.B.	brewer	1899	D.
St. Jean des Chaillons - Dore, W.	brewer	1899	D.
St. Jerome - Desormeau, S.	brewer	1899	D.
St. Roc Brewery, Meiklejohn, Wm. prop. (bottled ale)		1805	Ad.
St. Roch - Jameson's Brewery, St. Peter St.		1846-Ad.	1851-D.
St. Tite - Montgrain, E.	brewer	1899	D.
St. Therese - White Rock Brewing Co.		1909	D.
Three Rivers - Carigman, Onesime	brewer	1890	D.
Three Rivers - Duplesis, J.A. & Co.	brewer	1909	D.
Three Rivers - Dupont, J.A. & Co.	brewer	1899	D.
Three Rivers - Hart, Mose (brewery for sale)		1816	Ad.
Three Rivers - Rivard & Frere	brewers	1909	D.
Three Rivers - Rousseau, J.C.	brewers	1890	D.
Three Rivers - Rousseau & Co.	brewers	1909	D.
Three Rivers - Spennard, J.M.	brewer	1909	D.
Victoriaville - Gaudet, Athanase	brewer	1899	D.
Waterloo - Jenkins, Lyman B.	brewer	1899	D.
Yamachiche - Ricard, E.	brewer	1899	D.

Chemists, Druggists and Manufacturers

Hull - Davies, Dr. T.B.	druggist	1892-3	Directory
Montreal - Abbey's Effervescent Salt Co. Ltd.		1897	Ad.
Montreal - Ambrosse, John D.L.	chemist & druggist	1882	D.
Montreal - Baridon, L.R.	chemist & druggist	1882	D.
Montreal - Beall, Ross & Co. Whosl.	chemist & druggist	1882	D.
Montreal - Bent, George		1828	Ad.
Montreal - Binley, Wm.		1819	Ad.
Montreal - Birks, Rich.	chemist & druggist	1851, 82	D.
Montreal - Boulanger, G.	chemist & druggist	1882	D.
Montreal - Bowman, W.E.	chemist & druggist	1851	D.
Montreal - Boyd & Arnton (medicine manu.)		1870	Ad.
Montreal - Brayley, J.W. (medicine manu.)		1882	D.
Montreal - Brayley, Sons & Co.		1893	Ad.
Montreal - Breitin J. Bach Co. (Pepto-Mangan Gude)		1903	Ad.
Montreal - Brunet, Alf.	druggist	1882	D.
Montreal - Bulling, Wm. B.	druggist	1882	D.
Montreal - Campbell's Quinine Wine, prep. at Med. Hall		1873	Ad.
Montreal - Campbell, Kenneth & Co.		1882	D.
Montreal - Carter, Kerry & Co.	drugs, etc.	1851	D.
Montreal - Champlain, O.H.P.	drugs, etc.	1897-8	D.
Montreal - Contant, Jos.	druggist	1882	D.
Montreal - Coverton, C.J. & Co.	druggist	1882	D.
Montreal - Crevier, J.A., M.D.		1882	D.
Montreal - Curtis, H.H.	druggist	1882	D.
Montreal - Cundhill, Francis & Co's (Pancriatric Emulsion)		1869	Ad.

Quebec - cont'd

```
Montreal - Dawson, J.A.                          druggist        1882        Directory
Montreal - Desilets, C.M.                        druggist        1882        D.
Montreal - Desjardins, J.A., M.D.                                1882        D.
Montreal - Desrosiers, L.J.P., M.D.                              1882        D.
Montreal - Devins & Bolton                                       1874        Ad.
Montreal - Devins, R.J.                          druggist        1882        D.
Montreal - Dick & Co. (Dick's Liniment, Etc.)                    1894        Ads.
Montreal - Dubuc, Chas., M.D.                                    1882        D.
Montreal - Duckett, Wm. A., M.D.                                 1882        D.
Montreal - Dugal, Roch.                          druggist        1882        D.
Montreal - Edson, M.G. & Co.                     druggist        1882        D.
Montreal - Edwards, J. Baker, M.D.                               1882        D.
Montreal - Evans, Mercer & Co., (Phosfozone)                     1877        Ad.
Montreal - Evans, H. Sugden & Co.                druggists       1882        D.
Montreal - Finn, John A.                         druggist        1882        D.
Montreal - Fletcher, John (Fletcher's Cure for Coughs & Colds)   1844, 52    Ads.
Montreal - Gadbois, A., M.D.                                     1882        D.
Montreal - Gardner, John                         druggist        1854        Ad.
Montreal - Gianelli, A.M.F., Place d'Armes (Prop. Royal Italian Bitters) 1867  Ad.
Montreal - Giroux, Paul O.                       druggist        1882        D.
Montreal - Godfrey, R.                           druggist        1851        D.
Montreal - Gouldon, Jas.                         druggist        1882        D.
Montreal - Gravelle, A.E.                        druggist        1892-3      D.
Montreal - Gray, Henry R.                        druggist        1882        D.
Montreal - Harte, Jas. A.                        druggist        1882        D.
Montreal - Haswell, H. & Co. (man. Golden Fruit Bitters)         1883        Ad.
Montreal - Harper, John                          druggist        1882        D.
Montreal - Henry, J.F. & Co. (prop. Henry's Vermont Liniment)    1863        Ad.
Montreal - Jackson, Henry F.                     druggist        1882        D.
Montreal - Jouffray, Camille J.                  druggist        1882        D.
Montreal - Kerry, Watson & So.                   druggist        1882        D.
Montreal - Kohr, Dr. Medicine Co.                inc. 1899
Montreal - Lachance, S.                          druggist        1882        D.
Montreal - Lanctot, H.                           druggist        1892-3      D.
Montreal - Laport, Anselme                       druggist        1882        D.
Montreal - Laviolette & Nelson                   druggist        1882        D.
Montreal - Leblanc, Benj. H., M.D.                               1882        D.
Montreal - Lelerc, A.                            druggist        1882        D.
Montreal - Leduc, Jos., M.D. & Co.                               1882        D.
Montreal - Lewis, John & Co.                     druggist        1882        D.
Montreal - Loiselle, F.X.O.                      druggist        1882        D.
Montreal - Lyman, Lewis & Co.          drugs & medicines         1810        Ads.
Montreal - Lyman, Wm. & Co., St. Paul St.              1845-Ad. 1851-D.
Montreal - Lyman, S.J. & Co., Place d'Armes                      1851        D.
Montreal - Lyman, Sons & Co. (Royal Canadian Perfumes & satchets) 1890       Ad.
Montreal - McGale, B.E.                          druggist        1882        D.
Montreal - McKeon Drugs                                          1851        D.
Montreal - Meyer, Chemi de Paris (Meyer's Liquid Depilatory)     1892        Ad.
Montreal - Monckton, A.                          druggist        1882        D.
Montreal - Morin, C.D.                           druggist        1882        D.
Montreal - Muir, E.                              druggist        1882        D.
Montreal - Neil, Wm.                             druggist        1882        D.
Montreal - Nicolle, J.A.                         druggist        1892-3      D.
Montreal - Parker, M. & Co.                      Family Chemist  1844        Ad.
Montreal - Palardy, F.L.                         druggist        1882        D.
Montreal - Parkin & McLeish                      inc. 1899
Montreal - Perry Davis & Son & Lawrence                          1882        D.
Montreal - Picault, P.E.             chemist & druggist          1851        D.
Montreal - Picault & Co.             chemist & druggist          1882        D.
Montreal - Raymond, Oliver, M.D.                                 1882        D.
Montreal - Reaford,                  chemist & druggist          1846        Ad.
Montreal - Recamier Man. Co. (Recamier Sarsaparilla, 1880, Cosmetics, 1890)  Ad.
Montreal - Shrimpton, Chas., chemist. (inks & blacking)          1837        Ad.
Montreal - Savage, A. & Co.  manu. druggist            1839-Ads. 1851-D.
Montreal - Shuttleworth, E.B., Toronto                           1882        D.
Montreal - Richeleau, W., M.D.                                   1851        D.
Montreal - Skeith, John                          druggist        1882        D.
Montreal - Smallwood, Chas.                      druggist        1882        D.
Montreal - St. Antoine Drug Hall, Bourque, E.J., M.D. & Co., prop. 1882      D.
Montreal - St. Louis, F.                         druggist        1882        D.
Montreal - Thibault, A., M.D.                    druggist        1882        D.
Montreal - Tremble, J.E.                         druggist        1897-8      D.
```

Quebec – cont'd

Montreal – Trudeau, R.   druggist   1851   Directory
Montreal – Urquhart, A., Medical Hall, (Urquhart's Jamaica Sarsaparilla) 1847-Ads. 1851-D.
Montreal – Wadsworth, Romeo Drugs, Meds. etc.   1810   Ads.
Montreal – Workman, Benjamin & Co.   1846-Ad. 1851-D.
Montreal – Waller, S.   chemist & druggist   1851   D.
Quebec – Ardouin, G.G. Quebec Dispensary   1851   D.
Quebec – Bowles, Jos., Medical Hall   1851   D.
Quebec – Cruitshank's Drugs, etc. (Gowland's Lotion in qts. & pts.) 1808   Ad.
Quebec – Dilworth Drugs   1892-3   D.
Quebec – Giroux, O.   1851   D.
Quebec – Hall, J.L.   druggist   1851   D.
Quebec – La Roche, J.N.O.   druggist   1892-3   D.
Quebec – Lemieux, A.   druggist   1892-3   D.
Quebec – Musson, John, chemist, druggist & apothecary   1828-Ad. 1851-D.
Quebec – Quebec Chemical Works   inc. 1870
Quebec – Smith, Dr. Medical Hall   1846   Ad.
Quebec – Taylor, Henry   apothecary & druggist, Palace Gate 1764   Ad.
Quebec – Urquhart, John, Cul de Sac St., L.T. (Bitters Ad.) 1807
Stanstead – Lawrence, A.J. (prop. Harvard Bronchial Syrup) 1890   Ad.
Stanstead – Lydia E. Pinkham's Factory   1882   Ad.

Mineral Springs and Soda Water Manufacturers

Beeb Plain Bottling Works   s.w.   1899   Directory
Chicoutimi – Allan, Robt., 86 Dorchester W.   1909   D.
Chicoutimi – Godin, L.P.   1909   D.
Coaticook – Bouchard, J.A.   1909   D.
Drummondville – Berard, Arthur   1899, 1909 D.
Farnham – Monarch Bottling Co.   1899   D.
Farnham – St. Pierre, H.   1909   D.
Grand Mere – Paquet, Wilfred   1909   D.
Joliette – Lachappelle, Andre   spruce beer   1890-1   D.
Joliette – Lafortune, Goleo   1909   D.
Joliette – Lapierre, Adelard   1909   D.
Joliette – Latour, George   1890-1   D.
Joliette – Migue, Narcisse   spruce beer   1890-1   D.
Joliette – Ouimet, Jos.   spruce beer   1890-1   D.
Lachine – Priest & Johnson, 552 St. Joseph   1899   D.
Levis – Abenakis Mineral Water Co.   1909   D.
Levis – Marcotte, A.   1909   D.
Montreal – Allan, Robt., 620 Dorchester W.   1890-9   D.
Montreal – Allan, Robt., 81 Dorchester W.   1909   D.
Montreal – American Soda Water Co.   1909   D.
Montreal – Beaudoin, J.E., 109 Champlain   1890-1   D.
Montreal – Brossaile, Moise   1896-7   D.
Montreal – Caldwell, Wm., 23 Berchelet   1899   D.
Montreal – Campbell, Kenneth & Co., 84 St. Urbain, s.w.   1871-99   D.
Montreal – Canadian Aerated Water Co.   1899, 1909 D.
Montreal – Choquette, C., 384 Amherst   1899   D.
Montreal – Christen, Jos. & Co., 149 Sanguinet   1890-9   D.
Montreal – Christen, J. & Co., 21 St. Julie   1909   D.
Montreal – Clark, James   ginger beer   1851   D.
Montreal – Clow, Frank, 9 Edouard Charles   1899   D.
Montreal – Cooper, Arthur, 85 Papineau Rd.   1890-9   D.
Montreal – Cormond, F. & Co.   1890-9   D.
Montreal – Crepeau & Matte, 107 Wolfe   1890-1   D.
Montreal – Cusson & Lusignan, 1262 Notre Dame   1891   D.
Montreal – Dewitt, C.B., 97 Duke   1899   D.
Montreal – Diamond Mineral Water Man. Co.   1899   D.
Montreal – Dillon, R.& J. (Dillon's Bottled Cider)   1817   Ad.
Montreal – Domphouse, J., 2½ St. Dennis   1890-9   D.
Montreal – Farquhar, Mrs., soda water (see Wilson C.)   1851   D.
Montreal – Ferland, A. & Co., 151 St. Andre   1896, 1909 D.
Montreal – Flynne, root beer man. Chenneville & Craig   1844   Ad.
Montreal – Girouard, H. & Co., 77 Quesnel   1909   D.
Montreal – Goulet Bros., 157 Planet   1909   D.
Montreal – Gurd, Chas. & Co., 43-45 Jurors   1890, 1909 D.
Montreal – Harte, J.A.   1892-3   D.
Montreal – Hirschovitz, R., 349 Cardiex   1909   D.

Quebec - cont'd

Montreal - Joseph Bros., 168 St. Maurice	1899	Directory
Montreal - King Edward Soda Water Co.	1909	D.
Montreal - Lafreniere, Jos.	1890-9	D.
Montreal - La Riena Mineral Water Co. Ltd.	1909	D.
Montreal - Laurention Spring Water Co.	1899	D.
Montreal - London Mineral Water Co.	1909	D.
Montreal - Mascott, A. & Bros., 5 Place d'Armes	1890-1	D.
Montreal - Millar, Robt., 69 St. Antoine	1890-1	D.
Montreal - Millroy, P., 119 St. Andre	1890-9	D.
Montreal - Millroy, P.A., 121 St. Andre	1909	D.
Montreal Soda Water Co., 149 Sanguinet	1909	D.
Montreal - Paris Soda Water Man. Co.	1909	D.
Montreal - Pope, Thos. soda water man.	1847	Ad.
Montreal - Poulin, A. & Co., 8 Beaver Hall Hill	1890-1	D.
Montreal - Radnor Water Co.	1899-D. 1910-Ad.	
Montreal - Renwick, E. ginger beer	1851	D.
Montreal - Robillard, C. & Cie, 282 St. Andre	1890-1	D.
Montreal - Robillard, C. & Co., 9 Robillard Ave.,	1890, 1909	D.
Montreal - Roman, Jos.	1899	D.
Montreal - Rowan Bros. & Co., 618 Beaudry	1890-9	D.
Montreal - Rowan Bros. & Co., 22½ Vallei	1909	D.
Montreal - Rowe, Frank W. & Co.	1890-9	D.
Montreal - Savage, Alfred & Co., drug.& apoth. (aerated waters made by us) 1841 thru 1849 Ads.		
Montreal - Siminovitch, P. & Son, 157 St. Lawrence	1909	D.
Montreal - Standard Mineral Water Co.	1909	D.
Montreal - St. Leon Mineral Water Co., 54 Victoria Sq.	1890-9	D.
Montreal - St. Leon Mineral Water Depot, 346 St. James	1909	D.
Montreal - Tardy, L., 389 St. Catherine	1899	D.
Montreal - Therrien, J.F., 608 Cadieux	1899	D.
Montreal - Timmons, M. & Son, 306 Craig	1890-9	D.
Montreal - Turnbull Soda & Mineral Water Establishment	1817	Ad.
Montreal - Union Bottling Co., 297 William	1909	D.
Montreal - Vincent, Alfred, 12 Brondson la	1899	D.
Montreal - White, T. & Co., man. sarsaparilla & root beer	1845-8	Ads.
Montreal - Williams, Rich., ginger beer	1851	D.
Montreal - Wilson, Charles (late Farquhar & Wilson, est. 1845) 99 St. Urbain St., Montreal, ginger ale-1867, Ad.		
Montreal - Wilson, Charles, est. 1845 ginger ale	1871	D.
Montreal - Wilson & Recroft, ginger ale & soda water	1882	D.
Montreal - Winning, Hill & Ware, St. Paul St., min. water	1869	Ad.
Nicolet - Houde, J.L.	1909	D.
Papineauville - Belanger, A. & Co.	1909	D.
Pierreville - Pitt, Achille	1909	D.
Pointe aux Trembles - Archambault, M. (Hochelaga Co.)	1899	D.
Quebec - Asselin, I.J., 6 Buade	1890	D.
Quebec - Christie, Thos. (bottled Mountain Cider)	1816	Ad.
Quebec - Crauford, A. jr., 2 Carlton	1899	D.
Quebec - Deguise, Jos. ginger beer	1857	D.
Quebec - Dignard, P. & Cie, 86-88 St. Valier	1890-1	D.
Quebec - Fluet, F.A.	1909	D.
Quebec - Fortier & Co., 220 St. Valier	1899, 1909	D.
Quebec - Langlois, C.E.A., 9 Buade	1899	D.
Quebec - Paquet & Fluet, 63 des Prairies	1896-9	D.
Quebec - Shepherd, Rich., (bottled oxigenated gas water)	1810	Ad.
Quebec - St. Leon Water Co., 3 Port Dauphin	1890-1	D.
Quebec - St. Leon Spring Co., 9 Buade	1899	D.
Quebec - Timmons, M. & Son, 76 St. George	1890	D.
Quebec - Timmons, M. & Son, 90-92 Cote d'Abraham	1896, 1909	D.
Richmond - Bedard, G.A.	1899	D.
Riviere du Loup (Frazerville) - Darrise & Frere	1899	D.
Shawville - Eades, J.W.	1899	D.
Sherbrooke - Bryant, J.H.	1899, 1909	D.
Sherbrooke - O'Dell, C.J.	1899	D.
Sherbrooke - Wigget, W.H.	1899, 1909	D.
Sorel - Lafleche, Z.R.	1909	D.
Sorel - Marcotte, Arthur	1899	D.
Sorel - Rivet, Jos.	1909	D.
Thetford Mines - Rosseau, Achille	1899	D.
Three Rivers - Pacaud, E.L. (Caxton Springs prop.)	1838	Article ɤ on, Ads.
Three Rivers - Rousseau, J.C. & Co.	1899, 1909	D.
Three Rivers - Spenard, J.M.	1899	D.
Ste. Genevieve de Batiscan - Beillet, Urbain	1899	D.
St. Guillaume d'Upton - Lamy & Co.	1890	D.

Quebec - cont'd

Ste. Hyacinthe - Cordeau & Lajoie		1896-9	Directory
Ste. Hyacinthe - Menard, M., 86 Mondor		1899	D.
Ste. Hyacinthe Mineral Water Co.		1896-7	D.
St. Jerome - Desnorneau, S.		1909	D.
St. Johns - Audette, Julian		1899	D.
St. Johns - Tisdale, N. & Co.		1899	D.
St. Lawrence Mineral Water Co. Ltd.	inc. 1900		
St. Leon Mineral Water		1846 & on	Ads.
St. Leon Mineral Water Co. Ltd.	inc. 1899		
St. Louis - Jasmin, Arthur		1890	D.
St. Roch - Roger, Zotique, 295 St. Joseph		1890	D.
St. Therese de Blainville - Cloutier, Damase		1899	D.
St. Therese de Blainville - Duquette, Jos. A.		1890	D.
St. Tite - Marchand, L.P.		1899	D.
St. Tite - Piche, Jos.		1899	D.
Valleyfield - Belair, Eloi		1899	D.
Valleyfield - Delisle, J.P.		1909	D.
Valleyfield - Lauiel, T.		1909	D.
Valleyfield - Monette, V.		1890-9	D.
Varrennes Springs - Flight, Wm. & Co. props.		1842	Article & on Ads.
Victoriaville - Brunelle, J.		1909	D.
Waterloo - Ashton, W.		1899	D.
Waterloo - Forand, H.		1909	D.
Waterloo - Hills, Horace		1890	D.
Waterloo - Perkins, F.P.		1909	D.

SASKATCHEWAN

Brewers and Distillers

Moosejaw Brewing & Malting Co.		1909	Directory
Prince Albert - Golden Lion Brewing Co.		1909	D.
Regina - Drewry, E.L.	brewer	1909	D.
Regina Brewing Co. Ltd.		1909	D.
Saskatoon - Hoeschen & Wentzler	brewers	1909	D.
Saskatoon Brewing Co. Ltd.		1909	D.

Mineral Springs and Soda Water Manufacturers

Estevan - Macdonald Bros.		1909	Directory
Medicine Hat - Tracey, A.R.		1890-1	D.
Moosejaw - Crystle Spring Bottling Co.		1909	D.
Moosejaw - Seeley, E.W. & Co.	s.w.	1909	D.
North Battleford - Saskatchewan Mineral Water Works		1909	D.
Regina - Seeley, E.W. & Co.	s.w.	1909	D.
Saskatoon Soda Water Works		1909	D.

References - Canada Directory, by Robt. W.S. Mackay, Montreal Lovell, 1851; Canada Directory, John Lovell, 1857; Great Western Railway Gazetteer, Commercial Advertiser & Business Directory, Toronto, 1861-62; Grand Trunk Railway Gazetteer, 1862; Lovell's Ontario Directory, 1871; Times Business Directory, 1876; Lovell's Business & Professional Directory of the Province of Ontario for 1882, Montreal; Business Directory & Book of Reference for the Town & County of Peterborough for 1883-84 ; Directory of Town of Peterborough 1888 - 1889 ; Dominion of Canada Business Directory, pub. by R.L. Polk & Co. Toronto, 1890 -91 ; Ontario Gazetteer & Directory, Toronto, Might's Directory Co., 1892 -93; Vernon's Peterborough & Ashburnham Directory, 1895 - 97; Lovell's Business & Professional Directory for 1896 - 97; Canada & Newfoundland Business Directory, 1899 ; Might Directory Co., 1899; Canada Gazetteer & Business Directory, 1909; Incorporated Bodies - Baudoin, Philibert, Montreal Notary of Department of Agriculture, Montreal c. 1905 ; Index to Companies, Toronto (hand written - no pub., cont'd between late 1870's to 1906 or 07).

Taken also from the various newspapers mentioned in Bib., re advertising etc.

BOTTLE INDEX

HAVE
PAIN
KILLER

MEDICAL BOTTLES CONT'D

	no.	page
Jacobs F.A. Chemist,Toronto	344	33
Johnson & Johnson	234	21
Johnson's Liniment	188	16
K.D.C. for Dyspepsia	345	33
Kendall's Spavin Cure	228	20
Kendall's " "	298	28
Kennedy J.E. Cobourg, Ont.	258	24
Kennedy J. Hamilton, C.W.	311	29
Kepler (cod liver oil) misc.	7	1
Kepler " "	8	1
Kepler " "	9	1
Kerry Bros & Grathern	34	20
King St. Pharmacy	267	25
Knowles A. Pickering, C.W.	331	31
Kruchen	233	20
Kutnow's Powder	327	31
Lambert Pharma. Co.	122	11
Lee J.R. Toronto	187	16
Lehn S. Fink, Can. Ltd.	98	9
Liebigs Asthma Cure	202	17
Liquiozone Co. the	33	3
Lorentz Med. Co.	72	7
Lundin's Juniper Ade	226	20
Lyman Bros. & Co.	212	18
Lysol of Canada Ltd.	97	9
Lysol bottle	118	11
Lysol "	149	13
Lysol "	150	13
Lysol "	151	13
Macartney J.L. Niagara Falls,Can.	185	16
Magnesia bottle	108	10
Manley's Celery Nerve Compound	213	18
McDonald Medicine Co. Winnepeg	219	19
McNalty E.C. Niagara Falls	194	16
Medical bottle panelled	205	17
Merrill's Marvelous Medicine	313	29
Milburn T. & Co. Toronto	218	19
Milburn " " Ltd.	219	19
Mexican Corn Remedy	301	28
Milk Glass (fish on base)	340	32
Milton	101	10
Minard's Honey Balsam	290	27
Minard's Liniment	125	11
Minard's "	196	16
Monogram Square presc.	66	6
Moore G.A. St.John, N.B.	306	29
Morriss's Electric Fluid,Peterboro	312	29
Mother Graves Worm Exterminator	192	16
Munroe Fred,St.John N.B.	304	29
Musterol (milk glass)	106	10
National Drug & Chemical Co.	249	22
Northrop & Lyman Co.Ltd.Toronto	164	14
Northrop " " (Dr. Thomas)	171	15
Northrop " " "	172	15
Northrop " " "	173	15
Northrop " Toronto	50	5
Northrop " "	223	19
Northrop " Newcastle,C.W.	308	29
Northrop " Vegetable Disc.	303	29
Norton's (from ad.)	321	30
Nyal	230	20
Nyal (hair tonic)	119	11
Nyal Quality	166	14
Oil bottle (black)	74	7
Ointment (milk glass)	105	10
Ointment	113	10
"O" panel presc.	63	6
Oval (shape)	36	3
Oval "	159	14
Oval "	319	30
Owl Drug Stores, Toronto	324	30
Opeldeldoc	273	25
Ozone Co. of Toronto Ltd.	280	26
Paines Celery Compound	78	8
Panelled bottle	88	9
Pat. Dec.7,09	300	28
P.D. & Co. (round)	11	1

	no.	page
P.D. & Co.	129	12
Pew H.W. Niagara Falls,Can.	195	16
Phillips	222	19
Phillips Chas.H. Windsor	220	19
Phillips " "	221	19
Pierce R.V.,M.D.,Smart Weed	239	21
Pinex (cough med.)	170	15
Pinkhams Lydia E.	243	22
Pinkham's " 14½oz.	244	22
Poison (8 sided)	47	4
Poison Not to be Taken	79	8
Poison	82	8
Poison	83	8
Poison	142	12
Poison (panelled)	175	15
Poison Be Careful	329	31
Poison Not to be Taken	287	27
Polusterine Products Toronto	26	3
Polusterine Products Co., Tor.	284	26
Ponds Extract	259	24
Porter W.J. Cobourg	268	25
Potter Drug & Chemical	27	3
Prescription (round shouldered)	21	2
Prescription (square)	41	4
Prescription (panelled)	161	14
Prescription large	285	27
Princess Oval (presc.)	156	13
Putman's Corn & Wart Extactor	25	2
Radway R.R.R. & Co. Montreal	242	21
Radway " "	29	3
Radway " "	191	16
Radway " ,New York & Montreal	91	9
Raised shoulders (prob.Cosm.)	165	14
Rawlieghs	114	11
Rawlieghs	119	17
Red'g Applied for(Dominion G.)	250	23
Reed & Garnrick New York	179	15
Robinson W.S.Chem.,Yorkville	208	18
Round small	127	11
Round presc.	133	12
Round (12 panel)	137	12
Round (8 panel)	178	15
Round shouldered square	99	9
Round panelled (Dominion G.)	117	11
Rundles Liniment	55	5
Rundles	158	14
Salve jar	121	11
Salve "	136	12
Sanderson's H. Infallible Oil	28	3
Sanderson's Drugs,St.Mary's	51	6
Sandford's Ginger	8	1
Sandford's Jamaica Ginger	13	2
Scott's Emulsion	181	15
Scott's "	200	17
Scott's "	203	17
Shiloh's Consumption Cure,Tor.	333	32
Slocum's Coltfoot Expectorant	335	32
Smelling Salts bottle	95	9
Smither & Thurstone,Buffalo,N.Y.	216	19
Square base (wide mouth)	37	3
Square presc.	130	12
Square (double ring finish)	131	12
Squibb bottle	248	22
Staffords Inc.	235	21
Staminol (ladies leg)	38	4
Sterling Products Inc.	231	20
Stevenson T. Orangeville	254	33
Stringer's Nervine,Kingston Ont.	349	33
S & L (on base)	138	12
Swaim's Panacea	269	25
Syrop d'Anis Gauvin	339	32
Tayler J.& Co. (perfume)	23	2
Teaspoons (measured)	283	26
Temple of Health	260	24
Thompson R.S. Toronto	87	8
Three part mold (acid)	39	4
Three " " (small)	143	12
Tucker Geo.,Montreal	334	32
Turlington's Balsam	302	29

MEDICAL BOTTLES CONT'D.

SPIRIT BOTTLES (pages 65 to 98 incl.)

SPIRIT BOTTLES CONT'D

SPIRIT BOTTLES CONT'D.

SPIRIT BOTTLES CONT'D.

TOILET BOTTLES (pages 102 to 113 incl.)

INDEX CONT'D.

BOTTLERS and BOTTLES, CANADIAN
by O. URQUHART

First Edition.

Copyright © by S.& O. Urquhart, 1976.

S.& O. URQUHART, 10 FIR AVENUE,
TORONTO, ONTARIO,
CANADA, M4E 1B5.

INTERNATIONAL STANDARD BOOK NUMBER 0 9690604 0 8

Printed in Canada by Dancor Graphics, Toronto
Produced in consultation with Aegis Publishing and Film Scenarios, Toronto